MIRROR ON

1937

ISBN: 978-1-9993652-6-4

INDEX

INDEX - 2

INDEX - 3

INDEX - 4

THE DAILY MIRROR, Friday, January 1, 1937.

Daily Mirror

No. 10322 Registered at the G.P.O. as a newspaper. ONE PENNY

LATE LON. ED.

THE KING'S NEW YEAR MESSAGE

On this, the first New Year's Day of my reign, I send to all the peoples of the Empire my warmest wishes for their welfare and happiness.

In succeeding to the Throne I follow a father who had won for himself an abiding place in the hearts of his peoples, and a brother whose brilliant qualities gave promise of another historic reign—a reign cut short in circumstances upon which, from their very sadness, none of us would wish to dwell.

I realise to the full the responsibilities of my noble heritage. I shoulder them with all the more confidence in the knowledge that the Queen and my mother, Queen Mary, are at my side.

Throughout my life it will be my constant endeavour to strengthen that foundation of mutual trust and affection on which the relations between the Sovereign and the peoples of the British Empire so happily rest. I ask your help towards the fulfilment of this purpose, and I know that I do not ask in vain.

To repeat the words used by my dear father at the time of his Silver Jubilee, my wife and I dedicate ourselves for all time to your service, and we pray that God may give us guidance and strength to follow the path that lies before us.

GEORGE R.I.

GIRL WEARING LEAVES BANNED AT ARTS BALL

BY A SPECIAL CORRESPONDENT

With the greatest joy and hope Britain has known for years, millions greeted Prosperity 1937 early to-day.

GAY crowds in London's West End danced and sang; thousands went to the cathedrals and churches to give thanks.

One girl did not share the fun. Alone of 10,000 guests who went to celebrate at Chelsea Arts, an eighteen-year-old girl was excluded from the festival.

Her costume, consisting mainly of a few autumn leaves, was censored by the commissionaire.

As she was giving in her ticket at the main entrance to the Royal Albert Hall a commissionaire noticed her costume as a woodland nymph.

He decided at once that the girl had better not enter the hall until she had passed the eagle eye of the committee.

She told me: "This is a real disappointment. My costume is quite decent, and I think you will agree that it is charming.

"If you look round the hall, you will see many people who are dressed as I am, and in even less.

"I can understand the action of the commissionaire, who, after all, was acting upon orders, but my mother told me she thought the costume was both beautiful and proper.

"I think I should not have been excluded—I have always wanted to attend."

The "Naked Truth" was the theme of last night's revels.

Venus, a naked figure 120ft. high, hotly pursued by a caricature of George Robey, Mickey Mouse and other famous personalities, was drawn against a background of ships and sky, representing Chelsea Reach.

Men in leopards' skins, girls in Hawaiian costume and the briefest of beach panties leapt into the air with cries of joy at the presentation of this artists' conception of the coming year

Silence at St. Paul's

The West End has never been merrier. Hotels and restaurants, with extensions until two o'clock, were crowded. At one the diners ate strawberries grown under neon lights in Kent at a cost of 20s. for thirty berries.

Mounted police endeavoured to keep a way open for traffic, but found the task impossible long before midnight. Their horses were ridden broadside through the crowd from Regent-street to Leicester-square and back again repeatedly.

A solid ring of police guarded Eros, but it was the police themselves who were driven back to the very foot of the statue when the crowd made a concerted rush.

By contrast, St. Paul's, lacking the usual official welcome service, had the quietest New Year of recent times. Not a single voice echoed from the thousands of people who gathered to welcome 1937.

For the first time for many years, community singing was not part of the celebration.

As soon as 7 p.m. arrived the rush began and soon there was a delay of sixty minutes on calls to Glasgow and most parts of Scotland. There were also long delays on Irish and Bristol routes.

On the radio, British listeners were able to join for two minutes in the festivities of the Royal Sussex Regiment, broadcast from a canteen near Jerusalem. They heard the laughter of the men and the singing of their marching song followed by "Beside the Sea."

King George and his brother, the Duke of Windsor, both issued New Year's messages.

Far away in Schloss Enzerfeld, the Duke of

(Continued on back page)

ENDED WITH A BANG

Alresford (Hants) ended the Old Year yesterday with a bang—several bangs.

The Petty Sessions were being held in the Town Hall—and the hall was gaily decorated for the firemen's ball last night. In the centre hung nearly one hundred balloons in a cluster.

As the magistrates sat listening to the evidence there was a pop. The balloons were starting to go off.

AUSTRALIA WIN TOSS AND BAT—A WORLD'S RECORD CROWD TO WATCH

AUSTRALIA won the toss and decided to bat first in the third—and possibly decisive—Test match at Melbourne this morning.

An hour before the start 50,000 people had streamed into the ground, giving the new £100,000 grandstands a mass baptism. The world record of 68,238 spectators for a day's cricket seemed likely to be broken.

Crowds began to gather as early as dawn and the moment the gates were opened at 9 a.m. they began to jostle into the ground in their thousands.

The wicket, which was soft, was framed in a brilliant green setting, and looked innocent enough and probably slow and easy. But who could foretell Melbourne's notorious pre-lunch tantrums?

Australia's team was the first to be announced, says Reuter. Of the twelve chosen, C. L. Badcock stood down and took the position of twelfth man.

The team was therefore:—

D. G. Bradman (South Australia) (captain), W. A. Brown (Queensland), L. S. Darling (Victoria), J. H. Fingleton (N.S.W.), S. J. McCabe (N.S.W.), K. E. Rigg (Victoria), W. J. O'Reilly (N.S.W.), W. A. Oldfield (N.S.W.), L. O'B. Fleetwood-Smith (Victoria), F. Ward (South Australia) and M. W. Sievers (Victoria).

England's Team

England's team is: G. O. Allen (Middlesex) (captain), L. E. G. Ames (Kent), C. J. Barnett (Gloucester), W. R. Hammond (Gloucester), J. Hardstaff (Nottinghamshire), M. Leyland (Yorkshire), R. W. V. Robins (Middlesex), J. M. Sims (Middlesex), H. Verity (Yorkshire), W. Voce (Nottinghamshire), T. S. Worthington (Derbyshire). Twelfth man: L. B. Fishlock.

Allen decided to bring Worthington back for Fagg compared with the team which won the second Test. That was the only change.

THE DAILY MIRROR, Tuesday, January 5, 1937.

Daily Mirror

No. 10325 Registered at the G.P.O. as a newspaper. ONE PENNY

RICH MAN, BROKEN-HEARTED, LEAPS FROM AIR LINER

BY A SPECIAL CORRESPONDENT

MAX Victor Wenner, forty-nine-year-old Shropshire landowner, had everything money could buy. Then his wife died, and it broke his heart.

Yesterday he plunged 3,000ft. to death from the emergency door of a Cologne-London air liner as it passed over Belgium. Examination of the 'plane showed that he had tried to slash through the fuselage and open a door in the floor.

As he left for Germany last week to try to forget his grief, he told his housekeeper, "I shall be back for dinner on January 4—that is, unless anything crops up."

While his servants prepared a welcome at his beautiful home, Blatchcote Hall, Leebotwood, yesterday afternoon, a telegram told them he would never arrive.

Miss Nancy Humphrey, of Minsterley, his twenty-year-old housekeeper, told me last night that Mr. Wenner heard of his wife's illness when he was on a fishing holiday in Iceland in July.

A radio message was flashed to him and he raced home by steamer. But within a day or two of his arrival his wife died.

A strong-minded man, Mr. Wenner hid his grief from even his closest friends

To Try to Forget

"But now and again," said Miss Humphrey, "he used to clench his teeth and tears would well into his eyes as he thought of his dead wife. I have never seen a couple so devoted.

"He tried to occupy his mind by going out to his shooting ground, and one of the reasons for his going to Germany was to try to forget his great loss.

"When he went away last week he told my father, who was his land agent, and myself that he would be back to-night, and asked me to prepare dinner.

"One phrase he used, however, was strange. He said: 'That is, unless anything crops up.'

"He had everything that money could buy, but since July he has been really unhappy. He seemed restless and wanted to be on the move all the time.

"He was quite used to aeroplanes, as he was a flying officer during the war," she added.

Disturbed

Mrs. J. Cain, of Woodend, Clarence-road Hersham, Walton-on-Thames, who sat near Mr. Wenner in the 'plane as she travelled home from Germany with her husband, their three-year-old daughter and a nurse, told the *Daily Mirror* last night:—

"Mr. Wenner drove up in a taxi a few minutes before we left Cologne.

"When he came on board he was hatless and he seemed to be disturbed during the earlier part of the journey. He did nothing but write.

"Over Belgium he got up from his seat and hurried away to the compartment at the rear

(Continued on back page)

IN MID-AIR HE VANISHED

Max Victor Wenner, wealthy Shropshire landowner, was flying home from Cologne. Fellow passengers Mr. and Mrs. Cain.

Mrs. Cain noticed Mr. Wenner disturbed . . . writing . . . saw him leave the cabin. She heard a noise; Mr. Cain found damaged fabric, and open door.

Mrs. Cain . . . in mid-air she sensed tragedy.

TOSIES ARE THE LATEST

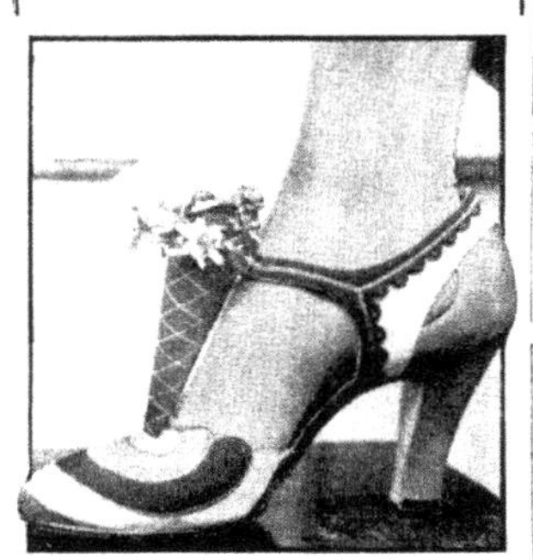

There'll always be flowers at her feet if Eve adopts the latest shoe fashion from Canada.

The dainty holder, made from the same material as the shoe, is filled with real blooms, packed in damp moss.

JOHN BARRYMORE PUT ON PROBATION BY HIS WIFE

FROM OUR OWN CORRESPONDENT

HOLLYWOOD, Monday.

SCREEN-LOVER John Barrymore has been "put on probation" by his wife. Reason—he walked out of her New Year party after a tiff.

When John stalked out of the gay Trocadero cabaret on New Year's Eve, no one thought anything about it. Nearly every one there was quarrelling, anyway.

"That's the whole trouble with us," Elaine Barrie told me to-day. "If Mr. Smith walks out when Mrs. Smith gives a party, who cares? But with us its front page news.

"Just a Lovers' Tiff"

"John was most abrupt in his actions that night. I told him to go to his trainer, Ken Kelly, until he decided to make amends. So the next move is up to him.

"We have not separated in the true sense of the word. I placed him on probation, that's all.

"But I hope he will come back home to-day," she added. "This is just a lovers' tiff. I do hope he comes soon."

Barrymore is reported to have been offended because he could not persuade Elaine to abandon a stage engagement for February

MAGISTRATE TOLD MEN TO HAVE A SCRAP—POLICEMAN AS REFEREE

BY A SPECIAL CORRESPONDENT

WITH solicitors as seconds, a magistrate as timekeeper and a police sergeant as referee, an epic boxing contest is in prospect at Crossmaglen, co. Armagh, Northern Ireland.

It all arises out of a feud between the Lavertys and the Keegans.

First one family, then the other drags the dispute into the local police court by issuing a summons for assault.

It was the turn of the Lavertys yesterday, and Major J. D. McCallum, the magistrate, thoroughly fed up with the whole affair, suggested that Owen Laverty and Pat Keegan should have a scrap, and thus get rid of the bad blood.

Evenly Matched

"If you want to continue this dispute, get the police-sergeant to act as referee in a decent stand-up scrap, with your solicitors as seconds, while I will act as timekeeper," he told them.

"They just grinned sheepishly," the Major told the *Daily Mirror* yesterday, "but I am hoping the police-sergeant of the Royal Ulster Constabulary—himself a fine boxer—will be able to persuade them to have a meeting.

"They both strip at about 9st. 10lb., and are about twenty-three years of age, so they will be evenly matched."

I think the fight is coming off—and it ought to be worth watching!

P.-C. WAS THERE WHEN TROUBLE "FERMENTED"

Hearing a muffled explosion and the smashing of glass in a chemist's shop yesterday, a Southampton policeman sent an S O S for assistance. Twelve policemen dashed to the scene and the building was surrounded.

When the proprietor arrived and opened the door, they found smashed glass but no sign of an intruder.

The chemist himself solved the mystery

On a shelf there had stood for years a jar of burnt sugar used for colouring. The sugar had fermented, the jar had burst and smashed other bottles.

NAME IN LIGHTS MEANT STARS TO HER!

FROM OUR OWN CORRESPONDENT

HOLLYWOOD, Monday.

SEEING her name in lights for the first time was a big moment in the career of a rising starlet, but it meant more than that to Jane Bryan.

In Hollywood boulevards to-night her name twinkled at her from a theatre marquee where her first starring film was showing.

She stepped back into the street for a better view of the entrancing sight, and was knocked down by a car.

She was taken to hospital to have abrasions attended to, and plans to view the pleasing scene to-morrow from the other side of the street.

COUNCIL FEARS A WAR

FEAR of a European war before the summer was one of the reasons Broadstairs Urban Council decided not to engage a seasonal concert party last night.

In the past the council has always engaged a concert party for the pavilion and a minstrel troupe on the pier, but this year the minstrel troupe will perform in the pavilion.

Cabinet prepares for crisis over Spain: back page.

FRIDAY, JANUARY 8, 1937

Daily Mirror

No. 10328 Registered at the G.P.O. as a newspaper. ONE PENNY

JULIANA GOES ON HONEYMOON BY BACK DOOR—ONLY 2 SAW HER

FROM OUR SPECIAL CORRESPONDENT.

THE HAGUE, Thursday.

WHILE a crowd of 2,500,000 went mad with joy here to-night, Princess Juliana and Prince Bernhard, cause of their rejoicing, slipped off on their honeymoon watched by only two members of the public.

They drove from the Royal Palace by a back door, accompanied by an equerry and a lady-in-waiting.

Two passers-by were the only people to see them as they headed for the Castle of Baron Bentinck at Amerongen, where the Kaiser first stayed when he fled to Holland.

To-day the Royal couple will continue their journey to Austria. Later they will visit the north of Scotland.

In The Hague the rejoicing grew as the night advanced.

Men, women and children, shouting and screaming, ran in solid blocks along the street carrying everything before them.

Marching Girls

Seeing children fall and hearing women's cries, the police attempted rescue dashes, but the crowd danced ring-o'-roses, picked victims up, raced on. They ran nearly two miles in the narrow streets before they were stopped by a police cordon.

When the soldiers came off guard duty in the streets to-day after the wedding, hundreds of pretty girls dived under the police ropes and linked arms with the marching regiments.

Arm-in-arm, soldiers and girls paraded the streets until a squad of police forcibly hustled the girls away. Several were arrested.

Ambulance men turned out to rescue swimmers who attempted to swim a race fully clothed in the river.

The manager of one cafe was locked in a cupboard while students wrecked the restaurant and took furniture into the street.

In contrast to the wild scale of the celebrations, simplicity marked the wedding itself.

Queen Wilhelmina, the solitary, proud woman who has held her country together with the power of her personality and her fixed determination to duty, cried quietly as the Prince's loud and clear "Ja" ("Yes") rang into every corner of the church. Her beloved daughter was happy with a worthy husband beside her.

(Continued on back page)

QUARTER OF WORLD SHAKEN BY 'QUAKE

BY A SPECIAL CORRESPONDENT

AN earthquake that shook a quarter of the world occurred yesterday—and the authorities don't know where.

It made the needle of the seismograph at Kew swing seven inches—only one inch short of the oscillation caused by the Quetta earthquake that destroyed towns and villages and killed thousands.

All officials could say was that they believed the 'quake was centred about 4,770 miles away from Britain.

A severe earthquake centred near Pyrgos, in Greece, is thought to have been a tremor from the larger one. Panic in the town is reported, but no casualties.

HAND-IN-HAND THEY PLIGHT THEIR TROTH

In St. James's Church, Cathedral of The Hague, Princess Juliana and Prince Bernhard making their marriage vows before Queen Wilhelmina, behind whom is the Earl of Athlone. More royal wedding pictures on pages 14 and 15.

SATURDAY, JANUARY 9, 1937

Daily Mirror

No. 10329 Registered at the G.P.O. as a newspaper. ONE PENNY

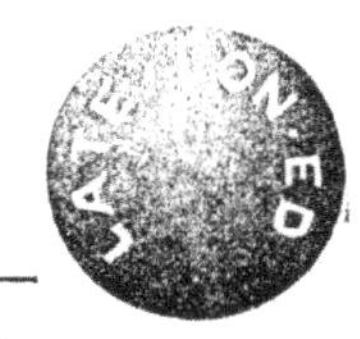

WOMAN WITH THE WORLD'S BEST JOB

BRITISH 'AMBASSADRESS' CAN SPEND WHAT SHE LIKES

BY A SPECIAL CORRESPONDENT

WITH three blank cheques in her bag with which she can buy anything and everything she wants, the woman with the world's best job sails next Friday for South Africa.

Mrs. Eugenie Daubeny, Great Britain's first Ambassadress of Trade, will be fulfilling every woman's wildest dream with:

Unlimited cash at her finger tips;

Unlimited opportunity to spend it in a country she has never seen—among companions who are waiting to entertain her.

For seven years she has never earned less than £1,000 a year and she now starts out as representative of a dress designer, an interior decorator and a jeweller with permission to spend an indefinite sum on her expenses.

Anything She Wants

"I can get anything in the world that I want," she told me as she made final preparations for her trip at the Savoy Hotel last night.

"I was looking for another exciting job when I left Grosvenor House, where I was hostess and interior decorator for three years, but I must say I never dreamt that I should tumble into anything like this."

And it is a flattering job, too. She is not taking out any specimen clothes or jewellery, she is simply wearing her own, provided for her by her employers.

I looked at her sparkling diamond ring, her diamond winged clasp at her neck and her specimen blue white diamond bracelet

Her simple black crepe dress was the smartest background for her jewels, which are valued at more than £20,000.

She is taking some evening dresses with her that would make any woman's mouth water.

Back for Coronation

"My chief pride is a dress called Lily of the Valley," she told me.

"It is of white silk organdie with green silk shoulder straps and an enormous green bow tied at the front."

This will be only a preliminary trip. Mrs. Daubeny is touring America in the autumn, and afterwards she hopes to visit Australia

Her nine-year-old daughter hopes to go with her to America so as to go on the films.

Mrs. Daubeny will be back in England in time for the Coronation.

Mrs. Eugenie Daubeny—a picture taken at her hotel last night.

BRITONS HURT IN BOMBED EMBASSY

THREE incendiary bombs fell in the British Embassy building in Madrid last night, injuring a British officer and an Englishwoman.

The refugees, who were formerly staying in the building, have, since the Embassy was transferred to Valencia, been transferred, otherwise the bombing would have been a great deal more serious.

Captain Edwin Lance, who has been acting as transport officer to the Embassy, was slightly injured by a bomb which fell on an annexe in which he was sheltering.

The name of the injured Englishwoman is Mrs. Norris.

Other incendiary bombs hit an apartment house in Montesquinza-street, in which the Acting British Consul, Mr. John Milan, and his wife, were at home. They were not hurt.

It is reported that a decree making the evacuation of Madrid obligatory for all non-combatants will be issued to-day.

French Fleet manœuvres off Morocco. See back page.

MAX WENNER'S LAST LETTER WAS NEVER FINISHED: MESSAGE BEGAN 'DARLING...'

FROM OUR OWN CORRESPONDENT

BRUSSELS, Friday.

LAST letter written by Max Wenner, wealthy Shropshire landowner, in the Cologne-London air liner a few minutes before he plunged 3,000ft. to his death last Monday, only adds to the mystery of his end.

It was recovered to-day when a peasant found his body in a pine wood near the Belgian village of Genck.

Addressed to Fraulein Olga Buchsenschutz, of Kusterdrebe, Essen, Ruhr, Germany, it contained only this message in German:

"Darling, thanks to you I have arrived in time at the aerodrome. Now I am writing to . . ."

There the note breaks off. Why it was not finished will never be known.

It is believed that Fraulein Buchsenschutz is the unknown lover Max Wenner journeyed to Germany to see, and for whom the authorities have sought in vain since his death.

Only Broken Arm

The letter was written on ordinary notepaper and was in a pre-stamped British envelope.

As it offers no clue, the Belgium Procurceur du Roi, which is equivalent to a coroner in England, has decided that to-morrow at two o'clock an autopsy will be held before the inquest.

When it was discovered by the peasant Max Wenner's body was curiously unmarked.

The doctor's impression is that Wenner must have been dead before he touched the ground owing to heart failure.

The only apparent wound was a scratch on the forehead, probably caused by a branch of a tree, and a broken left arm.

Apparently his 3,000-ft. fall was broken by the trees and undergrowth.

BABY BORN AS SHOT MOTHER DIES: FATHER CHARGED

FROM OUR OWN CORRESPONDENT

NEW YORK, Friday.

SURGEONS raced with death in Oakland, California, to bring about the birth of a child before its nineteen-year-old mother, rushed to hospital with a bullet wound in the head, died.

Ten minutes after a healthy seven-pound boy was born, the girl, Mrs. A. L. Randall, died. Her husband was at once arrested and charged with murder.

According to Mrs. Randall's aunt, Miss Hohnhaus, she was with her niece in their apartment when Ray Randall, an aviator, who had been estranged from his wife, entered and demanded reconciliation.

"My niece said she would never return to him. Then he raised a revolver, shot her and vanished," said Miss Hohnhaus

100 ARRESTS IN RAID

Nearly 100 arrests were made when scores of police officers raided a social club in Commercial-road, E., at midnight.

The arrested people, including several women, were taken to Arbour-square Police Station in lorries, and charged under the Gaming Act.

"I AM NOT A PERFECT WIFE"

"I KNOW I am not a perfect wife," confessed Mrs. Grace Barwell of Southchurch-road, Southend, bride of ten months, at Southend Matrimonial Court last night. "You have not given me time to learn."

She asked for a separation order on the grounds of the cruelty of her husband, Victor Barwell, radio employee. "What is a wife for?" he had queried. "Why do I pay you wages?"

Mrs. Barwell replied: "She has to wait on you hand and foot You should have more consideration, married so short a time."

The husband's brother said "His trouble is selfishness. He will not give way. Everyone must be perfect. He is something like a soldier, and the little things upset him. He has no tolerance. He is bull-headed. Instead of having things straight out and finished, he will sit and sulk for a fortnight."

Mrs. Barwell was granted an order of 25s. a week

Mrs. Barwell.

LORD MAYOR HAS 'FLU

The Lord Mayor of London is confined to his bed with influenza, announced Lady Broadbridge yesterday.

JULIANA IN "HIDING"

Princess Juliana and Prince Bernhard have "disappeared" on their honeymoon.

They have left Holland, but their destination remains a secret. A report yesterday that they had arrived at Innsbruck on their way to Igls, Austrian Tyrol, was incorrect.

A telegram was received at the Hotel Iglerhof, Igls, signed by the Prince's secretary. It said: "The Prince and Princess have changed their plans, and therefore, for the time being, will not arrive at Igls."

According to one source, they passed their wedding night in the Noordeinde royal palace.

A news reel of the wedding, which was sent to Berlin by aeroplane yesterday to be shown to members of the Dutch Club, has been confiscated by the German authorities.

MONDAY, JANUARY 11, 1937

Daily Mirror

No. 10330 Registered at the G.P.O. as a newspaper. ONE PENNY

HEIRESS AND HORSEWHIPPED SALESMAN ELOPE, MARRY

FROM OUR SPECIAL CORRESPONDENT

SHIPSTON-ON-STOUR (Worcs), Sunday.

A PRETTY twenty-three-year-old heiress, whose fortune is estimated at £80,000, has eloped with a twenty-five-year-old ironmonger's salesman who, for her sake, suffered a horsewhipping without flinching.

Noreen Neilson, a niece of the late Canon R. J. B. Irwin, vicar of Lillington, Leamington, ran away from here with William Kennett to get married a' Oxford Register Office

The couple took with them two of Kennett's friends, members of the local cricket club, to act as witnesses. They were Mr. John Smith and Mr. Ray Padbury.

The four motored to Oxford in Miss Neilson's car. Afterwards Kennett and his wife left for a motoring honeymoon in North Devon and Cornwall

Dark and Handsome

Kennett, who is a strikingly handsome, dark-haired young man of twenty-five, with an athletic figure, is a native of Worcester. He has lived here for eleven years, working as a salesman at the general store and ironmongery department of Mr. H. F. Sale and Son, Sheep-street, Shipston.

His father, who was a coalman, was killed some years ago, and the Ministry of Pensions sent the children of Mrs. Kennett to various villages around the district. Kennett was apprenticed to the general store, and it was there he first met Miss Neilson eight or nine months ago when she lived in the village.

At that time she lived in a large house opposite the tiny stone cottage where Kennett lodged with Mr. and Mrs. East.

Gradually their friendship ripened into love and often they were seen motoring off to Oxford in Miss Neilson's car.

The Thrashing

To-day Mr Ray Padbury told me that shortly before they ran away Mrs. Neilson had tried to break the friendship between Kennett and the girl.

"I know," he said, "that a man had spoken to Bill about his friendship with Noreen. Bill said he could not stop speaking to her if she came into the shop to buy things as he would have to serve her.

"After this episode there was some more trouble.

"The man went to the house where Bill was lodging and thrashed him with a horse crop.

"Bill, although he is a big strong fellow

(Continued on back page)

ON THEIR HONEYMOON

On honeymoon after their elopement. Mr. William Kennett and his heiress bride, Miss Noreen Neilson, photographed last night at Exeter.

Squirrel Goes Nuts!

IT sounds like a nightmare, but it happened—a squirrel chased a man and terrorised a town in U.S.A.

The town was Rockford, Illinois. The squirrel evidently "went nuts," so to speak. It pounced from a rooftop and attacked men, women and children in a street, trying to bite their faces. It succeeded—with five of them.

Crowds ran screaming into buildings to escape it. Then it attacked a man. He fought it, threw it off, and ran. The squirrel chased him along the street until—

Howard Smith, of the local Humane Society, lassoed it and broke its neck. Howard is now the hero of Rockford!

Britain's singing mouse may broadcast. See back page.

BRANCH KILLS WIFE AS HUSBAND HANGS 20 FEET UP

FROM OUR OWN CORRESPONDENT

HEREFORD, Sunday.

"HELP! Mummie's dead," shouted eleven-year-old Bernard Atkins, yesterday, as he rushed into the stables of Bryngwyn Manor, Wormelow, near Hereford.

Bernard had left his mother lying on the ground half a mile away, felled by a branch, from a tree, and his father hanging from another branch 20ft. from the ground.

Mr. Atkins, forty-three-year-old bailiff at the Manor, had been trimming the tree while his wife held the ladder.

When the branch fell, killing Mrs. Atkins instantly, it smashed the ladder and her husband only saved himself by clutching another limb.

Soon after his son ran up his hold gave and he fell beside his wife, fracturing his pelvis and receiving severe head injuries. It is feared that he has fractured his skull.

Mr. Ernest Oakley, his employer, told me:—

"Bernard was playing, some distance away, when his father called to him to get help. He shouted, 'Quick boy, I can't hang on much longer.'

"I have not yet been able to break the news to Atkins of his wife's death."

The Atkins had been married for fourteen years. They were an ideally happy couple.

PREMIER'S LONG TALK WITH THE KING

MR. Stanley Baldwin, who, with Mrs. Baldwin, is staying at Sandringham, had a long private interview with the King on Saturday night.

The Duke of Kent was also a guest there this week-end.

Nearly 8,000 people saw the King and Queen as they walked through the park to church yesterday.

The sermon was preached by the Bishop of Jarrow.

Arrangements have been made for the King and Queen to return to London to-day by royal coaches attached at Wolferton to a train from Hunstanton, arriving in London about 8.20 p.m.

The King goes to church—page 15.

YARD ENDS BRIBE INQUIRY

Scotland Yard detectives have completed secret investigations into allegations of bribery made against officers attached to West End stations

'During the week-end they made their report to Sir Philip Game, the Commissioner of Police. He will decide whether a Court of Inquiry shall be held.

29—LOST TWO WIVES IN 18 MONTHS

FOUND drowned in the sea at Westcliff yesterday, William Walter Abel, twenty-nine-year-old hotel worker of Burdett-avenue, Southend, had lost two wives in the past eighteen months.

His second wife died in childbirth in Southend Hospital a few weeks ago. The child also died.

Abel's two children by his first wife live with his mother at East Dereham, Norfolk.

SIX DIE IN AVALANCHE

A girl is the only survivor of a party of seven skiers who were swept to their deaths by an avalanche yesterday on the Driesen Mountain in the Uri Canton. The party were all Swiss, says Central News.

TUESDAY, JANUARY 12, 1937

Daily Mirror

No. 10331 — Registered at the G.P.O. as a newspaper. — ONE PENNY

MURDER OF KIDNAPPED BOY INFLAMES U.S.—HUNT IN SNOW

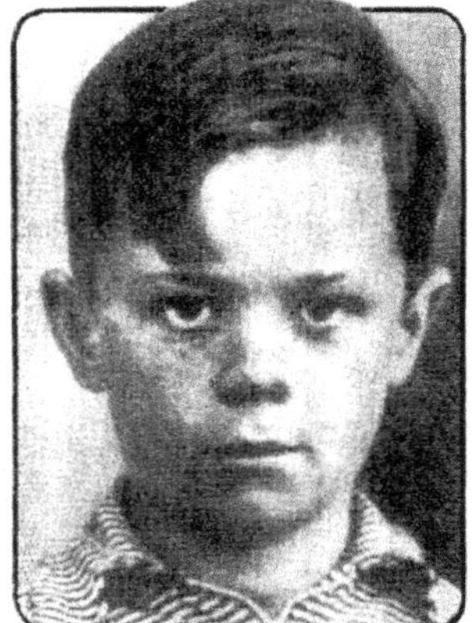

Ten-year-old Charles Mattson. His kidnappers killed him: £5,600 ransom was waiting.

FROM OUR OWN CORRESPONDENT

TACOMA (Washington), Monday.

Naked, beaten to death, flung from a speeding car, the broken body of ten-year-old Charles Mattson was found to-day half-buried in snow in the foothills of the Rocky Mountains, fifty miles from his home in Tacoma, from which a masked, bearded gangster kidnapped him sixteen days ago.

TO-NIGHT, as the news set the United States aflame with rage, wealthy Dr. W. W. Mattson, Charles's father, raced to Everette, nearest town to the spot where the body was found.

To detectives who broke the news, Dr. Mattson cried: "I will believe nothing until I have seen with my own eyes." He advertised only a few days ago that he would pay the £5,600 ransom demanded by the kidnapper.

Sheriff Fears Lynching

Mrs. Mattson collapsed, speechless with grief, when she was told of the murder.

Sheriff Bjorklund, of Tacoma, swore: "Our hunt will be as relentless as that for the murderer-kidnapper of the Lindbergh baby.

The entire police force of the county, headed by picked G-men, have been mobilised to track down this brutal killer.

"Volunteers who know the countryside round Everette will help the police.

"My only fear is that justice will be baulked if these men get hold of the murderer. There is no doubt that they would lynch him.

"Charles Mattson's body was found by a young man who was hunting rabbits in the woods.

"As he came into a clearing 200 yards from the main highway he saw a tiny arm protruding through the snow."

The coroner declared that the boy died on January 7 or 8, and that his body was frozen before he was dumped in the woods.

Charles Mattson was kidnapped on the night of December 27. He was sitting with his fourteen-year-old sister when a masked man burst into the room.

Mrs. Mattson, fearful that her son would die of exposure—the temperature was well below zero when he was carried away—issued an appeal to the kidnapper:

"Keep my son warm. Save him from harm. He has just had a severe cold."

Muriel, sister of the boy, who, with a girl friend, saw him kidnapped, and (right) Dr. W. W. Mattson, his father.

HITLER'S PLEDGE TO FRANCE—RESPECT FOR SPAIN'S INTEGRITY

HITLER and the French Ambassador to Berlin, M. Francois-Poncet, yesterday exchanged assurances that the integrity of Spain and Spanish Morocco would be respected.

This move, which eases the tension which has arisen between the two countries in the last few days, was made informally at the diplomatic reception given by Hitler, says Reuter.

The Ambassador, replying for the diplomats to Hitler's welcome, emphasised Europe's anxiety over events marking the New Year.

Afterwards Hitler and M. Francois-Poncet had an informal talk, during which the mutual assurances were exchanged.

U-boats off Morocco—page 3.

WOMAN APPOINTED POLICE SURGEON

DR. Eleanor M. Reece has been appointed a surgeon to the Metropolitan Police. Her chief duty will be to look after the health of the women police.

Between seventy and eighty women officers will be under her charge.

Dr. Reece lives in Kensington Park-road, W. She qualified in 1919, and has been an L.C.C. schools medical officer, honorary physician at the Elizabeth Garrett Anderson Hospital, and resident surgeon at the Royal Sea Bathing Hospital, Margate.

A PRINCESS IN TROUSERS

The honeymooners photographed yesterday.

JULIANA OBEYS MOTHER-IN-LAW, SPENDS SLIMMING HONEYMOON

FROM OUR SPECIAL CORRESPONDENT

KRYNICA (Poland), Monday.

OBEYING her mother-in-law's advice, Princess Juliana is spending a slimming honeymoon. She has gone on a three-meals-a-day diet—with no sweet foods, no cream, no puddings, plenty of ski-ing.

Asked why she wants to slim, Princess Juliana smiled and said: "My mother-in-law, Princess Lippe, advised me to get a bit thinner. I want to be a good daughter-in-law—besides, my honeymoon is sweet enough."

Doctor's orders agreed with mother-in-law's advice.

So Prince Bernhard, declaring that if his wife were thinner it would be good for her, requested the cooks of the Hotel Oatria here, where they are staying, to amend their famous red beet and tripe speciality dinners to simple, slimming foods.

Result—here are the meals Princess Juliana had to-day:—

BREAKFAST.—Boiled egg; brown bread and toast with very little butter; coffee with a little milk and no cream.

TEA.—Plain English tea served at 4.30.

DINNER.—Soup; fish; meat and vegetables; fruit. Champagne.

Princess Juliana is anxious to lose at least a stone in weight.

She has taken up winter sports in earnest to help her slimming. Her ski-ing costume is navy blue trousers, a pullover and a scarf.

Calling her holiday a "sporting honeymoon," she has given up using powder.

SIR WILLIAM RAY, M.P., RESIGNS

SIR William Ray, M.P. for Richmond (Surrey), has decided to resign his seat immediately on the grounds of ill-health.

He announced his decision in a letter to the executive committee of Richmond Conservative Association.

Sir William Ray has held the seat since 1932.

He was re-elected at the last General Election, when the figures were: Sir William Ray (C.), 30,433; L. Gassman (Soc.), 10,953; Conservative majority, 19,480.

The Socialist candidate at the by-election will be Mr. E. T. Lancaster.

MAJOR FINDS HIS WIFE SHOT

RETURNING from a hunt, Major C. Pepys, of Knowle House, Knowle (Devon), found his wife shot through the head.

She was lying in a downstairs room with a shotgun which had been discharged nearby.

For some time Mrs. Pepys, forty, had been suffering from a nervous breakdown.

Suicide while of unsound mind was the verdict at last night's inquest at Budleigh Salterton, Devon.

Major Pepys and his wife have lived in the district for several years.

There are two children, a girl aged ten and a boy aged six.

THURSDAY, JANUARY 14, 1937

Daily Mirror

No. 10333 Registered at the G.P.O. as a newspaper. ONE PENNY

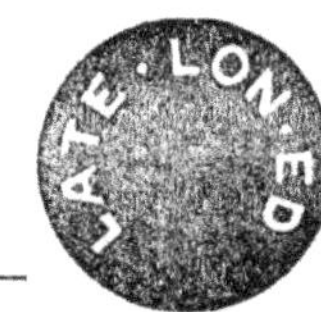

MR. SIMPSON CHARGES SLANDER AGAINST A COLONEL'S WIFE

Mr. Ernest Simpson, husband of Mrs. Wallis Simpson, has issued a writ for alleged slander against Mrs. Joan Sutherland, wife of Lieutenant-Colonel A. H. C. Sutherland, O.B.E., M.C., of Connaught Square, London, W.

MR. SIMPSON WAS THE RESPONDENT IN DIVORCE PROCEEDINGS AT IPSWICH IN OCTOBER WHEN MRS. SIMPSON WAS GRANTED A DECREE NISI ON THE GROUNDS OF HER HUSBAND'S ADULTERY WITH AN UNNAMED WOMAN.

The action is based on a remark alleged to have been made concerning the Ipswich divorce proceedings.

Mr. Henry North Lewis, of the firm of solicitors, Middleton, Lewis and Clarke, of Leadenhall-street, London, E.C., who advised Mr. Simpson in the divorce proceedings, told the *Daily Mirror* last night:—

"I can only confirm that a writ has been issued.

"I cannot tell you where Mr. Simpson is at the moment. He is somewhere in London, but I do not know his address."

Mr. Ernest Aldrich Simpson, who is thirty-nine, was born in New York. His father was English and his mother Canadian

In Coldstream Guards

After graduating at Harvard he entered the Coldstream Guards in 1918. He later went to work in the ship-chartering firm of his father, Simpson, Spence and Young. He married Dorothea, daughter of Arthur Webb Parsons, member of an old New England family and there is a daughter now aged twelve.

After the dissolution of this marriage he was transferred by his firm to London, where he married in 1928 Mrs. Wallis Spencer—wife of Lieutenant Spencer, a U.S. naval airman.

Through the introduction of Mrs. Benjamin Thaw and Thelma Lady Furness, sisters of Mrs. Gloria Vanderbilt, the Simpsons were invited while living in London to dine with the then Prince of Wales at Fort Belvedere.

They were often guests when the Prince of Wales dined at the Farm-street, London, house of Mr. and Mrs. Thaw.

As a close friend of Thelma Lady Furness, Mrs. Simpson was often a member of parties given at Fort Belvedere and St. James's Palace.

When Mr. and Mrs. Simpson took a flat at Bryanston-court, W., in 1934, they entertained a great deal and the Prince was a regular guest.

In August last year Mrs. Simpson was one

(Continued on back page)

Mrs. Joan Sutherland.

Mr. Ernest Simpson. A Harvard man, he was later an officer in the Coldstream Guards

"BRITAIN HAS FIVE MONTHS TO PREPARE" WARNS ARMY CHIEF

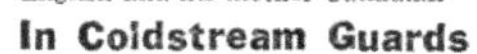

"Your country is in danger. Some people say we have five years in which to prepare. I would feel an optimist if I said five months from to-night."

FIELD-MARSHAL Lord Milne struck this warning note last night at a dinner in support of the London (City and County) and Middlesex cadet movement at the Mansion House.

The time had arrived, he declared to train the youth of the nation so that it would be ready for that greatest of all services—service for the country.

"The next ten years will probably decide the fate of the British Empire and the British people," he said.

Referring to "another period of madness when every effort was made to throw away all forms of preparedness," Lord Milne declared that the youth of the nation had its patriotism and instinctive desire for service damped

Lord Milne was Chief of the Imperial Staff for seven years from 1926 until 1933

TO SHARE HORSE OF MAN THEY LOVED

BY A SPECIAL CORRESPONDENT

RUSSETT, favourite horse of Mr. Charles Vivian Jackson, who was killed in a sleigh accident at St. Moritz, has now become the joint property of the two women who mattered most in his life—his widow and Miss Peggy Hopkins Joyce, the actress.

Mr. Jackson gave four of his horses to Miss Joyce, but in Russett, on which he won his first steeplechase, he kept a half interest.

As he has apparently left no will that half interest automatically passes to his wife.

"I am certainly going to keep my interest in the horse," Mrs. Jackson told me at her London home last night.

"I have an affection for the horse."

FRIDAY, JANUARY 22, 1937

Daily Mirror

No. 10340 Registered at the G.P.O. as a newspaper. ONE PENNY

'PLANE HITS SHIP: CREW SEE PILOT DROWN BUT SAVE MECHANIC

FROM OUR SPECIAL CORRESPONDENT.

Belfast, Friday Morning.

Battling frantically to reach the Belfast steamer Corrib (624 tons), as her engines threatened to fail over the Irish Sea, a 'plane piloted by Captain Eric George Stuart, of London, crashed into the rigging of the ship and plunged under the forecastle head.

A boat hurriedly lowered from the steamer snatched Cyril Poole, of Asquith-road, Cheltenham, mechanic on the machine, from the sea, but the crew saw Stuart sink "like a stone" as they drew alongside.

THE STORY WAS TOLD WHEN THE CORRIB DOCKED WITH THE SURVIVOR AT BELFAST AT 2 A.M. TO-DAY.

Seven lifeboats and forty trawlers had joined in the search when radios flashed a message that Stuart was missing on a flight from Liverpool to Belfast.

Captain Archibald Wilson, master of the Corrib, told me when he landed: "The mate was on deck at the time of the accident. He gave the alarm, and I hurried to the bridge.

"The 'plane was evidently struggling to reach the ship. It seemed as if the pilot was nursing the engine.

"It came down alongside and actually struck the rigging and crashed under the fo'castle head. We were going full speed at the time, but we hove to at once.

"Poole was washed clear of the 'plane, and was drifting helplessly in the sea. My ship's boat rushed to the rescue.

"The crew reached him and then pulled for the wreckage. But it was their bitter experience to see Stuart sink when they were within a few boats' length of saving him.

"We cruised around for a considerable time, but there was no hope of recovering the body, and we reluctantly proceeded on our journey."

"Declined Lifebelt"

When Poole was landed he was suffering from exhaustion, and was rushed to hospital.

In his bed he told me: "We ran into really bad weather soon after leaving Liverpool, and another 'plane which was following turned back. Captain Stuart decided to continue to Belfast.

"Wind and rain forced us down, and at times we were within a few feet of the sea.

"I saw that disaster lay ahead. I adjusted my lifebelt, and handed another to Captain Stuart. "Thanks, I won't bother," he told me.

"Hardly had he uttered those words when the 'plane crashed. It had been a race with death to reach the steamer.

"Captain Stuart clung to the wreckage, and I was swept away almost immediately, but my lifebelt stood me in good stead.

"I can honestly tell you that I tried to loosen my lifebelt to end it all, but I went into oblivion, and the next thing I knew I found myself being hauled out of the water."

Captain Stuart, who was a New Zealander, lived at Earl's Court, London, with his wife and

(Continued on back page)

Rumours spread over Chicago yesterday that Katherine Hepburn was marrying Howard Hughes (left), Texas millionaire. And all day long thousands of people thronged the Marriage Bureau corridors to see the show. But the couple remained secluded in a hotel suite—the Hepburn taking Garbo's "silence" cue.

But late at night, when she was due to go down to the theatre for "Jane Eyre," the Hepburn issued a statement. "Miss Hepburn says she won't marry Hughes to-day," it said.

Mr. George Legassick, aged eighty-three, oldest fisherman of Hope Cove, kisses the bride. Her groom, Mr. Ernest Powlesland, stands at her left hand.

SHE FORFEITS LIFE OF LUXURY TO BE "PERFECT WIFE" IN A FISHERMAN'S COTTAGE

FROM OUR SPECIAL CORRESPONDENT

HOPE COVE, DEVON, Thursday.

WHEN she whispered the words "I will" in the tiny Holy Trinity Church here to-day a young woman gave up a life of travel and luxury to become the cottage bride of a handsome but humble fisherman.

"I mean to be the perfect fisherman's wife," she told me in the little white-washed cottage which will be her home, after the wedding.

The heroine of this story-book romance was Miss Joan Mary Ellison, whose late father was director of several Yorkshire colliery companies and whose mother lives in a large, well-staffed house at Broadway, Worcestershire.

The man whom she promised to obey was fair-haired, stockily-built Ernest Edward Powlesland, whose good looks, athletic ability and prowess as a fisherman have made him the idol of this little village.

She is thirty and he is twenty-five.

All Over World

"Don't run away with the idea that I have made any sacrifice," were the first words she said to me.

"True, I have had an expensive education, have travelled more or less all over the world and mixed with so-called society people, but what are those things compared with a happy home life with the man you love?

"I met Ernest three years ago when I came to Hope Cove for a holiday. We became so friendly that I have never left Hope Cove from that day to this.

"I bought myself a little cottage called The Turrets and changed the name to The Crab Pot in honour of my husband's calling.

"We are going to live there, and I can tell you I mean to be the perfect fisherman's wife. I have a tiny private income of my own, and

(Continued on back page)

ALL-MOUSE OPERA IS HIS AMBITION

FROM OUR OWN CORRESPONDENT

NEW YORK, Thursday.

AN all-mouse opera company is the ambition of Gil C. Brown, of Bloomington, Illinois, who, impressed by the "epidemic" of singing mice, wants to turn marriage broker.

Brown employs Mickey, Chicago's singing mouse, for £7 a week at his Bloomington theatre, and wants Mickey to become the husband of Minny, the singing mouse of Woodstock.

He believes their offspring would produce a race of "warblers," thus founding an all-mouse opera.

America's reply to Mickey of Devonport, England, who was trapped twelve days ago, has been to find two more singing mice.

Edith, caught last week in a farmhouse at Salisbury, Maryland, has already broadcast and sung for a talkie.

DUKE OF KENT SPEAKS OF: "HAPPILY MARRIED PEOPLE"

Seventy thousand British children are neglected at home; another 10,000—many of them babies—are cruelly ill-treated.

"THAT is sad hearing to people like myself who are happily married and have children," said the Duke of Kent, speaking in London last night.

The Duke mentioned the figures when he appealed for higher public contributions to help the National Society for the Prevention of Cruelty to Children.

SATURDAY, JANUARY 23, 1937

Daily Mirror

No. 10341 Registered at the G.P.O. as a newspaper ONE PENNY

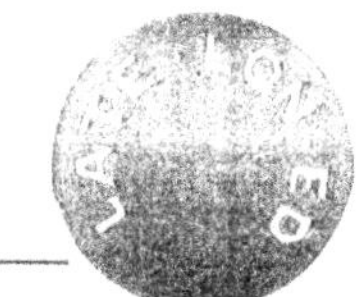

'I'LL NEVER RE-MARRY,' SAYS WIDOW OF 19 AWARDED £1,165

Mrs. Mildred May Small and her three-year-old daughter.

FROM OUR SPECIAL CORRESPONDENT

SPALDING (Lincs.), Friday.

With tragedy stamped on her young face, a dark-eyed widow of nineteen, awarded £1,165 damages for the death of her husband in a road smash, told me to-day that she will never marry again.

COUNSEL in the case had called her young and pretty—with a good chance of re-marriage.

Bitterly she gave me this answer: "How does that counsel know how I feel in my heart for Bill, my husband? How can he know what it is like to have a baby who will only know her father by a picture on the wall which she calls a nice picture of Uncle Bill? She calls her grandfather 'Dad.'"

Mildred May Small, now living with her father, Mr. Fowler, at Gedney Hill, near here, had claimed damages from John William Hirst, a garage proprietor, of Burnley, for the death of thirty-four-year-old William Henry Small.

A year ago her husband was riding a motor-cycle between Sutton and Holbeach when he was killed by a car owned by the garage.

Mrs. Small was left with a baby girl now aged three and no home and no money.

"All I Loved"

Hard work and hard times have made her face life bravely. Simply dressed in black with a white frill at her throat, she looked around the little labourer's cottage where she has taken refuge since her husband's death.

"There are eight in the family living here," she said. "People are cynical about money and think that a young and pretty woman who claims damages can have a good time.

"Can money really make up for loss or damages for a broken life?

"Bill was all I loved, and I shall never forget him, and unless I change my character completely I shall never marry again.

"Mother is ill. We buried grandfather yesterday.

"My place is here by my parents and with my child"

"Money for Education"

A sum of over £1,000 has probably never been seen in that cottage before. When Mrs. Small received the telegram from Northampton, where the judgment was delivered to-day, there was no rejoicing in the family.

The money will probably be used for the education of three-year-old Pamela Mavis.

"We are simple folk, but my daughter shall never lack a home as long as I am alive." Mr. Fowler said quietly.

CORONATION BROADCAST

New plans for the Coronation are announced this morning.

Street radio is to broadcast the Abbey ceremony to London's crowds.

Seven thousand seven hundred guests will fill the Abbey. One-piece carpet, 173 feet long, will cover processional way.

See page 3.

FATHER'S SECRET

Miss Mabel Beetham, of Bedford Park, W., whose father yesterday sued Reginald Harry James (right), of Shepherd's Bush, for damages for her alleged seduction.

During the hearing her father admitted that his statement that he had been married thirty-four years was untrue—and that there had been no marriage.

See story on page 4

"PLAY FOR ENGLAND AS YOU NEVER PLAYED BEFORE" IS DYING WOMAN'S LAST REQUEST TO HER GRANDSON

WHEN W. W. Parr, twenty-one-year-old Blackpool outside right, plays for England to-day against Wales at Portsmouth in his fourth amateur international game, he will be complying with the dying wish on Thursday of his grandmother, Mrs. Mary Ellen Sharples.

Mrs. Sharples, who was seventy-five, called Parr to her bedside, and said to him: "I want you to play in this game—and you must play the game of your life."

An hour later she died.

Parr lived with his grandmother most of his life, and no one watched his football career with greater interest.

Yet, it was football that caused the death of her husband. Two years ago as he was watching Parr playing in a junior football match the ball struck him in the face, and a few hours later he died.

"MAN WITH SEVEN WIVES" IS CITED IN DIVORCE SUIT

"DAILY MIRROR" SPECIAL NEWS

A MAN who was said to have had seven "wives" will figure as respondent in a divorce action at Leicester Assizes next week.

He is John Ainsworth Christien, who was sentenced to twenty months' hard labour for bigamy and fraud at the Old Bailey last week.

The suit is being brought by his legal wife, whom he married at Hornsea, Yorkshire, in October, 1932. The case is listed as "Elliott v. Elliott."

It was in the name of John Barry Elliott that Christien went through the ceremony, his wife being Miss Marjorie Yvonne Wilson.

They went to Barcelona for their honeymoon.

While in Spain Christien met Senorita Rosita Rivero whom he afterwards bigamously married

2 DEAD IN LOST 'PLANE WRECK

Seventeen hours after it had vanished a Channel 'plane was found wrecked on a hillside near Oxted, Surrey, late last night. The pilot and wireless operator were dead.

See BACK PAGE.

TUESDAY, JANUARY 26, 1937

Daily Mirror

No. 10343 Registered at the G.P.O. as a newspaper. ONE PENNY

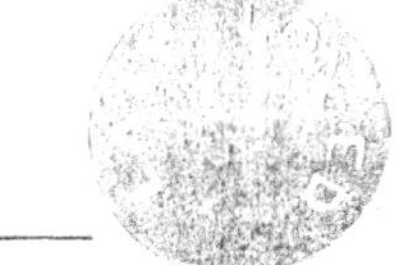

70-FOOT SWIM UNDER PIT FLOOD TO TRAPPED MEN

FROM OUR OWN CORRESPONDENT

PENZANCE, Monday.

Into black flood water filling the gallery of a Cornish tin mine, ex-sailor Clifford Bawden plunged to-night and swam 70ft.—head below the surface—to the ledge on which three miners had been trapped for more than fifty hours.

AS he took his last deep breath before diving he knew that he was risking his life. On that perilous swim, 300ft. below ground, there was no chance of being able to come to the surface to breathe.

For there was no room for a man's head between the surface of the water and the roof of the V-shaped working.

With bursting lungs he broke the surface at the other end of the gallery. He switched on the electric torch he carried.

The circle of light picked out the faces of John Bates, George Williams, David Sedgeman—all safe, after being trapped since Saturday afternoon in the darkness of the Whealreeth Tin Mine Co.'s mine.

Bawden gave them some stimulants from a watertight container, told them safety was near. Then he plunged back into the water.

Rescuers' Cheers

The men waited nearly an hour until pumps had reduced the level of the water, and then waded breast high through the floods to safety.

They were surprised to learn it was Monday evening. They had lost all count of time and thought it was Sunday afternoon.

The rescue parties at the mine shaft end of the gallery had never thought Bawden would succeed in his daring attempt to reach the ledge. Others had attempted to reach the men by wading up to their necks in water. All had been compelled to turn back.

There had been silence as Bawden disappeared below the surface. Minutes passed. . . . Then cheers echoed as he reappeared.

Survivor's Story

Last man to arrive at the surface was John Bates, twenty-three, of Helston. Lying on a stretcher at the pit-head Bates told the *Daily Mirror*:—

"The first thing I knew about the accident was a man shouting 'Look out. Run for your life.'

"I turned to run, and was struck in the back by a mass of falling water.

"I clutched some iron pipes in the mine shaft, and climbed the tunnel.

"We performed feats of climbing which we could never have done without being driven by danger, and finally we got above the level of the water. We sat in the darkness and waited, and later on were encouraged by tappings from above."

Bawden himself, was among the party who were trapped by the flood on Saturday afternoon. He was rescued, however, after three hours.

John Bates (centre), last of the three rescued men to reach the surface, smilingly greeting the colleagues who had shared in the rescue

'POPE WILL NEVER RESUME NORMAL LIFE'

A grave turn of the Pope's illness was revealed late last night when a Vatican prelate in close touch with the Pontifical Department made this statement:—

"Although the last few days have brought no actual change in the local symptoms of the illness they have confirmed the impression previously formed that a complete recovery can no longer be hoped for.

"The Holy Father may be left to guide the Church for many months to come, but he will remain incapacitated and will never be able to resume his normal life.

"On the other hand, he may be the victim of a sudden cardiac or circulation attack which his medical adviser cannot prevent."

After last night's examination (says the Exchange) Professor Milani expressed satisfaction at the result of the treatment intended to prevent the spread of gangrene.

THEY BURNED THE MASTER'S CANE

BOYS have raided schools at Southend. At one school the master's cane was put on top of a heap of books, maps and pencils in the main hall, and the pile was set on fire.

Pinned to the wall of a classroom by a knife was an envelope on which was written "Death to Tyrants."

From the store-room of another school a French sabre and a bayonet were taken and placed beside two tiny children found asleep in a shed after they had been reported missing

SHE DOESN'T LIKE HERSELF

Ruth Chatterton never sees one of her own films, because she says: "It's agony to see myself blinking my eyes"—a mannerism which has helped to make her the star she is.

RUTH CHATTERTON 'HATES' HERSELF ON THE SCREEN

BY A SPECIAL CORRESPONDENT

CHIC, ultra-attractive film star Ruth Chatterton hates herself on the screen so much that she hasn't seen the last six films in which she has starred.

She confessed this to me last night when I saw her in London on her arrival from Paris.

Ruth Chatterton is Ruth Chatterton's worst fan.

"I've got a lot of bad habits and mannerisms which they seem to like to photograph in Hollywood," she said. "I blink my eyes a lot, for instance. To see myself doing that is just agony. I hate it.

"Then I've got a funny nose with a bump on the end of it. Since I first saw all this of myself on the screen, I just don't go and see my pictures."

Miss Chatterton, who is forty-three, thinks that age doesn't matter if you are an actress.

"I've been playing mothers and grandmothers since I was sixteen. Good acting is above age. And I am an actress first. I couldn't pretend to be a beauty like some of those people in Hollywood."

Her tonic before an arduous day in the studio is a half-hour above Hollywood in her 175 m.p.h. monoplane. She got her pilot's certificate three years ago

B.B.C.-BAITING SPLITS RADIO LEAGUE

SIR Patrick Hannon, Conservative M.P. for Moseley, Birmingham, threatened to resign from the chairmanship of the Listeners' League at a private meeting of League members held at the House of Commons last night.

Sir Patrick stated that he differed profoundly from some of his colleagues on the question of the League's policy. He refuses to be a party to attacks on the B.B.C. unless there are good reasons for doing so.

The League, it is understood, is critical of the internal administration of the B.B.C., but Sir Patrick considers that this is not the League's business.

Another special meeting of the League, to which several thousand listeners belong, is to be held. Unless Sir Patrick can get full support for his view, he states, he will resign.

Postmaster-General turns down B.B.C. "political bias" inquiry—page 7.

MONDAY, FEBRUARY 1, 1937

Daily Mirror

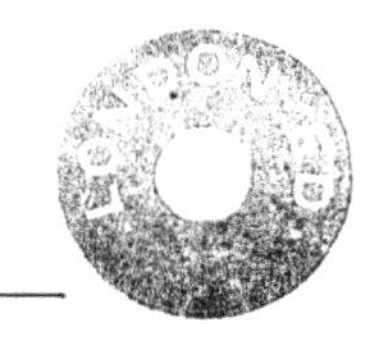

No. 10348 — Registered at the G.P.O. as a newspaper. — ONE PENNY

MARRIAGE AT NINE SHOCKS U.S. WOMEN

FROM OUR OWN CORRESPONDENT

NEW YORK, Sunday.

WOMEN of America are launching the greatest outcry in their history to end the marriage of nine-year-old Eunice Winstead and 6ft. twenty-two-year-old Charles Johns, of Sneedville, Tennessee.

President Roosevelt himself is known to be shocked. But he is powerless to act. No law forbids such a marriage.

The United States Constitution would have to be changed to provide a law. Prominent American women plan a campaign to change it.

The League for Woman president will take the case of Eunice and Charles to the Supreme Court and will seek to have the marriage annulled on the grounds that it conforms to a law not in the public interest.

Miss Lillian Rock, president of the League, told me to-day:—

"We are going to fight. It is a national scandal repugnant to every woman in the civilised States of America.

"I say 'civilised' because Tennessee is the sort of place where anything can happen. They denied the laws of evolution there once. Now they have allowed this poor child to marry a man twenty-two years old when she isn't old enough to find her own way to school.

"But don't let England imagine that the women of America are prepared to do nothing about it.

"We are. Unfortunately, every State in America is able to make its own marriage laws. And that is Tennessee's idea of a 'law.'

"We Will Get Busy"

"Every women's organisation in the country will be getting busy, and when that happens over here, something usually gets done.

"There's the future of a human being at stake, and that's enough for us."

Charles and Eunice, who were married by a travelling minister at the side of a mountain road, are now in a honeymoon cottage.

Charles says he will fight anyone who tries to take Eunice away from him.

He said to-day: "Eunice does not know what this marriage business is all about yet, but for a while I am going to try to make things easy for her."

"I married her because I loved her and wanted a home. She married me because she wanted to. Her parents don't mind, so it is nobody else's business.

Eloped at 13

"If anyone tries to interfere with us they'll get a fight."

Eunice, who doesn't look a day older than her years, was wearing a dress that did not reach to her knees. She adjusted the bonnet of her doll—wedding gift from Charles—and prattled. "Charlie's going to build me a house and I am going to learn housekeeping. Soon I shall put away my doll and get to work. I can already make a bed."

Eunice's is the second child marriage in the district within two weeks. Ella Green, thirteen-year-old schoolgirl, eloped with Charles Newbery, seventeen.

Just before Christmas, Irvene Rhoades, aged twelve, married Clarence D. Leach, a young factory worker at Wabash, Indiana.

Mrs. Ellen Walker, of Panacea, Florida, married in 1935 at twelve, has born a son to her husband of twenty-two, Cullen Walker, a surveyor.

Scandal of child marriage was attacked by the famous American authoress, Katherine Mayo, in her book, "Mother India."

HIS WEDDING GIFT TO HER WAS A DOLL

Nine-year-old Mrs. Johns (Eunice Winstead, of Tennessee) with her twenty-two-year-old farmer husband. He gave her a doll for her wedding present.

WOMEN—OVER THIRTY

"It is not true that the usefulness of women is finished at thirty. If it were, it would be a dreary thing to look forward to," said Miss Dorothy L. Sayers, the novelist, in a broadcast last night in aid of the Over Thirty Association.

The King's First Honours List

YOUNGEST KNIGHT FOR 26 YEARS

BY A SPECIAL CORRESPONDENT

THE New Year's Honours issued to-day—King George VI's first list—is almost unaltered from that approved by King Edward just before his abdication.

The Queen becomes a Dame Grand Cross of the Royal Victorian Order and Grand Master of the Order.

The Duke of Kent and Lord Louis Mountbatten become personal Naval Aides-de-Camp to the King.

The Duke of Connaught, the Duke of Gloucester, the Duke of Kent, Prince Arthur of Connaught, the Earl of Athlone and the Earl of Harewood become personal Aides-de-Camp.

The Duke of Gloucester is granted a commission as an Air Vice-Marshal.

The list, which includes one Viscount, three Barons, two Privy Councillors, six Baronets and twenty-nine Knights Bachelor (exclusive of overseas), is in PAGE FOUR.

Fifty-six women appear in it.

Mr. Malcolm Stewart, ex-Commissioner for Special Areas, who drew up the report, becomes a baronet, and Mr. Walter Monckton, K.C., legal adviser to the Duchy of Cornwall, who figured prominently during the Abdication, becomes a Knight Commander of the Royal Victorian Order.

Industry's two chief representatives are Sir Harry McGowan, one of the new peers, and Henry Philip Price (knight), head of Price (Tailors), Ltd., of Leeds, the Fifty-Shilling Tailors and donor of £20,000 to Bradford Grammar School.

Youngest Knight

Sir Harry McGowan, who is sixty-two, started work as an office boy at 5s. a week when fifteen at Nobel's Explosives. Twenty-six years later he was a director and in 1918 he was made managing director and knighted.

Now he is chairman and managing director of £76,000,000 Imperial Chemical Industries, Ltd., which employs 50,000 people in the United Kingdom alone.

Thomas Cook, M.P. for North Norfolk and great-grandson of the founder of the famous tourist agency, receives a knighthood. At thirty-four he is youngest knight for twenty-six years.

He has done probably more than any other man in this country to improve the standard of the fire-fighting services in rural areas.

He organised the first International Fire Brigades' Conference, and on his estate—Sennowe Park, Guist—Mr. Cook maintains a fully-equipped motor fire-engine and brigade which is available to surrounding villages.

For Courage

Courage gets its reward in the list.

Squadron-Leader F. R. D. Swain, aged thirty-three, receives the Air Force Cross for his magnificent achievement in setting up a new height record for heavier-than-air craft last September at 15,223 metres, of 49,944ft.

A pioneer in X-ray research whose experiments have resulted in permanent injury and ill-health, receives the O.B.E.

He is Dr. Bernard Hart, fifty-three, of Armthorpe, West Yorks, who began experiments in X-ray in 1905—"the dangerous days of X-ray research."

As a result of his experiments he was severely burned, but immediately on his discharge from hospital he began his work again. Time and time again he was injured and lost a finger due to extensive burns.

"My health has been broken by my experiments," Dr. Hart told me, "but I'd go through it all again.

"Anyone would have done the same if they'd had the opportunity.

"I was terrifically bucked when I learnt that

(Continued on back page)

A HALT FOR RUNNING REPAIRS: And if you had driven from John o' Groats to Monte Carlo, like Miss Parnell, here, you'd want a compact with your complexion.

PASSENGERS LOOKED ON AS BUS WAS STOLEN

A GLEAMING new twenty-seater bus, "The Favourite," stood in one of the main streets of Selby, Yorks, on Saturday night. A man got in the driver's seat and in full view of dozens of people, drove off. Intended passengers thought he had gone for petrol for the bus, which was not due to start its next journey to Carwood for fifteen minutes.

In Ploughed Field

Five minutes later the owner-driver of the bus came up. It was then the waiting passengers realised that the bus had been stolen.

The bus was found yesterday in a ploughed field several miles away. It took twenty men working with blocks and tackle to get it back to the road.

'BLATANT REPUDIATION OF SEX MORALITY,' SAYS BISHOP

"There has been an almost blatant repudiation of Christian standards, especially as regards sexual morality, within the last thirty years."—the Bishop of St. Albans (Dr. M. B. Furse) at St. Martin's-in-the-Fields last night.

SATURDAY, FEBRUARY 6, 1937

Daily Mirror

No. 10353 Registered at the G.P.O. as a newspaper. ONE PENNY

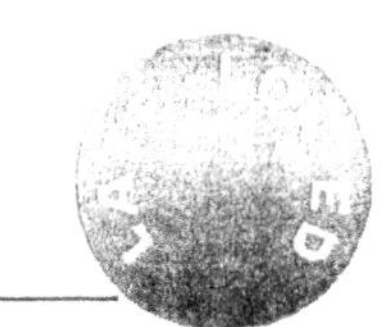

STALIN'S SECRET GUARD OF 1,000 AS ARMY PLOT TO CURB HIS POWER

SMILING 'NAPOLEON' OF RUSSIA

Klimentyi Yefremovitch Voroshiloff, Marshal of the Soviet Union, is the Napoleon of Russia.

Handsome, quick to smile, with dancing blue eyes and black curly hair, he looks younger than he is—fifty-six.

At seven he was herding cattle. At twelve he was only just learning to read. Then followed years of revolutionary work, banishment to Siberia—freedom.

His rise to fame, with the coming to power of Lenin, was swift—though Trotsky once said of him, "He might at a pinch command a regiment, but never an army."

To-day, still the least educated of all the Marshals, he is a dashing leader, an idol of the people.

Rides a high-spirited cavalry horse—but drives in a Rolls-Royce when he acts the popular hero.

FROM OUR OWN CORRESPONDENT

WARSAW, Friday.

With rumours of a Red Army revolt growing in Moscow, Stalin to-day installed a bodyguard of 1,000 picked soldiers at the doors of the Kremlin, which houses his own apartments and Government headquarters.

During the day about 50 Ogpu agents have been arrested.

MARSHAL Voroshiloff, head of Russia's great army, has summoned all the Soviet Russian Marshals to a conference in Moscow to-morrow.

To Government officials and Army leaders the change of the Kremlin guard came as a great surprise. It was kept secret and occurred unexpectedly at midnight.

Not even the highest officers of the guard knew anything about it until they were told to clear out and the new regiment arrived to keep guard at the Kremlin.

Army's Demand

All of them are trustworthy soldiers from Georgia—Stalin's home country. All the five gates of the Kremlin Fortress are stated to have been strengthened, particularly the main one, called Salvation Gate, which leads to the Red Square.

Marshal Voroshiloff, after paying a hasty visit to Leningrad, held a conference with the generals there. As soon as he returned to Moscow he summoned the conference of the five marshals.

It is believed that Voroshiloff and Stalin are anxious to avoid a serious clash, but the military are anxious that Voroshiloff should obtain a proper share in the Government.

The next few days will be decisive. Bloodshed is said to have accompanied the arrest of the fifty Ogpu officials.

30 Fires in Day

A number of them tried to protect themselves with pistols and were shot. All are believed to be followers of Woronin, the director of the Lubianka Prison, who was arrested earlier in the week. Woronin was a friend of Piapakoff, and was suspected of plotting to free Piapakoff before his execution on Monday morning.

Reports published in Berlin of students' riots are not denied.

Thirty more fires are reported to have occurred in Moscow during the last twenty-four hours.

Owing to the feeling of panic prices of food are rising heavily. A pound of butter was quoted to-day at about fourteen shillings.

Marshal Voroshiloff, chief of the Red Army, who has summoned all Soviet Russia's Marshals to a conference.

£100 REWARD FOR TRAPPING "MURDER-IMPULSE" FIEND

REWARD of £100 will be paid by the Royal Society for the Prevention of Cruelty to Animals to anyone who gives information leading to the conviction of the cat-slaying fiend of Fulham who, this week alone, has strangled twelve cats.

One fear is that if the killer is not caught soon he may turn to killing children.

For it is believed that the fiend is suffering from a "murder impulse."

A London psychologist told the *Daily Mirror* last night: "The cause of this person's mental affliction is probably inferiority complex.

"The murder impulse here is directed towards cats.

"These cases generally have their roots in some youthful illness. It is a disease modern psychological methods can cure."

One of the twelve cats killed in the past week was impaled on railings alive and dragged itself free to died in agony.

Sometimes the fiend snares a cat with cord and hangs it.

Inspectors are patrolling the streets of South-West London day and night.

ON THE WAY TO SEE HER BROTHER

The Princess Royal arriving in London from Leeds last night on the first stage of her journey, with her husband, the Earl of Harewood, to visit the Duke of Windsor at Enzesfeld Castle, near Vienna.

There had been some doubt as to whether the Earl of Harewood would accompany the Princess, but the "Daily Mirror" was informed officially at Harewood House that he was to make the trip to see his brother-in-law.

The Earl travelled to London in the Pullman coach attached to the 1.10 p.m. express from Leeds to King's Cross and the Princess followed on the Queen of Scots Pullman from the same station.

THURSDAY, FEBRUARY 11, 1937

Daily Mirror

No. 10357 Registered at the G.P.O. as a newspaper. ONE PENNY

BACHELOR M.P.S HEAD DEMAND FOR HIGHER BIRTH RATE

BACHELOR M.P.s demanding an official inquiry into Britain's falling population heard Mr. R. A. Pilkington (Con., Widnes), himself twenty-six, unmarried, ask the Chancellor of the Exchequer in the House of Commons last night to put a tax on bachelors to end the problem.

"I recently learned with amazement and horror," he said, "that even in the House of Commons, where the age limit is fairly high, there are nearly 200 bachelors. Members should take immediate steps to remedy that."

It was thirty-year-old Mr. J. R. H. Cartland, unmarried Member for King's Norton, who moved the demand for the inquiry—and blamed love of luxury for the modern small family.

Mr. H. '. Parker (Soc., Romford), bachelor of twenty-eight, supported him—but he blamed war. Mothers would not bear sons to fight.

But it was left to Mr. Henderson Stewart, East Fife's bachelor member, to explain in an interview later why more M.P.s did not take a personal interest in the problem.

"IT MAY BE THAT, LIKE MYSELF, MANY OF THE :00 ARE BLESSED WITH SUPERB MOTHERS IN COMPARISON WITH WHOM IT SEEMS IMPOSSIBLE TO FIND A MODERN YOUNG WOMAN FIT TO BE A WIFE.

"The Scottish mother born in the last generation is unsurpassed."

Of the nine women M.P.s only three—the Duchess of Atholl, Lady Astor and Mrs. Tate—are married; not one of the nine spoke in the debate.

Meanwhile, Mr. Arthur Hayday (Soc., West Nottingham), who has had eighteen children, sat quietly on his bench and listened to the bachelors talking.

Government Accept

Their demand was accepted on behalf of the Government by Mr. R. S. Hudson (Parliamentary Secretary, Ministry of Health), who promised to "intensify" an inquiry which had been continuously studying the subject. He appealed for any society to help in the research.

He mentioned that "the one deserving thing about the birth-rate" was that since 1933, for the "first time in our history," it had remained stable. "In fact, the total in the last few years has shown a slight rise."

Mr. Cartland, moving that an inquiry be held, said that the birth-rate had been falling persistently since 1875.

We had about twenty years' breathing space in which it was possible, if it was desirable, to reverse this trend.

What was the reason for the tendency towards smaller families? Was it incompatible with an increase in families that we should have radio, small cars, visits to football matches, and cinemas, silk stockings and permanent waves?

Mr. D. Sandys (Cons., Norwood), seconding

(Continued on back page)

Mr. R. Cartland, M.P. (left) and Mr. R. Pilkington, M.P.

HER £50 A WEEK TRICK

Vavien Gaye fell off her horse as film director Herbert Wilcox's car came by . . . now she's his new star.

STAGED FALL FROM HORSE—AND IT WON HER FILM STARDOM

BY A SPECIAL CORRESPONDENT

AS a result of staging a fall off her horse in front of film director Herbert Wilcox's car, a beautiful young Chester girl has won a three-year film contract starting at £50 a week.

The resourceful actress is nineteen-year-old Vavien Gaye, and she has just completed working in her first film role opposite Gordon Harker in a screen version of "The Frog."

Last night Miss Gaye, who is to be Mr. Wilcox's new star, told me how she thought up her ruse to get an appointment with Mr. Wilcox at the studios. "My father, who taught us all to ride, always said that you have to learn to fall before you can ride," said Miss Gaye.

"I can fall off a horse with as much skill as the next girl, so after a lot of disappointments in not getting interviews at the studio, I decided to fall off a horse as a last resort.

"I knew when Mr. Wilcox's car was due to come down the lane I had chosen near Pinewood. Along came the car and off I fell. As he helped me up I said, 'At last we meet'

"I had a test soon after and have just finished the first picture I have ever appeared in."

Miss Gaye came to London with her family from Chester when she was fourteen

LONDON MAY HAVE WORLD'S FINEST BOULEVARD

The "finest boulevard in the world" making a traffic artery right across London from north to south may be built if the Municipal Reform Party is returned to power in the coming L.C.C. elections.

Such a road was foreshadowed by Mr. William Webbe, the Party's leader, speaking in London last night.

The boulevard, he said, would cost millions, but that was not extravagance.

If they were returned to power they should plan a great traffic artery which would come as far south as the Elephant and Castle and go right away across London to Euston-road or Hampstead-road.

Two girls, both only nineteen, tell to-day how they earn £50 a week.

Crooner Evelyn Dall "just yells into the microphone and somehow the boys like it." She's going to retire when she's twenty-five.

Actress Vavien Gaye just fell off a horse—as a film director was passing in his car. The ruse won her a contract and stardom.

GIRL CROONER TO RETIRE AT 25

BY A SPECIAL CORRESPONDENT

PLATINUM blonde Evelyn Dall nineteen-year-old, £50-a-week American crooner, who won fame in London, plans to retire when she is twenty-five.

When I talked to her last night in her dressing-room at the New Cross Empire, London, she said:—

"Boy, I'll tell you all I know. I'm working now to get money to retire. No one wants a girl when she's over twenty-five. She loses her sex appeal then.

"Sure, I earn £50 a week. Many times it has been twice that amount.

"I send cash home to educate my young brother. He has ambitions, like me.

"It Gets Over"

Evelyn smiled, showing her pearly teeth and rolling the blue eyes that have won her thousands of "fans."

"People consider I croon well," she said. "Between ourselves, but this is a secret, I just yell into the mike.

"Somehow it gets over and they applaud, and, boy, how that makes my heart glad.

"I didn't start my career as a singer. I began as a dancer when I was fifteen.

"If luck holds out, I am not going to work after I am twenty-five. No, siree! I'm saving to put my money into something sound. Then, perhaps, one day I'll settle down.

"My crooning days will be over, and, maybe, I can croon to something that will go to sleep. You know, in a cradle."

Miss Evelyn Dall, £50 a week crooner.

FRIDAY, FEBRUARY 12, 1937

Daily Mirror

No. 10358 Registered at the G.P.O. as a newspaper. ONE PENNY

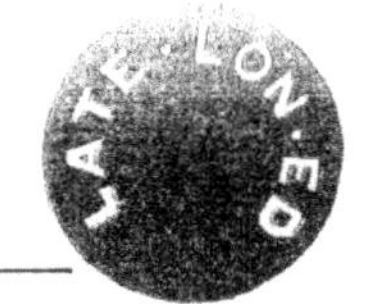

PRISONERS LEAVE GAOL TO GO DANCING AND MOTORING

FIVE SONS OF PERFECT MOTHER STAY SINGLE, SAY 'NO PLACE LIKE HOME'

BY A SPECIAL CORRESPONDENT

The " Perfect Mother " whose five grown-up sons and one daughter are so happy at home that they do not want to marry and have homes of their own told me last night of her non-marrying family.

SILVER-HAIRED Mrs. M. D. Stewart is the mother of Mr. James Henderson Stewart, thirty-nine-year-old M.P. for East Fife, who after the Bachelor Tax debate in the House of Commons on Wednesday night said he was blessed with a mother " compared with whom it seemed impossible to find a modern young woman fit to be a wife."

The first thing I learned when I called at Birchwood House, Woldingham, Surrey—the home of the Stewarts—yesterday was that James's view is shared by his four brothers and only sister. These are:—

William, thirty-four, farm inspector; Jack, thirty, engineer; Valentine, twenty-six, dance band musician; Sophie, twenty-four, actress; and Ronald, twenty-two, B.B.C. engineer.

All are strikingly good-looking. All are in good jobs. Yet none of them is married or engaged.

No Quarrels

And their reason is exactly the same. They say: " We are so happy in our home that we do not want any other."

The mother who binds this remarkable family together is small and active for her years. Her smile is kindness itself, her voice soft and low, and her eyes behind her spectacles fill with love whenever they rest on her devoted children.

" I think it is simply wonderful of James to say that about me in the House," she said to me. " He's a good boy—no mother ever had a finer. But then all my children are splendid; I have no favourites; I love them all equally well.

" Do you know we have never had a quarrel in our house. I have never had to say a harsh word to any of them, and as for punishing them—well, it simply hasn't been necessary.

" You see, both my husband and I have tried to set them a good example. We have taught them to be thrifty without being mean, to appreciate the decent things of life—music and friendship—and above all to be useful.

Milking Cows

" They all take their share of the housework; even Sophie, who is doing so well with her film acting that she is soon going to Hollywood. They can all milk a cow and play some musical instrument or another

" Music has done as much as anything else to bind our home together. We used to have our own little band and give concerts in the evenings."

And Sophie Stewart, slim, elegant, with red-brown hair, has played an important part in " As You Like It," the film in which Elisabeth Bergner starred. She is shortly to start work in a new British picture in which she will play the lead opposite Clive Brook.

" No, I have no wish to be married just yet," she declares. " I agree with my brothers that home is the best place, and I must say that what is said about the flightiness of modern girls also seems to apply to most of the modern young men."

Mrs. M. D. Stewart with her film actress daughter, Sophie Stewart, who is shortly to play the lead opposite Clive Brook.

The happy family of the Stewarts at their home at Woldingham, Surrey. A to B: William, Ronald, Sophie, Mr. and Mrs. Matthew Deas Stewart, Jack, Valentine and Mr. J. Henderson Stewart, M.P. for East Fife.

IF YOU WANT TO BE A PERFECT MOTHER, TOO—

Don't neglect the homely things.

Look after your husband and children.

See they get good food.

Make their home comfy and don't be too keen on frivolous pleasures, such as pictures and dancing.

✦ ✦ ✦

—That is Mrs. Stewart's advice to brides-to-be.

FROM OUR OWN CORRESPONDENT

GUERNSEY, Thursday.

AMAZING stories of how prisoners " played truant " from the gaol here, walking out at night, going home or going to dances, and then returning to prison in the early hours of the morning are the subject of an official inquiry.

The full truth of these alleged night excursions will not be known until the end of the inquiry.

The prison is on the outskirts of the town, and it is stated that on occasions the prisoners escaped for a visit to the outer world. The escapes were discovered when a police-sergeant saw a gaol door left open.

A former prisoner told the *Daily Mirror* that on leaving the prison the usual plan was to go to the nearest car park and borrow cars.

The cars were generally returned or left somewhere near the prison in the early hours of the morning.

Wore Warders' Coats

There was no hope of getting off the island, and no attempt was ever made.

The prisoners always went back to prison.

Once a prisoner was recognised at a dance. A friend spoke to him by name.

He calmly replied: No. I'm his brother. He is in prison. Didn't you know ? "

One of the prisoners—a good-conduct man—is believed to have made keys to fit various locks in the prison, and after warders had made the rounds for the night this prisoner released himself and his friends.

Other reports from people in the island state that when the prisoners wanted a " night out " they put on warders' overcoats the night before, and with upturned collars boldly walked out and posted letters asking friends to supply them with clothes.

Then when they returned to the gaol the prisoner with the key locked them in their cells again.

£5,000 CORONATION CLAIM

Westminster Hospital is claiming £5,000 from a City firm of underwriters under an insurance policy referring specifically to the coronation of King Edward VIII.

SAVED BY MAN HE WAS ARRESTING

POLICE-INSPECTOR Tribe told the magistrate at Clerkenwell Police Court yesterday that Seaman Harry Tait, thirty-two, against whom he was giving evidence, saved him from crashing through a church ceiling, 70ft. high, as he was arresting the seaman.

Tait and William Andrews, twenty-three-year-old waiter, were committed for trial at the London Sessions on a charge of having been concerned together in breaking and entering a lock-up shop in Caledonian-road, Islington, N., with intent to commit a felony.

Inspector Tribe said he saw the two men on the roof of the block of six shops.

Andrews came down through a sky-light and was arrested. Tait was found in the roof of the church.

" He refused to come down," said the inspector. " I got through a fanlight into the roof, but I lost my footing on a joist. My foot slipped through the ceiling.

" I had got hold of the prisoner, and he assisted in preventing me from falling through."

PETROL UP TO-DAY

FROM to-day the price of petrol will be advanced by a halfpenny a gallon on all grades.

The price was increased by a halfpenny a gallon recently.

The present price of first grade petrol is 1s. 6½d. a gallon, which—with the exception of 1930—is the highest since the war. From to-day first grades will be 1s. 7d. a gallon.

SATURDAY, FEBRUARY 13, 1937

Daily Mirror

No. 10359 Registered at the G.P.O. as a newspaper. ONE PENNY

JEKYLL AND HYDE PREACHER

LEFT PULPIT TO DEFRAUD

BY A SPECIAL CORRESPONDENT

Lover of children, eloquent lay preacher of the Gospel, cunning crook, Albert George Owen stepped down from the pulpit to defraud the people in his congregations.

HIS double life was ended at the Old Bailey yesterday with a sentence of twelve months' imprisonment on charges of fraud.

Owen is forty-eight, handsome and cultured. Last night I learned from the minister of Brixton Hill Methodist Church, where he was on the roll of preachers, and from his few friends, of the religious side of his character.

They said that he had converted many to Christianity by his fervent exhortations.

"Man of God"

Yet he represented himself as an agent of the London Passenger Transport Board. He called on small shop-keepers, who knew him as the respected man of God, and asked them to set up a time-table agency.

The condition of holding the agency was that they should put advertisements in the time-table.

His victims never guessed that their charming visitor was to be revealed in court yesterday as a man with five previous convictions.

"He came to me about a year ago with the finest recommendations," the Rev. Leslie C. Fogg, minister of Brixton Hill Methodist Church, told me.

"He was charming—one of the finest talkers I have ever met. His recommendations were of the very best, and we placed him on the roll of preachers.

"I cannot guess how he got his references, but I certainly will make sure that no other Methodist congregation will ever have to listen to a fake of this kind.

"Fortunately he never preached in my church, but preferred to go round small congregations and missions."

Owen has been on the Methodist Circuit for the Streatham district since 1917. Brixton Hill Church, where he often visited, is facing Brixton Prison, where he spent last night.

At Blegborough-road, S.W., where Owen lived with Mr. and Mrs. Moore, I learned another surprising fact about his character.

"He would never swear in front of my kiddies. He loved children and went out of his way to give them a copper or two," said Mr Moore.

Albert George Owen.

Salome (played by Miss Pamela Foster) quailing before the spears of the Temple guards.

A scene at the dress rehearsal at the Albert Hall of the "King of Glory" pageant, which is to have its opening performance there on Monday.

The roles of the Temple guards are taken by men of the Welsh Guards.

NEW CHARTER FOR SERVANTS

Cardiff Council offered a solution of the servant problem yesterday—a scale of hours, wages and conditions for domestics.

For untrained girls of 14 to 15 they suggest 6s. a week; 15 to 16, 7s.; 16 to 17, 9s.; 17 to 18, 11s., and for trained girls in all classes 1s. extra.

Nine-hour days, half a day off a week and two weeks' annual holiday with pay are recommended.

PRISON 'TORTURE' ALLEGATIONS: M.P. TO DEMAND DENIAL OR INQUIRY

BY OUR POLITICAL CORRESPONDENT

GRAVE allegations against the present prison system in this country are made by Mr. G. R. Hall Caine (Con., East Dorset). He tells me that he has information from a most reliable source that convicts are subjected to what can only be described as torture.

For the most trivial offence, such as failing to return a book to the prison library, a convict is liable to have his warm clothes removed and then be placed alone in a cold cel for three days and be fed on bread and water.

"If that is true," said Mr. Hall-Caine, "and I have reason to believe it is, there is something very wrong with our prisons. Men are imprisoned for misdemeanour, there is no question of vengeance.

"In Sir John Simon we have a humane Home Secretary who takes the greatest interest in prison life. That is why I am asking a question on this matter next Monday. I want him to deny these allegations or to order an immediate inquiry.

"If a British subject was tortured in a foreign prison in the manner I have described, there would be an immediate outcry."

Mr. Hall-Caine would like to be quartered in the cells set aside for prisoners undergoing solitary confinement just to "see for himself."

ITALY'S ROYAL BABY—9 lb. 3 oz.

BIRTH of a sturdy, dark-haired boy—he weighs 9lb. 3oz.—to Princess Marie Jose, wife of Crown Prince Umberto, sent a wave of joy over Italy yesterday. His coming ensures the succession to the Throne.

The Crown Prince and Princess have been married for seven years, and until now had only one child, Princess Maria Pia, born on September 24, 1934, says Reuter.

The Salic Law prevents a woman from succeeding to the throne in Italy, and if Crown Prince Umberto had died without a son, the throne would have passed to his cousin, the Duke of Aosta.

King Victor Emmanuel, after whom the boy will be called, was immediately rung up and told the news of the event, and thereupon conferred on his grandson the title of Prince of Naples, which he himself held before he ascended to the throne.

The King also signed a sweeping amnesty Bill under which most prisoners serving terms up to three years' imprisonment will be released, and all fines will be suspended, adds British United Press.

Monday has been declared a public holiday, and public buildings will be beflagged.

The Duce has telegraphed to the King and Queen and to the Prince and Princess the jubilation of the Fascist Government at the birth of a Prince.

BLUE DANUBE SUNG TO PRINCESS ROYAL

THE Princess Royal was the guest of the famous Vienna choirboys at their hostel near Vienna yesterday.

After a day spent in sightseeing with the Duke of Windsor, the Princess heard the boys give a concert in her honour, reports Reuter.

At the Princess's special request they sang the "Blue Danube" waltz.

MONDAY, FEBRUARY 15, 1937

Daily Mirror

No. 10360 Registered at the G.P.O. as a newspaper. ONE PENNY

TWO FRIENDS DIE BECAUSE ONE FELL IN LOVE

BY A SPECIAL CORRESPONDENT

Two young men, devoted to each other for five years, died together in a gas-filled room at Station-road, Finchley, N.W., yesterday, because one had fallen in love with a girl. This threatened to break their "perfect friendship."

JAMES T. Rich, twenty-one, lay on the bed as though death had surprised him sleeping. His friend, Albert J. Grimes, twenty-four, a gag in his mouth, to muffle a possible call for help, was sprawled across the pillows, his arm round Rich.

On a table by the bed were two notes written by Grimes.

One was addressed to Miss Dorothy Bonner and read: "Don't take my pal away from me."

The other, to Grimes's mother, said: "Bury us together. No flowers."

The girl, pretty twenty-three-year-old Dorothy Bonner, of Barnet, met Rich at his twenty-first birthday party three weeks ago in the home of Grimes's sister.

She attended as a "last-minute guest," taking the place of another. Though Miss Bonner went to school with Albert and Gertrude Grimes, she was not a close friend, but she lived in the same road and was invited to even the numbers of boys and girls.

Rich was very attracted by Miss Bonner. It was the first and last time they met.

A few days ago she received a letter from Rich asking to meet him again, but she did not either meet him or answer the letter.

She was prostrate with grief last night.

Her brother told me: "My sister can explain nothing. It is a complete mystery to her. She only met Rich once at the party.

"Several other men were there and they all had a good time together. She is not engaged to anyone—not as far as I know in love with any man. Certainly not Rich."

When Rich told his friend of his affection for Dorothy it brought the first cloud to their friendship.

"Terrier" Friends

Grimes and Rich met as "Terriers" in the same unit. Rich lived at Aveton-road, East Finchley, and worked in a Cricklewood brick-yard. Grimes was unemployed.

"Last Saturday night they returned to the lodgings early," Mr. Arnaboldi, their landlord, who discovered the tragedy, told me.

"They played the gramophone for hours, and the last tune I heard was the one they always played—'When the poppies bloom again.'

Police believe that fear of being parted from his friend by the girl caused Grimes to act.

James Rich (standing) and Albert Grimes.

FILM STAR'S 2 DIVORCE SUITS —AT ONCE

So anxious is Miss Arlene Judge, the film star with "Hollywood's most perfect figure," to be married again, that she is off to Reno this week to get a divorce from her husband, Mr. Wesley Ruggles, film director, though she already has a divorce suit pending against him in California.

Her Reno reason is that she doesn't want to wait the year demanded by Californian law, when she can be freed in six weeks by Reno.

Prospective husband No. 2 is the New York millionaire sportsman, Mr. Daniel Topping.

ONLY TRUNCHEONS FOR MEN GUARDING £1,000,000 JEWELS

NINE policemen armed only with truncheons, and two commissionaires were the guards at Olympia during the week-end for jewellery worth nearly £1,000,000.

The jewellery is part of the priceless display by the Birmingham Jewellers' Association at the British Industries Fair, which opens to-day at Olympia, the White City and Birmingham.

At the White City eight policemen and a sergeant watched over a display of jewels including diamonds and rubies studding a pair of shoes valued at 600 guineas.

C.I.D. men patrolled the Fair buildings at Birmingham—aided by a squad of firemen, who cycled along the passages between the twelve miles of stands.

From Morocco

From all over the world people are coming to the Fair.

One of the most picturesque visitors is Si Ahmed Hadji, a bronzed, bearded Moroccan merchant from the little town of Sale, near Rabat.

With his son, in his flowing Arab robes, he will be a guest at the Fair and banquet to-night, when the Duke of Kent will be the principal speaker.

The Queen will visit White City to-day; the King and Queen, Queen Mary and the Princess Royal go to Olympia to-morrow.

On Thursday the Queen, Queen Mary, the Princess Royal and the Duchess of Gloucester will make another tour of Olympia.

MOTHER OF TWINS ANGRY AT "INSULTS" IN LETTER-BOX

FROM OUR SPECIAL CORRESPONDENT

HARMONDSWORTH (Middlesex), Sunday.

EXPECTING her third set of twins soon, thirty-seven-year-old Mrs. Long, mother of five children and wife of the village chimney sweep, proudly told her friends.

Since then Mrs. Long and many married couples in the village have been inundated with pamphlets on birth control. They were pushed through letter boxes by men, who drove through the village in a car. Villagers are indignant.

Mrs. Long told me to-day: "Sending such pamphlets to me is the biggest insult I have ever had. It is a disgrace and ought to be stopped.

"Here is the Government telling us they want more babies and yet they allow such literature to be pushed upon people who do not want it.

"Though I have been married only seven and a half years, I have a boy aged six, twin boys aged four, and twin girls aged two. I am proud of my children."

Mr. Long, younger than his wife, was a chauffeur, but lost his job and became a chimney sweep.

He said: "I do not know why we should be sent such pamphlets. It is nobody's business but our own."

THE SOAP CAN'T PLAY TRICKS ON YOU NOW

One of the world's great problems—how to take a bath without losing the soap—has been solved at last.

Americans are now buying a pretty cord necklet, on which is threaded a cake of soap.

On entering the bath they put this round the neck. Then they always know where to find the soap.

FOG THRILLS FOR 400

CHANNEL BOAT IN CRASH

GROPING her way out of Boulogne in thick fog at 7.30 last night, the Southern Railway steamer Isle of Thanet, carrying 198 passengers, bound for Folkestone, crashed into the new breakwater outside the French harbour, buckled her bow and rudder plates and had to anchor in the roads.

She lay-to for five hours, then put back to Boulogne and landed her passengers just before midnight.

It is believed that the Isle of Thanet will be sent to dock.

In the roads close by her sister-ship, Maid of Orleans, carrying 189 passengers and crew from Folkestone, had anchored because the fog sirens and lights had failed and she was unable to enter harbour.

On the other side of the Channel the British steamer Llanover and the Belgian steamer Mambika collided off Dungeness, Kent.

(Ship Blows Up.—See page 2.)

NUNS SPY FOR HITLER

Discovery that nuns from Berlin who have been travelling in Poland are Nazi representatives spreading propaganda is causing a sensation in Warsaw, cables the *Daily Mirror* Warsaw correspondent.

Under the pretext of maintaining itinerary ambulance organisations, these nuns have been spying for Hitler.

WEDNESDAY, FEBRUARY 17, 1937

Daily Mirror

No. 10362 Registered at the G.P.O. as a newspaper. ONE PENNY

£1,500,000,000 IS ARMS BILL FOR NEXT FIVE YEARS

BY OUR POLITICAL CORRESPONDENT

Britain's arms bill in the next five years will be £1,500,000,000.

The Government White Paper issued last night, on the eve of to-day's full-dress debate in the House of Commons on the £400,000,000 Loan Bill, says that it would be " imprudent to contemplate " anything much less.

THE taxpayer will therefore have to find money for defence at the rate of £220,000,000 a year.

The keynote of the White Paper is to be found in the following passage:—

" Modern forces, whether on land, at sea, or in the air, must, if they are to be effective, be provided with arms and defences more ingenious and more formidable and far more costly than any conceived a generation ago."

The expenditure will apply to all three Services, but the heaviest immediate increase will be for the Navy. The provision for the Services will be, in brief:—

NAVY (1937 programme).—Three new capital ships costing £8,000,000 each, seven cruisers, two aircraft carriers, existing vessels to be modernised, large increase in personnel, substantial increase in Fleet Air arm.

ARMY.—Two new tank battalions, modernisation of all arms, complete system of motor transport, immense reserves of ammunition, increase of strength, equipment of Territorials with Army's weapons, modernisation of barrack accommodation.

ROYAL AIR FORCE.—Large numbers of new aerodromes, seventy-five operational training and other stations at home and abroad, large increase of personnel.

The White Paper stresses that this country has become increasingly vulnerable to air attack and adds: "The strength of the Royal Air Force has become a matter of paramount importance and no effort has been or is being spared to bring it up to the strength and standard of efficiency which the Government deem requisite for our safety."

Miss Margaret Ann Watney.

LEFT MONEY TO THE MAN IT TOOK FROM HER

BY A SPECIAL CORRESPONDENT

BEAUTIFUL, twenty-one-year-old Miss Margaret Ann Watney, of Heath End House, Baughhurst, Hants, has left a share in her fortune of £52,000 to the man from whom it parted her—Patrick Stevenson Blackwood.

Mr. Blackwood, twenty-four-year-old kinsman of the Marquis of Dufferin and Ava, had been her friend since childhood.

Hid Illness from Him

A friend of Mr Blackwood's said last night:

"Mr. Blackwood went abroad, and while he was away Miss Watney contracted the illness that caused her death.

"Mr. Blackwood, from whom I believe she had tried to conceal her illness, hurried to England.

"He was overwhelmed by grief. After attending the funeral he went abroad again."

Another friend of Mr. Blackwood's said:

"I always felt that Miss Watney's wealth was a bar to her engagement to Mr. Blackwood. He was far from wealthy."

In her will Miss Watney has left him £400 a year for five years, £300 of which she asks him to apply to the study of medicine.

At the end of the five years he is to have the capital sum entirely.

After other bequests, totalling £2,600, Miss Watney left the residue of her estate to her mother.

£1,500,000,000

If you had as many pennies as this was pounds you would have £6,250,000.

£1,500,000,000 is enough to give every man, woman and child in this country £34 each.

And it is enough to pay for the building of a fleet of 300 liners the size of the Queen Mary

U.S. CURATE HOLDS CORONATION OFFICE

FROM OUR OWN CORRESPONDENT

NEW YORK, Tuesday.

PROUDEST curate in America to-day is twenty-eight-year-old Rev. James de Wolf Perry, who has been invited by the Archbishop of York to serve as one of his two chaplains at the Coronation.

The Rev. Mr. Perry is a humble, hard-working member of the staff of the Episcopal Church at Norfolk, Virginia.

He was astonished one morning to receive unheralded, a letter from Dr. Temple asking him to take part in the greatest ceremony of the century.

"The Archbishop's kindly invitation was a tremendous surprise," he told me. "I could hardly believe it was true. I met Dr. Temple when he was visiting America, and accompanied him on part of his tour in Virginia."

Mr. Perry spent a year at Cambridge University.

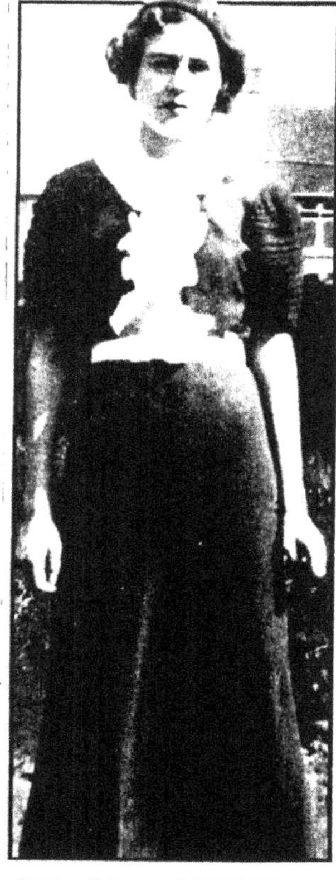

Kathleen Holloway and (left) Ted Morgan.

GIRL VANISHES AFTER DEFYING PARENTS FOR SWEETHEART

FROM OUR SPECIAL CORRESPONDENT

HOUNSLOW (Middlesex), Tuesday.

PRETTY Kathleen Holloway, seventeen-year-old typist, of Burns-way, Hounslow, who defied her parents to continue friendship with a youth of her own age, vanished to-day.

Earlier she had given evidence in defence of her sweetheart when he was summoned on a charge of assaulting Kathleen's mother.

The boy, Ted Morgan, of Leysfield-road, Shepherd's Bush, W., is an unemployed machine-minder.

He was fined 20s. at Brentford Police Court for assaulting Mrs. Holloway while he was out walking with her daughter.

Kathleen supported his denial that he struck the blow. She told the Court that her parents had done everything they could to stop her friendship with Morgan, and that she no longer loved her father and mother.

When the case ended Morgan agreed not to see his sweetheart for two months, on the advice of the probation officer.

He went home. Kathleen did not. Nor has she been seen by relatives or friends since she left the court.

Her father told me to-night:—

"I did not appeal to Kathleen to return to us. I have made so many appeals in vain. She has left this home, where she had every comfort, for the sake of this youth.

"We Can Do Nothing"

"There was no question of an engagement. I would never have allowed him to enter my house.

"The appalling thing is that here is a girl of only seventeen going her own way, and we, her parents, can do nothing about it."

Ted Morgan, surprised and alarmed by Kathleen's disappearance, said to me: "I think she spent last night at a friend's house. This morning I told her on the way to the court that I thought it would be better if she did not come to my home again.

"I can only hope that she is staying with friends."

MONDAY, FEBRUARY 22, 1937

Daily Mirror

No. 10366 Registered at the G.P.O. as a Newspaper. ONE PENNY

PILOT PARTS FROM VILLAGE BEAUTY, THEN GOES TO DATE WITH DEATH

FROM OUR SPECIAL CORRESPONDENT

CAMBRIDGE, Sunday.

A PRETTY girl called at the Cromwell Hotel here this morning to keep an appointment with handsome, well-dressed air pilot Eugene L. Currey, about to leave for Spain. Waiting police met her; told her that Currey lay dead in a gas-filled bedroom on the next floor and took her to the station to be questioned.

The couple came to the hotel late last night and Currey, who was married and had a child, booked a room. Early this morning they said good-bye in the front hall and the girl drove back in her car to the village home of her parents at Shelford, near here.

Currey, once a bus driver, then business man, and, finally, a civil air pilot, ordered tea to be served in his bedroom at nine o'clock next morning.

Then, whistling, he walked to his room and bolted the door

Farewell Note

When the maid went up with the tea this morning she saw a wedge of light shining under the door; smelled gas, and called the proprietress, Mrs. Quick.

Police broke in and found Currey sprawled across the bed in his underclothing, dead.

Gas was hissing from a ring near the bed. In his pockets police found a few shillings, a farewell letter and his airman's licence.

A few minutes afterwards his girl friend called for him.

Papers in Currey's pocket gave an address in Westland-road, Darlington. Police inquiries showed that Currey, his wife and daughter had left that address a month ago.

Mrs. Currey, who had been staying with relatives at Kingsgrove, Stoke, near Coventry, arrived here to-night with two friends.

"Flying to Spain"

Mrs. Currey owned a large confectioner's business in Gladstone-street.

Mr. Currey took up civil flying and obtained his pilot's "A" licence at Cramlington and Croydon

Mrs. Currey yesterday received a telephone call saying that her husband was going to fly a bomber to Spain.

"Mr. and Mrs. Currey had been married for about nine years," a friend told me to-night.

"They seemed to be an ideal couple.

"No one knows who Mr Currey's girl friend is."

SPORTS CLOTHES FOR MRS. SIMPSON'S TROUSSEAU

FROM OUR OWN CORRESPONDENT

NICE, Sunday

Mrs. Simpson has ordered sports clothes to be sent from Chanel's, of Paris, to the villa of Mr Herman Rogers, Lou Viei at Cannes, so that she can make a choice for her trousseau.

Mr. Rogers said to-night that Mrs. Simpson will not go to Paris because she wishes to avoid attracting attention.

Duke of Windsor Inspects Two Villas—page 3.

Where the boy jumped from one bungalow roof to another (shown by white arrow) and climbed to a chimney stack (indicated by broken line).

BOY IN PYJAMAS DEFIES POLICE FROM CHIMNEY

FROM OUR OWN CORRESPONDENT

ROMFORD, Sunday.

BAREFOOT, clad only in pyjamas, a thirteen-year-old boy who had escaped from Essex Remand Home, sat defying Romford police pursuers with witty back answers on the chimney-pot of a bungalow in Harold's Park, Essex, for more than an hour.

Early yesterday morning he climbed thirty feet from the window of his dormitory and fled.

Police saw him running and chased him along the railway

When the chase closed on him he climbed forty feet to the roof of a bungalow in Greenways-avenue and jumped six feet across a paved alley-way to the next-door bungalow. Then he squatted on the chimney.

Men with ladders, policemen and officials from the remand home pleaded.

"You'll get killed if you're not careful," they said. "It'll be my funeral and not yours if I am," the bad boy rapped back.

Shivering, his pyjamas mud-coated, and his feet cut and bleeding, the boy clung to the chimney pot.

Took Flying Leap

When men with ladders got too near, he shook them off, took a flying leap and safely reached another bungalow and again sat on the chimney

Mrs. J. Silver, cooking breakfast, "thought a ton of bricks had fallen on the roof."

Later, with the men approaching him from all sides the boy calmly slipped down the tiles and gave himself up.

VIVIENNE ELDERS PICKED UP IN 'PLANE 35 MILES AT SEA

TUNIS, Sunday.

LOVELY French air ace Vivienne Elders was picked up in the Mediterranean last night thirty-five miles from land, after hours afloat on the sea. She was unhurt.

For the second time in a year an accident brought discovery that saved her life.

As she flew to the international air meeting at Cairo yesterday her petrol failed. She was forced to land her 'plane on the water, says Reuter.

For hours she drifted. Then the lights of the little Greek steamer Chelatross came slowly up in the night. The crew heard her cries. Again she had cheated death.

Last May Mlle. Elders was in a 'plane with three companions when a choked petrol feed forced them to land in the Sahara. For three days they were missing.

Italian Air Force flyers found them near Mount Talmut, with hardly any food or drink left.

They were far from the motor routes across the desert and would have starved in a few days.

SON FOR CROWN PRINCE

A son was born to Crown Prince Olaf and Princess Martha of Norway in Oslo yesterday. The baby is second in line to the Norwegian Throne.

Princess Martha is a cousin of the Crown Prince of Sweden.

TUESDAY, FEBRUARY 23, 1937

Daily Mirror

No. 10367 Registered at the G.P.O. as a Newspaper. ONE PENNY

BLONDE SCALES GAOL WALL

TO ALL-NIGHT LOVE TRYST IN KILLER'S CELL

FROM OUR OWN CORRESPONDENT

NEW YORK, Monday.

LOVE tryst in a cell in Detroit (Michigan) Gaol was revealed to the astonished warders to-day when they found slender, brown-eyed Lucille Turner hiding in the shower bath of "Triggerman" Dayton Dean, self-confessed executioner to America's night-riding Black Legion.

With a laugh and a shrug as they grilled her in the warden's room, seventeen-year-old blonde Lucille told how she cat-climbed to the window of Dean's nine-story cell last night from the women's detention room below.

"I've been there all night," she boasted. "We had dinner together and a real good time."

Dean, gaoled for life for kidnap and murder, is now disclosed to be living happily in a luxury cell, furnished complete with radio and shower. Inside they found jars of fruit and a selection of choice drinks.

Here's what Lucille told Policewoman Eleanor Hutzel:

"Oh, sure I kissed Dayton many times. He sure had a nice room, and as we became better acquainted he kissed me passionately again and again.

"We got to know each other about six days ago, when I was playing the piano in the rest room, and he hollered down: 'Come up and see me some time.'

Inquiry Ordered

"I had never seen him before, but I was real interested, having heard so much about him. So last night I climbed up the grill from my window to his.

"Every time a warder passed the door I ducked into the shower bath and Dayton looked out of the window."

Police Commissioner Pickert, fearing that an orgy of love trysts has been going on, has ordered a thorough investigation into the scandal.

BLACK LEGION BLAMED FOR 50 MURDERS

America's Black Legion, secret society rivalling the terrors of the Ku-Klux-Klan, is blamed for fifty murders in Michigan alone.

With 135,000 members in a single State, its tentacles reach through the whole nation to wield huge political power, with death as the penalty for those who disobey.

WITH HER PUBLIC SCHOOL HUSBAND

"Here's to us"—Manuel del Campo, Mexican actor, and Mary Astor, of film and diary fame, drinking a toast to their future happiness.

They were married in America last week, and if Mary has her way they will honeymoon in England and visit Clifton College, Bristol, Manuel's old school.

PARTED

Convulsed with grief and with tears streaming down her face she says good-bye Mrs. Virginia S. Tomlinson, whose husband, Tommy Tomlinson, experimental flyer, was awarded a divorce at Kansas City, U.S., sees daughter Sheila for the last time before the child is given to the custody of the Sisters of Notre Dame

ITALY WILL BOYCOTT THE CORONATION IF HAILE SELASSIE ATTENDS

BY OUR POLITICAL CORRESPONDENT

CORONATION problem No. 1 was created yesterday by the decision of the Government to invite an Abyssinian representative to attend the ceremony.

Haile Selassie and the Empress, now living at Bath, are practically certain to be there, in which case Italy is just as certain to refuse to attend.

Still King in League Eyes

Haile Selassie is still officially regarded by most nations as official King of Abyssinia until the League recognises Italy's annexation of Ethiopia.

So Mussolini will have to decide quickly whether to sink his pride and attend or—stay away.

(Commons storm over Coronation invitation to Germany, page 2.)

OFFICE BOY NOW PRAYS—AND PAYS

TWO thousand hard-boiled business men attended an Oxford Group meeting in London last night to talk about the effect of religion on business.

"Better Relations"

Mr. George Becker, a managing director, who presided, said that religion bettered relations between employers and workers.

Then spoke Charles Korts, stockbroker's office boy. Since he took up religion, he said, he has been paying for his private telephone calls.

GERMANY'S "NO" TO RAW MATERIALS PARLEY

Germany has definitely refused to take part in the forthcoming League of Nations conference on re-dividing the raw materials of the world it was announced from Geneva yesterday.

'PLANE CRASHES IN SNOWSTORM: 2 DEAD

TWO men were killed and two seriously injured last night when a Royal Air Force 'plane crashed in a blinding snowstorm at Ewell Minnis, between Dover and Folkestone.

The machine hurtled into a field, swept through two hedges, across a road, then overturned.

Wreckage was strewn over nearly a quarter of a mile, and the machine's two engines were hurled 50 yards.

The dead men were Sergeant-Pilot G. J. Maurice and Aircraftman S McCabe. The injured are Flight-Lieutenant G. E. Strangman and Flight-Lieutenant R. J. Cooper.

The machine, which belonged to No. 48 Squadron, Manston, was returning to Manston Aerodrome, near Broadstairs, when it ran into the storm. A graphic description of the accident was given by ex-Police-Sergeant H. Roberts, who lives close to the scene. He said:

"We found two of the occupants badly injured, one on each side of the machine, and in the machine we found one man dead. Fifty yards away was another body."

This was the thirteenth R.A.F. accident this year.

JEWEL ROBBERY IN THE QUEEN MARY

NEW YORK, Monday.

Mrs. Dorothy Busch, of Los Angeles, has reported to the police the loss of 500 dollars in cash and 500 dollars' worth of jewellery from her stateroom on the liner Queen Mary when the vessel was a day out from Southampton.

She was dining with Zazu Pitts, the film star, when the robbery took place, adds Central News.

SATURDAY, FEBRUARY 27, 1937

Daily Mirror

No. 10371 — Registered at the G.P.O. as a Newspaper. — ONE PENNY

NATIONAL ANTHEM PLAYED TO END WILD ICE HOCKEY SCENES

THE National Anthem, blared out above the roar of the crowd, stopped amazing scenes at Harringay last night three minutes before the end of the world championship ice-hockey match between Great Britain and Canada.

For fifteen minutes a hostile crowd of 10,000 held up the play, showered orange peel, apples, pennies, programmes and newspapers on the ice.

Frantic appeals for silence went unheard amid the booing.

Then, from the band came the strains of "God Save the King."

At once there was silence. The crowd stood to attention.

The anthem ended and the game went on. Canada won 3—0.

The night had begun with a stampede for seats after people had waited in queues for nearly eight hours. Panes of glass had been smashed, doors broken in as hundreds rushed forward. Police, hidden in a car park, were called to restore order.

Players in Mix-up

Then, three minutes from the end of the game, the trouble began. There was a hectic mix-up between four players on one of the barriers.

A British player, E. Brenchley, received a cut over the eye. One of the two referees immediately sent a player from each side to the penalty box for one minute.

His action in sending the British player off incensed the crowd.

Amid the excitement one of a party of Canadian bluejackets climbed over the barrier and walked on to the ice to talk to Gordon Dailley, the British captain.

The crowd was shouting for the referee and nothing could be heard above the demonstration.

"The British players request that you behave like British sportsmen," exclaimed an official.

Invaded the Ice

"Unless you stop throwing things on the ice the president of the International Federation will stop the game."

The threat had no effect, and with officials, coaches and players, spectators began to invade the ice. It was then that the National Anthem was played.

In all the National Anthem was played three times during the evening: before, during and after the game.

Among the spectators was Sir Austen Chamberlain.

(Pictures on back page.)

This Girl Foretold Her Death in a Poem. *Story on Page Two.*

£150,000 FROM FAMILY FUNDS FOR EX-KING

BY OUR POLITICAL CORRESPONDENT

BEFORE the King left London for Windsor last night, he gave final approval to the secret compact reached by members of the Royal Family to provide for the Duke of Windsor.

It is proposed to give ex-King Edward VIII a capital sum of £150,000; an annual income of £25,000.

All this money will be found by members of the Royal Family, King George VI himself bearing the major share, by allocating much of the revenue of the Duchy of Cornwall.

Agreement has been reached after long negotiations, during which the Duke of Windsor has been visited by Sir Walter Monckton, attorney-general to the Duchy of Cornwall, Mr. A. G. Allan, solicitor to the Duke, the Princess Royal and her husband the Earl of Harewood, and the Duke of Kent.

In the *Daily Mirror* of January 18 I forecast that provision for the Duke of Windsor would be made privately and that taxpayers would not be called on to pay a penny for him in future

S O S FOR TWINS' FATHER AT SEA

FROM OUR SPECIAL CORRESPONDENT

SOUTHAMPTON, Friday Night.

S O S messages in English and French were broadcast by the B.B.C. to-night telling Mr. Oscar Hansen, of Athelstone-road, Southampton, skipper of the motor-yacht Arania, cruising somewhere off southern France, that his twin baby son, aged seventeen months, is lying seriously ill in the South Hants Hospital here.

The father does not know that his other twin son, Tony, died in the same hospital last night.

To-night Mrs. Hansen was praying by the bedside of Michael, her surviving son.

Film-star Rosita Diaz: Shot as a spy.

FILM STAR SPY'S "STUDIO POSE" IN FRONT OF SPANISH FIRING SQUAD

ROSITA Diaz, red-blonde screen star, has played her last role—target of a firing squad in Seville. Cigarette between her crimson lips, taunting her executioners with a smile, she walked to her doom with the lithe, provocative grace that she had shown in the white glare of the studio lights.

She was shot as a Government spy. But no confession was wrung from her, no hint of her accomplices.

Secret Information

Insurgents said that her spying activities brought death to more than sixty people in Seville.

Information which Rosita was alleged to have given to a secret radio station in the city was passed on to Madrid. The result was two successful air raids which caused havoc in Seville.

Rosita's acting career reached its peak last year, when she was signed up by Fox Films in Hollywood.

She made a series of French pictures, including a short film with Maurice Chevalier.

SHE SANG OPERA IN HER SCANTIES

AUSTERE, arty patrons of the Metropolitan Opera, New York's musical Mecca, laughed themselves hoarse last night when beautiful twenty - three - year - old soprano Natalie Bondanya did an involuntary strip-tease act in the middle of an opera aria.

Her crinoline slipped, fell, left her standing in her intimate Fifth-avenue scanties.

Clenching her tiny hands, she—just went on singing, but the riot of laughs drowned her voice.

"Was I flabbergasted," Natalie almost blushed over the transatlantic 'phone to the "Daily Mirror."

"I was Elisetta in 'The Clandestine Marriage' when the crinoline fell. In a panic I just opened my mouth wide and sang.

"It was my first big part, so I just gave a good kick to get out of the wreckage, and thought of mother cowering in her box."

But after the show the audience paid like good sports in crates of flowers. Natalie had made good.

MONDAY, MARCH 1, 1937

Daily Mirror

No. 10372 Registered at the G.P.O as a newspaper. ONE PENNY

50 STRANDED TEN HOURS IN BOAT-TRAIN, HELD UP BY SNOWDRIFT

FIFTY passengers were prisoners for ten hours when the Irish boat train plunged into a five-feet snowdrift on the way from Stranraer to Glasgow. A dance band entertained them through the night.

They were victims of the seventy-miles-an-hour blizzard which raked Britain yesterday, wrecking communications, leaving a trail of destruction, paralysing shipping off the coast.

Several deaths were reported.

For six hours the Irish boat train was "lost," as far as railway officials at Glasgow were concerned

One hundred workmen toiled with picks and shovels to dig out the stranded travellers.

Exhausted and hungry, the passengers arrived in Glasgow at ten o'clock yesterday morning—ten hours late.

The steamer that brought them from Larne to Stranraer had run aground for two hours. Then at Maybole, Ayrshire, the engine came up against a solid wall of snow.

After the guard staggered a mile through the blizzard to a signal-box to give the alarm, another engine was sent from Girvan to push the train through. It could not get nearer than 200 yards from the stranded train.

Ships, white under sleet, snow and hail, raced for the shelter of British ports.

There are fears that a ship was sunk with all hands in Berwick Bay.

Over south-west England the worst storm for 100 years raged during the evening. The railway from Plymouth to Princetown was buried 10ft. deep in snow. Scores of moorland villages were isolated.

Ilfracombe pier was partly wrecked and tea rooms at Hillsboro were blown over a 600ft. cliff into the sea.

Villages Isolated

Fed by heavy rains since Saturday afternoon the Thames has risen and more floods are threatened.

Owing to blocked roads, only about 1,500 gallons of milk could be dispatched to London last night from the Leyburn depot of one firm.

Week-end electricity black-outs occurred in Yorks, Dorset, Lakeland and the west counties: dozens of villages were isolated.

Distress signals were seen by the Goswick coastguards, but Holy Island lifeboat searched for hours in a terrific gale without finding the vessel.

An SOS was broadcast by the B.B.C. at the end of a musical programme yesterday afternoon. It read:—

"Vessel in distress N.N.E., from Huntcliff, East Yorks, impossible to communicate with life-saving authorities. Will any person near Saltburn, hearing this message, notify the coastguards and life-saving authorities at once?"

Within a few seconds Saltburn Exchange was besieged with calls from listeners trying to get in touch with lifeboat headquarters.

All over Lancashire, Yorkshire, Wales and Lakeland and many parts of the south hill roads were impassable, causing bus services to be suspended.

While on his way to attend service at Bath Abbey, a retired clergyman, the Rev. H. A. Westrop, aged about seventy, who had been staying at the Westbourne Hotel, fell dead on the Grand Parade.

HE THRASHED MAN WHO SCARED WIFE IN BEDROOM

FROM OUR OWN CORRESPONDENT

COPENHAGEN, Sunday night.

A FORMER English public schoolboy who flew here from England when he learned that his wife had been pestered by an Austrian Jew, told me to-night how he had thrashed the man in one of Copenhagen's smartest hotels.

Mr. Clement Jackson Howells, of The Pantiles, Golders Green, N.W., flew over to protect his wife, who had come here for a rest cure after an operation.

"The trouble began in a ship when my wife was on her way to Copenhagen," said Mr. Howells.

"The second day out an Austrian Jew kept pestering her. He asked if he could dance with her, if she would have a drink with him, and if she would meet him on the boat deck.

"She became so frightened that she told the wireless officer and a steward. They looked after her for that particular reason.

"One morning when she woke up my wife

(Continued on back page)

Unable to live in their downstairs rooms because flood water lies 3ft. deep there, families in a Bath street took to the bedroom floor. But the floods persisted, and children are being rescued by police in punts, and taken to more comfortable quarters.

Iris Cruttenden

VILLAGE GIRL FOR EGYPTIAN COURT

FROM OUR SPECIAL CORRESPONDENT

HASTINGS, Sunday.

SEVENTEEN-YEAR-OLD Iris Cruttenden, daughter of a chauffeur, has left her humble home in the Sussex village of Brede for an Egyptian palace.

She has been appointed personal maid to the four young sisters of King Farouk.

Iris, who has never been far from her native village, will accompany the Princesses and King Farouk to Switzerland, Paris, and then to England for the Coronation celebrations.

She Longed to Travel

"Iris always longed to travel. Now her dream has come true," the Rev. P. W. Hill, rector of Brede, told me to-night. "She obtained the post through a friend who is a retired nurse.

"This friend has a nurse relative at King Farouk's palace, and when the Princesses asked if she knew of an English girl who would like to be their maid Iris was recommended."

'SPIRIT' MAY DIRECT NORMA

Lovely Norma Shearer, believing that Irving Thalberg's spirit survived the grave, may act in films under the "guidance" of her late husband.

Friends quote her as saying that in her return to the screen Thalberg's spirit will guide her acting in every scene, just as his presence inspired her during his lifetime.—Reuter.

AUSTRALIA'S 604 TEST RECORD

MELBOURNE, Monday morning.

AUSTRALIA were all out for 604 shortly after play opened in the third day of the final Test.

This was Australia's highest score in this country against England.

More than 45,000 saw Farnes dismiss Fleetwood-Smith, who scored 13, McCormick being not out 17.

Barnett and Worthington opened England's fight against tremendous odds. Barnett began to hit out, smashing McCormick's first ball to the boundary, and late-cut the second for a four. He was out for 18 from a "bumper" by Nash which was caught by Oldfield, England's score being 33 for 1.

Fast scoring continued when Hardstaff joined Worthington, and in twenty minutes the score reached 40.

SHE WILL NOT COPY SHIRLEY

Irene Price, the twelve-year-old Mitcham girl who has been signed on long-term stage contracts at £50 a week, starts rehearsals to-day.

"I'm going to be myself, and not an English imitation of Shirley Temple," she said to a *Daily Mirror* representative.

THIRD "CAT" RAID

Jewels worth £1,000 were the spoils of a cat-burglar at Windsor—and his tactics tallied with those used in two Chelsea raids a few days ago.

Apparently he climbed a stack pipe to break into a dressing-room at Queen's Acre, home of Sir George Crichton, late Comptroller of the Lord Chamberlain's Office.

WEDNESDAY, MARCH 3, 1937

Daily Mirror

No. 10374 Registered at the G.P.O. as a newspaper. ONE PENNY

STREET CAR PARKS WILL GO

SAYS THE MINISTER OF TRANSPORT

"I do not think it fair that the peace of inhabitants in quiet streets should be invaded by cars"

STREET car parks in the London traffic area are to go, Mr. Hore-Belisha, Minister of Transport, announced last night.

"I shall consider," he said, "fixing a date after which the leaving of cars in streets, except for the purposes of taking up and setting down at houses and shops, will be prohibited."

Mr. Hore-Belisha made his announcement in a speech at the Chartered Surveyors' Institution dinner in London.

He added that he would give local authorities time to take advantage of the Ribbon Development Act, which gives them power to supplement private enterprise in providing car parks.

Then, he declared, he would appoint no more parking places, and would "progressively diminish the number of existing parking places."

A stationary vehicle, he pointed out, immobilised a whole line of traffic, and he did not think it fair that the peace of inhabitants in pleasant squares and quiet streets should be invaded by cars which had no real claim to be there.

Mr. Hore-Belisha also announced that no Ministry of Transport grants would be given for the construction of a new road or the improvement of an old one, unless it complies with the Ribbon Development Act.

The boundaries of roads should be expansible and not rigid

"I announce publicly," he added, "that so great an importance do I attach to the restriction of indiscriminate access to, and freedom from building along, our roads, that I will not ordinarily be prepared to contribute to the construction of a new road, or the improvement of an existing one, unless the provisions of this Act, in the interests of movement, safety and amenity are applied."

£20,000 "Garage"

Mr. Hore-Belisha's parking proposals apply only to that part of the London traffic area of about 1,800 square miles in which he has power to appoint or cancel parking places.

In other parts of the country, parking places are appointed by the local authorities under the Public Health Act, 1925.

According to Ministry of Transport statistics, the capital value of the land surface put out of use by a stationary motor-coach in a busy London street is about £40,000, and by a private car about £20,000.

In the London traffic area, there are between 300 and 400 officially appointed parking places at present.

Commenting on Mr. Hore-Belisha's "no parking" proposal, the Automobile Association in a statement last night said:—

"To abolish existing parking accommodation, which is already inadequate, and where it causes no hardships or inconvenience either to traffic or residents, is in our opinion arbitrary and unjustifiable.

"Many shopping and trading centres are almost entirely dependent upon motoring patrons.

We can't play cricket, perhaps, though it's our national game. . . We're not much good at golf . . . and we aren't a wow at swimming, though we're an island.

But on the ice, which is the snow countries' national playground, one of our girls last night skated off with the women's world championship cup—sixteen-year-old Cecilia Colledge, daughter of a Hampstead doctor.

Congratulations ! Good skating !

SECOND-STRING GIRL SAYS "I'LL GO ON"

BY A SPECIAL CORRESPONDENT

"I INTEND to go on and on, and am going to be a champion some day," Miss Megan Taylor told me, just after the announcement of the results in the women's world ice-skating championships at the Empress Stadium, Earl's Court, last night.

Megan was once again runner-up to Cecilia Colledge, sixteen-year-old daughter of a London surgeon.

"I have no intention of turning professional until I have won the world title," added Miss Taylor.

Megan, who looked just as attractive off the rink as when she delighted the 8,000 audience with her perfect timing and remarkable accuracy, took her latest beating in true sporting fashion.

She has become a perpetual second-string, having been runner-up to Cecilia in both the British and European championships this year.

It is thirty years since Britain could claim the woman skating champion of the world. Now we have the two best.

POLICE SEEK BLONDE AND 3 MEN: BURGLARIES RIDDLE

POLICE of three counties were searching last night for a blonde girl and three men believed to be responsible for a number of burglaries near Bognor.

They are believed to have been staying at a bungalow in the district.

Last night a saloon car containing four people was seen leaving the district at a fast speed. The driver disregarded police signals to stop. Later a car was found abandoned.

CHILD'S BODY EXHUMED BY TORCHLIGHT

FROM OUR SPECIAL CORRESPONDENT

PRESTON, Tuesday.

POLICE supervised the exhumation of the body of a little girl from Preston Cemetery last night.

It was that of Mavis Marie Woof, aged three and a half. The child is stated to have been ill for some time in a nursing home about a mile from Preston. Her mother is in service near Blackpool.

Mavis was buried last Wednesday in the Church of England section of the cemetery. Only three people were present at the funeral —a young woman, an elderly woman and a nurse.

Strict Secrecy

There were three wreaths, one of which was marked "from Dr. Paget."

The police are maintaining strict secrecy.

Secret preparations for the exhumation were made yesterday afternoon.

A Home Office order had been obtained by the Preston coroner, and the grave was opened by the light of police officers' torches.

The coffin was afterwards taken from the cemetery by car. Arrangements were made to carry out a post-mortem examination.

FIRE ENGINE SKIDS INTO SHOP: SIX HURT

SIX people were injured last night when a fire-engine skidded in Portland - road, South Norwood, hit a street refuge, mounted the pavement, tore down fencing and crashed into a bootmaker's shop.

Two firemen were flung through the shop window and landed on customers.

Mrs. Louisa Parker, sixty, of Haddington-road, South Norwood, was detained in Croydon Hospital with a broken leg and head injuries.

Mrs. Bertha Payne, wife of the occupier of the shop, received treatment for shock. Driver Edward William Sales, twenty-nine, of the Woodside Fire Station, also suffered from shock.

Mr. H. G. Payne, occupier of the shop, told the *Daily Mirror*:—

"Two firemen somersaulted through the plate-glass window and fell right on top of us."

AUSTRALIA KEEP THE "ASHES"

AUSTRALIA won the fifth Test—and retained the Ashes—at Melbourne this morning by an innings and 200 runs.

England's second innings closed for only 165 runs.

A surprisingly large crowd was eager to be "in at the kill," says Reuter.

There were 10,000 people in the ground.

MONDAY, MARCH 8, 1937

Daily Mirror

No. 10378. Registered at the G.P.O. as a Newspaper. ONE PENNY

ADVENTURER-AUTHOR DEAD IN YACHT WRECK: WIFE MISSING

FROM OUR SPECIAL CORRESPONDENT

EXMOUTH, Sunday.

AFTER a life of thrilling adventure, Serge Zolo perished here to-day fighting desperately to reach the shore in a dinghy after the gale had driven his 44-ton yacht Rona on the sands.

His wife is missing and is believed to have died with him.

Zolo, whose real name was Constantine Serge Zolotoohin, was only eleven when his father, a White Russian general, was killed by the Bolshevists.

Zolo escaped, disguised by faithful servants of his father, and became first a fur trader in the Arctic, then a policeman, a smuggler of Chinese into the U.S., and a rum-runner.

Recently he had written revue scenarios for the B.B.C.

Zolo's Canadian wife, Phyllis, was his only companion when he set sail from Dartmouth on Friday in the Rona.

Experienced seamen came to his aid, warned him: "A man and a woman alone can't handle a 44-ton vessel."

Their warnings would have been graver still had they known that a few days before Zolo had stripped 200lb. of lead ballast from the keel. If that ballast was not replaced the yacht risked turning turtle in a rough sea.

"Soon She Will Know"

But the much-travelled, splendidly built Zolo was confident. He repeated his intention of making for a French port to try to pick up a crew before leaving for the West Indies.

A few hours after Zolo sailed a south-east gale sprang up.

And this morning coastguards found the yacht stranded here.

Zolo's body was washed up at Dawlish.

"Sentenced to Adventure," was the title of Zolo's latest book, published by Harraps, which he dedicated to his wife, a singer and dancer who appeared in last year's Radiolympia.

"Mother thinks I have come home for good," runs the last paragraphs. "And I haven't disillusioned her—yet," he added.

"She doesn't know that I am planning to cruise the world in a sixty foot schooner because I want to write about strange people and photograph strange places.

"Soon she will know."

Little did he dream of the way in which his mother, who lives in London, was to learn of his plan

SENTENCED TO ADVENTURE

things that I had done—only some of them. She will read about the rest. It is easier that way.

Mother thinks I have come home for good, and I haven't disillusioned her—yet. She doesn't know that I am planning to cruise the world in a sixty-foot schooner because I want to write about strange people and photograph strange places. Soon she will know

The end—the last paragraph in Zolotoohin's recently published book, "Sentenced to Adventure."

Five words haunted this girl—sixteen-year-old Marie Platt. See story on back page.

Constantine Serge Zolotoohin. A picture from his autobiography.

Wrecked off Exmouth — Zolotoohin's yacht Rona, swept by the waves yesterday.

On the deck was strewn woman's clothing, while nearby floated a lifebelt and the wreckage of a dinghy.

A mile away the body of Zolotoohin was washed ashore —of his wife there was no trace.

SCHOOL DESK BABY-GIRLS ON PARADE

FROM OUR OWN CORRESPONDENT

NEW YORK, Sunday.

TWO mistresses walking into a classroom of fashionable Far Rockaway Girls' School, New York, heard cries coming from a desk. They opened the lid and found inside—in an improvised crib—a newly-born baby girl.

As one woman tried to hush the baby's cries, the other, fearful of the scandal that might wreck the school's good name, called the headmistress.

At once the whole school was assembled—row upon row of wide-eyed, mystified girls. They were told by the head, "The mother must confess."

No one confessed. Instead, the girls, aged thirteen to eighteen, sent up the cry: "Make the baby the school mascot!"

To-morrow morning the hundreds of girls at the school will be lined up in the assembly hall while doctors and police attempt to trace the baby's mother.

STORM HITS CRACK LINER: 30 OF CREW HURT

ARRIVAL of Italy's crack liner Rex at Genoa yesterday after a terrific battle with Atlantic storms let loose a flood of rumours.

According to Reuter, thirty of her crew were injured on the voyage from New York to Naples.

Two Killed

A report from Naples states that two people were killed by the buffeting, says Reuter message from Rome.

One is said to have been a passenger, British or American; the other a member of the crew.

The body of a passenger was landed at Naples and the body of a seaman at Genoa, says the British United Press.

This report says that sixty people in all were injured.

WIFE IN CABIN SCENE

HUSBAND'S FRIEND FOUND DRUGGED IN BED

MR. Falk Feilberg, a Danish friend of Mr. Clement Jackson Howells, the London club proprietor whose wife died in a Copenhagen hospital of an overdose of sleeping draught last Friday, is now in hospital suffering from a similar complaint.

Last night Mr. Feilberg was found unconscious in a room at the Copenhagen hotel where Mr. Howells is staying. He was taken to hospital, where his illness was diagnosed as an overdose of sleeping draught, and he has been placed on the danger list.

Police state that Mr. Feilberg had sat up until the early hours of the morning talking with Mr. Howells.

According to the newspaper *National Tidende*, Copenhagen police have ordered a post-mortem on Mrs. Howells, says British United Press.

It was Mr. Feilberg who met Mrs. Howells upon her recent arrival in Denmark, when she complained that she had been molested in her cabin aboard ship by an Austrian traveller.

Mr. Feilberg then called Mr. Howells, whose home is The Pantiles, Golders Green, N.W., to Copenhagen, and the latter flew there, went to the hotel where the Austrian was staying and thrashed him.

DAUGHTER FOR EILEEN BENNETT

Mrs. Marcus Marsh, formerly Miss Eileen Bennett, the lawn tennis player, has given birth to a girl weighing 6½lb.

Late last night it was stated that mother and baby were doing well.

Mrs. Marsh is the wife of Mr. Marcus Marsh, well-known racehorse trainer. For months past Mrs. Marsh has been preparing a pink and blue "dream nursery" at her home at Lambourn, Berks.

Before she married Mr. Marsh she was the wife of Mr. E. O. Fearnley-Whittingstall.

SATURDAY, MARCH 13, 1937

Daily Mirror

No. 10383 Registered at the G.P.O. as a newspaper. ONE PENNY

DUKE OF WINDSOR COMPLETES WEDDING PLANS—IN FRANCE, IN MAY

SPECIAL "DAILY MIRROR" NEWS

THE Duke of Windsor has almost completed the plans for his wedding to Mrs. Simpson, which will not take place in Austria, but in France.

He does not wish in any way to interfere with, or distract from, the celebrations connected with the Coronation of his brother, and so he has decided not to get married until after the Coronation.

In all probability he will marry Mrs. Simpson about ten days after the Coronation.

He is planning to leave Castle Enzesfeld, near Vienna, where he has been staying since his abdication, and go to a chateau near Rouen, where the wedding will take place.

The Duke has had many offers of castles all over Europe for his honeymoon, but he has decided to spend it in the Austrian Alps.

He has leased, from the beginning of June, Count Paul Munster's castle, high up in the mountains on the Austrian-Italian frontier in Carinthia.

This castle lies in the heart of a deer forest, ten miles from the nearest railway station, at Arnoldstein.

The Duke visited the castle recently, and decided it would be ideal.

It is decorated with a great number of antlers from deer shot near the castle, but, at the Duke's request, several of these are being taken down, as he does not like antlers on the walls.

A Quiet Life

The Duke, who is in the best of health, is living very quietly at Enzesfeld.

Never since he went there has he been to Vienna at night, nor has he taken any part in the gay night life of the city.

His only visits to Vienna have been to the British Legation, the Turkish baths, and the Bristol Hotel for tea.

He spends most of the day playing golf or ski-ing, and in the evening sits in his bedroom typing letters to his friends.

(WORLD COPYRIGHT.)

MRS. SIMPSON STUDYING FRENCH VERBS

Mrs. Simpson gave an interview yesterday in the Chateau de Cande library.

She is polishing up her French, she said—and laughed over her struggle with irregular verbs.

Looking out at the heavy rain, she announced that she was anxious to take up golf again when better weather came.

Spain's war was another topic.

Obviously she takes keen interest in newspaper stories about her, for she said to the British United Press interviewer:

"You can see I am a much better motorist than the newspapers give me credit for. I don't look a bit pale and wan, do I?"

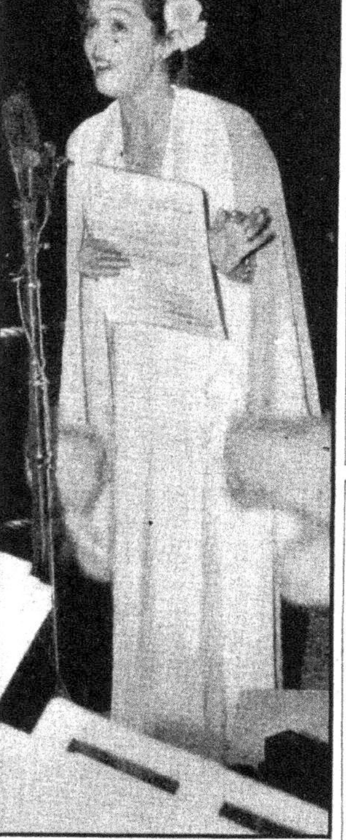

Star of stage and screen, Miss Jessie Matthews singing into the microphone at the Gaumont-British annual film ball at the Albert Hall last night.

The revelry was tinged with sadness, for the ball was in the nature of a farewell to many employees—under the new Gaumont-British production curtailment.

THE QUEEN'S TRAINBEARERS

Among the ladies invited to carry the Queen's train at the Coronation are Lady Iris Mountbatten (left) and Lady Ursula Manners (below, left)

Lady Iris Mountbatten is the seventeen-year-old daughter of the Marquis of Carisbrooke.

Lady Ursula Manners, who is twenty-one this year, is the elder daughter of the Duke and Duchess of Rutland

LOST BARONET SAFE

Sir Charles Ross, Bart., for whom coastguards searched when he vanished on a fishing trip in a cabin launch, arrived safely yesterday at Key West, Florida, says Reuter.

Sir Charles, who invented the rifle used by Canadians during the war, had been missing since Tuesday.

GANG GIRLS SENT HERE, DUPE MEN

FROM OUR OWN CORRESPONDENT

NEW YORK, Friday.

THE hectic adventures in England of two New York gangster girls, who duped handsome young Englishmen, enjoyed aeroplane joy rides and frequented gay night clubs, were revealed to me exclusively to-day

Beautiful, fair-haired Nancy Prosser and Thelma Jordan are girls notorious in New York's underworld. Yet they have recently been enjoying London's night life in the company of the cream of European society.

They were sent to England with first-class tickets in the liner Samaria by Special Prosecutor Dewey and his colleagues after giving evidence that led to the conviction of Lucky Luciano, New York's Tsar of Vice. "You'll be safer there," said Dewey.

Returned Penniless

They returned home, third-class, with not a halfpenny in their elegant handbags, when they were informed by their New York "fairy godfathers" that "there was no more dough."

To-day these girls are being kept in hiding in New York while Luciano's brilliant lawyer, Moses Polakoff, is demanding a new trial for his client on the grounds that they have retracted their evidence.

Americans wonder how it was that Britain

(Continued on back page)

"BOY-BIRCHING MUST BE STOPPED!" 2,000 WOMEN PROTEST TO PREMIER

FROM OUR OWN CORRESPONDENT

DORCHESTER, Friday.

HORRIFIED at tales of the effect of birching, 2,000 Dorset women are to protest to the Prime Minister and the Home Secretary against the birching of boys under magistrates' orders.

They are to send a resolution, which will also go to the four Dorset M.P.s, asking for the repeal of the Act which permits magistrates to order this punishment.

The women, members of Dorset Co-operative Societies, are also to ask for the appointment of younger magistrates who understand the temperament of juvenile offenders.

"We regard birching as a relic of the past which, instead of being beneficial, is more likely to be detrimental to the boys," one of the women said to me to-night.

"While many of us know, as mothers, that transgressors have to be dealt with, we believe that birching may result in beating badness in.

"If the criminal records are studied, the remedy in the past would not seem to have been very successful.

"More modern magistrates are needed in place of the old people, who live in the past and inflict the punishments of the past."

'PLANE 'LANDS' ON AIRSHIP

Colonel Udet, German air ace, yesterday successfully "landed" an aeroplane on a special "trapeze" arrangement suspended below the Zeppelin Hindenburg while the airship was in flight near Frankfort, says the Central News.

MONDAY, MARCH 15, 1937

Daily Mirror

No. 10384 | Registered at the G.P.O. as a newspaper. | ONE PENNY

GIRL NURSE TELLS OF BATTLE TO DEATH WITH NAKED MAN IN BATHROOM

FOUGHT FOR KNIFE

FROM OUR OWN CORRESPONDENT

NICE, Sunday.

TWENTY-SIX-YEAR-OLD Nurse Margaret Hill, daughter of Colonel W. J. M. Hill, D.S.O., of Withyham, Sussex, told me to-day of her struggle in an hotel bathroom in a desperate but vain effort to prevent a naked man from cutting his throat.

The suicide was James Baker, eighty-three, a blinded British engineer.

Miss Hill was sent by the Queen Victoria Hospital here to bring Mr. Baker to hospital.

Miss Hill, whom I saw at her hospital to-night, said:—

"I walked into the bathroom. Mr. Baker was sitting in the bath with a penknife in his hand.

"He had cut his throat.

"I grabbed at his wrist to try to take the knife away from him.

"He pushed me aside, but I sprang forward again as he struggled to his feet in the bath.

"I was trying to stop his slashing his throat again.

"But he was fighting to die—fighting with surprising strength. He was too strong for me.

"He slashed his throat once more—before I could grasp his wrist, twist it and snatch the knife from his weakened grasp.

"Then I knew it was too late.

Shocked, trembling, the girl was herself rushed to hospital.

But, first, she had sent seventy-five-year-old Mrs. Baker there. Mrs. Baker's condition is described at the hospital to-night as "critical."

Mr. Baker, blind and crippled in a motor-car accident four years ago, was ill—but extraordinarily strong for his age and condition.

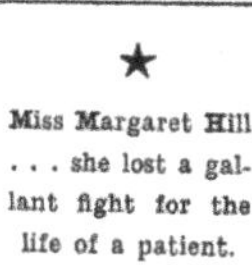

Miss Margaret Hill . . . she lost a gallant fight for the life of a patient.

POLICE FIND 'JAMES HUNT' IS WOMAN

BY A SPECIAL CORRESPONDENT

POLICE who questioned a "man" on Saturday night after a dispute at a house in the West End where he was employed, found on taking him to Vine-street station that he was a woman.

She was charged in the name of Mrs. Valerie Arkell-Smith, of Grafton-street, St. Pancras, and will appear at Great Marlborough-street Police Court to-day, accused of stealing £5 from the house of Mrs. Adrienne Scott, of George-street, Hanover-square, where she was employed.

She had been known as James Hunt.

For months residents in Grafton-place, Euston, have admired the tall, well-built figure of a "man" about thirty years of age, always well dressed and with dignified bearing, who left his house each morning as though going to business

Mrs. Mattioda, the landlady of the house where Arkell-Smith lived, told me: "I can hardly believe that she is a woman.

"She has lived here for a year and seemed to be very much attached to a woman with whom she had been living and whom I understood to be Mrs. Hunt.

"'Mr. Hunt' was always well dressed and appeared to be wealthy. I understood that he was connected with some business in the West End.

"'Mr. Hunt' often spoke of his military career, and certainly carries himself like a soldier."

"He always addressed 'Mrs. Hunt' as Betty. The pair spent most of their evenings in their room. Occasionally they went to a cinema together.

James Hunt.

VICAR ANSWERS RUNAWAY WIFE AND A THIEF FROM PULPIT

"I left a good husband in a fit of exasperation and stayed with another man. Can I expect my husband to take me back?"

THAT heart cry from a woman, one of many human problems sent to him, was read from the pulpit at Christ Church, Claughton, Birkenhead, last night, by the vicar, the Rev. H. R. Bates.

He had invited written questions and a congregation of 500 heard him deal with them.

"What do you men say?" the Vicar asked, "of the unfaithful wife.

"If she means 'good' by worldly standards he may not take her back, but if she means the standard as the attitude of Christ he will take her back."

Prayers were offered for this woman and for a convicted thief.

These were other questions, and the Vicar's answers:—

A woman: I have lost two fiances, one killed in the war the other dying of pneumonia. Why have I been denied love?—It is not really correct she was denied love. That she has known love twice is something for her to be thankful for.

The thief, just completing a long sentence: Can I regain the affection of my children and wife?—Not until he confesses to her that he has done wrong can he ask his wife to take him back.

For a trivial offence, his father pushed this little boy's fingers into the fire.

SEE STORY ON PAGE 4.

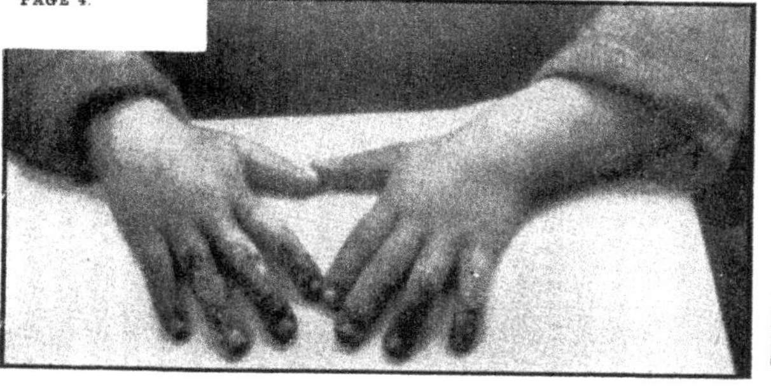

FIRM SPENDS THOUSANDS TO CURE MEN'S RED NOSES

Samuel Fox's steelworks at Stocksbridge, near Sheffield, are to spend thousands of pounds remodelling their furnaces, because they mean to see their workmen free from the embarrassment of red noses.

It has been found that a new cooling system minimises the irritation to the blood experienced by men working on the melting process—and keeps their noses a natural hue.

WEDNESDAY, MARCH 17, 1937

Daily Mirror

No. 10386 Registered at the G.P.O. as a newspaper. ONE PENNY

SIR AUSTEN CHAMBERLAIN, 73, DROPS DEAD IN HIS HOME

BY OUR POLITICAL CORRESPONDENT

SIR Austen Chamberlain, seventy-three-year-old "Father" of Conservative statesmen, fell dead in his London home, Egerton-terrace, Kensington, last night.

For the past few days he had been suffering from lumbago. Yesterday he said he felt better and soon after six o'clock decided to go downstairs to his library.

He was walking down a flight of stairs when he suddenly clutched at his breast, staggered, pitched forward and fell heavily to the foot of the stairs.

He died in a few minutes from a heart attack without regaining consciousness.

The news was at once flashed to the House of Commons.

Mr. Neville Chamberlain, Chancellor of the Exchequer, Sir Austen's half-brother, was dining there. He was the only man to be told Sad-faced he drove to 11, Downing-street.

M.P.s Talk On

The House, unaware of the tragedy, went on discussing Army estimates while the nation's greatest apostle of peace lay dead in his library.

The monocled, top-hatted, orchid-loving Sir Austen, best dressed and most-caricatured man in the House, had died with the Chamberlain family's greatest aim—the Premiership—almost within the grasp of its now only surviving politician-member.

It will be as Foreign Secretary that Sir Austen will take his place in history. People jeered at him when he once said "I love France as a woman."

Lady Chamberlain

But they cheered him when he returned from Locarno in 1925 after signing the Treaty that was to have ended war in Europe. The King and Mr. Baldwin met Sir Austen, too.

The Order of the Garter was conferred on him and he shared the Nobel Peace Prize for 1925 with General Dawes

His Help Mate

Lady Chamberlain daughter of the late Colonel Henry Lawrence Dundas, was a great help-mate to him throughout his career, and her part in the Locarno negotiations was recognised by the award of the Grand Cross of the Order of the British Empire.

They had two sons, Joseph, who was born in 1907, and Lawrence Endicott born in 1917, and one daughter, Diane.

"For twenty-two years," Sir Austen said in 1928, "my wife has been my partner in private life, and if in that time I have been able to

(Continued on back page)

Sir Austen Chamberlain—he always wore a monocle like his father, and a topper.

'BE READY TO FLY,' RADIO WARNS FENLAND FAMILIES

Families of every town and village in 250 square miles of Fenland waited last night for orders to abandon their homes before the advance of millions of gallons of water.

WARNING to stand by was broadcast by the B.B.C., who sent out a bulletin every fifteen minutes in the danger period. An announcer said:

"The River Great Ouse Catchment Board warns residents in all Fen areas to stand by and be ready to evacuate in case of breaches of river banks.

"The Board cannot guarantee to prevent an overflow, and a breach may occur. Areas to which this applies are those below river level in Cambridgeshire, including the Isle of Ely"

While the families prepared to flee, hundreds of volunteers, directed by expert engineers, fought to stem the rising floods in rivers and dykes.

At midnight an official of the Board told the *Daily Mirror*:

"So far all our defences have held out. We cannot say that we are safe. The crisis will not be over for at least another day.

"We cannot tell from hour to hour where the burst-through will occur or what disaster will happen if it does."

But by 2 a.m. to-day came more reassuring news.

The central office at Ely announced that wind and rain had ceased and the tide showed every sign of falling.

"Every hour that the banks hold now is an hour gained," it was stated.

Two Hamlets Emptied

Two hamlets—Welches Dam and Puri Bridge, near Ely—have already been evacuated by the villagers

Their cottages, just below the middle level bank were in danger of being washed away by a mile-wide lake of flood water, caused by the overflow of two reservoirs, the Hundred Foot and the Old Bedford.

Reserves of men were rushed to prevent the bank breaking, but the situation was so critical that all residents in the area were hurried from their homes to refuge in houses found for them by the police at Manea.

"Slow Down Pumps"

Chief engineers of the Ouse Catchment Board broadcast an urgent appeal to farmers to stop pumping water from dykes a d ditches into the swollen rivers

They appealed:—

"Will all pumps in the southern level slow down between 8.30 p.m. and midnight as the position is critical. The safety of the Fens may depend on this."

Six rivers encircling the Fen country have been steadily rising. One breach at a critical point on the fifty-mile front may bring disaster.

Cambridge undergraduates raced twenty miles in cars to Earith, near Ely, yesterday afternoon to help hundreds of farm labourers in the battle to save Fenland.

They toiled ankle deep in mud and water In Ely a bugler was on duty all day—ready to sound the alarm.

Zero comes twice daily to the weary fighters when the tide is running in from the Wash.

(Pictures on page 16)

SEVEN KILLED, 400 WOUNDED, AS PARIS POLICE FIRE ON RIOTERS AT MIDNIGHT

SEVEN people were killed and 400 wounded when Paris mobile guards opened fire last night on 10,000 rioters outside Clichy Town Hall. The trouble began in a cinema where Colonel de la Rocque, leader of the Fascist "French Social Party" was holding a rally of his supporters.

Almost as soon as the audience had taken their seats violent fighting broke out. Stones were thrown and bottles and pieces of iron were used. Then shots were fired.

The cinema became a shambles and fighting spread outside to the road.

Ambulances sounding sirens rushed up and down the street removing the wounded from the "battlefield."

Fifty police were injured. Mobile guards had to charge the crowds, a number of whom took refuge in the Town Hall.

M. Leon Blum, the Premier, went personally to the scene. His Secretary-General, M. Blumel, was wounded three times.

Messages from Reuter and British United Press.

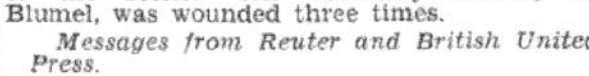

FIGHTING THE FLOODS in Fenland. Cambridge undergraduates filling sandbags at Earith to reinforce the dykes, over which the waters are already sweeping Further flood pictures are on page 16.

DUKE GOES TO BED BY CANDLELIGHT

THE Duke of Windsor went to bed in Enzesfeld Castle by candle-light last night.

When the Duke returned from Vienna he found that the electric light in the village had failed. A gale had blown overhead cables across one another, causing a short-circuit, the *Daily Mirror* Enzesfeld correspondent telephoned last night.

The village electrician was preparing to climb the high pylon in the darkness to try to restore the current, but when the Duke heard of his plan, which might have meant death, he insisted that the man should not do so until this morning.

"I don't mind using candle-light to-night," the Duke said, and then, in common with the villagers, he sat in his room with a candle as the only means of light.

Rumours that the Duke is planning shortly to leave Austria are denied here, and it is expected that he will remain in Austria until well into next month at least.

LANDSLIP: RAIL WATCH

The Southern Railway main line between Folkestone and Dover, threatened by Monday's landslide, was closed last night.

At one point the slide approached to within less than fifteen feet of the actual track and new cracks appeared in many places yesterday. Engineers kept watch all night. It is expected that the service on the line will be resumed to-day.

TUESDAY, MARCH 23, 1937

Daily Mirror

No. 10391 Registered at the G.P.O. as a Newspaper. ONE PENNY

8-COUNTY HUNT FOR FLYING DUCHESS, 71, LOST ON SOLO TRIP

Police of eight counties sent out every available patrol car last night to search for the Duchess of Bedford, Britain's seventy-one-year-old flying Duchess, whose green Moth aeroplane had been missing ten hours.

IN Bedfordshire all police reserves were on duty early to-day. Flying Squads were busy on every road. Flight-Lieutenant R. C. Preston, the Duchess's private pilot, announced, "If she is not found by daybreak, I shall take up a 'plane and search for her myself."

Appeal to Police is Broadcast

At 3.30 p.m. yesterday the Duchess stepped into her 'plane, marked G-ACUR, and took off from the beautiful lawn in front of her house, Woburn Abbey, near Bedford, which has been converted into a landing ground.

She needed only half an hour to complete her 200 hours' solo flying. Flight-Lieutenant Preston had mapped out for her a trip around Cambridgeshire.

"I watched her take off," Flight-Lieutenant Preston told the *Daily Mirror*. "She was cheerful and smiling happily. As the 'plane roared by me she waved her hand. That was the last I saw of the Duchess."

The weather was then bright and good for flying. But soon afterwards the sky became overcast. A snowstorm blew up.

When the Duchess had not returned by 5.30 p.m. her relatives became very anxious and communicated with the police.

The B.B.C. broadcast an appeal to police authorities to send out patrol cars.

The appeal was soon answered with these reports:—

AMPTHILL (Beds), six miles away: 'Plane, believed to be that piloted by the Duchess, seen about four o'clock. 'Plane heard again just after six. Snow was then falling.

PETERBOROUGH: Gamekeeper in Monks Wood, Woodwalton, thirteen miles away, said that he saw a machine flying very low over the wood and heard the engine fail.

FARCET (two miles from Peterborough): Man telephoned that he saw a 'plane circling over the town as though trying to find somewhere to land

Over Fens?

Police cars were at once rushed to these districts, and searchers set out with lamps.

It was thought that the Duchess may have flown on over the flooded Fenlands. An R.A.F. official said that flying conditions there had been ideal. The snowstorm had been confined to Northamptonshire and Bedfordshire.

Meanwhile, at Woburn Abbey, the seventy-nine-year-old Duke, who had said good-bye to his wife as she walked to her 'plane, was waiting anxiously for news.

"He is keeping calm," said Miss Green, com-

(Continued on back page)

The Duchess of Bedford in the cockpit of an open 'plane.

"WHAT WILL BE, WILL BE" —THE BEDFORDS' MOTTO

Though the Duchess is now missing a few miles from her home she has:—

Flown within 50ft. of the seething crater of Vesuvius;

Made a record flight to India and back by daylight in seven and a half days.

Covered the 19,000 miles Capetown and back in twenty days—tramping miles by torchlight in a lion-infested jungle to sleep in a native hut after a forced landing

CABINET WILL COST COUNTRY ANOTHER £30,000: PREMIERS' PAY TO BE DOUBLED

BY OUR POLITICAL CORRESPONDENT

SALARIES of Prime Ministers will in future be doubled.

This is the unexpected feature of the Ministers' Salaries Bill to be presented in the House of Commons to-day, and published to-morrow. Cabinet increases will cost the country another £30,000.

Mr. Baldwin, it is understood, will not accept the increase, but has paved the way for his successor, Mr. Neville Chamberlain.

Mr. Chamberlain, when he succeeds him in May, will receive £10,000 a year instead of the £5,000 which is Mr. Baldwin's income.

All Cabinet ministers' salaries will be put on a basis of £5,000.

It is probable that the Leader of the Opposition, Mr. C. R. Attlee, will receive a salary of £2,000.

Pensions of the same amount will, I hear, be made available to former Prime Ministers.

The Men and the Money

This is how Ministers will be affected:—

£5,000 RISE

The next Prime Minister.

£3,000 RISE

Mr. Hore-Belisha, Minister of Transport.
Earl Stanhope, First Commissioner of Works
Mr. Ernest Brown, Minister of Labour.
Mr. W. S. Morrison, Minister of Agriculture
Mr. Oliver Stanley, Education Minister.
Mr. Walter Elliott, Secretary for Scotland.
Lord Halifax, Lord Privy Seal.
Mr. Ramsay MacDonald, Lord President of the Council.

£500 RISE

Sir Samuel Hoare, Admiralty First Lord

'B.B.C. SENSATIONALISED FENLAND NEWS'

BY OUR POLITICAL CORRESPONDENT

B.B.C. officials may be criticised in the House of Commons to-night for "sensationalising" their news broadcasts on the Fenland floods.

Commander R. T. Bower, Conservative member for Cleveland, hopes to raise the point when M.P.s debate the question of land drainage.

"If I have an opportunity in the debate," he said to me last night, "I shall criticise the B.B.C. for dramatising the floods in their broadcasts which might have made some people think that the Fens were experiencing a sort of Ohio disaster.

Reference will also be made to the *Daily Mirror* plea that workless miners should be given employment in draining the Fens.

Mr. W. Dobbie, Socialist M.P. for Rotherham, told me that he intends to urge this proposal

NEVER TO HAVE A CHILD AGAIN

—Mother's Vow

FROM OUR SPECIAL CORRESPONDENT

TUNBRIDGE WELLS, Monday.

A YOUNG mother who was bluntly told by the local coroner to-day that her ignorance led to the death of her six-week-old son, Francis, vowed before me to-night that she would never have another baby.

"I did everything I could for my baby," said Mrs. Alice Phyllis Adie, a pretty, auburn-haired girl of twenty-two, to me.

"I loved him," she added tearfully. "Now I have been rebuked."

"Starved to Death"

Recording a verdict that her baby died of malnutrition, the coroner said to Mrs. Adie:—

"This child was starved to death, but I am prepared to believe that you thought you were doing the right thing. I am prepared to put your complete failure down to ignorance.

"You and your husband are both young, and I hope you make a better job of it next time.

"Motherhood is a job which has to be learned just the same as dress-making or brick-laying, and you cannot have a child and become an experienced mother at the same time."

Mrs. Adie, who admitted to the coroner that she guessed the amount of artificial food she gave her baby, said to me:

"Doing My Best"

"I thought I was doing my best. I have had nursing experience as an under-nurse and I brought up a child on artificial food from the age of one month.

"I knew nothing about baby clinics, and I did not worry because I thought Michael was all right. Last Friday morning he was well, chuckling in his bed. In the afternoon he was dead.

"After what the coroner told me, with all the people in the court listening, I decided never to have another child."

In the hall to-night stood a shiny new perambulator with the coverlet thrown aside. And I saw a half-finished cot, which the proud father had been making for his son.

Yesterday was the first anniversary of Mrs. Adie's wedding. There was to have been a celebration party at their home in Lime Hill-road here—a house they took eight months ago to give their baby every chance.

Instead it was a house of mourning

Mr. and Mrs. Adie.

WEDNESDAY, MARCH 24, 1937

Daily Mirror

No. 10392 Registered at the G.P.O. as a Newspaper ONE PENNY

MUSSOLINI WILL NOT QUIT SPAIN: IS ANGRY WITH BRITAIN

BY OUR POLITICAL CORRESPONDENT

Ministers are anxious about the strained relations existing between Britain and Italy.

I hear that the Italian Government has now announced its intention not to withdraw any of her volunteers from Spain.

That development is regarded as most significant in view of the fact that only a few days ago Italy was prepared to discuss withdrawal.

IT is feared that present hostility of Mussolini to this country will be aggravated by to-morrow's debate in the House of Commons, on the Socialist motion censuring the Italian massacre of Abyssinians at Addis-Ababa.

There was strong feeling among Conservative members last night that the debate should be called off, and that the Opposition should be given an opportunity to raise their motion after the Easter recess, when, it is hoped, a calmer atmosphere will prevail.

So far, the Socialists give no sign of withdrawing. They seem determined to launch a fierce attack on the Italian policy in Abyssinia.

At yesterday's meeting of the non-Intervention sub-committee lack of unity among those present was only too apparent.

Bewildered Committee

Count Grandi, the Italian Ambassador, told the committee that his country was not prepared to remove volunteers from Spain.

Then M. Corbin, the French Ambassador, remarked that the whole position was made very difficult by that statement, and Herr von Ribbentrop, German Ambassador, said that his Government had not reached any decision about withdrawing volunteers.

The sub-committee broke up, bewildered and apprehensive about the future.

Of the Italian Press silence about the Pope's Apostolic letter to Germany the Vatican newspaper *Osservatore Romano* is critical, reports the British United Press.

"The greater part of the Italian Press," it says, "published meagre items which were evidently inspired by the briefest and most inexact communique from an official agency.

(Continued on back page)

TENT IS TWINS' HOME

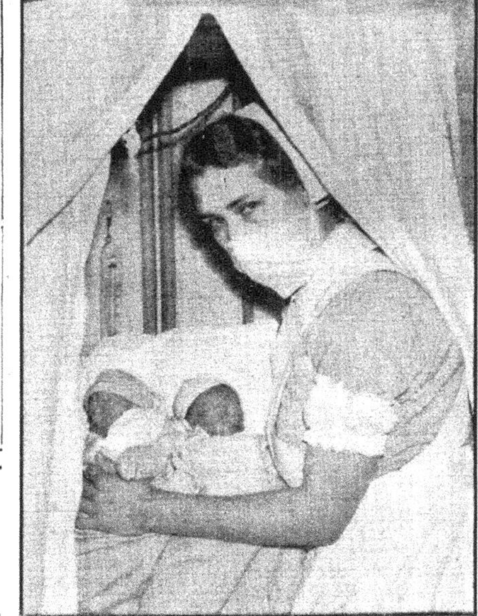

Attended by a nurse wearing a respirator, Mrs. Batchelor's second pair of twins in their tent at King's College Hospital.

MOTHER HAS FIVE CHILDREN UNDER 2½: HER SECOND TWINS IN 10 MONTHS

BY A SPECIAL CORRESPONDENT

HUDDLED together in a special little tent in King's College Hospital lie the second pair of twins born within ten months to Mrs. Margaret Batchelor, of Lilford-road, Camberwell.

Mrs. Batchelor now has five children under two and a half.

The new twins are girls (3lb. 12oz. and 3lb. 9oz.), and they were born yesterday. All three were last night "doing as well as could be expected."

"It Was a Tremendous Surprise"

Mrs. Batchelor told me, "It was a tremendous surprise, but I'm ever so glad all the same. I'm not feeling so bad. I expect it will be a bit of a struggle to keep things going, but apart from that I am so glad everything has gone well. My other twins are both boys."

At the Batchelors' home, where the twins' health was drunk in a glass of beer, Mr. Batchelor told me: "I believe this is a world's record. The twins are not quite ten months old.

"We've Got Nothing Ready"

"I must say it comes as a bit of a shock. We didn't expect another baby to be born for at least two months or so. We've got absolutely nothing ready for the new arrivals.

"I'm only in part-time employment in the building trade, but I suppose we shall have to rub along somehow.

"I've no idea what we shall call them."

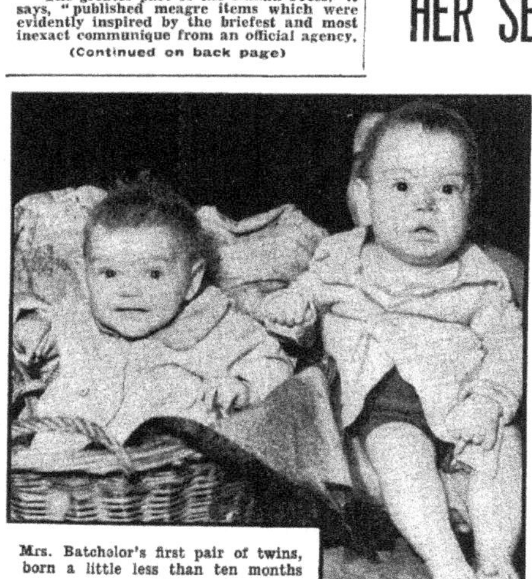

Mrs. Batchelor's first pair of twins, born a little less than ten months ago.

Flying Duchess Still Lost

STRAIN OF VIGIL TELLS ON DUKE, 79

BY A SPECIAL CORRESPONDENT

THE seventy-nine-year-old Duke of Bedford was last night showing signs of strain after a thirty-hour search by more than 1,000 police and R.A.F. 'planes had failed to find any trace of his wife, the seventy-one-year-old Flying Duchess, missing on a solo flight.

The Duke has been in poor health recently, and a nurse is living at Woburn Abbey, his Bedfordshire home.

Outlying parts of the grounds of the Abbey were being searched by torchlight throughout the night.

The Duchess was taken slightly ill while flying a few weeks ago, a member of the estate staff told me last night.

"She had one or two attacks of giddiness recently, and had complained of head pains," I was told.

Search Extended

B.B.C. last night broadcast a message from the Chief Constable of Bedford asking for the search to be extended to the Norfolk coast and the Yorkshire Moors in case the Duchess may have lost direction and landed there.

The area to be covered will extend south to St. Albans, west to Bicester, and east to Mildenhall. From Grantham 'planes will fly to the Wash and out to sea.

Bedford police had earlier searched in vain after a woman had telephoned that she saw a blazing aeroplane over Stagsden, Bedfordshire, at 5 p.m. on Monday.

The task of searching may take several days because of severe weather and extensive flooding in the area. I reached this conclusion after ninety minutes in the air circling round the woods and thickets which abound in the area surrounding Sawtry (Hunts) where the Duchess was seen last.

SHIRLEY TEMPLE "OPERATION": MOTHER'S DENIAL

BY A SPECIAL CORRESPONDENT

(By Transatlantic Telephone)

NEWS flashed round the world from Hollywood at 2 a.m. this morning that Shirley Temple, world's baby sweetheart, had been rushed to hospital to have an operation for abdominal trouble.

When I put through a call to her home from the *Daily Mirror* office her mother came to the 'phone.

"There's nothing wrong with Shirley—I am the one who's to have the operation.

"I want you to tell the world now that there's no operation to Shirley on the way.

"Shirley doesn't even know that I have been to the doctor. It is such a slight operation that I am not worrying in the least, but I do thank the *Daily Mirror* for having telephoned and cleared the matter up.

"Shirley is as fit as a fiddle and is working on her film, 'Wee Willie Winkie.'"

When I asked if Shirley would talk about her mother, I was told that she had been in bed since 8 p.m. (American time), and could not be awakened. She has to be on the set at six this morning.

THURSDAY, MARCH 25, 1937

Daily Mirror

No. 10393 Registered at the G.P.O. as a Newspaper. ONE PENNY

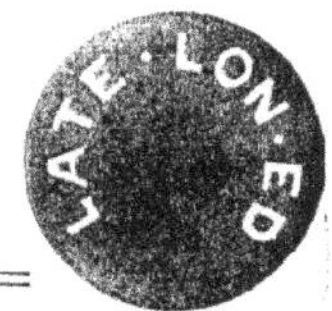

LONDON BUS STRIKE THREAT

ON EVE OF EASTER HOLIDAY

ON the eve of the Easter holidays, London is threatened by one of the largest stoppages of passenger transport since the General Strike eleven years ago.

Midnight meetings of bus drivers will be held at garages throughout the East London area to-morrow. It is likely that they will decide not to take their buses on the roads on Saturday.

Trouble in the bus depots over the 1932 speed-up agreement which the Transport and General Workers' Union accepted on behalf of the men is the cause.

To relieve the situation and prevent the men taking unofficial strike action, the Transport and General Workers' Union prepared a new scheme, and put it before London Transport.

Reply in Sealed Envelope

The reply was sent in a sealed envelope to the union yesterday. It will be considered by senor officers of the Union at Transport House to-day.

If strike action were decided on only fourteen garages would stop work at first, but there is so much dissatisfaction that the strike might rapidly spread through London.

Garages in the eastern district are: Upton Park, Old Ford, Forest Gate, Loughton, Leyton, Dalston, Barking, Hackney, Palmers Green, West Green, Athol-street E., Enfield, Seven Kings and Romford.

Blackpool hotel workers decided early to-day, after a three hours' meeting, to strike at once. All hotels in the resort where the workers' union is not acknowledged, and where immediate pay increases are not granted, will be picketed.

An official said: "It will be a ruthless struggle. The gloves are off."

After the Crash

The wrecked Capricornus lying among pine trees on the snowclad mountainside into which it crashed in France.

On the right is her pilot, Captain A. Paterson — a picture taken shortly before the flying-boat took off from Southampton.

CRAWLS 2 MILES, TELLS OF AIR-BOAT DISASTER

AN injured man slowly dragged himself yesterday two miles along snow-covered tracks to a lonely farmhouse in the Beaujolais Mountains, near Ouroux, France.

He brought first news that disaster had overtaken eighteen-ton, £40,000 Capricornus, Imperial Airways' Queen Mary of the skies, a few hours after she had left Southampton on her maiden trip.

Her mighty engines had sent her full speed into a hill-side as driving snow blotted out the pilot's view. Four of her crew and the only passenger, fifty-five-year-old Miss B. M. Coates, of Lyminge, near Hythe, perished.

The man who crawled for help is radio operator James Cooper, sole survivor. He collapsed when he reached the farmhouse. He has a broken arm, leg and face injuries, but last night his condition was reported satisfactory.

Unconscious in the wreckage as Cooper's warning sent farmhands racing to the Capricornus lay Miss Coates.

The rescuers found Captain A. Paterson, the pilot, dead with his hands on the controls.

His dead comrades were First Officer G. E. Klein, of Warrington, Lancs; Flight-Clerk D. R. O'Brien, of Home Lodge, Downsway, Sutton; Steward F. A. E. Jeffcoats, of Kynaston-avenue, Thornton Heath.

Farm-carts drawn by horses and oxen were

(Continued on back page)

Only passenger aboard the Capricornus when it crashed—Miss B. Coates.

THE KING GIVING MR. BALDWIN HIGHEST HONOUR POSSIBLE

SPECIAL "DAILY MIRROR" NEWS

THE King has decided personally to confer the Order of the Garter on Mr. Stanley Baldwin when he retires from the premiership after the Coronation.

This is the highest order the King can bestow on a Minister. Unless, as is expected, Mr. Baldwin goes to the House of Lords, he will be the only commoner in the Order.

The decision to honour Mr. Baldwin in such fashion is a personal expression of thanks from the King for the special services rendered by the Premier during the last few months.

The only other commoner ever to hold the Order was Sir Austen Chamberlain.

M.C.C. IN EARTHQUAKE

A slight earthquake at 5.30 this morning (local time) shook the beds throughout the hotel at which the M.C.C. are staying in Wellington, New Zealand, says Reuter.

They were awakened at a much earlier hour than usual, but the cricket was resumed later as if nothing had happened.

CAT BURGLAR TAKES £2,000 NECKLACE AS FAMILY DINE

A string of pearls valued at £2,000 was taken by a cat burglar who last night entered the house in Avenue-road, St. John's Wood, of Mr. G. Lowenstein.

The intruder climbed a stackpipe at the side of the house, entered the bedroom by a window and ransacked the room while members of the family were dining in a room immediately below.

'NO' TO CORONATION OFFER

Executive of the Mineworkers' Federation of Great Britain decided in London yesterday that they will refuse to accept any of the tickets sent to the Trades Union Congress for seats at the Coronation.

MONDAY, MARCH 29, 1937

Daily Mirror

No. 10395 Registered at the G.P.O. as a Newspaper. ONE PENNY

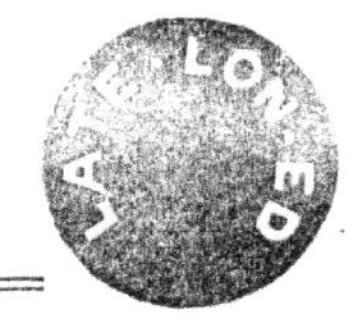

WAR ACE SEES HIS WIFE SHOT DEAD IN PACKED BAR PARLOUR

Mrs. Godby.

FROM OUR SPECIAL CORRESPONDENT

HIGH WYCOMBE (Bucks), Sunday.

WARTIME flying ace Robert Godby, leaning against the bar of the Hour Glass Inn at Sands, Bucks, last night, spun round at the sound of a revolver shot, saw his wife lurch forward dying over a game of dominoes, a bullet through her brain.

A glass tinkled to the floor, the scattered dominoes slid from the tilted table into the dead woman's lap. That broke the spell.

MEN AND WOMEN CROWDING ROUND THE BAR HEARD GODBY CRY OUT IN ALARM, AS HE LEAPED TO HIS WIFE'S SIDE AND GATHERED HER IN HIS ARMS.

Then uproar broke out in the bar.

Mrs. May Godby was thirty-seven, attractive, smartly dressed, soft spoken.

Albert Boddy, thirty-seven, a bricklayer, of Lane-end, High Wycombe, was later arrested. He will appear at High Wycombe Police Court to-morrow, accused of murdering Mrs. Godby.

Flying-Officer Godby told me to-night at his home in Mile End-road, High Wycombe:—

"This is terrible. I loved my wife dearly. We had been married for eight years. We have no children."

A friend told me: "The Godbys returned from New Zealand only ten-days ago. They had been there a year.

LYNCH THREAT EXILES 'GROOM

NEW YORK, Sunday.

LYNCH - THREATENING Klu - Klux-Klansmen, infuriated by the marriage a week ago of a fifty-seven-year-old mill foreman and a schoolgirl of twelve, last night exiled the bridegroom from his home town for ever.

Chandler Revell, of Manatee, Florida, cowered with his child bride behind locked doors at their newly furnished home when the Klansmen wearing civilian clothes, forced their way in with the ultimatum:

"Get out of Florida, stay out. Come back —you'll be strung up."

Snatching his few belongings Revell, an ex-Klansman, fled.

The bride has been taken from Manatee by her sister to avoid publicity.

State authorities are taking steps to annul the marriage.

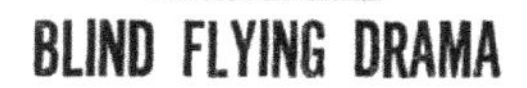

BLIND FLYING DRAMA

Drama of the skies was played over Sheffield in the early hours yesterday, when two flyers, an instructor and a learner, had to make a forced landing in a blinding snowstorm.

When they ran into the storm Mr. R. J. Pattinson, of Leeds, who was inexperienced in blind flying, had to rely on his instructor, Mr. A. W. Vincent, of Imperial Airways, although the latter was not in a position to see the blind flying instruments, which were behind him.

Vincent shouted directions to the pilot through the speaking tube, and the machine was safely landed.

SHE'S TOO BIG TO FLY

She wanted to learn to fly, did 25st. Miss Doris Burge — and went to Hanworth Flying School. They took a look, and said she was too big to fly. Anyway, they hadn't a plane with a cockpit into which she could get Her only hope of learning to fly, they said, was a bomber. See story on page 3.

QUADS' MOTHER GRANTED WISH FOR GIRLS: 2 LIVE

BY A SPECIAL CORRESPONDENT

HE was to be called David . . . but an hour before he was to be baptised, one of the quadruplets—three girls and a boy—born to a London wife yesterday, died. One of the girls survived only for a few minutes.

"My wife wanted a girl. Well, we have got them, and we are very happy," said Mr. William Chapman, the husband, of Garnham-street, Stoke Newington, N., last night.

His wife, Florence, thirty-eight years old, gave birth to the babies in the Royal Northern Hospital, Holloway, N.

The babies were born within two hours of each other. The boy, who was first, weighed $4\frac{1}{4}$lb. He died twelve hours after The girl, who died weighed only $1\frac{1}{2}$lb.

"We had known for the past three months that my wife was going to have three babies," said Mr. Chapman.

"Florence had already been in a Stoke Newington nursing home three weeks. She is only a little woman.

"We knew we could hardly afford them, but we looked forward happily to the prospect of three new children. My wife longed for one of them to be a little girl. We have two sons, Arthur, aged fourteen, and Roy, ten.

"One of our girls is 5lb. and the second is just short of that.

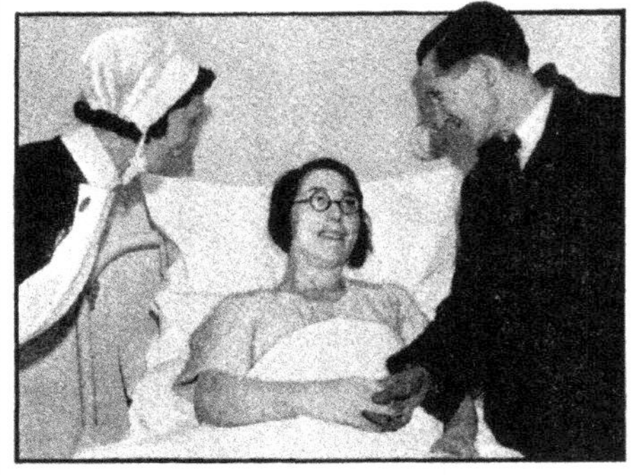
Mrs. Florence Chapman.—A handshake from her husband.

MYSTERY BRITON IN TRIPLE FLAT MURDER

FROM OUR OWN CORRESPONDENT

NEW YORK, Sunday.

BLONDE Veronica Gedeon, a well-known mannequin, and her mother, Mrs. Mary Gedeon, aged fifty-four, were found strangled in their apartment here to-day. An Englishman who boarded with them was found dead in another room—stabbed through the ear.

Veronica, who in New York's fashion salons was known as Ronnie, and her mother were in their night attire.

The Englishman, Frank Byrnes, aged thirty-five, who came here about twelve years ago, was regarded locally as a mystery man. He was employed as a waiter in New York's Racquets Club.

The tragedy was discovered by Mrs. Gedeon's estranged husband and their daughter and son-in-law, Mr. and Mrs. Joseph Kudner, who are now being questioned at the police station.

THURSDAY, APRIL 1, 1937

Daily Mirror

No. 10398 Registered at the G.P.O. as a Newspaper. ONE PENNY

MAN 22, WEDS BRIDE 65, BECOMES "GRANDFATHER" OF EIGHT

"DAILY MIRROR" SPECIAL NEWS

SMART blue hat perched on her blonde curls, sixty-five-year-old Mrs. Charlotte E. Brooks nodded "Yes," married twenty - two - year - old draper's assistant Stanley G. Searle at Fulham Register Office yesterday, made him grandfather of eight children and father of six adults older than himself.

Elderly women crowded round the register office cheering, shouting to the smiling bride dressed in royal blue, as she came out hugging her husband's arm.

They pelted them with rice and confetti and followed them —recruiting others on the way—to the bride's flat in Anselm-road, Fulham, where their demonstration became so noisy that special squads of police were called out.

Less than a year ago Mrs. Searle's eighty-four-year-old husband died.

Her second marriage was a sequel to a lightning courtship with the handsome, well-built, blond young shop assistant whom she met while buying groceries at the shop round the corner where he used to work.

The wedding taxi raced the well-wishers back to Anselm-road, where the bride's six children, her eight grandchildren—the eldest a woman, twenty-one, the youngest a baby in arms—waited among a crowd of grandfathers and grandmothers to congratulate them.

S O S to Police

While dance tunes were being strummed on the piano in the drawing-room hundreds of people arrived and blocked the street outside.

Rumour had spread that the bride and bridegroom were leaving for their honeymoon.

But as Mr. Searle has to be back at work behind the counter of the Fulham draper's shop this morning the honeymoon was only a one-evening event.

The demonstrations of the crowd outside became so lively that an S O S was sent to the police by the bride's family.

By that time the road was blocked, people were spilling over into North End-road, a main thoroughfare, and a police car with special reserves was needed to keep it clear for traffic.

The bride and the bridegroom were both modest about their romance.

Laughingly they admitted it, and said, "We are married and we have nothing to say."

But one of the bride's many young grandchildren told me with a burst of pride, "I've got a grandfather now, and he's only five years older than I am."

For many years Mrs Searle practised as a midwife

DUCHESS OF BEDFORD'S SON, the Marquis of Tavistock, leaving after yesterday's memorial service to his mother at St. Mary's Church, Woburn (Beds), close to Woburn Park, where the seventy-one-year-old Duchess took off on the flight from which she never returned.

★

Daughter of H. B. Warner, English film star, fourteen-year-old Lorraine—seen in London last night—thinks film stars, in the main, a lot of saps.

★

FILM STARS ARE A LOT OF SAPS SAYS "SORRELL'S" DAUGHTER

BY A SPECIAL CORRESPONDENT

FOURTEEN-YEAR-OLD Lorraine Warner, self-assured American daughter of English film star H. B. Warner, sprawled on her stomach, blonde head between cupped hands, in their Savoy suite last night—and renounced films for ever.

"No, sir!" said Lorraine. "I've seen too much.

"I've had my chance, you know. They gave me an audition for 'Cavalcade.' Yep, as long ago as that.

"I suppose I could have muscled in if I wanted to, but nothing doing. No sir!

Mr. Warner, star of "Sorrell and Son," the Judge in "Mr. Deeds Comes to Town," is here to work in the picture "Victoria Regina" at Iver, Bucks.

From the depths of an armchair he grinned proudly as Lorraine wise-cracked, gave me the low-down on film stars whose names are world-famous.

Lorraine rolled slowly over on her side, smiled slyly, rolled back again—"Lot of saps," she summed up.

"Now this is what I am going to do.

"When I've finished school I'm going to college to study to be a doctor.

"I used to have a woman doctor myself, and I guess that's what I'd like to be—at the moment, anyway.

"I ought to be at school now, as a matter of fact. But I took my holiday early. I'll have to make it all up when I get back home —still, I'll have seen the Coronation.

"The nicest thing about London that I've seen so far is the Australian soldiers.

Mr. Warner broke in, "First people who rang me up on arrival were Scotland Yard.

"I suppose they felt protective, and it was nice of them. But I think Lorraine and I can look after ourselves."

"I guess so," said Lorraine.

I'm sure of it.

THE FISH ARE TOO SMART

The fish of the River Don, near Aberdeen, unlike the taxpayer, are not to be caught.

For the third successive day the Chancellor of the Exchequer fished there yesterday, but he has not yet made a catch.

£5,597,000 BUDGET DEFICIT

BY OUR POLITICAL CORRESPONDENT

Budget deficit of £5,597,000 is shown in the final Treasury returns for the financial year issued last night.

It was a big blow to M.P.s' hopes of a £4,000,000 surplus. But the position might have been worse. Some pessimists had forecast a £20,000,000 deficit.

TAXPAYERS must, however, expect unpleasant surprises on Budget Day, April 20.

Income tax will not be increased by more than 3d., but additional indirect taxation is certain.

During the past year income tax showed an increased yield of £19,163,000 on the previous year.

Expenditure Rises

Realised revenue for the year was £797,289,000. Expenditure has jumped to £802,886,000. It includes a large sum applied to debt redemption.

Total ordinary revenue shows a net increase of £44,369,050 over last year although that was the highest since 1932.

Votes for the Army, Navy and Air Force fall below the estimate, being £186,072,000 against an expected £188,204,000

THURSDAY, APRIL 8, 1937

Daily Mirror

No. 10404 Registered at the G.P.O. as a Newspaper. ONE PENNY

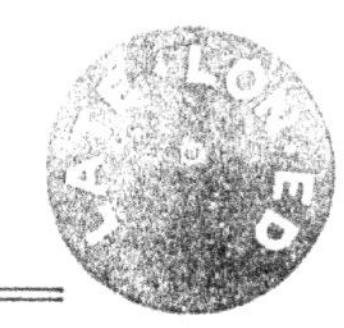

PEER WITH VAST ESTATES KEPT BY WIFE ON 35/- A WEEK

FROM OUR SPECIAL CORRESPONDENT

DUBLIN, Wednesday.

THE SENSITIVE BLUE EYES OF FORTY-TWO-YEAR-OLD LORD MASSY—PENNILESS PEER AND HEAD OF ONE OF IRELAND'S OLDEST FAMILIES—BRIMMED WITH TEARS AS I TOLD HIM TO-DAY THAT HE WAS THE OWNER OF A VAST EXPANSE OF MOUNTAIN LAND IN NORTH LEITRIM, THAT THE SHOOTING AND MINERAL RIGHTS OF SOME OF THE FINEST COUNTRY IN IRELAND WERE WAITING TO BE CLAIMED BY HIM.

EVER since he succeeded to the title eleven years ago Lord Massy has had to fight ill-luck. "Sometimes as I sit here in my loneliness and poverty I believe that the title has been nothing but a curse," he told me.

We were talking in Beehive Cottage—a labourer's 10s.-a-week house on his old estate—which Lord Massy has made his home, and as we chatted, he stirred a pot of stew on the wood fire.

"Do you know," he said earnestly, "I always thank God these days that I went to Harrow. I am sure it is the experience I had there of being a fag that enables me to do this."

It was here that I had found the man for whom Leitrim County Council have been searching for two years to collect unpaid rates of £41 on Lord Massy's estates.

He was amazed to hear that they had despaired of finding him and were about to raise a mortgage on the property, let the shooting rights and work the minerals for the benefit of the ratepayers.

Tried to Get Work

"I know that my grandfather owned a lot of land in North Leitrim," he said. "I remember hearing years ago how famous people from England came over to join his shooting parties.

"But I had always been told that the land had been sold to the Irish Land Commissioners—that everything had gone.

"Of course, I can't possibly find all that money for the rates now," he said. "But if I could prove my claim to it and be given time, I could try to raise a mortgage on the land, clear it of debt, and have enough to live on—decently."

There was a catch in the voice of this haggard, friendless, cultured Irishman.

He and his wife struggle to exist and keep their sixteen-year-old son and heir at school on 35s. a week that Lady Massy earns as a clerk in Dublin.

He spends his days tramping the mountains in search of firewood to keep his family warm.

He looked around the bare walls of his room, saw the coats he was using for bedclothes, and added:—

"I have tried for years to get a job—anything," he said, "but for my wife we should be starving.

(Continued on back page)

Lord Massy's present home, Beehive Cottage, tucked away in the desolate hills of Kilakee.

Peer, head of one of the oldest families in Ireland, Lord Massy (right) sitting by the fireside of his 10s. a week cottage on his old estate.

Above, his ancestral home, Kilakee House, and (below) Lord Massy with his sixteen - year - old son and heir, the Hon. Hugh Massy.

SAUCEPAN ON FIRE: HE LEARNED HIS COOKING AT HARROW

250 ITALIANS REFUSE TO FIGHT: IMPRISONED IN SHIP

—Traveller's Report

IMPRISONMENT of 250 Italian troops in a Spanish rebel steamer, because they refuse to go to the front, was reported yesterday at Gibraltar by a traveller from Seville.

He states that the Italians are in a ship named Arcila (says the British United Press). It is anchored in Seville port.

No Arcila is listed in Lloyd's Register. Other travellers arriving in Gibraltar tell of terrible conditions among the rebels.

Hundreds of wounded are said to be arriving every day from the front near Cordoba. Hundreds more are reported to be suffering from disease through long exposure to bad weather and lack of medical supplies.

Garland, a destroyer, was ordered yesterday to Palma, Majorca, where the British Vice-Consul will ask General Franco for an explanation of the bombing of the British warship Gallant on Tuesday.

"CHRIST IS GERMANY'S PUBLIC ENEMY"

—Says Pastor

"Christ Himself is regarded as a public enemy in Nazi Germany. All the persecution of Christians and of Christ is being carried out under a law which is entitled 'a law for the protection of people and State,'" ex-U-Boat Commander Oscar Niemoeller told a congregation at his church in Dahlem, Germany, last night.

He quoted instances of persecutions of the Evangelical Church, of which he is now a pastor, and named twenty-three Church workers labelled, "Enemies of the State" by the Nazis, Reuter says.

MARIE TEMPEST SELLING HOME

FAMOUS actress Marie Tempest has decided to sell the beautiful home in Avenue-road, Regent's Park, where she and her idolised husband, the late Mr. Graham Browne, spent so many happy years

A month ago Mr. Browne died after a brief illness Miss Tempest, heartbroken, bravely appeared in "Retreat from Folly" at the Queen's Theatre, London, the same night, playing opposite her husband's understudy.

They made the home in Avenue-road together, extensively modernised it and redesigned its charming garden.

Every nook and corner has eloquent sad memories for the widow.

There are three sitting-rooms and seven bedrooms in the house.

MRS. SIMPSON'S PET DOG KILLED BY SNAKE

FROM OUR SPECIAL CORRESPONDENT

PARIS, Wednesday.

SLIPPER, Mrs. Simpson's Cairn terrier, has died after being bitten by a snake in the grounds of the chateau where she is staying.

The news was telephoned to the Duke of Windsor at St. Wolfgang to-night.

When Mrs. Simpson left England shortly before the Duke's abdication she left Slipper behind in her hurry.

The Duke of Windsor took Slipper with him to Enzesfeld and a fortnight ago—shortly before he moved to St. Wolfgang—he sent the little Cairn back to Mrs. Simpson at Tours by special messenger.

They were both very attached to the dog.

FRIDAY, APRIL 9, 1937

Daily Mirror

No. 10405 Registered at the G.P.O. as a Newspaper. ONE PENNY

2,000 HUNT 15 NEGROES WITH ORDER "SHOOT TO KILL"

"DAILY MIRROR" SPECIAL CORRESPONDENT

JACKSONVILLE (Fla.), Thursday.

FIFTEEN DESPERATE NEGRO CRIMINALS ESCAPED FROM DUVAL COUNTY GAOL ARE FLEEING FOR THEIR LIVES THROUGH THE MARSHES OF SANTA FE LAKE: 2,000 ARMED MEN AND BOYS ARE HARD ON THEIR HEELS WITH OFFICIAL ORDERS "SHOOT TO KILL."

Three of the fugitives are murderers, two of them gang killers and the rest "lifers."

They escaped in their underwear, at dawn to-day, sawing through cell bars in the temporary gaol, where they have been herded while the big main block is being cemented.

Fifty desperadoes formed a human rampart and fought back warders as the prison-breakers escaped, walking over the temporary barricades on long planks.

Fusillades followed them from the look-out tower as they raced through the darkness to the cover of the swamps.

Screams from the prison siren brought smallholders tumbling from their beds. In a flash the alarm was spread by police radio over the borders of Georgia and Alabama.

Close behind the alarm came official summons from big, gruff Virginian Sheriff Bohon to "decent citizens of the Southern States" to hunt down the criminals.

"Shoot them down on sight," he ordered, "they deserve all that is coming to them."

Skirmishing Line

Farmers from Alabama, cotton planters from Georgia, orchardists and hill farmers from Jacksonville grabbed guns, reaping hooks and axes and mobilised for the greatest man hunt since the slave days.

Few waited to clothe themselves fully before they raced by car and horse shay to join the army of revenge, their lust to kill inflamed by news that two of the negroes were Alvin Baker

(Continued on back page)

Helen Burgess, who has died as she won film fame. She was Buffalo Bill's wife in "The Plainsman."

FILM BEAUTY LOVES, PARTS, DIES IN YEAR

FROM OUR OWN CORRESPONDENT

HOLLYWOOD, Thursday.

Beautiful eighteen-year-old Helen Burgess, ex-high school girl, who leaped to stardom as Buffalo Bill's wife in "The Plainsman," died to-day in an oxygen tent at Hollywood while specialists were fighting to save her.

FAME, love, marriage, disillusionment and death have crowded into the short drama of her life in the past ten months.

As soon as "The Plainsman" was filmed she eloped to Yuma, Arizona, to wed a young penniless piano tutor, Herbert Rutherford.

Romance died before it was born. Three weeks later they parted. The unkissed bride secured an annulment. The bride found her husband had married her to spite another woman.

A sudden attack of pneumonia early this week rushed to a quick climax, and Helen died almost before the Paramount studios knew she was ill. The crisis came so swiftly that there was not time to move her from home to a hospital.

Last July Mr. Cecil de Mille tested her for the screen. Film scouts had found her playing at a little amateur theatre.

Her beauty and voice fascinated them. "In a year," they prophesied, "you will be famous."

Without any previous film experience she was given a star's part in "The Plainsman."

FEARS MORE BABES, SEPARATED FROM VANISHING HUSBAND

WIFE who had been left with four children by a husband who came back to her and disappeared in three days feared, "It might mean more children and the same thing all over again."

She is Mrs. Florence Grace Dawkins, of Springfield-place, Wandsworth, S.W. She was granted a separation order at London South-Western Matrimonial Court yesterday.

Mrs. Dawkins applied for the order on the grounds of her husband's neglect to maintain her and his desertion of her.

"Don't you want to go back to your husband?" asked Mr. Clyde Wilson, the magistrate, himself a bachelor.

"No, it might mean more children and the same thing all over again," she replied.

Mrs. Dawkins said her husband left her in December with four children; returned at Christmas, and then left her for good three days afterwards.

The wife was granted an order for 18s a week for herself and her children.

Mrs. Dawkins told the *Daily Mirror* last night: "I think I have done my share of motherhood. My husband would not mind having fifty children, but I think I have done enough. That was really the whole trouble

"I have already had a long spell in hospital and a serious operation, and I do not want any more trouble."

THREE OF THE 300 spinsters who attended a meeting in the Memorial Hall, Farringdon-street, London, last night to demand pensions at fifty-five for spinsters—on an equal footing with widows. See story on back page.

DUKE OF KENT WILL BE BEST MAN

FROM OUR SPECIAL CORRESPONDENT

TOURS (France), Thursday.

THE Duke of Kent has been asked by the Duke of Windsor to be best man at his wedding, which will take place in Tours at the end of May.

Princess Mary has been asked to attend the wedding.

The Duke of Windsor has sent a special message of sympathy to Mrs. Simpson on the death of her dog, Slipper, which he had with him in Vienna for several months.

POLICE CHIEF DISMISSED

A senior detective-inspector of the City of London Police was dismissed the force last night after an all-day sitting of the Disciplinary Board.

It was alleged that he improperly associated with a prisoner on remand.

SEZ YOU!

Eighty-six-year-old Mr. Herbert Williams, Church-street, Eccles, shopkeeper, was knocked down near his shop, taken to hospital and detained with multiple injuries.

While he was still seriously ill he was told how firemen had to break through the roof of his shop to quell flames. Last week he left the hospital, cured, and told everybody as he marched through the gates. "No more trouble for me. I am going to be lucky for a change."

Last night he fell from a tramcar in Church-street and is again in hospital with head injuries.

SATURDAY, APRIL 10, 1937

Daily Mirror

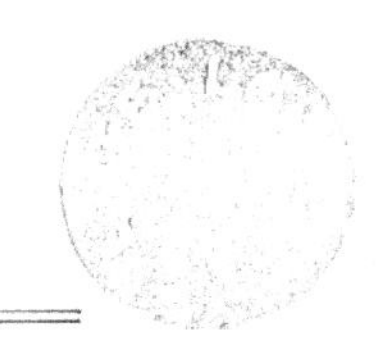

No. 10406 Registered at the G.P.O. as a Newspaper ONE PENNY

ANZAC V.C. SIGNS AUTOGRAPH AND STEPS TO DEATH

Sir John Stuart Knill, Baronet . . . sweeps Chelsea streets . . . works on a stall in Caledonian Market.

WHY ? IT'S TOLD ON PAGE 3.

BY A SPECIAL CORRESPONDENT

AUSTRALIAN V.C. GUNNER ARTHUR PERCY SULLIVAN, WHO TRAVELLED 50,000 MILES TO SERVE THE EMPIRE, FOUGHT IN THE GREAT WAR, AND WON THE HIGHEST MILITARY HONOUR FOR RESCUING FOUR COMRADES UNDER INTENSE FIRE IN RUSSIA, WAS KNOCKED DOWN AND KILLED BY A BICYCLE IN A QUIET LONDON STREET LAST NIGHT.

Humming happily he strode along Birdcage-walk, paused near the entrance to Wellington Barracks to sign a small boy's autograph book.

He stepped back into the roadway, into the path of the cyclist. Then came the crash and the man who had defied death lay dead beside the path.

He had come to London with the Australian Coronation contingent to do a sacred duty. He brought with him the ashes of another V.C. for burial.

Sullivan's ashes will be taken back to Australia to be buried with military honours.

They Talked of Traffic Dangers

Shortly before he was killed the gunner's friends sat in the mess talking about the dangers of London traffic.

"If anyone dies on trips like this," one of them remarked, "it is usually the most popular man in the regiment."

"Sully," as he was known, was the best-liked man among the 150 soldiers, sailors and airmen in the troop.

"We never dreamed when we sat talking that our grim prophecy would come true," one of them told me.

Late last night a cable was sent to Mrs. Sullivan, who is staying with friends in Sydney.

It reached her three days ahead of a letter Sullivan had written to her and their four children telling them of the wonderful time he was having in London.

Major C. E. Prior, Adjutant to the Australians, said, "Sullivan was the most popular man in the party. His death was a terrific blow to us all, and has spoiled for us the wonderful time we have had in London.

"After the accident Sully's body was carried into the guardroom, and our medical officer, Lieutenant-Colonel Barton, raced to his aid, but he was too late. There were deep scalp wounds."

Gunner Sullivan in civil life was manager of a bank at Casino, a country town of New South Wales. He was forty-one.

Gunner A. P. Sullivan, V.C.

£30,000 'LUCK' WRECKED HER HAPPY HOME

BY A SPECIAL CORRESPONDENT

"When my husband lived on four pounds a week we were happy. But when fortune came 'overnight' and he lived at the rate of £200 a week—then our happiness went."

THAT tragic epitome was spoken by a little, grey-haired woman—fifty-five-year-old widow of a man who won £30,000 in the Irish Sweepstake, and died two and a half years later from chronic alcoholism, most of his fortune gone.

When George Herbert Cuffin, of Huntington, Cheshire, won his prize he was a labourer.

"It's the Money I Blame"

Mrs. Cuffin, mother of seven grown-up children told me: "Before the fortune came my husband was devoted to his children, fond of his work and of our little home. But that money changed him immediately.

"In less than three years he spent nearly two-thirds of the thirty thousand—one-third he settled on his stepson. And then he died from too much drink."

Mrs. Cuffin.

Mrs. Cuffin sighed.

"The change from being poor to owning more money than he thought existed, was too much for him. It's not him that I blame—or the drink. It's the money."

In the Chancery Division yesterday settlement was announced in an action by the personal representative of Cuffin against Francis Joseph Calderbank, licensed victualler, of the Bowling Green Hotel, Chester, for a declaration that three conveyances of land made by Cuffin to Mr. Calderbank were null and void and should be set aside.

Publican Clears Name in Court—page 9.

GALE SWEEPS YACHT TO SEA—COLLEGE MASTER, WOMAN AND 2 BOYS ON BOARD

CAUGHT in a gale off the coast of Devon last night, a master of Cheltenham College, two of his pupils, and the mother of one of the boys, were swept to sea in a small yacht, and early to-day are still missing.

Those on board are: The Rev. J. Best, Mrs. A. Holborn (wife of Commander Holborn, of Membland Cottage, Newton Ferrers), Arthur Holborn, her fourteen-year-old son, and another boy from Cheltenham College.

Called Out Lifeboat

They set out from the harbour at Hooe, near Plymouth, at five o'clock. When the gale blew up and they had failed to arrive after two hours, Commander Holborn called out the lifeboat.

"The yacht is a small yawl called the Nanette, and has a little auxiliary engine," Commander Holborn told the *Daily Mirror*.

"The gale is rising every hour. If it gets much worse there is little chance of their surviving unless they have put into a cove."

DUKE OF WINDSOR

THE *Daily Mirror* learns that the unexpected visitor at the lakeside cottage of the German film star, Emil Jannings, at St. Wolfgang, Austria, was not, as reported in our issue of April 2, his Royal Highness the Duke of Windsor.

We are informed by Messrs. Allen and Overy, solicitors, of 3, Finch-lane, E.C.3, who are acting for the Duke of Windsor, that the Duke has never met or communicated with either Emil Jannings or his daughter.

We much regret having given publicity to the report, and take this the earliest opportunity of unreservedly withdrawing the statements, which we now find were quite inaccurate, and we beg to tender our apologies to his Royal Highness

"HONEST JOHN" FOUND, TO GET £9

"HONEST John" Hardie, homeless, penniless, who found £9 in a street at Coatbridge, Lanarkshire, handed it over to the police and tramped on, without claiming a reward of £1, was found yesterday at Dalkeith.

He did not know that a greater reward for his honesty is waiting for him at Coatbridge.

It is £9—the sum he found—sent as a tribute to him by people who read of his honesty a week ago.

Last night "Honest John" was on his way to Coatbridge.

Sir William Younger, who sent £1, described Hardie as "a splendid fellow," and added, "I hope he will get the work he is looking for."

TUESDAY, APRIL 13, 1937

Daily Mirror

No. 10408 — Registered at the G.P.O. as a Newspaper. — ONE PENNY

HUNT FOR BEAUTY'S SLAYER

Houses within a hundred yards, a busy road, with a lamp lighting a junction, only a few feet away a cottage in which lived two people. . . .

But nobody heard the cries or the struggle of beautiful **Ruby Keen** (left), whose body, with clothes torn off in fight with her murderer, was found early yesterday at the spot (marked with an arrow) in this picture.

POLICEMAN-FIANCE WILL JOIN IN

BY A SPECIAL CORRESPONDENT

LEIGHTON BUZZARD, Monday.

TWENTY-THREE-YEAR-OLD Police-Constable Pat Smith, heart-broken, yet filled with rage, will join in the great police hunt for the murderer of the beautiful girl who was shortly to become his wife.

His sweetheart, twenty-three-year-old Ruby Keen, was discovered strangled with her own scarf, half-naked and outraged, in Lovers' Lane, 300 yards from her home, this morning.

Police-Constable Smith is overcome with grief.

"He has been unable to eat a thing all day," a colleague told me. "He has been given a few days' rest because of the terrible loss he has suffered. But his heart is filled with rage against the murderer of this sweet young girl.

"As a man and a police-constable he feels it his duty to help to track down the murderer of his bride-to-be."

Tears streamed freely down the cheeks of the handsome young constable when I saw him at the home of Ruby's mother to-day.

"We were to have been married in August," he said, brokenly.

"I have seen the priest. We were so happy—now this terrible thing has happened—poor Ruby!"

Seen with Strange Man

A statement to the police to-night by Mrs. L. Andrews, who lives near the Keens in Plantation-road, reveals that the last time Ruby was seen alive a strange man accompanied her.

"I saw her walking down Plantation-road towards Lovers'-lane with a man at about 10.15 p.m. last night," Mrs. Andrews said.

"The man was slightly taller than Miss Keen. He wore no hat and had his hair

(Continued on back page)

WEDDING PRESENTS FOR MRS. SIMPSON

FROM OUR SPECIAL CORRESPONDENT

TOURS (France), Monday.

WEDDING presents for Mrs. Simpson are already arriving at the Chateau de Cande, where Mrs. Simpson is staying.

One American woman, an enthusiastic supporter of Mrs. Simpson in U.S., who lives at Richmond, Virginia, sent a picture of a Madonna because she says Mrs. Simpson is the perfect model for the Madonna.

"Has anyone ever told you that you are a Leonardo da Vinci? Not the Mona Lisa; there is something sinister in her smile," she explained to Mrs. Simpson.

"But the picture of St. Anne and of a Madonna might have been painted from yourself, so I would like to send you a little copy of the Madonna as a wedding present if you will let me."

'GET MARRIED—ALL OF YOU!'

—The Boss

ALL administrative officials over twenty-five in Pommerania (Germany) must marry, orders the Nazi Governor there, Herr Schwede-Koburg.

His decree was made because of the "shocking number who are bachelors," though salaries were enough for supporting a wife, and because so many married officials were childless.

He announced this at the annual meeting of officials at Stettin, Reuter says.

TUBE ATTACK ON BOY: AN ARREST

POLICE charged a man at Hampstead Police Station early to-day with the attempted murder of fourteen-year-old Dennis Thorp, pupil of South London Borough Polytechnic, who was found in Hampstead tube station yesterday with throat wounds.

The man will appear at Hampstead Petty Sessions to-day.

Last night Thorp's parents, who live at Haverstock-hill, N.W., watched at his bedside in New End Hospital, where a successful operation had been performed on the boy.

In his neck was a wound three inches long.

Boy's fight for life: See page 4.

FRIDAY, APRIL 16, 1937

Daily Mirror

No. 10411 Registered at the G.P.O. as a Newspaper. ONE PENNY

TOMMY FARR'S LEFT PUNCHES BAER INTO OBSCURITY

FIGHTING the greatest battle of his career, twenty - three - year - old British heavy-weight champion Tommy Farr beat ex-world champion Max Baer, odds-on favourite, on points over twelve rounds at Harringay Stadium last night.

Baer scarcely won a round.

Farr's form was a revelation. When Mr. Douglas, the referee, lifted the British champion's arm for victory, 14,000 spectators rose to their feet cheering hysterically and singing " Land of My Fathers."

It was the greatest popular British boxing win since the war.

More women than at any previous fight were among the crowd —the most fashionable for years.

Notabilities at the ringside included the Marquis and Marchioness of Queensberry, Lord Hewart, the Lord Chief Justice, Lord Burghley, Lord Stanley and Walter Neusel, the German heavy-weight.

Overwhelmed by Crowd

As Farr and his bodyguard forced their way back to his dressing-room they were overwhelmed by the crowd. Police and attendants had to rescue them.

Farr, smiling broadly despite his cut left eye, kept muttering his delight, but nobody could hear a word he said, so great was the din.

Silent, almost deserted Baer walked to his dressing room, a cigarette drooping from his puffed lips, left eye swollen and cut—but smiling still.

Wales went crazy with enthusiasm.

In Tonypandy, Farr's home town, there were radio parties in kitchens, sitting-rooms and clubs to follow the fortunes of the "hero" from this little Welsh mining village.

Enthusiasm mounted to such a pitch as the news of Tommy's ascendancy was told in the story of the rounds that cheers often blotted out the loud-speakers in hotels and clubs.

Danced in the Streets

When the result was announced the population of Tonypandy rushed into the streets.

Men and girls, boys and women hugged each other and danced down the road shouting the tidings.

Many of Farr's relatives listened in at the villa in Slough where the Welshman has made his home.

Here is what the boxers said:—

TOMMY FARR : "I knew from the very first round I was on the road to success.

"I was expecting Max to show me something, but it never came. I am terribly delighted, and I am glad that I gave British boxing a good show."

MAX BAER : "I guess I am not the same guy that fought those big men Schmeling and Carnera.

"This is the first time I have had a cut on my face. I guess Buddy, my brother, is going to be stepping in my shoes. I'm through.'

"This fellow Farr is rugged and a good puncher. If he meets Neusel he will win."

LEN HARVEY commented: "Max was going in the fifth round.

"That injured eye had a lot to do with his defeat. Farr boxed spendidly."

LEFT HAND WAS 'RIGHT'!

Crowds of Farr's supporters, bursting through a cordon of police and attendants as he left the ring, shook his hand—the left hand which had battered Baer to defeat.

BATTERED FACES . . .

but Baer took defeat with a laugh —as he stood with one arm round Farr's neck after the fight was over.

Other fight pictures are on the back page and page 34.

FIRST ROUND PROVED FARR OUR BEST HEAVYWEIGHT FOR 10 YEARS

By PETER WILSON

TOMMY Farr proved himself the best heavy-weight champion Britain has had for a decade when he out-boxed, out-fought and out-generalled Max Baer, ex-heavy-weight champion of the world, over twelve rounds at Harringay Stadium last night.

In the first minute Farr closed Baer's eye and opened the spectators' when a vicious right-cross skidded off the American's left eyebrow, ripping it open as neatly as though it had a zip-fastener over it.

From the first gong the Welshman, his fair head lowered, bored in like a wild animal forcing the burly American—he was a stone the heavier—to break ground.

Baer, slow, lethargic almost, started by grimacing and snarling in his customary fashion.

After the first few rounds had passed it was his supporters who were making the faces, and he saved his breath for the battle that was on.

In some ways that sensational first round, with the Welshman leaping in and out and

(Continued cn page 34)

MRS. DOYLE SAID ENOUGH FOR FIVE DIVORCES

Film star Judith Allen, granted an interlocutory decree of divorce at Los Angeles yesterday, was interrupted by the Judge as she was telling of the love affairs of her boxer husband, Jack Doyle.

"You have said enough for five divorces," declared the Judge.

Judith declared, says Reuter, that Jack gave her such a black eye she had to wear dark glasses for a fortnight.

"He just took you as a sparring partner," commented the Judge, who dismissed her application for £20 a week alimony, saying she had a good job, could keep herself.

WHILE MAIDS LISTENED-IN : £5,000 JEWELS STOLEN

WHILE maids downstairs were listening to the radio, waiting for the big fight commentary, a burglar entered the home of Mr. Percy Illingworth, in Eaton-place, Knightsbridge, S.W., last night, and calmly walked out with £5,000 worth of jewellery.

"The burglar seems to have got in by the back door," Mr. Illingworth, twenty-seven-year-old nephew of Lord Illingworth, stated.

"He must have walked past the servants' hall, where two maids were sitting, gone straight up to a bedroom on the second floor, rifled the jewel case and walked straight out of the front door—leaving it open.

"My wife and I were out at dinner. Discovery of the burglary was made by the nurse, who found the front door open when she came in, saw the light still on in the bedroom, and went upstairs to investigate.

The haul included three pearl necklaces—one a rope of some eighty graduated pearls; the other of five rows of seed pearls; and a third a pearl necklace with diamond clasp.

"The burglar touched nothing but the jewels," said Mr. Illingworth. "After all, he'd done a good night's work.

"The whole 'job' was perfectly timed, planned and executed."

THURSDAY, APRIL 22, 1937

Daily Mirror

No. 10416 — Registered at the G.P.O. as a Newspaper. — ONE PENNY

CLARK GABLE SAYS "I'M NO PAPA—GOT 2 WIVES TO PROVE IT"

FROM OUR OWN CORRESPONDENT

NEW YORK, Wednesday.

CLARK Gable grinned at the reporters as he pushed his way through a clamouring horde of women fans outside Los Angeles court-house for the Norton trial to-day. "I'm no papa," he wise-cracked, "and I'll show you two wives to prove it."

In court his attorney announced that Gable's first wife, Josephine Dillon, and his second, Ria Langham, from whom he separated "on a friendly footing" in 1935, have offered to give evidence for him against forty-seven-year-old Violet Wells Norton, the Englishwoman who accused him of being father of her love-child in an Essex romance.

Women are rallying to their hero. This morning he got up to find a record mail. Rabbits' feet, sacred statues, lucky coins and psychic handkerchiefs poured in from admirers all over America as tokens of sympathy and good luck in the trial.

With them came letters begging Clark to wear the lucky symbols in court.

One girl sent him the first verse of Kipling's "If," which includes the lines: "If you can trust yourself when all men doubt you . . . or being lied about don't deal in lies . . ."

At the court house Clark sought refuge behind locked doors in a private room. His peace ended when Frau Deorfleur, a friend of the old days, got leave to enter with a band of Pressmen.

"He Was with Me"

"I'll do anything to help Clark," she cried. "He's always been the swellest guy I know."

She told reporters he couldn't have lived with Mrs. Norton in Essex, as is alleged, because at that time he happened to be with her.

Many men joined the throngs of women in court hoping to hear Mae West give evidence of a letter written by Mrs. Norton which said: "You will be surprised to know Gable is the father of my daughter Gwendoline, who looks exactly like him. Now, Miss West, would you be a fairy godmother to my girl and put Clark to shame?"

At the start of to-day's hearing the defence failed in a move for a directed verdict acquitting Mrs. Norton and Jack L. Smith, a private detective, who are accused of attempting to obtain money from Gable by fraud.

Miss Adele Royle, actress-mannequin, who is suing Lord Kingsborough for alleged breach of promise.

FAITHFUL MARY SAYS—

"FATHER DIVINE AIN'T NO GOD! JUST A MAN"

"He ain't God! He's just a damned man—no more God than anybody else."

THIS was how "Faithful Mary," middle-aged mulatto wife of Father Divine, debunked the black, self-styled Messiah, to New Yorkers yesterday, says British United Press.

Father Divine is being sought by the police following the stabbing of Harry Green, white process server, who tried to thrust a writ into his hand at a sacred banquet in the Harlem temple.

The charge against him is "felonious assault."

Faithful Mary revealed that after the stabbing Father Divine asked her to hand over to him the deeds of a hotel and its 165 acres of ground at High Falls, New York State. She refused.

Next to Father Divine, Faithful Mary has been the most powerful figure in the sect which hails him as God.

Scores of different properties are in her name, including "Heavens," "Promised Lands," farms, dress shops, and "Glory Be to Father Divine" restaurants.

VISCOUNT DENIES PROMISE TO WED

VISCOUNT Kingsborough, thirty-nine-year-old heir of the Earl of Kingston, is being sued by a West End actress-mannequin, Miss Adele Royle, for damages for alleged breach of promise to marry her.

The action is in the list for hearing before a special jury in the King's Bench Division. The defence is a denial that any promise to marry was ever made.

Titian-Haired Beauty

Miss Royle, who is thirty-four, is tall and good-looking, with long Titian hair which she wears coiled in plaits. She lives at The White House, Albany-street, Regent's Park, London, N.W.

Lord Kingsborough is the Earl of Kingston's only son. He has three sisters.

He was educated at Eton and at the Royal Military College becoming a lieutenant in the Royal Scots Greys and serving in the war.

In 1927 he retired from the Army owing to ill-health.

He is a keen yachtsman, and in 1930 won the endurance race organised by the Marine Motoring Association at Poole.

The Earl of Kingston, who lives at Kilronan Castle, Keadue, and Oakport, Boyle, Co. Roscommon, is the ninth earl and is a Deputy-Lieutenant for Co. Roscommon.

He served in South Africa in 1900 and 1902 and also served in the Great War, when he was wounded.

Viscount Kingsborough.

"YOU SILLY BLIGHTER" AND "YE GODS!" BROADCAST MYSTERY

BY A SPECIAL CORRESPONDENT

VARIETY had just ended in the B.B.C.'s London Regional programme yesterday afternoon at 4.45.

Then that 'tween-items silence . . . but crashing through it came a protesting voice. It said clearly, if rather more-in-pain-than-in-anger:—

"You silly blighter."

. . . the 'tween items silence descended on the air again, but then the listener heard:

"Ye Gods!"

. . . silence once more, then the same voice, not so much in pain as in anger this time, said:

"Give me the—"

—but what listeners will never know.

The voice, to their regret, faded out and a clear, correct polite announcer announced urbanely a reading from the works of Edmund Spenser.

* * *

Answer by the B.B.C. to a question by the *Daily Mirror*: "There does seem to have been a slight hitch during the change-over. Oh! no, we cannot confirm, nor would we deny, that unintended remarks were broadcast."

STRIKE WILL HOLD UP LINERS

SURPRISE strike order threatened to stop the Queen Mary sailing from New York yesterday—but a two-hour truce enabled her to leave to schedule.

Mr. Joseph Ryan, president of the International Longshoremen's Association, later informed Reuter that the strike was to be resumed because members of the independent union at Montreal returned to unload the Andania and the Alaunia.

A hundred and fifty dockers at once ceased work on the Cunard cargo steamer Maidan at Boston.

A strike has also been called against all vessels of Furness, Withy and Co. and associated lines in North American ports.

FASCISTS IN STREET CLASH

Fighting broke out in St. George's High-street, Shadwell, last night, when about 600 Blackshirts, marching to the Limehouse headquarters, passed an anti-Fascist meeting. Police soon cleared the fighters and one arrest was made.

MONDAY, APRIL 26, 1937

Daily Mirror

No. 10419 Registered at the G.P.O. as a Newspaper. ONE PENNY

6-FT. TYPIST FOUND IN RIVER:

HEIGHT WAS HER CURSE

RIVER police patrolling the Thames at Wapping, yesterday, found the body of Irene Filmore, 6ft., twenty-two-year-old Dulwich typist. For twelve days she had been sought by Scotland Yard and the police of all England after vanishing from a Streatham dance-hall, and the hunt was intensified by the receipt of a £600 ransom demand.

Discovery of her body reveals that the ransom notes were a cruel hoax. Experts say she had been in the water nearly a fortnight. She still wore the pink dance frock and the grey fur coat in which she vanished. Scotland Yard announce they are satisfied there was no foul play.

ONLY ONE EXPLANATION CAN BE FOUND FOR IRENE FILMORE'S DEATH—SHE WAS 6ft. TALL. HER HEIGHT BLIGHTED HER HAPPINESS AND HER LIFE.

Police-Constable Perkins, the Deptford officer who was with Irene at the dance-hall when she disappeared, was greatly upset by the news of the discovery. "I know her height worried her," he told the *Daily Mirror* last night.

"We had no quarrel. She simply left me after making an excuse, as I thought, to go to the cloakroom. It was only when she did not return that I became alarmed

"I Had Little Hope"

"It is a mystery to me how she could have gone so far away, although the body may have drifted down the river."

Constable Perkins himself is over 6ft.

War-widowed Mrs. Edith Filmore, Irene's mother, told the *Daily Mirror* last night in Bassano-street, East Dulwich:

"She was never the same after her illness Her height had always made her acutely sensitive. It preyed on her mind"

Mr. George Filmore, Irene's brother, who went with Mr. Baker to identify the body, said last night:—

"In my fruitless search for Irene I really had little hope of finding her alive."

House Searched

Scotland Yard joined the search when two ransom notes demanding £600, were sent a week ago to Mr. Gerald Baker, at whose home in Bassano-street, East Dulwich, Irene was living.

A police patrol reported on Saturday night that he saw Miss Filmore entering a house in Coptic-street, Bloomsbury, with a man.

Mr. Gerald Baker was summoned by the police to accompany them to the house.

Thorough search of the house revealed no trace of the girl.

Another girl vanishes after dance—page 2

Irene Filmore—six feet tall . . . "her height preyed on her mind," her mother told the "Daily Mirror" last night.

Mr. Reuben Levy, with his daughter Dora, after he was told of his win.

WON £30,780 FOR SIXPENCE—HE THINKS IT'S A DREAM

BY A SPECIAL CORRESPONDENT

TO a dazed little fifty-two-year-old Jewish wood-carver sitting half-asleep on the side of his bed in a Council house in Shore-road, Hackney, E., last night I broke the news that he had won £30,780—for sixpence.

By making four away wins in his Littlewood's coupon, Mr. Reuben Levy scooped the pool at odds of 1,231,200 to 1 and won what Messrs. Littlewood's claim is the world's record football dividend.

Mr. Levy, who works in a Tottenham cabinet factory, fumbled for his spectacles as I told him the news. His first words were to his grey-haired wife:—

"Don't worry, Esther, it is all a dream."

"Not Going to Work in the Morning"

But later, when he had pulled on some clothes, he told me just what his feelings were about that £30,780.

By his side was his twenty-five-year-old daughter Dora, who is a shorthand typist in the City.

"Please tell me, first of all, whether you are kidding me," he said, "because if it is true, I am *not going to work in the morning*."

"I know nothing about football. I have only entered these pools this season and have spent about 15s. so far.

"All I go by are the four numbers—sixteen, seventeen, twenty-one, and twenty-nine in pool five.

"I have never been to a football match in my life. This morning as I shaved I told my wife, who was getting the breakfast, that I might have won a few shillings.

"Now I feel as if I shall wake up in the morning and find that this £30,000 business is

(Continued on back page)

BROOK REACHES CAIRO

Mr. H. L. Brook, the Yorkshire airman who is attempting to beat the Cape flight record, arrived at Cairo at 11.5 p.m. (G.M.T.) last night from Rome, says Central News. **See page 2.**

CAUGHT OUT WITH BLONDE : WIFE DOG-WHIPS HIM

FROM OUR OWN CORRESPONDENT

NEW YORK, Sunday.

THIRTY-SEVEN-YEAR-OLD Mrs. William R. Seymour had never seen her husband with another woman in all their thirteen years of married life, when she dropped into fashionable Restaurant la Rue early this morning and saw him with a blonde.

Mrs. Seymour, New York and Palm Beach society hostess, had with her a dog and two sisters—and a dog leash.

Eye-witness Mrs. John Best, tells the story.

"Mrs. Seymour drew a dog leash from her coat, lashed her husband and his companion.

"At the same time her sisters hurled plates, chocolates and bottles at their brother-in-law's girl friend, who managed to flee from the restaurant."

Police restored order. Mrs. Seymour and her sisters were arrested—to be bailed out later by the husband they had attacked.

TUESDAY, APRIL 27, 1937

Daily Mirror

No. 10420 Registered at the G.P.O. as a Newspaper. ONE PENNY

M.P. SAYS RUSH-HOUR TUBES ARE UNFIT FOR GIRLS

GIRLS and men are packed like cattle into peak hour tube trains running to Highgate and Edgware.

They are crowded together in such a manner that even decency is in question.

Rochdale Socialist, Mr. Kelly, after making these charges in the House of Commons last night moved that the L.P.T.B. Bill be rejected.

During busy hours passengers were so crowded that if cattle were transported in such a way action would be taken before the Courts Mr. Kelly declared.

"I wouldn't like a young daughter of mine to travel during the rush hours on the Morden tube," he told the "Daily Mirror" last night.

"Horrible Experience"

"Young folk of both sexes are pressed together breast to breast in the compartments. Without going into unpleasant details it must be a horrible experience for a nice young girl to travel in such a way face to face with a man whom she instinctively knows to be 'not quite the right sort.' I have known such a condition in the train that people are unable even to raise their hands if they want to sneeze."

The Bill proposed to extend the Morden-Edgware Tube to Aldenham. If that were allowed conditions would become even worse.

As a resident in the area, Mr. Attlee said he was on the Stanmore line every day, and he found it difficult to get a seat

He did get a seat as far as Wembley Park, but thereafter the crowds came in and more often than not he had to stand. What should have been part of the green belt of London had been covered with small houses or by garage accommodation with living accommodation attached.

This would never be cured until there was real planning in outer London.

This reckless development and the consequent extension of railway lines were destroying the health of people who had to endure hours of torture each week in overcrowded trains.

Mr. Robert Morrison said that a promise had been made that the next line to be dealt with would be that of the L.N.E.R. system between Liverpool-street and Enfield. Antiquated conditions on that line were the greatest traffic scandal in the world.

New York Tube "Hell"

Captain A. Hudson, Parliamentary Secretary to the Ministry of Transport, said: "I have always had the New York system in the rush hours held up as the most intensified form of hell, and I do not think they have managed to solve this problem.

"They employ men to throw the passengers into the carriages one on top of the other, to crush them in and shut the doors in a way we would not tolerate here.

Since April 8 the Board had already provided extra trains on the Edgware line, and they hoped that when all their plans were matured it would mean about 40 per cent. increase in the accommodation."

The motion for the rejection of the Bill was defeated by 134 votes to 55. The Bill passed the report stage, and was ordered for third reading.

REBELS STOP BRITISH SHIP 'DEVELOPMENTS EXPECTED'

The Newcastle steamer Greathope (2,297 tons), bound for Antwerp, was stopped by rebel armed trawlers a few hours after leaving Gibraltar yesterday, says Reuter.

The message adds: "Developments are expected."

Greathope arrived at Gibraltar from Valencia earlier in the day with a cargo of fruit.

Britain Protests to Franco: Page 2.

Wearing toeless shoes and carrying a jam-pot-shaped handbag to match. Lady Warwick on her arrival at Plymouth yesterday.

THE PILOT CRAWLED OUT

This is all that was left of an R.A.F. fighting 'plane after a crash yesterday at Montsford, Berkshire. The 'plane hit an overhead electric wire. The pilot crawled out of the wreckage practically unhurt. See his unopened parachute in the front of the picture?

COUNTESS OF WARWICK SAYS: "IT'S GOING TO BE DIVORCE"

BY A SPECIAL CORRESPONDENT

"I GUESS we're through. . . . Yes, it's going to be divorce. I may get married again and I may not. Freedom is something a woman gets to like.

"So far there's no romance in my life, and if people imagine it they are wrong."

Beautiful, dark-haired, vivacious Countess of Warwick told me this when I interviewed her on her arrival from America last night.

At the present time she is staying with her mother, Lady Rosabelle Brand, at Lewes, Sussex.

"As far as I know," she said, "Lord Warwick is still in Hollywood. I don't know what he is doing, but then wives who are going into the divorce courts don't know what their husbands are doing, do they?

"I guess the divorce suit will be heard in England. May be sometime in July.

"I have returned home to be with my son for his third birthday."

"No Romance"

When I asked Lady Warwick if she had any romance she said, with a laugh:—

"Gee, you newspaper men always look for that. . . . As a matter of fact, I haven't. You may have seen photographs of me with a handsome man, but that doesn't mean romance. . . . No, sir.

"At present I am looking forward to the freedom. It will give me a chance if I wish to make a career.

"Some people have suggested I might like doing commercial photography . . . well, I might, and I might not.

"So far I am through with marriage, but, like all women, I have the option of changing my mind . . . and you never know, do you?"

PETROL UP ½d.—5-YEAR RECORD

BY A SPECIAL CORRESPONDENT

A RISE of a halfpenny a gallon in the price of petrol came into force at midnight last night—bringing it to the highest level since 1932

Third increase within four months, it is due to the continued rise in world prices and the rise in freight rates, which have trebled in the last six months.

An official of the R.A.C. described the increase as "very regrettable" last night.

"Coming just at the opening of the motoring season, it is hard luck on the working-man motorist. It does seem a pity that the companies can't try to stabilise the price."

Mr. A. J. Pegg, secretary of the Phœnix Oil Co., gave the viewpoint of the producers:—

"It now costs 30s. ton to bring petrol by tanker from the Black Sea, as against 10s. a ton six months ago.

"There is every justification for the increase."

WEDNESDAY, APRIL 28, 1937

Daily Mirror

No. 10421 Registered at the G.P.O. as a newspaper. ONE PENNY

NATIONAL COAL STRIKE WILL BE CALLED: RAIL MEN THREATEN

BY OUR POLITICAL CORRESPONDENT

Notice of a general strike throughout the coalfields—to begin two days after the Coronation—will be handed in on Friday after miners' delegates have met in London. Decision to stop work in fourteen days is regarded as inevitable.

Nottinghamshire coalowners show no sign of agreeing to recognise the Mineworkers' Federation, and unless recognition is generally forthcoming, the miners are determined to strike in sympathy with Harworth men

RAILWAYMEN are being urged to strike during the Coronation period. Stoppages throughout the engineering industry in sympathy with the London busmen—whose strike is due on Friday—are also being planned secretly and unofficially.

Threat of a railway strike comes from a section of the Associated Society of Locomotive Engineers and Firemen.

A resolution urging strike action was carried unanimously at a meeting of the London locomotive men, addressed by Mr. Elliot, member of the National Executive of the union, and by Mr. J. V. Sweeney, district organiser.

This action is advocated on the eve of negotiations between the three railway unions and the four main-line companies

Influential shop stewards are backing the sympathetic strike movement among motor and aircraft engineers in Coventry, Birmingham, Wolverhampton.

The executive of the Bank Officers' Guild will meet in London this week and will give sanction for a strike to enforce recognition of the Guild.

Sir Stafford Cripps yesterday accepted an invitation to defend the members of the Notts Mineworkers' Federation who are being prosecuted in connection with the Harworth Colliery dispute. The National Council for Civil Liberties made the invitation.

Notts County Council, at its meeting next Tuesday, will consider a resolution urging the Home Secretary to open an inquiry into the Harworth disorders.

Three more men, alleged to have been concerned in the Harworth Colliery riot last Friday, were arrested yesterday and remanded.

Strikers Hold-up Bus—page 3.

M.P.s DISCUSS DISPUTE

M.P.s from the mining areas discussed the Harworth Colliery dispute with officials at the House of Commons last night. Considerable secrecy was observed over the meeting.

Eighteen-year-old Kenneth Gibson, He struck down with a poker his married landlady in London, whose lover he had become.
(See story on page 3.)

LEVINSKY'S WALTZ AMAZED DOYLE

By PETER WILSON

AFTER the greatest travesty of boxing I have ever seen, Jack Doyle, handsome Irish crooner, film star and boxer, beat King Levinsky, ex-fishmonger from Chicago, at Wembley last night.

The fight—if one can call it that—contrary to expectations, lasted the full twelve rounds and is the first that Doyle has ever won on points.

As the American, with blood streaming down his swollen, distorted face, reeled and lurched around the ring, the usual crowd of fashionable ring-siders yelled and screamed for the kill which never came.

Levinsky showed pluck in staying on his feet. But that was all he did show. A navvy at a street corner would have displayed as much acquaintance with the finer points of boxing.

Such a farce did the whole thing become that in the final round Doyle twice waltzed round the ring, pulling the American with him, to show that his opponent was holding him.

After he had done it the second time, Levinsky entered into the spirit of the thing and, parted by the referee, continued a solo waltz of his own while Doyle gazed at him amazed.

Full story, page 26.

Jack Doyle (centre), the Irish heavy-weight, with King Levinsky, of America, whom he defeated on points, after their fight at Wembley Stadium last night, in which, says Peter Wilson, "boxing skill was notable for its absence." (See report on page 26.)

"NOTCHED" HIS GUN FOR EVERY DEAD MAN—BUT THE LAST

IN the dim light of a little room in Bloomsbury, an old man, lovingly handling a long-barrelled old six-chambered revolver, would point to the notches on the butt and tell how every one meant a man's life.

For "Professor" Harrison had been a sheriff in California in the days when outlaws were shot on sight.

Yesterday he was found shot dead in a room he rented in Guilford-street, W.C. The big six-shooter lay, with his sheriff's star, beside him.

The "Professor"—his real name was John Harrison—made two fortunes in his lifetime, and lost both.

A friend said last night: "The 'Professor' came to England about twenty years ago on a world-seeing tour. He made a fortune in America in the 'Wild West' days of the 'nineties, but by the time he reached England all his money was gone.

"So he started in business as a herbalist and sold a treatment for rheumatism and other maladies.

"At one time he had a shop in the Haymarket and employed a number of assistants, but of late he had financial worries.

GENTLEMEN PREFER BRONZE

This summer gentlemen prefer bronze, says Jack Dawn, M.-G.-M. make-up expert at Hollywood. He has devised the "bronze flecks" complexion Harlow is featuring, and advises red copper lipstick and natural copper nailpolish to go with it.

'MY WIFE MADE ME A DANCE WALLFLOWER'

"DANCING has been my wife's downfall. I have taken her to dances, but she won't have me as a partner. After being a wallflower all night I have waited outside for her in the car."

This was the complaint of forty-two-year-old Edward Palmer, of Park-drive, Hanworth, Middlesex, yesterday unsuccessfully summoned by his wife for desertion.

Mrs. Palmer, married fifteen years, with two children, aged twelve and fourteen, said her husband had refused to sleep with her

"Because she has been flirting with a lance-corporal of the R.A.S.C.," retorted Palmer. "She even refused to be driven home from a dance. When I arrived home I found her in the kitchen flirting with this soldier."

"Go back and woo your wife," the Bench advised Palmer.

"That's always meant everything to us," Palmer told a *Daily Mirror* representative last night, pointing to a white marble dove—emblem of peace—hanging in the porchway of his home. And he waited for his wife to return.

CAPE ATTEMPT FAILS

Mr. H. L. Brook, the Harrogate flyer who was trying to beat Miss Amy Johnson's record for the England-Cape flight, has abandoned the attempt on the outward record, Reuter understands.

He was delayed yesterday by a thunderstorm which forced him down for the night 100 miles from Juba, Sudan. He is now there with a damaged tail wheel, but intends to go on to the Cape as soon as it is repaired

THURSDAY, MAY 6, 1937

Daily Mirror

No. 10428 Registered at the G.P.O. as a Newspaper. ONE PENNY

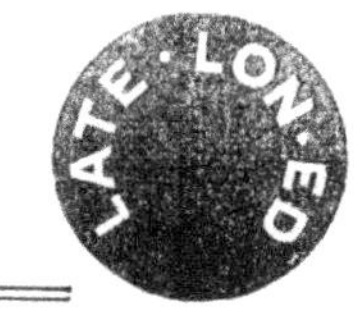

THOUSANDS MASS AT PALACE FOR FIRST COURT

BY A SPECIAL CORRESPONDENT

Thousands of Coronation visitors reinforced London sightseers last night when a record crowd massed at the gates of Buckingham Palace to see debutantes arrive for the first Court.

TWO hundred superbly-gowned debutantes curtsied before King George and Queen Elizabeth in the white and gold Throne-room of Buckingham Palace last night at the first Court of their reign.

The King wore the scarlet and gold uniform of a field-marshal. Queen Elizabeth's gown was of deep golden brocade in a small scroll design. With it she wore a glittering Indian-embroidered train of gold lame and coloured sequins.

Thousands of visitors to the Coronation were among the crowd that watched the arrival of the debutantes at the Palace for last night's first Court of George VI's reign.

Princess Stays Up Late

Set on her black hair was a magnificent tiara of diamonds and rubies. She wore a necklace of the same gems.

The Queen also wore the pale blue riband of the Order of the Garter, conferred on her in the New Year Honours.

The Queen's dressmakers had been at Buckingham Palace in the afternoon for a final fitting of her lovely Court gown.

Traditionally, before the Court the Queen allows a few privileged people to see her in her robes and garments. The most interested to see her in her royal splendour last night was Princess Elizabeth, who had been given special permission to stay up late.

Five thousand people swarmed round the Palace gates to see the "debs" arrive. Many of them were overseas visitors brought in motor-coaches by tourist-firms.

"Musical Chairs"

They saw a game of motoring musical chairs round the Victoria and Albert Memorial, for most of the debutantes arrived well before 7.30 p.m., and cars were barred from the Palace quadrangle until that time.

But traffic arrangements broke down, and police ended the "musical chairs." Cars had to join a crawling procession which occupied more than half The Mall from Trafalgar-square.

As 7.30 boomed, the first car passed through the Palace gates

The crowd surged forward and police had difficulty in keeping free a passage for the cars following.

The police closed Buckingham Palace-road before the Palace gates were opened. It was the first time that such drastic action had been taken on the night of a Court but the plan worked well.

Traffic chaos was worse when the Court ended. Police holding up normal theatre traffic so that cars could leave the Palace caused a serious jam in all directions.

Crowds cheered the Duke and Duchess of Kent, the Duke and Duchess of Gloucester as they left the Palace. Queen Mary left later.

★ Leaving for last night's Court . . . Mme. Malbran, wife of the Argentine Ambassador, with her daughter Celia (beside her) and the daughters of the Argentine Ambassador in Belgium. ★

NAZI CROSS FOR THE KING

It is stated in Berlin that King George VI is to be the first recipient of the Grand Cross of the German Eagle Order of Merit, created by Herr Hitler last May Day to provide an honour for foreigners.

It is believed that the honour will be presented by Field Marshal von Blomberg, head of the German delegation to the Coronation, says Exchange.

VITRIOL-THROWER IN WEST END BURNS YOUNG WIFE

BY A SPECIAL CORRESPONDENT

AS the gay throngs from Soho's clubs and cabarets were going home yesterday a woman in evening dress screamed and fell to her knees—burnt by vitriol which a man had thrown at her. Her husband leapt in pursuit of the man, who took to his heels and escaped in the maze of side streets.

The woman, attractive twenty-eight-year-old Mrs. Gwendoline Phyllis Crow, wife of a magistrate in the Burma Frontier Service, was taken to a nearby chemist, where her injury was treated.

Through Dress

The vitriol had burnt through her dress and stockings to her leg.

Mrs. Crow said afterwards: "I didn't take much notice of the man. He seemed perfectly ordinary. As he drew abreast of me, he took his pipe from his mouth and flicked it in front of my knees.

"I felt my dress burning.

"My husband chased the man, but he escaped."

RESCUE DIVE IN CRICKET PADS

INTO the River Lea at Clapton last night plunged a young man wearing cricket pads.

Alfred Castle, twenty-five, of Grosvenor-road, Highbury, playing in a match on Clapton Marshes, heard screams.

He raced to the river bank, found a boy struggling in the water.

And five-year-old Derek Pleasant, of Millfield-road, Clapton, owes his life to Mr. Castle's quick courage.

The boy recovered after artificial respiration.

"It was a very plucky rescue," the Lea Bridge Weir-keeper told the *Daily Mirror*.

"Although the man was handicapped by his cricket pads he ran about 100 yards to the river before plunging in, and swam strongly to the boy.

"He grasped him as he was going down for the third time."

Mr. Castle was given a change of clothing at a boathouse, then went home.

CANADIAN TRAIN WRECKED

Several people were killed and many injured when the Ocean Limited express struck coal trucks, and was wrecked near Springhill Junction, Nova Scotia, yesterday says Reuter.

Among those killed were tramps who were "riding the rods" underneath the carriages.

FRIDAY, MAY 7, 1937

Daily Mirror

No. 10429 Registered at the G.P.O. as a Newspaper. ONE PENNY

HINDENBURG EXPLODES —NEARLY 100 DEAD

The German airship, Hindenburg, in flight.

FLAMING WRECK FALLS ON AIRFIELD: CHILDREN VICTIMS

From Our Own Correspondent

Lakehurst, New Jersey, Thursday

Hindenburg, biggest airship in the world, exploded and crashed in flames with the loss of 96 lives—eight women and three children among them—as she was about to moor in a thunderstorm here to-day.

Only four people escaped—by jumping from a window—while the rest of the passengers and crew were trapped in the blaze.

BUFFETED BY A GALE AND WITH LIGHTNING FLICKERING AROUND HER, THE HINDENBURG APPROACHED THE AERODROME AND TOSSED HER NOSELINES TO THE GROUND READY TO BE MADE FAST, WHEN THERE WAS A TERRIFIC ROAR.

Flames burst from the stern, the giant ship hovered for a moment, then crashed to the ground from 300ft., shaking the whole neighbourhood. Within a few minutes her steel frame had collapsed into a twisted mass.

According to ground watchers, passengers were laughing and waving from the observation windows when a bomb-like explosion sent out clouds of red and black billowing smoke. Within a few seconds screams filled the air.

For half her length her girders lay bare while the other half was hidden by clouds of smoke. Flames lighted up the wreckage.

Spectators stood sobbing, many of them hysterical, as army trucks, with screaming sirens, sped to the still blazing wreckage.

The Hindenburg, making her first flight over the Atlantic this season, was carrying thirty-nine passengers in addition to a crew of sixty-one. Captain Max Pruss was in command with Captain Lehmann, acting in an advisory capacity. Among the passengers, most of them Germans or Americans, were:—

Mr. Charles Seymour Higgens, of London.

Mr. J. Grant, assistant manager of the Hamburg-America Line, London.

Colonel Nelson Morris, Chicago meat packer millionaire and former U.S. Minister to Sweden.

Caught like rats in a trap, with the only exit from the airship barred by flames, not one passenger is believed to have escaped.

Mr. Ira Nelson Morris, Chicago meat packer millionaire, one of the dead passengers.

Four members of the crew, two of them cabin boys and one a steward, saved themselves by jumping from a window as the airship neared the ground. They are Clifford Osburn, Joseph Spahs, Philip Mungun and Herbert O'Laughlin.

"Flames were leaping round me, and I saw the only thing for it was to jump," said O'Laughlin. "I waited till the ship was ten feet above the ground."

Harry Wellbrook, a member of the ground crew, said

"We got three bodies from the stern of the ship.

"All were burned beyond recognition, but one, whose features were unrecognisable, was still breathing. The clothing on all three was burned to a cinder and their skin had been scorched off."

A photographer on the spot told me: "I ran towards the ship and saw it enveloped in flames.

"I saw a man walking towards me assisted by two other men. He had no clothes on."

Louis Krantz, another witness, said: "I have seen hell. Hindenburg exploded in the air and

(Continued on back page)

ZEPPELIN FACTS

THE Hindenburg was 803ft. long—nearly as long as Britain's crack liner Queen Mary—and as wide as Nelson's Column is high. She was constructed partly from the wreckage of the R 101.

Empty, she weighed 100 tons, 200 when loaded.

Flames on her crash were fed by the 7,062,800 cubic feet of gas in her envelope

She cost £500,000 and took two years to build.

A sister ship, almost a replica of the Hindenburg, is now under construction in Germany. It is to be completed by the end of this year.

SATURDAY, MAY 8, 1937

Daily Mirror

No. 10430 Registered at the G.P.O. as a Newspaper. ONE PENNY

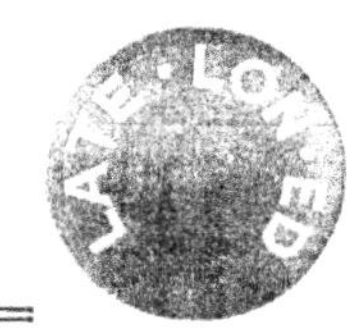

WE'RE HAPPY AT LAST

"We are always happy," said Mrs. Simpson when, yesterday, on the terrace of the Chateau de Cande, Tours, she and the Duke of Windsor posed together for the first time for photographers. Mrs. Simpson's statement came in answer to a request for "a happy picture." As she said it, Mrs. Simpson turned to the Duke and he replied, "Of course. Isn't that evident?" *See page 5 fcr story and another picture.*

THURSDAY, MAY 13, 1937

Daily Mirror

No. 10434 Registered at the G.P.O. as a Newspaper ONE PENNY

THE CROWNING OF GEORGE VI
KING AND EMPEROR

The moment of Majesty: " The Archbishop, taking the crown from the Dean of Westminster, places it reverently upon the King's head. At the sight whereof the people, with loud and repeated shouts, cry, GOD SAVE THE KING."

FRIDAY, MAY 14, 1937

Daily Mirror

No. 10435 Registered at the G.P.O. as a Newspaper. ONE PENNY

BRITISH DESTROYER MINED: SEE PAGE 3

CROWD OF THOUSANDS MOBS THE KING AND QUEEN

Enormous crowds pressing round the King and Queen's car during their tour of North London Story on back page and other pictures on pages 17 and 32.

The King's 'Heartfelt Thanks' to His People

"At the conclusion of the Coronation ceremonies in London, the Queen and I wish to express our deep gratitude to all those who have contributed to their successful accomplishment, both inside and outside Westminster Abbey.

"We know well that the planning, no less than the execution of the essential arrangements, entailed months of careful preparation and imposed an immense volume of work on all branches of the Public Services.

"I have nothing but praise for the fine bearing and discipline of those representatives of my Naval, Military and Air Force, who were on duty. It was a special satisfaction to me that they included so many splendid detachments from the Overseas Forces, whose presence here we all welcome.

"On such an occasion as this, the duties of the Police are extremely arduous. On them rests the double responsibility of making possible the successful fulfilment of the ceremonial programme, and of ensuring the safety and comfort of a vast concourse of spectators.

"Great credit is due to the members of the Police Forces concerned for the unfailing patience and tact shown by them in the performance of their long and tiring task—a task in which, as usual, they have been assisted by the orderliness and good humour of the crowds themselves.

"The Queen and I wish also to pay a tribute to the devoted services given to their fellow citizens through a long day by the members of voluntary organisations, in particular the St. John Ambulance Brigade, the British Red Cross Society and the Boy Scouts Association.

"Finally we would like to say how greatly we admired the decorations in the streets. We congratulate the responsible authorities and householders; and we are touched by the thought that all over the country so much care has been devoted by our people to decorating their homes in celebration of this day.

"For all the help so willingly given to ensure the success of the Coronation ceremonies, the Queen and I tender our heartfelt thanks. "GEORGE R.I."

SATURDAY, MAY 15, 1937

Daily Mirror

No. 10436 Registered at the G.P.O. as a Newspaper. ONE PENNY

KING GEORGE VI AND HIS QUEEN

ROYAL CORONATION PORTRAIT

Their Majesties King George VI and Queen Elizabeth, with their daughters, the Princess Elizabeth and Princess Margaret Rose—a Coronation portrait specially taken at Buckingham Palace. A Coronation portrait of the Royal Family is on pages 14 and 15, with pictures of the presentation of Coronation medals to members of the Overseas contingents by the King and Queen. Further pictures of this ceremony are on pages 5, 12 and 17.

TUESDAY, MAY 18, 1937

Daily Mirror

No. 10438 Registered at the G.P.O. as a newspaper. ONE PENNY

MOTHER SLAYS BABE IN WOODS TO MAKE ROOM FOR LOVER

FROM OUR OWN CORRESPONDENT

NEW YORK, Monday.

CIGARETTE drooping from her lips, blonde, twenty-eight-year-old mother, Mrs. Helen Tiernan, told detectives to-night how she burned her seven-year-old daughter Helen to death, then slashed her son Jimmy, five, with a table knife in an attempt to murder him—so that she could find room in their flat for her lover.

"Our three-roomed apartment was too small for the four of us," she drawled, "so the children had to go. I was madly in love with George. Nothing mattered as long as I had him.

"I took the children out to the woods at Brookhaven (Long Island), and when they were not looking I attacked Helen.

"She dropped when I hit her on the head, and Jimmy ran. I chased him and struck him down with a knife. Then I poured petrol over them both and set it on fire.

"They didn't seem to move, so I threw leaves over them, and went by train to a beach close to the wood and met George there.

"We sat on the beach and talked until after dark and then motored back to New York."

At this point in the woman's story the door opened and George Christie, handcuffed to police, was led in. Mrs. Tiernan's calm deserted her; she trembled, burst into sobs, and was taken away to the cells screaming "I love him! I love him!"

She was accused of the murder of Helen and attempting to kill Jimmy.

Christie was locked up as a material witness. Police declare he is Mrs. Tiernan's lover.

"Mummy Hit Me"

While the confession drama was being played at police headquarters little Jimmy Tiernan, delirious, was chattering to detectives in hospital—"Mummy hit me and Helen." He spoke over and over again of his "two daddies."

Mrs. Tiernan is believed to be a widow. District Attorney's officials say that if the leaves and grass had not been wet both children would have been burned to cinders and the crime would never have been discovered.

ATLANTIC AIR RACE BAN

The U.S. State Department has notified France, through the French Embassy in Washington, that the United States Government will not permit the Atlantic air race to start from the United States, says British United Press.

MURDER IN A TUBE TRAIN

Beautiful Laetitia Toureau (picture above) was in a Paris Apache dance hall. A soldier was heard to say to her: "If you deceive me I'll kill you." They left the hall together, were seen to part at a tube station. Five minutes later she was found dying from murderous wounds in a train. Police have accounted for all her day's movements except three and a half minutes. The soldier has vanished. (Story on page 3.)

Dancing to a one-man accordion band in Trafalgar-square last night.

PREACHED HIS OWN FUNERAL SERMON

Five thousand mourners heard farmer Wade Millman, aged eighty-eight, preach his own funeral sermon from the pulpit of a church at Coatsville, Indiana, U.S.A.

With the empty coffin resting on trestles before the altar, and with minister, undertaker and pall-bearers in attendance, he threw himself with zest into the service.

"Now I'll Die"

Millman paid glowing tribute to his own life, patiently sucking an orange to clear his throat. "Let me die unremembered" he concluded: "Let me lie in the grave unmolested."

Then he sang the hymn "When the roll is called up yonder I'll be there."

After the service Millman said: "'Twas all very moving All I've got to do now is die."

WHERE THEY WENT YESTERDAY

There were 20,853 visitors to Westminster Abbey, 36,000 to the Houses of Parliament, 10,000-15,000 to the Windsor Castle State Apartments, and 5,000 to the tomb of Queen Victoria and the Prince Consort at Frogmore.

CROWDS GO HOME IN COMFORT

LONDON'S police and railways won their race with the "floodlight" crowds by half an hour this morning.

A special service had been put on and the last train did not leave until 1.40 a.m.

But half an hour before this the crowds had dispersed and the last few trains left for the suburbs only half full.

Earlier London had been invaded by holiday-makers who arrived in fifty special trains, hundreds of motor-coaches and thousands of cars. It was a city on the march as the crowds made a farewell tour of "London by floodlight."

Six thousand were waiting at the doors of Westminster Abbey when they opened at 10 a.m. At 8 p.m., when they closed, there was still a half-mile queue of sightseers who had to be turned away by the police

Police had previously announced that at 9 p.m. many streets in the West End and the

(Continued on back page)

THE KING AND QUEEN SEE COMMAND SHOW OF 2-HOURS CORONATION FILM

FOR nearly two hours last night the King and Queen, Princess Elizabeth and Princess Margaret watched the showing of the full-length Coronation film in the Throne Room at Windsor Castle.

They were delighted with it, their Majesties remarking especially on the excellence of the interior scenes at the Abbey. Several incidents when the Royal Family were grouped on the Palace balcony amused them very much, and the little Princesses laughed aloud at some of the shots of themselves.

Fifteen thousand people who toured the State Apartments during the day—a record number—had seen workmen fitting up the film apparatus without realising they were seeing the preliminaries to a command performance.

Among fresh thousands who arrived in Windsor last night to see the floodlighting were the Duke and Duchess of Kent, who motored over from The Coppins, Iver (Bucks), and walked round unrecognised by a large crowd.

THURSDAY, MAY 20, 1937

Daily Mirror

No. 10440 Registered at the G.P.O. as a newspaper. ONE PENNY

NAVAL HONOUR IS PLANNED FOR PRINCESS ELIZABETH

The "Daily Mirror" understands that Princess Elizabeth, who to-day will inspect the Fleet at Spithead with the King and Queen, may receive honorary Naval rank shortly.

THE matter is being considered. Such an honour would be the first of its kind in history.

Vast crowds thronging Britain's first naval port roared her a welcome yesterday as she arrived with her father, who fought at Jutland, and like his father, is a sailor King.

Greatest massing of Britain's naval might since the war will await the Royal visitors to-day. Side by side with 160 British ships will be thirty-three foreign war craft representing seventeen nations.

Most of Portsmouth's citizens were surprised when the Princess arrived in the city with her parents.

Smiling Queen

And Portsmouth had a surprise for the Princess.

It was the model of a battleship which had been built in the middle of the main square.

The Princess could not take her eyes from it. "Isn't it beautiful?" she cried delightedly.

A woman in the crowd passed her a sprig of lilies-of-the-valley and she carried them in her hand.

Princess Elizabeth, sitting between the King and Queen in a big grey car, dressed in pink.

The King wore an Admiral's uniform, and the Queen, in pale blue, looked radiantly happy.

In the second car rode the Duke and Duchess of Kent.

The Duchess wore dark blue.

After their welcome at the Guildhall the royal party drove to the dockyard.

As they embarked on the Victoria and Albert the Royal Standard was run up, and the guns from the battery thundered their salute.

The King gave a dinner party on board the yacht.

Chartered a Train

The seventy-six miles of road from London to Southampton were packed with 30,000 cars yesterday as Londoners went south to get a glimpse of the greatest naval review Britain has staged for a generation.

Crowds began to leave London at 6 a.m., and by seven o'clock people were trying to find alternative routes to the port.

So great was the crush of rail travellers that one man chartered a special train for his guests.

Royal Drive to the Guildhall, page 4; To-day's Naval Review Timetable, page 5.

The King, followed by the Queen and the Princess Elizabeth (the Princess's hat is just visible), boarding the royal yacht, Victoria and Albert, at Portsmouth.

The spray of lilies-of-the-valley for luck in the Princess's hand in the picture on the left was given her by a woman in the crowd which greeted the royal visitors. Stepping forward, the woman put the sprig into her hand, and received a smile of thanks.

BUSIEST DAY OF THE KING'S REIGN

For King George yesterday was the busiest and most varied of his reign.

It began with an audience with Prince Chichibu, who on behalf of the Emperor of Japan conferred on the King the Order of the Chrysanthemum.

The King then drove to the C ildhall, where he was the guest of the Lord Mayor and the Corporation of the City of London at luncheon.

Soon after he set out for Portsmouth, where he entertained at dinner, on board the Royal yacht, the principal officers of the Fleet.

To-day King George will attend the Naval review at Spithead.

FRANCE'S BIGGEST SEAPLANE CRASHES: 5 DEAD, 5 INJURED

FIVE men were killed and five seriously injured when France's largest seaplane, the Loire et Olivier, crashed in taking off from the sea at Cap d'Antibes last night.

The 'plane, carrying a crew of five and five passengers, was on its last test flight before going on the Atlantic service.

As it left the water, about fifty yards from its base, the right pontoon came loose and the right wing collapsed. The 'plane plunged, hitting the water with terrific force.

There was an explosion and the seaplane began to sink.

The names of the dead are:—Lucian Bourdin, the pilot, who held the world's seaplane altitude record; M. Bloin, the telegraphist, and M. Brochet, the radio engineer. They were trapped in the machine and drowned. The bodies have not been found.

Two other victims were later washed ashore.

The Loire et Olivier is a four-motored all-metal monoplane with total horse power of 3.540.

DIED IN HER BOTTOM DRAWER

SPRAWLED in the open bottom drawer of a chest in which she kept her savings and treasures, sixty-eight-year-old retired governess Miss Emma O'Meara was found dead in her little cottage at Chideock, Dorset.

The room was in disorder. The table was overturned, chairs upset, and on the floor was a muddled heap of belongings. The money was untouched.

She had been decorating the cottage for the Coronation, and when, on Whit Monday, her neighbours, Mr. and Mrs. Roper, heard a strange tapping, they paid no heed.

Victor Huxter, milkman, was the last to see Miss O'Meara alive. She complained of feeling unwell, but refused to let him send for a doctor.

"Miss O'Meara must be putting up more decorations," joked Mr. Roper.

MONDAY, MAY 24, 1937

Daily Mirror

No. 10443 Registered at the G.P.O. as a newspaper. ONE PENNY

ROCKEFELLER DIES LEAVING £200,000,000, BUT THWARTED MAN

"DAILY MIRROR" SPECIAL

NEW YORK, Sunday.

Richest man in the world, John D. Rockefeller, worth £200,000,000, though he gave away £150,000,000, died a few minutes after 4 p.m. to-day, just as tea was being served in his mansion at Ormond Beach, Florida.

ONE of the last remarks the dying millionaire made before he sank into coma was:

"I'M VERY, VERY TIRED."

First tidings to the outside world were signalled when a youth employed on the estate, aided by the estate's superintendent, hoisted a worn American flag to the flag polehead and then half-masted it.

When the news was flashed over the radio, hundreds of residents and tourists flocked to the Rockefeller home, but found all roads to the estate blocked by guards.

Rockefeller was ninety-seven. Greatest ambition of his life was to live to 100 and he lavished a fortune in vain on specialists.

Though a message to John D's bankers made the financial world tremble, this withered dyspeptic old man lived the last twenty years of his life by sheer will power.

From his early days in Cleveland, Ohio, when he began to amass his huge fortune in oil, beginning as a book-keeper's clerk, earning 18s. a week, he has suffered constant bad health.

All that remains of John D. will go back to this starting place. His body will be taken by car to Cleveland for burial. The millionaire will end where he began.

Rockefeller would have been ninety-eight in six week's time. No relatives were with him when he died.

Last Friday he had a heart attack. He rallied afterwards and was in good spirits, but a relapse came at midnight on Saturday, and he became unconscious, and so remained until he died.

End Was Peaceful

"His death could not have been more peaceful or more beautiful," a member of his household said.

As the illness was not thought serious, the old man's son, John D. Rockefeller, junior, stayed at his Tarrytown (New York) estate and had not planned to go to Florida.

Until a few days ago Mr. Rockefeller had been more active than at any time in recent years.

John D. Rockefeller's annual income has been estimated at £10,000,000. The £150,000,000 he gave away has financed amazing philanthropic schemes in a battle to immortalise his name in all parts of the world.

Rockefeller's health broke down when he was fifty-five, and he took over his "new business of living to be a hundred and doing good work."

In recent years this ambition to conquer the years became so overwhelming that he lived surrounded by medical experts, medical charts, and on scientific diets. He had special oxygen apparatus feeding the air in his houses and his motor-cars also.

There were special windows to increase the power of the sun's rays in the various rooms of his beach home, where he hobbled from point to point, following the sun round all day.

The Magic Spell of Rockefeller—page 4

With his great-grandchildren on his knees.

John D. Rockefeller and Elizabeth and John de Cuevas, children of the multi-millionaire's grand-daughter.

MARY, MARY MILITARY

Pill-box hat, tunic, swagger-stick, sash and gauntlet gloves—the Coronation troops have left Hyde Park, but this visitor yesterday ensured that the military atmosphere remained.

NAZI OFFICIAL HEARD THROUGH FLAT WALL

A man who criticised the Nazi regime in his own home has been sent to prison for three months by a court at Wesermuende, North-West Germany.

The wall of his apartment was so thin that a Nazi official in the flat next door was able to overhear what he said, says Reuter.

HOTTEST DAY: LONDON PACKED

THOUSANDS of sightseers, many of the men with jackets over their arms, promenaded the West End of London last night, after the hottest day of the year.

Five thousand had waited for three hours outside Buckingham Palace to see the King and Queen return from Royal Lodge, Windsor.

They formed a cheering avenue as the royal car moved towards the Palace courtyard.

Queues formed at every West End Tube station towards midnight. At Marble Arch the queue was a quarter of a mile long.

Maximum temperature in London yesterday was 71deg. Resorts in the south-east enjoyed the year's hottest day, too—Herne Bay and Tunbridge Wells had twelve hours' sunshine. So had Stonehaven, in Kincardineshire.

If to-day is fine the King and Queen will drive in an open carriage to St. Paul's Cathedral for the Empire Day and Coronation Thanksgiving service.

She Loved the Sun

Ninety-two-year-old Mrs. Emma Carlish got out of bed at her home in Romford-road, Forest Gate, yesterday and flung up the window to let in the bright sunshine.

She overbalanced, fell from the window, crashed through a glass canopy. She died in hospital.

WOMAN ISSUES WRIT AGAINST GENERAL BOOTH

A WOMAN has served writs through her solicitors on General Eva Booth and Commissioner John MacMillan, the new Chief of Staff of the Salvation Army.

Commissioner Mapp, the dismissed Chief of Staff, said last night that the writs are not in connection with his dismissal.

He issued a statement declaring:—

"The real reason why I have been dismissed from the Salvation Army is my letter to General Booth of March 16, 1937, in which I asked to be allowed to retire because of my health, and referred to certain matters which the General desired to be kept secret.

"Suddenly Decided"

"Later I had long talks with the General and I agreed for the sake of the Salvation Army to keep silent.

"She agreed to facilitate my retirement by granting an immediate furlough.

"This she did with the full knowledge of the facts on which she later purported to dismiss me.

"There would have been no public scandal if General Booth had not suddenly decided to take disciplinary action against me on the basis of allegations which have never been proved nor admitted."

SATURDAY, MAY 29, 1937

Daily Mirror

No. 10448 Registered at the G.P.O. as a newspaper. ONE PENNY

DUCHESS OF WINDSOR WILL NOT HAVE ROYAL RANK

When Mrs. Wallis Warfield weds on June 3, she will become the Duchess of Windsor, but she will not rank as a member of the Royal Family. That was made clear last night in a notice in the "London Gazette."

LETTERS patent had been issued, defining application of the title of Royal Highness, it was announced.

These declare that the King wishes his brother, the Duke of Windsor, notwithstanding the abdication, personally to enjoy the title of Royal Highness.

This will not extend to his wife or to possible children.

Full ministerial responsibility is taken for the notice. It says:—

"The King has been pleased by letters patent under the Great Seal of the Realm bearing date the 27th day of May, 1937, to declare that the Duke of Windsor shall, notwithstanding his instrument of abdication executed on the 10th day of December, 1936, and his Majesty's declaration of Abdication Act, 1936, whereby effect was given to the said instrument, be entitled to hold and enjoy for himself only the title, style or attribute of Royal Highness, so however that his wife and descendants, if any, shall not hold the said title, style or attribute."

Letters patent concerning the title of Royal Highness were issued by Queen Victoria seventy years ago. It was laid down that the title was enjoyed only by near relations of the Sovereign who are "in the succession to the throne."

The Wedding Room

The room in which Mrs. Warfield is to be married is only 20ft. long and about 15ft. wide, says the *Daily Mirror* correspondent at Tours. It is panelled in pale green and has a parquet floor, and a very fine Carbusson rug.

Bride and bridegroom will have their faces to the light, for, in the bay to the south window of the room, the table behind which the Mayor will sit is to be placed.

Facing the Mayor will be two heavy antique chairs from the Chateau de Cande for the Duke and Mrs. Warfield.

On each side of these will be chairs for Mr. Rogers, who acts as Mrs. Warfield's witness, and Major E. D. Metcalfe, best man.

Behind will be rows of small chairs for the guests.

The door leading into the library will be left open so that the music from the organ shall be heard. Marcel Dupres, famous French organist, is to play. He arrives to-day.

The room will be banked on each side with flowers chosen to match its eighteenth century charm.

There will be no wedding cake for the Duke and Mrs. Warfield, and no wedding feast at the reception—just a buffet with champagne and sandwiches.

THE WHOLE B.B.C. IS LIT UP

"I had it in my mind to spend my time proving to you that the B.B.C. is human, but my task has been simplified by the fact that certain recent events have 'lit up' that side of the B.B.C.

"You can now take it for granted that the B.B.C. is a very human concern."

That was John Coatman, chief news editor of the B.B.C., speaking—addressing the Manchester Luncheon Club yesterday.

They're Happy Now!

Richard Jobey and Elsie Farrer, with their lucky black cat, smiling happily after the magistrates had yesterday granted permission for them to marry.

BOY LOVER, DISOWNED BY MOTHER, WILL WED HALF-CASTE SWEETHEART

SPURNING his nother's threat—"You are finished with us for ever"—Richard Jobey, twenty-year-old engineer, of Cross-street, Bradford, Manchester, yesterday gave up his home to marry his attractive dark-skinned half-caste sweetheart, nineteen-year-old Elsie Farrer.

As the chairman of the Manchester City magistrates granted the boy permission to marry, Richard and Elsie fell into each other's arms and kissed.

And the boy's mother went storming down the court corridor after the cry with which she disowned her son.

Then the boy and girl left the court together, Elsie taking Richard to her mother's home in Ascot-road, Newton Heath, where they are now preparing happily for the wedding.

"All children are born under the same God," said Mr. Nathan Laski, chairman of the magistrates, "and the girl can't help her colour.

"The boy tells us that he loves the girl, and I do not think that the mother's objection is fair. She has said nothing against the girl's respectability."

As Elsie took her lover to her mother's home, a black kitten came running to her.

"It came into the house this morning," she

(Continued on back page)

BRITISH SHIP HIT IN AIR RAID

BOMB fragments struck the London steamer Pinzon when rebel 'planes raided Valencia Harbour yesterday. Her port bow was holed but none of her crew was injured.

A ship named Cabin, which was sunk with the loss of seven of her crew, was flying the British flag, says Reuter, and it was announced by the Spanish Government that she was registered at Cardiff.

But no ship of that name is registered in Britain, and Mr. Thompson, first secretary at the British Embassy in Valencia, told the British United Press: "The only British ship damaged by bombs in to-day's air-raid is the Pinzon."

The Pinzon, a ship of 1,365 tons, is owned by MacAndrews and Co., Ltd.

Italian-Type 'Planes

The air raid, the worst Valencia has experienced, was carried out, according to a military observer attached to one of the foreign Embassies, by two squadrons of thre bombers each.

One squadron appears to have concentrated first on the business section of the town and then on outlying districts and the other on the poorer parts of Valencia.

Afterwards they linked up and flew away to the east.

They were all three-engined 'planes of the Italian Caproni type, and are believed to have come from the Balearic island of Iviza.

By last night thirty-seven bodies had been recovered, and seventy-three wounded received in hospital. Many people are believed to be still buried under debris

Houses were wrecked over a three-mile area and fires broke out in many quarters of the town.

SICK PEER BETTER —SON HONOURED

Lord Runciman lies on a sick bed. But yesterday he felt much better—probably because son Walter had been created a viscount.

The family record is believed to be unparalleled: father and son have been created peers in their lifetimes.

Said Lord Runciman, ninety-year-old shipowner: "Naturally, I am delighted. My son is one of the greatest national and commercial financiers in the country. He will have no double dealings and no trickery."

Cabinet shuffle and new honours—page 3.

AUDIENCE DIDN'T KNOW: SINGER HAD FOOT IN BATH

THE audience listening to the Song of the Bird in the second act of "Siegfried" at Covent Garden last night did not dream that the singer, Miss Stella Andreva, was sitting in the wings with a swollen foot in a bowl of warm water to ease her pain.

A few moments before she had sprained her ankle behind the scenes as she was arriving to take up her place in the wings.

Miss Andreva was attended by a doctor. A bowl of water was brought and when the moment came for her song, she pluckily carried on sitting in a wooden chair, her foot all the time immersed in the steaming water.

The bird in "Siegfried" sings almost to the end of the second act. When the curtain fell Miss Andreva was carried away, and, as she had no further part in the opera, was able to go to her hotel.

Mlle. Alicia Markova, the ballerina, was prevented by a chill from dancing at a matinee at His Majesty's Theatre yesterday in aid of the Nijinsky Foundation.

TUESDAY, JUNE 1, 1937

Daily Mirror

No. 10450 Registered at the G.P.O. as a newspaper. ONE PENNY

ITALY JOINS GERMANY, SMASHES SCHEME FOR SPAIN CONTROL

FEARS that the entire system of Spanish non-intervention and control will be smashed, with the gravest consequences, by the bombing of the German battleship Deutschland and the retaliatory shelling of Almeria, were expressed last night by diplomats.

Germany and Italy announced yesterday that they have withdrawn from the system of control of the Spanish coast until they receive guarantees that incidents like the bombing of the Deutschland will never be repeated.

Whitehall and Paris are seriously alarmed. As long as Italy and Germany remain outside the control system they can send volunteers and armaments to Franco. If they do, France, Britain and Russia might feel compelled to stop them on the high seas.

Mr. Eden Trying to Save the Situation

Britain's Foreign Minister, Anthony Eden, is working desperately to save the situation. He is trying to persuade the Spanish Government not to attack German or Italian warships.

"Italy is solid with Germany in the Spanish situation. The shelling of Almeria is fully approved." This statement was made in Rome last night after Mussolini had flown back from his country home for a consultation with his principal lieutenants.

He is prepared to send more warships to Spain if necessary.

In Berlin it was officially stated that the shelling of Almeria was the end of the retaliation for the bombing of the Deutschland, but it was later announced that further German battleships were being sent to reinforce those already in Spanish waters.

Eleven German warships were reported to be steaming full speed through the Bay of Biscay last night, on their way to Spain. One French warship was hurrying there, too, and four others had steam up at Toulon.

In Paris it was rumoured that another port, Cartagena, had been bombed.

The opinion was expressed in Government quarters in Berlin that the bombardment does not constitute an act of war: First, because there are no diplomatic relations between Berlin and Valencia; secondly, because "one can not wage war on a band of pirates."

Mr. Eden discussed the situation last night with M. Corbin, the French Ambassador in London, Dr. Woermann, the Minister of the German Embassy, Count Grandi, the Italian Ambassador, and the Spanish envoy.

He had separate interviews with all four.

Mr. Eden stated in the House of Commons last evening that he had asked the German Charge d'Affaires to represent to his Government that the German Government would take no action which would render the present grave situation still graver.

British and French Foreign Office officials were in touch all night.

Berlin reports claimed that the bombardment of Almeria destroyed the harbour works and silenced the batteries.

The Spanish Government announced that 200 shells were fired into the town, destroying forty houses and killing twenty people.

Messages from Reuter and British United Press.

MRS. WARFIELD IN HER NEW CLOTHES

Wearing part of the new wardrobe she has bought for her wedding to the Duke of Windsor on Thursday.

Mrs. Wallis Warfield in a blue and white sequin coat over a white dress. On her left hand is her emerald engagement ring.

On the right she is seen on the steps of the Chateau de Cande, in a dark blue dress decorated with black butterflies and carrying Slippers II, the Cairn terrier given her by the Duke of Windsor to replace her dog that was killed by a snake.

FALSE AIR RAID WARNING SAVED THOUSANDS

A FALSE air raid warning saved the lives of thousands of people in Almeria, says British United Press.

The alarm sent them hurrying into the bomb-proof shelters for the night.

While they were there the German warships appeared off the coast in battle formation and began their reprisals.

DYNAMITED WIFE AND EIGHT CHILDREN

A "LIE detector" machine has betrayed a father of ten children and forced him to confess he blew up his home with dynamite, killing his wife and eight of the children.

He did it after quarrelling with his wife "because she kept having more kids."

John Waszak, of Waukesha, Wisconsin, is quoted as saying: "I plotted the explosion last March. None of the children helped me with the farm work, so when the family was gathered round the wireless I went to the cellar and lighted a one-foot fuse attached to low-grade dynamite, known as pyrotol," says British United Press.

TYPHOID CASE IN SPANISH REFUGEE CAMP

FROM OUR OWN CORRESPONDENT

SOUTHAMPTON, Monday.

A CASE of typhoid fever was confirmed to-night in the Basque refugee children's camp at North Stoneham—temporary home during the last week of 3,000 children.

It is the first case of infectious disease reported there. The victim is Ricardo Garcia, aged nine. He was rushed to Southampton Isolation Hospital.

Mr. Henry Brinton, organiser of the camp, told me to-night: "We do not take a serious view of the matter. Precautions have been taken to prevent the disease spreading.

"I was in communication with the Ministry of Health to-night and was told that it was all right to proceed with the evacuation arrangements."

FRIDAY, JUNE 4, 1937

Daily Mirror

No. 10453 Registered at the G.P.O. as a Newspaper. ONE PENNY

...The Duke and Duchess of Windsor...

ON THE STEPS OF A NEW LIFE—TOGETHER

His Royal Highness the Duke of Windsor and his bride walking down to the terrace of the Chateau de Cande at Tours—their first public appearance after their wedding yesterday.—Other wedding pictures on pages 3, 4, 16, 17 and 32.

TUESDAY, JUNE 8, 1937

Daily Mirror

No. 10456 — Registered at the G.P.O. as a Newspaper. — ONE PENNY

JEAN HARLOW DEAD

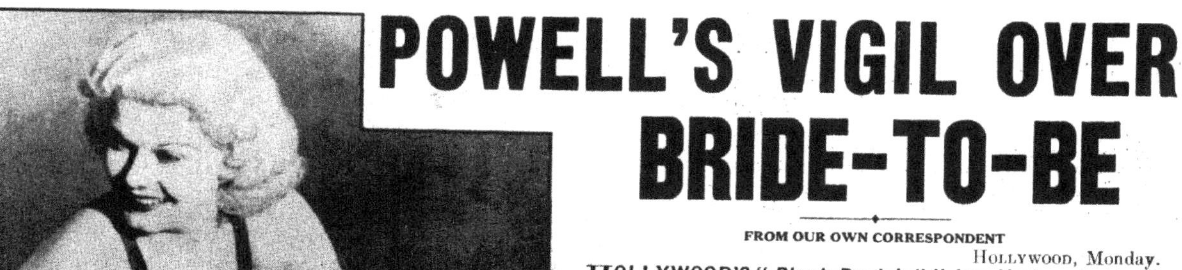

POWELL'S VIGIL OVER BRIDE-TO-BE

FROM OUR OWN CORRESPONDENT

HOLLYWOOD, Monday.

HOLLYWOOD'S "Blonde Bombshell," Jean Harlow, died fighting for life under an oxygen tent in the Good Samaritan Hospital here to-day. She was twenty-six.

At her side her mother, hysterical, collapsing, called to her again and again to fight on; screen hero William Powell—he was to have married her in a few weeks—watched silent, gripping her hand.

Jean tried to answer. From the tent came a few mumbled, incoherent words. Then coma and the end.

A doctor touched Powell on the shoulder. "She's gone, Bill," he said. Mother and lover were led gently away.

Hollywood was stunned by the news. Clark Gable, working with her on her new film "Saratoga" when she fell ill on May 29, is reported prostrate with grief. Jean was suffering from internal inflammation but on Friday she was much better.

"In a few days I'll be back on the set," she said. This morning there was a sudden relapse. Uræmic poisoning started a swelling of the brain. Rushed to hospital she was twice given blood transfusions and injections. Within an hour she was dead.

Eloped at 16

The original "platinum blonde," Jean Harlow, a Kansas dentist's daughter, eloped from school at sixteen to start the hectic career that carried her from an extra to an £800-a-week star and through three romantic marriages in ten short years.

She entered films for a bet. A friend in a film studio wagered her that she would not dare present a letter from a studio official to the casting director.

She saw the director—and got a job.

She had just left an exclusive school at Lake Forest, Illinois—by eloping with a youngster named Charles McGrew. The marriage was dissolved soon after she entered films.

She was playing as an extra in a Clara Bow film when Howard Hughes picked her from a hundred applicants as leading woman in his anti-war spectacle, "Hell's Angels."

Jean wanted to act. She grew tired of being a "platinum blonde." She changed her hair to brown—just to show, as she said, "Talent has nothing to do with the colour of my hair."

Then Hollywood wanted her to turn into a "redhead." Jean flatly refused.

She said: "I'm brown-ette. Not blonde, not red—just brown-ette."

Her second husband was Paul Bern, the film director. They married in July, 1930. Two months later Bern shot himself before a mirror in their home. He left a note which said: "Dearest Dear,—This is the only way to make good the frightful wrong I have done you and wipe out my abject humiliation. You understand last night was only a comedy." A year later she eloped with Harold Rosson, a Hollywood cameraman. The marriage ended in divorce after eight months.

(The Blonde and her last bombshell—by Ivan Goff: page 12.)

Happy in the joy of life only a fortnight ago, full of vitality and glamour, high up in the rank of film stars and, at twenty-six, rising to that hierarchy which rules the box office, Jean Harlow died in Hollywood yesterday . . . by her side William Powell, who was to have brought again Romance into her life.

RISING AGAINST STALIN: MOBS SLAY OGPU AGENTS IN REPLY TO PURGE

FROM OUR OWN CORRESPONDENT

WARSAW, Monday.

STALIN, from the Kremlin, has ordered stronger repressive measures against "comrades" rising in revolt against his new Red Army purge.

Unrest is spreading in the military garrisons as more and more officers are arrested, while in the streets the mobs are growing.

In six places, including the Don Basin, Ogpu chiefs have been murdered and State food stores looted.

Konstantynow workers have destroyed local factories and killed the managers.

At Szczerbanowsk, an industrial centre about 200 miles from Moscow, rioters, aided by soldiers, attacked Ogpu headquarters, tied up the officials, poured petrol on the walls and set fire to the building.

More than twenty-two Ogpu officers were burned to death. Those who tried to escape were shot down by the waiting crowd.

It is said that Stalin has imprisoned Marshal Tukharzevski, arrested Marshal Blucher, and caused more than 300 officials to be flung into gaol during the last few days. Twenty Foreign Office servants were imprisoned during the week-end.

PETER, 3, RAN AWAY TWICE : LOOKING FOR 'TWAINS'

BY A SPECIAL CORRESPONDENT

VANISHED from his home in Lodge-avenue, Romford, three-year-old Peter Garvan was later found sitting demurely in a first-class carriage at Liverpool-street Station.

When his father came to fetch him home by car, he was most unwilling to go. Quite unperturbed, he remarked calmly that he wanted to catch another train.

"I had to use a lot of persuasion to get him away," his father said. "He is passionately fond of trains."

When he got home his mother locked him in the sitting-room for safety. An hour later she went to fetch him out for his walk, and found he had disappeared again, this time through the window, a five-foot drop from the ledge.

After another frantic search, he was found waiting on Romford station for another train.

Peter, fresh from his adventure, was holding an audience of envious and admiring friends in his quiet little Romford home last night.

"Twains," he murmured ecstatically, "twains, wif lots of black smoke and noise. And going fast, fast all the time.

"I wish," he sighed deeply, "I wish I could live in a twain for ever. I wish I were an engine man.

One of the last pictures to be taken of Jean Harlow, with William Powell.

WEDNESDAY, JUNE 16, 1937

Daily Mirror

No. 10463 Registered at the G.P.O. as a Newspaper. ONE PENNY

PRINCESS JULIANA TELLS ON RADIO SHE EXPECTS A BABY

Princess Juliana of Holland broadcast proudly to the world last night the news that she is expecting a baby. She is the first Princess in history to announce personally the forthcoming birth of an heir in line of direct succession to the throne.

JUST back from her honeymoon, which ended with the Coronation celebrations in London, the Princess hurried through the delighted welcome of the capital to retirement at her home outside Amsterdam.

Rumours that her health had broken down were exciting the Dutch people. She cancelled all engagements, and last night, to allay anxiety, she explained the reasons over the radio.

Nobody knew what the broadcast was to be. The Princess asked that arrangements be made for a special relay from her summer palace at Foest.

Everyone expected that the message would be simply formal thanks for her welcome home from her honeymoon.

Only Prince Bernhard to whom she was wed on January 7 this year, shared the surprise she had for the nation.

He sat at her side and held the microphone. He spoke a few words after the Princess.

The Princess began by thanking Amsterdam for its loyal welcome.

Then she said: "I am very very sorry that I have forced to be absent from some of the events in the welcome programme. The reason I know you will approve; it will make you happy. My health makes it impossible for me to keep public engagements."

Then the Princess told her secret.

Palace Message to the "Daily Mirror"

As soon as the broadcast concluded Amsterdam began a wild night of celebration. Palace officials warned the Dutch newspapers that the law forbade any quotation of the Princess's message.

Speaking over the trans-European telephone last night a palace official told the *Daily Mirror*:—

"The broadcast news of this happy event is typical of the democratic spirit which endears our Princess to the nation. We are all very happy."

The Princess was in England for the Coronation and last week returned home.

After the honeymoon Princess Juliana lost all her Dutch reserve and had acquired a French style of dressing.

CONSERVATIVES WIN

By the victory of Lieutenant-Colonel the Hon. Henry Guest in the by-election in the Drake Division of Plymouth, the result of which was declared last night, the Government gains its third success in the miniature "General Election" of twelve contests.

Lieutenant-Colonel Guest had 15,778 votes and his Socialist opponent, Mr. G. T. Garratt, 11,044. The by-election was caused by the death of Captain F. E. Guest, the new M.P.'s brother. At the General Election he had 21,446 votes and Mr. J. J. Moses (Socialist) 15,368.

The "sit-down" knock-out of Neusel, when he was beaten by Tommy Farr, the Welsh heavy-weight.

Neusel Knocked Out in Eight Minutes

FARR'S WINNING BLOW STARTS WOMEN SCREAMING AND KISSING

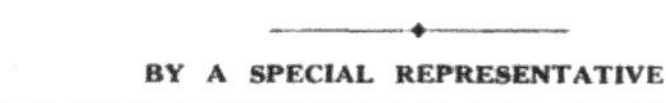

Farr (left) and Neusel exchanging blows in the first round.

BY A SPECIAL REPRESENTATIVE

WHEN Tommy Farr beat Walter Neusel in seven minutes fifty-eight seconds at Harringay last night, beautifully-gowned women leapt to their feet, screamed, threw their arms round men, kissed them, and shrieked again.

Neusel went down in the third round to a right cross to the jaw, following a hail of blows. That blow had everything—faultless timing and fourteen stone seven behind it. The "Iron Man" dropped like a pole-axed bull. But the iron came out.

Before the referee had counted two Neusel was sitting up with one arm on the ropes. He looked to his corner and said in gesture, "I'm finished."

"Get up, Walter," they shouted wildly, but Walter was looking up at the referee, mentally counting with him.

As soon as "ten, out" was called, he got to his feet and walked to his corner.

Farr won this fight with his brain.

His advisers official (from his corner), and his advisers unofficial (half the big names of society, stage, cinema and the ring), shouted to him to box.

Farr never heard them. He in-fought mixed it, and slugged Neusel all over the canvas. He knew how he wanted to fight.

He used his ramrod left, and never missed his target. But he also used his right.

Neusel was out-fought and out-boxed any way you look at it.

Before the fight started every star of the boxing world came into the ring. The two Baers, Schmeling, Petersen, Foord, Harvey, Ernst Koeblin.

Description of the fight—Page 30.

P.-C., ENGAGED, WED ANOTHER, SAYS GIRL

"I do hope and pray that God will help me to put right what wrong I have done. Now, my dear, try to cheer up and be better. I am going to try and be a better man and right the wrong I have done you, sweetheart."

This letter, stated to be from a London policeman, alleged to have married one girl while engaged to another, was read at Monmouth Assizes yesterday.

Henry Harvey Rich, a Metropolitan Police constable, of Larkhall Rise, Clapham, S.W., was the defendant in a breach of promise action brought by Miss Ada Ann Phillips, of Portskewett-road, Newport, Mon.

Mr. Campbell Lloyd Davis said that Rich met Miss Phillips in 1927

In October, 1929, Rich was home at Newport on leave and the couple decided to marry. He bought her a ring, which she wore until August, 1936, when Rich told her that he had been married since July of that year.

Case was adjourned till to-day.

THURSDAY, JUNE 17, 1937

Daily Mirror

No. 10464 Registered at the G.P.O. as a Newspaper. ONE PENNY

BRITISH SHIP WITH NO PORT HAS £10,000,000 CARGO ON BOARD

BY A SPECIAL CORRESPONDENT

THREE miles off the Biscay coast of France, in the roads of the River Gironde, a treasure-ship rides at anchor with £10,000,000 in gold and securities sealed in her holds—but with no port to go to.

The ship is the 1,400-ton British cargo steamer Seabank, an insignificant, rusty-plated tramp, whose home port is Cardiff.

Three weeks ago the Seabank was chartered by the Basque Government after she had run the blockade into Bilbao with food.

Neither Captain Maber, master of the tramp, nor his crew knew at the start that their outward cargo was to be the entire liquid assets of the Basque provinces, including the deposits from three banks.

They were told that at dusk a fortnight ago when loading began.

Stole Out to Sea

Under cover of night, flanked by British destroyers and carrying treasure worth £10,000,000 sealed up in the holds under her hatches, the Seabank stole out to sea from Bilbao and steamed north.

Then the radio crackled out a dramatic change of orders to Captain Maber. He was ordered to drop anchor in Gironde roads.

The Basque Government feared that wherever the Seabank's precious cargo was unloaded, there was a danger that it would be confiscated.

In the King's Bench Division, London, it was ruled last Friday that the Basque Government had no authority to land the cargo in London.

If the cargo were unloaded in a French province the same circumstances would stand—except that France is anti-Franco, and Basque authorities fear that the treasure would be confiscated for use by the Spanish Government.

So the Seabank lies in the Bay of Biscay, "marooned," with no country in Europe to take her golden cargo.

In a fortnight's time the Basque Government's charter on the ship lapses.

Following a letter sent by an official representing the three main Basque banks to Sir Henry Chilton, British Ambassador at Hendaye, a British destroyer has been sent to lie at anchor near the Seabank.

Owner of the tramp is Mr. A. J. Pope, proprietor of the Seabank Hotel, Porthcawl.

AUDIENCE MISSED A FIRE —SO DID THE M.P.S

Five fire engines gave M.P.s a laugh last night. The brigade men dashed into Palace Yard looking for flames in the House.

But there was no fire. A false alarm had been 'phoned by a voice that said it was a policeman.

Other people who did not see a fire last night were the audience of 500 in the Westminster Theatre. They missed a real one.

Firemen dealt with it tactfully—it was in the scenery workshop—while the 500, just beyond the wall, heard nothing but dialogue.

WIFE IS LOYAL TO P.-C. WHO JILTED GIRL

BY A SPECIAL CORRESPONDENT

ATTRACTIVE brunette wife of Henry Harvey Rich, a Metropolitan police constable who has been ordered to pay £100 damages for breach of promise, told me last night:

"I love Harry and will stand by him to the end of my days."

This loyal and devoted wife, when I saw her at her Fulham home, was clad in a dressing gown and looked very frail.

Only ten days ago she lost her baby and nearly sacrificed her own life.

"I discharged myself from hospital on Monday," she said, "so as to be at home when Harry got back. He does not know I am here."

Mrs. Rich told me that she first met her husband in 1933. "I would have married him very soon," she said, "but my mother was very ill and I had to look after her until her death.

"We got married in July of last year."

Mrs. Rich's fine, dark eyes flashed with scorn. "I should like to emphasise," she said, "that the disgusting rumours circulated in certain quarters that my husband had to mai.. me because I was expecting to become a mother are absolutely untrue."

Miss Phillips

Police-constable Rich, who lives at Larkhall-rise, Clapham, S.W., was ordered at Monmouth yesterday to pay £100 damages and costs, for breach of promise, to Miss Annie Phillips, of Portskewett-road, Newport, Mon.

"I thought more of my wife than Miss Phillips," Rich pleaded.

ANXIETY FOR BARRIE

The condition of Sir James Barrie, who is in a West End nursing home suffering from bronchial pneumonia, was still causing anxiety last night.

Mlle. Jeanne Manet, casino girl who says that crooner-heavy-weight boxer Jack Doyle is engaged to HER. "He called himself Romeo and called me his Juliet," is her story.

DOYLE, TOLD HE IS ENGAGED, SAYS, "I NEVER HEARD OF THE GIRL"

LIGHTNING lover Jack Doyle, crooner-heavy-weight-boxer, once wed to film star Judith Allen and unsuccessful claimant to a tobacco heiress, Libby Holman, and an automobile heiress as his future brides is now declared by Mlle. Jeanne Manet, a casino girl, to be engaged to her.

But Doyle, who is now in New York, declared last night that he had never heard of her.

"This is terrible," he exclaimed in alarmed tones, when told of Jeanne.

"Who is the lady?" he asked. "What is she like? Somehow I feel she's just a gag.

"Take it from me, I'm not going to marry a woman I've never met, even if she crosses the ocean for me."

Doyle contradicted previous statements that he would marry an heiress. "I've no matrimonial intentions just now," he said, "but I'm Irish, so I might do anything suddenly."

Jeanne Manet is a blonde, blue-eyed girl of nineteen. She left school only a year ago, and started her stage career last January.

Her mother told the *Daily Mirror* in Paris last night:—

"He flew from England every week-end to see her at her Paris flat, and proposed

DROWNS IN TOWN'S NEW POOL

FROM OUR SPECIAL CORRESPONDENT

MARGATE, Wednesday.

THREE policemen and three civilians struggled to-night to rescue thirteen-year-old Robert Setterfield, of Buenos Ayres-road, Margate, from the eight-foot end of the new municipal pool here.

He was alive when they got him out, but died a few minutes after he had been taken to hospital.

To-day the Mayor of Margate is officially to open the pool, which is tidal, and built right on the sands.

At the time Robert was bathing the tide was so high that waves were washing over the outer wall

FRIDAY, JUNE 18, 1937

Daily Mirror

No. 10465 — Registered at the G.P.O. as a Newspaper. — ONE PENNY

CHILDREN IN HOSPITAL PRAY, "MAKE THE PETER PAN MAN WELL"

BY A SPECIAL CORRESPONDENT

CHILD patients in Great Ormond-street Hospital were praying last night for Sir James Barrie, greatest children's author of his day, who is dangerously ill in a London nursing home, and is feared to be dying.

Prayers were offered, too, by the staff of the hospital, of which Sir James is patron, and to which since 1929 he has given all royalties from his immortal "Peter Pan."

Sir James has been a frequent visitor to the hospital. The matron said to me last night:—"Many of the children told me that they had prayed for 'the Peter Pan man' to get well and to come and see them again soon."

For some time Sir James, who is seventy-seven, had been in bad health. He was too ill to see "The Boy David," his first play since 1920, when it opened at Edinburgh last November.

A week ago, suffering from pneumonia, he was taken to the nursing home from the top-floor flat in Adelphi-terrace House, overlooking the Thames, where he had lived for thirty years.

Last night relatives and friends were at his bedside, and this morning, after a midnight visit from Lord Horder, the King's physician, and Dr. McKay Huey, a bulletin was issued saying that his condition had become "very grave."

Divorce Broke His Heart

Sir James has been famous for nearly fifty years, since he wrote "Auld Licht Idylls."

But he never enjoyed his fame. He has always shrunk from the limelight, and has been known as "the shyest man in Britain."

And the author who brought smiles to so many faces is a man who has rarely been seen to smile.

His books and plays—on happy themes—have been written with a broken heart. He never recovered from his ordeal of twenty-eight years ago, when he had to give evidence in the Divorce Court that resulted in his obtaining a decree against his wife, Mary Ansell, an actress, who appeared in one of his first successful plays.

Sir James had married her thirteen years previously at Kirriemuir, the little Forfarshire weaving town where he was born

Increasing fame and wealth came to him as if to compensate for the wreck of his marriage. "Peter Pan" earned him £50,000 in British royalties alone, in twenty-one years. He was created a baronet in 1913, and nine years later admitted to the Order of Merit.

But no honour, no fame, no increase in the wealth for which he had never sought have ever consoled him for that day in the Divorce Court.

MAULED BY LION—BUT WON A GIRL

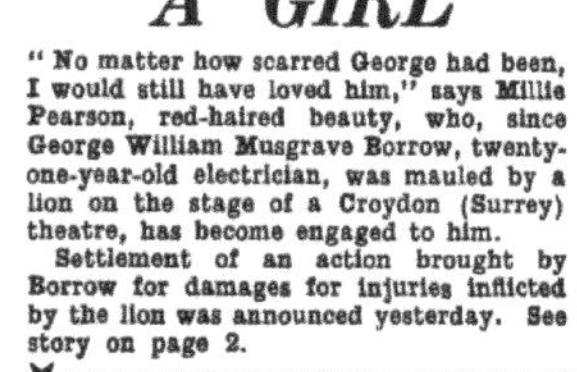

"No matter how scarred George had been, I would still have loved him," says Millie Pearson, red-haired beauty, who, since George William Musgrave Borrow, twenty-one-year-old electrician, was mauled by a lion on the stage of a Croydon (Surrey) theatre, has become engaged to him.

Settlement of an action brought by Borrow for damages for injuries inflicted by the lion was announced yesterday. **See story on page 2.**

18 KILLED IN SPANISH BATTLESHIP

EIGHTEEN of the crew were killed and more than 100 were injured when an explosion, followed by fire, occurred on the Spanish Government battleship Jaime I, it was announced in Valencia last night

The Jaime I is undergoing repairs at Cartagena.

Senor Prieto, Minister of National Defence, flew to Cartagena to examine the ship.

The Minister visited the wounded in hospital and then visited the mortuary.

He ordered an immediate examination, by a special Judge, into the causes of the explosion and the fixing of the responsibility.

The chief of the port of Cartegena showed the Minister a film that he had taken away from a foreign observer on a Non-Intervention boat. From the bridge of a ship the photographer had obtained "shots" of the Jaime I when the explosion took place, of the first relief work, and of the position of the other Republican fleet in the port.

Jaime I, the Spanish Government's crack battleship, is a cruiser of 15,452 tons.

She has played a big part in the war. She put into Cartagena after being damaged in a clash with rebel ships.

—Reuter and British United Press.

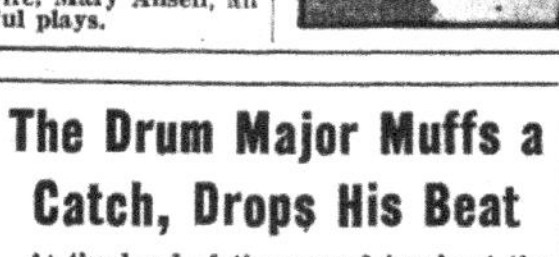

The Drum Major Muffs a Catch, Drops His Beat

At the head of the massed bands at the Aldershot Tattoo last night marched majestically the senior drum major.

Twirling his staff in his fingers, he tossed it aloft, made a grab as it came down—and missed.

He hastily stooped and picked up his symbol of authority.

And among the 69,250 who saw him do it were Secretary of State for War Hore-Belisha, Prime Minister Neville Chamberlain, Princess Helena Victoria, Princess Marie Louise and Prince Arthur of Connaught.

CHILD AGED THREE SHOT DEAD AT PLAY OUTSIDE HER OWN HOME

FROM OUR OWN CORRESPONDENT

DARTFORD, Thursday.

WHILE playing with the little son and daughter of a farm labourer living in cottages adjoining Rabbits Farm, Horton Kirby, near here to-night, Margaret Miles, aged three, was killed by a shot through the head.

Hearing a report the mother of Ronald James Sparks, aged four, ran out of the house, and found Margaret in a pool of blood in the road.

Mrs. Flack, a neighbour, who was working in the fields, told me: "I heard the report, and thought it was someone driving the birds away from the strawberries. When I learned of the tragedy I ran and told Mr. Miles, who was working on strawberries.

"He was stunned, for Margaret was a lovely child. She was one of a family of five children."

DOROTHY PUTS LOVE FIRST

BRITAIN'S No. 1 tennis ace, Dorothy Round, served a love game yesterday.

As a result she's not going to play against the U.S. in the Wightman Cup match at Forest Hills in August

But yesterday's love was real love, love for Dr. Douglas Little, of Dudley, whom she is marrying in September. And preparations for the great event, she says, will make it impossible for her fight for the trophy.

"I've lots and lots of things to do," Dorothy told the *Daily Mirror* last night.

"But I'm looking forward to Wimbledon."

Sports comment.—Page 30.

DIDI BATTYE: "NO KIDNAP EVIDENCE"

THE police have no evidence to show that Miss Diana (Didi) Battye, the society beauty who was missing for eight days, was a victim of kidnappers.

This was started by the Home Secretary, Sir Samuel Hoare, yesterday in reply to a question in the House of Commons by Mr. A. Short (Socialist, Doncaster).

Miss Battye's stepfather, Mr. Leonard Hackett, told the *Daily Mirror* last night that she was still ill, "fighting for her memory."

WEDNESDAY, JUNE 23, 1937

Daily Mirror

No. 10469 Registered at the G.P.O. as a Newspaper ONE PENNY

30 SHIPS READY TO BOMBARD VALENCIA: NEW ARMY FOR FRANCO

IT'S 10 TO 1 "HE" WAS DOING THE SAME THING

There's nothing like a cigarette to steady your nerves, say smokers.

Not that Miss Audrey Bateman-Champain seems to be suffering from stage fright . . . but a cigarette was in her hand as she left for her wedding to Mr. Alfred Brailsford Woodburn at Holy Trinity, Sloane-street, yesterday.

BOMBARDMENT OF VALENCIA, SPAIN'S CAPITAL, BY THIRTY GERMAN AND ITALIAN WARSHIPS.

ITALIAN REGULAR ARMY DIVISIONS OPENLY SENT TO GENERAL FRANCO, REBEL CHIEF.

THESE prospects were discussed by worried European diplomats last night as Hitler and Mussolini met their war chiefs to consider the first diplomatic rebuff they have received since the Spanish civil war broke out.

Britain and France had turned down the Fascist States' plan for an immediate naval demonstration off the coast of Valencia as a protest against the alleged torpedo attack on the German cruiser Leipzig.

Communique issued at the British Foreign Office after the Four Power conversations between Mr. Eden and the French, Italian and German ambassadors had broken down, said:

"It was unfortunately found impossible to reach agreement on the measures which should be adopted in this case."

Britain Rebuffs Hitler

The communique followed Mr. Eden's blunt statement, cheered by the crowded House of Commons:

"I can say definitely that the Government have no intention whatever of joining in naval demonstrations off Valencia."

So Germany and Italy will hold a naval demonstration off Valencia on their own. It will take place within the next twenty-four hours

Thirty German and Italian warships, showing the Swastika and Italian flags, will demonstrate. The Leipzig, the Deutschland, and the Von Scheer and another pocket battleship, with destroyers will represent Germany

More Men for Franco

Italy will send, in addition to battleships, a cruiser squadron and destroyers.

It is possible that Hitler and Mussolini will decide within the next twenty-four hours to change the pacific demonstration into something more serious. They may decide to open fire.

And in Rome last night it was thought that Mussolini would send regular army divisions to General Franco.

Messages: "Daily Mirror," Reuter, British United Press Central News, Exchange.

'SECRET SON' CLAIM IN MENACES CASE

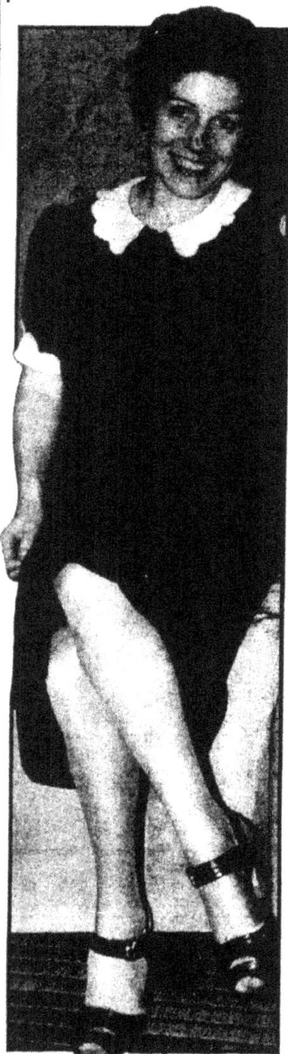

Mrs. Jenette, whose husband, Terence Jenette, a Londoner, was sent for trial, at Alton (Hants) yesterday, on a charge of demanding £50 by menaces from Mr. William Winter, nephew of the late Sir James Barrie.

Jenette declared that he was the son of Mr. Winter's wife and alleged that his existence had been kept a secret from Barrie. See story on page 3.

RIOT SQUADS PATROL 'BLACK BELT' AS CHICAGO GOES FIGHT-CRAZY

FROM PETER WILSON

CHICAGO, Tuesday.

IF ever there has been a fight-crazy town, it's Chicago to-day. No one talks or thinks of anything else, and quite a few people look as though they are going in for a practical demonstration. The day's entertainment started at noon, when Braddock and Louis weighed in.

There was only a quarter of a pound difference between them, Louis having that advantage, and Braddock scaling 14st. 1lb.

Both men were in great shape and shook hands amiably. Braddock remarked: "You need a shave, Joe," to which Louis replied, "I'll get it to-night."

It is a glorious day here, not too hot, so that it is estimated the crowd will be around 70,000, paying roughly £120,000 to £140,000, of which Braddock gets half and Louis £20,000 to £25,000.

Squads 300 strong, trained in military formation, are stationed at four quarters of "Black Belt" and all picked men.

Nevertheless, when I said I would like to ride through the coloured section after the fight I was told that if Louis is beaten it would be as well to keep out unless I wanted to go home in a box.

Certainly there is an air of tenseness, with the negroes all excited as children going to a party.

Odds have shortened sensationally. A day or two ago one could get 3 to 1 against Brad

(Continued on Back Page)

GERMANS DETAIN BRITISH AIRMEN

AN English flying instructor, Mr. A. H. Abbot, and three pupils on a week-end flight in Europe, are being detained, says Reuter, at Frankfurt, where they flew by mistake to the military airport, until photographs taken on their flight are developed.

Mr. Abbot, who is employed by Air Service Training, Ltd., had with him Mr. A. G. Nicholson, Mr. T. M. Walters and Mr. J. H. White.

GEDDES, AXE MAN, DIES

Sir Eric Geddes, the "Axe" man, famous organiser of munitions and railways during the war, died last night, aged sixty-one.

Story of his life, and picture, page 2.

THURSDAY, JUNE 24, 1937

Daily Mirror

No. 10470 Registered at the G.P.O. as a Newspaper. ONE PENNY

NAZI, ITALIAN FLEETS MEET IN SECRET, DEFY BRITAIN

UNDER sealed orders, Nazi and Italian Fleets are meeting in the Mediterranean this morning for a demonstration against Valencia, the Spanish capital. At midnight the Germans sailed from Lagos, where their Fleet had gathered in secret.

Mr. Eden, British Foreign Minister, had kept in touch all night with other Cabinet Ministers, as well as the French Ambassador. They were considering these facts:—

(1) In spite of Berlin denials, the German Fleet that had taken part in the Naval Control Scheme off the Spanish coast anchored secretly in the port of Lagos, on the south coast of Portugal, yesterday morning.

(2) These German warships were sailing to the Mediterranean to join the Italian Fleet off the Spanish Coast.

(3) Berlin announced that the pocket battleship, the Admiral Graf Von Spee, sailed last night for Spain.

(4) The gathering of the Fleets and the sailing of the Graf Von Spee are going on in face of a warning to Hitler by Britain and France that hostile action against the Spanish Government would be regarded as a step likely to have serious consequences.

The German Fleet in Spanish waters consists of the pocket battleship Admiral Scheer, the light cruisers Koeln, Nuernberg and Karlsruhe, three destroyers and a tanker.

The visit to Lagos was authorised by the Portuguese Government.

But a Berlin spokesman denied that German warships were at Lagos. It was added that nothing would be made known of the movements of the warships until they had taken up new positions.

The warning to Hitler was carried to Hitler last night by Ambassador von Ribbentrop, who flew from Croydon Airport.

Von Ribbentrop was passing on to Hitler a blunt statement that public opinion in Britain and France would flare up against Germany and Italy in the event of a demonstration by the Nazi and Italian fleets.

"From now on," said a Berlin statement, "the German Government takes care of the protection of its interests against the Bolshevist incendiaries in Valencia, and will

(Continued on back page)

Two-and-a-half-year-old Buddy Guldahl, son of the American open golf champion, practising on the roof of a London hotel to "beat the socks off the old man"—his own words. For the reason—read below.

Monkey Has "Day Out"—Wrecks Shop

Mrs. Rawlings's first impulse was to run for the fire brigade when she saw the crowd outside her husband's pet-shop in Clapham-road, London, S.W.

But they were watching a monkey which had escaped from its cage and was having a "field day" in the shop.

These were its activities:—

Opened bird-cages;

Turned over gold-fish bowls and jumped on the fish;

Stamped on wire cages and squashed them flat;

Danced round the shop with a kitten in its arms;

And finally—bit an assistant.

It did £30 worth of damage.

BABY GOLF MASCOT TO KNOCK SPOTS OFF HIS CHAMPION FATHER

BY A SPECIAL CORRESPONDENT

BUDDY Guldahl, two-and-a-half-year-old mascot of the American Ryder Cup golf team, was throwing a temperament when I called to see him with his mother at the Savoy Hotel last night.

Three feet of brawn and determination, his big brown eyes expressed resentment against life in general, and he refused for a long time to say anything.

Cause of the trouble was that his father, 6ft. 2½in. Ralph Guldahl, American open champion, had taken a mean advantage, gone off to play a practice round at Trent Park while Buddy was having his afternoon nap.

Buddy hates to be away from his father when he plays golf. His miniature golf-bag trimmed with Scotch tartan propped up against the settee, he swung his midget 22in. driver at random "just to let you folks know how mad I am."

Since he was fifteen months old Buddy has travelled all over the United States and Canada watching his father play in tournaments. In his grey tweed knickerbockers and Homburg hat he often steals most of the glory.

Whenever he sees a crowd round his father he stands a little way off, swings his tiny driver in professional style and waits for the crowd to collect.

"You just wait," he said to me in between wild swings, "I'll beat the socks off my old man when I grow up. I'm just a natural born golfer, that's what I am."

Buddy's particular ambition at the moment is to drive a ball off the roof of his hotel into the Thames.

"I guess I'm off my drive, or sump'n," he said. "I couldn't seem to hit a ball properly this morning."

LORD SYSONBY

IN the report published in the *Daily Mirror* of June 11 of a blood transfusion from Lord Sysonby to his butler, Alfred Jackman, in an effort to save the latter's life, it was stated that Lord Sysonby was shooting with Mr. Jackman at the time when the latter was wounded.

This was incorrect; Lord Sysonby was not with Mr. Jackman at the time of the accident.

We desire to express our sincere regret to Lord Sysonby for any misapprehension which may have arisen.

ON THE WARPATH?

General Goering, German Air Minister (wearing civilian dress) driving to the Cabinet meeting yesterday, at which Germany's course of action in regard to Spain was decided.

MONDAY, JUNE 28, 1937

Daily Mirror

No. 10473 Registered at the G.P.O. as a Newspaper. ONE PENNY

4 KILLED, 20 HURT, AS TRAIN CRASHES INTO TRUCKS

Piled-up wreckage of the two leading coaches of Southern Railway train which crashed into two stationary trucks at Swanley Junction just before midnight. Four people were killed.—Special "Daily Mirror" picture.

FROM OUR SPECIAL CORRESPONDENT

THREE WOMEN AND A MAN WERE KILLED AND TWENTY PEOPLE WERE INJURED WHEN THE FOLKESTONE - LONDON EXPRESS JUMPED THE POINTS AND CRASHED INTO A SIDING AT SWANLEY JUNCTION, KENT, AT 11.20 LAST NIGHT.

The engine hit two stationary trucks and an electrical transformer, mounted the transformer, and the two leading coaches were telescoped.

The driver and fireman escaped, although the engine rolled over on the permanent way.

The train was travelling via Ashford.

Just before the crash the driver leaped from the footplate. The fireman was buried under the wreckage of the driver's cab, while behind him maimed and shattered passengers struggled for life out of a mass of twisted steel and crushed woodwork.

Steel corridor coaches saved the rest of the train. All the dead and seriously injured were in the first and second coaches.

The occupants of the first three compartments directly behind the tender were uninjured.

They were thrown 10ft. into the air as the coach snapped its coupling and reared above the smashed engine and tender.

Only the rear portion of the first coach was wrecked. It bored its way right through the second coach. The second coach was stripped of its seats and wrecked. It looked as if it had been blown up by dynamite.

The dead man's name was Brewer.

Two women are unidentified. The third woman had "D.R." initials on her handkerchief.

Dr. Dawson Crawford and Dr. Smith, of Swanley Junction, and station officials worked for twenty minutes with handsaws releasing the trapped passengers until fire brigades from Dartford, Ewnsford, Swanley and Wilmington arrived.

Ambulances from Orpington, Dartford and Farningham were rushed to the scene. Police came from Dartford, Farningham and Bromley in cars.

By 1.30 all the injured had been treated.

L.P.T.B. ran buses from Swanley garage to take passengers to the district home.

Mr. F. Meredith, of Maidstone, a passenger, told me:—

"We were doing about forty-five when there was a terrific crash and we were all thrown on top of each other.

"We worked our way out of the carriage and struggled to release as many passengers as we could. Their courage was magnificent.

"One man with a broken leg laughed and chatted with us while we were digging him out.

"Nearby a woman, her legs terribly smashed, bled to death before we could get her out.

"The train was full.

"All passengers who could helped in the rescue work for half an hour before firemen and police arrived."

Mr. Ernest Cook, of Billet-lane, Usk, who had been waiting for a train at Swanley Junction, said:—

"I saw the driver staggering down the line. He seemed dazed, and kept muttering, 'Where's my mate?'

"We sent him away so that he shouldn't see the worst. For by that time I saw the front of the train was smashed to matchwood.

"I couldn't believe that anybody could be alive in the second coach. A middle-aged man was pinned down in one of the compartments, but he managed to squeeze his head out of the window and shout out directions as to how to release the others.

"It was the bravest thing I have ever seen.

"One girl who had her legs terribly crushed did not murmur. When we carried her out she had a smile on her face.

Doctors, nurses and ambulances were mobilised and arrangements were made for the injured to be taken to Dartford County Hospital.

TUESDAY, JUNE 29, 1937

Daily Mirror

No. 10474 Registered at the G.P.O. as a Newspaper. ONE PENNY

BRITAIN MIGHTIER THAN EVER: READY FOR ANY DANGER OF WAR

SIR THOMAS INSKIP, MINISTER FOR DEFENCE, REVEALED YESTERDAY THAT BRITAIN IS NOW FULLY PREPARED AGAINST WAR.

He announced at a meeting of the London Chamber of Commerce that :—

Our Navy is the most powerful and efficient in history;

One hundred and twenty-three new air squadrons have been formed in the past eighteen months;

The Regular Army is expected to be at its peak strength by the end of this year.

Vast reserves of fuel and other essential commodities that might be cut off by blockade have been accumulated to meet any emergency.

"What we are doing," said Sir Thomas, "marks another stage in the attainment of peace. The more determined we are to defend ourselves the more we shall be able to co-operate with the nations for the maintenance of peace."

The Navy's Power

Dealing with the progress of Britain's rearmament, Sir Thomas Inskip said :—

"The Navy's readiness for her task is much greater than it was twelve months ago.

"Our battleships will be the best-protected yet built. Our cruisers and destroyers will provide the highest standard of efficiency in gun-armament that is possible to-day.

"One of the things that hinders recruiting for the Army is the fear that when a man comes out he will not find a career satisfactory to him or his family.

"I hope that the City of London will do something to diminish that apprehension. These men are the salt of the population. They should be helped and encouraged as much as possible.

"We will get the men into the Service when they know that their future is assured.

3,400 More Pilots

"The Air Force has done very well indeed. Since the beginning of 1935 we have had over 3,400 entrants as air pilots and 28,000 airmen have been enlisted, whilst 123 squadrons have been formed at home.

"Considerable supplies of essential commodities are now available for any emergency."

General Goering complained in a Berlin speech yesterday that Germany had not enough essential commodities, and declared that she needed colonies to provide them. He added:

"Just as Germany must be able to rely finally upon her own sword alone to defend her territory, so must she be economically self-supporting, if she is to preserve her independence, her honour and her international prestige."

Plague of caterpillars is devastating trees in the Broads in Suffolk. Here is a tree, every leaf eaten away and the trunk covered with a web of ghostly white. other pictures on pages 14 and 15.

CATERPILLAR HAVOC ATTACKS TWO AREAS IN BRITAIN

PLAGUES of millions of caterpillars are attacking two widely-separated areas in Britain.

The affected areas are along the banks of the River Waveney, in Norfolk and Suffolk, and between the Ochil Hills and Kirkcudbright in Scotland.

Willow trees on the river banks extending from Beccles to Burgh St. Peter, Norfolk, are covered with a small brown caterpillar believed to have arrived from the tropics last year.

Their webs have coloured trunks and branches a fantastic silver while every piece of green foliage has been eaten away.

The menace is heightened by the fact that the birds do not appear to feed on the caterpillars.

The Only Hope

"We tried spraying the trees with a solution," Mr. Mobbs, borough surveyor of Lowestoft, told the *Daily Mirror* last night, "but this had little effect.

"We are afraid the insects might extend operations inland. The only hope of repelling them is a very severe winter, during which their nests would be destroyed."

Valuable pasture land in Scotland is being laid waste by a species of caterpillar sometimes two inches long.

The pests are able to cover a mile a day, and in some parts of the Dollar Area are two feet deep. One farmer has lost 1,000 acres of pasture.

Rain has washed thousands of the caterpillars into reservoirs—leading to fear of contamination.

Mrs. Freestone.

Bath Scene Ban Doesn't Worry Marlene Dietrich

Marlene Dietrich is not worried because the U.S. censor's office have heavily cut the bath scene in her new British-made film "Knight Without Armour."

Scene shows Marlene in her bath—covered with foam up to her neck.

"They know their business, and perhaps they know best," she told the "Daily Mirror" New York correspondent yesterday.

CHILD BRIDE, WED TO GIVE HER BABY A NAME, ISSUES "WARNING TO GIRLS"

"I AM not afraid of the whole country knowing about this. I hope it will be a warning to girls everywhere to be very careful about men. I have gone through a terrible time since I knew everything."

A lovely sixteen-year-old bride, who is soon to be a mother, yesterday told the *Daily Mirror* of her experiences, in order to save other young girls from similar unhappiness.

Married on February 13 at the Roman Catholic Church of St. Marie, Bury, Elizabeth Freestone, of Gigg-lane, Bury, was granted a separation order at Bury Police Court yesterday.

Mrs. Eaton, Elizabeth's mother, will care for her during the birth of the baby.

Elizabeth told the "Daily Mirror" :—

"I am going to be brave.

"I know this means publicity, but I am glad because I do hope that it will be a lesson to other young girls.

"I met Bill at the mill where I was working as a weaver.

"He fascinated me, and I, knowing little of what love meant, thought I loved him. Now I know that it was not love.

"He used to take me home from work and we went out in the evenings. It was a change from dancing, and I thought we would be happy.

"But I knew before we were married that I did not love him. I married him to give my baby a name.

"I had not been out with boys before, and I say to all young girls—be very careful and always confide completely in your mothers. I have made a terrible mistake, and I hope that it will save other girls from what I am going through."

A Baby Next Month

Mrs. Freestone added that she lived with her husband only seven weeks before they parted.

She stated in court earlier in the day that her husband, William Freestone, twenty-four, warehouse hand, of Ford-street, Stockport, hit her three times in five weeks and had tried to choke her.

When the case was called the clerk handed the girl a letter from her husband. She read it, then said firmly: "I think the case should be heard."

"Efforts had been made to bring the couple together," said the clerk. The girl said she could not go back to her husband.

"He has been beastly with me," she told the Court, adding quietly: "I am expecting a baby next month."

The separation order was granted on the grounds of persistent cruelty, and Freestone is to pay his wife 10s a week.

FRIDAY, JULY 2, 1937

Daily Mirror

No. 10477 — Registered at the G.P.O. as a Newspaper. — ONE PENNY

FOILED AT GRETNA BY FATHER'S 'PLANE DASH, LOVER SOBS, "I LOVE HER"

BY A SPECIAL CORRESPONDENT

"WON'T you please tell Mr. Carr from me that I love his daughter, that I know Martha loves me, and that all we want to do is to put this terrible affair straight?"

This was the sobbing appeal made to me last night by Herr Richard Strausz-Hupe, handsome thirty-four-year-old Austrian, back in London after a futile dash to Gretna Green with Miss Martha Carr, seventeen-year-old daughter of an American millionaire, Mr. George Russell Carr.

Chartering an aeroplane from Croydon at dawn yesterday, Mr. Carr flew to Carlisle, motored to Glencaple, a little seaside resort forty miles from Gretna Green, found his daughter, and flew back with her.

Mr. Carr told the whole story last night at Claridge's Hotel, where he is staying with his daughter.

Started Flight at Dawn

It was late on Wednesday night, he said, when Martha 'phoned him from Glencaple, where, she explained, she was staying with a friend.

"I 'phoned a friend," continued Mr. Carr, "and when he told me Glencaple was near Gretna Green, I rang up Croydon and chartered a 'plane.

"At dawn I started.

"I flew to near Dumfries, and motored from there to Glencaples and found her."

"She was on one floor of the hotel, and her man friend on the other. You should have seen her face when I tapped on her door!

"She was darned glad to see me. She's feeling a little sorry for herself. You know what these moonlight romances are.

"Well, we didn't give her friend time to think, I hustled her into the car, and raced for the 'plane."

Herr Strausz-Hupe followed by the first train for London.

"It was just a perfectly ordinary attempt to get married," he said to me. There was no elopement—nothing secret.

"It is simply this. Martha and I love each other—dearly. We just want to get married. We thought we could do it quickly in Scotland and the only way of finding out how was to go up there and try.

"We did not attempt to conceal that from Mr. Carr. Martha telephoned him saying exactly what we were going to do. And there was nothing improper about it—a friend of mine was with us all the time.

(Continued on back page)

THE QUEEN'S DEBUTANTE COUSIN GOES TO COURT

Making a charming picture with the breeze blowing her veil around her . . . Miss Sarah Susannah Bowes-Lyon, seventeen-year-old cousin of the Queen, leaving for the Palace to attend last night's Coronation Court. Below: Miss Mauricette MacGillecuddy, of Melbourne, an Australian debutante.

The Queen's gown was of gold brocade in a scroll design with a train of cloth of gold.

FARR-LOUIS FIGHT IS FIXED

MR. Ted Broadribb, manager for Tommy Farr, the British heavy-weight champion, announced last night that he had accepted terms over the radio telephone from New York for Farr to meet Joe Louis for the world heavy-weight championship early in September in New York.

Asked about the proposed fight between Schmeling and Farr, Mr. Broadribb said, "That's out."

Mike Jacobs, manager for Joe Louis, stated in New York last night, reports British United Press, that he had guaranteed Farr a certain sum or 20 per cent. of the net receipts.

"I wanted Schmeling," Jacobs added, "but, apparently, Max does not want to fight. Anyway, he will not reply to my cables, so I am going ahead with Farr, and I have cabled him to be ready to sail in two weeks."

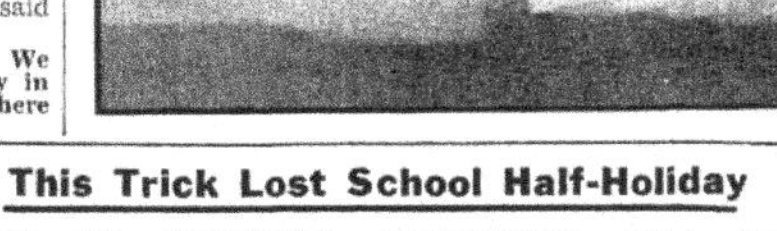

This Trick Lost School Half-Holiday

'BEER IS BEST' NOTICE ON DESK

BY A SPECIAL CORRESPONDENT

BOYS and girls of Southall County School, Middlesex, had the biggest laugh of the term yesterday. Alderman E. B. Hamblin, J.P., Mayor of Southall, had just finished his address and stepped forward to remove the sheet from a reading desk, a Coronation gift from the Town Council. Suddenly the respectful silence was broken by peal upon peal of laughter.

The headmaster and officials on the platform became uneasy. One of them leaned forward and gazed at the desk in horror.

Across the front, in bold red letters, was the slogan: "BEER IS BEST."

Councillors present smiled, but the school staff sat in stony silence.

Afterwards, Mr. C. G. Vernon, headmaster, said to me:

"The act was one of gross impertinence on the part of a boy not yet known.

"I cannot say what action I will take but the half-holiday promised to the school to-morrow afternoon has been cancelled."

The King Honours R.A.F.

For the first time since her Coronation the Queen wore her crown last night at the third Court of the Coronation season at Buckingham Palace.

And the King created a precedent by wearing the grey-blue uniform of Marshal of the Royal Air Force.

Never before has it been worn at a Court by the Sovereign.

The arches of the Queen's crown were removed to form a regal circlet in diamonds of cross-patees and fleur-de-lys.

NORROY KING OF ARMS

We have been asked to point out that the picture published in the *Daily Mirror* yesterday as Sir Gerald Wollaston, was a photograph of Algar Howard, Esq., Norroy King of Arms. We regret any inconvenience caused by this error

SATURDAY, JULY 3, 1937

Daily Mirror

No. 10478 Registered at the G.P.O. as a Newspaper. ONE PENNY

LATE LDN ED.

"LADY LINDY'S" OCEAN SOS:

FUEL FOR THIRTY MINUTES

"I HAVE ONLY HALF-AN-HOUR'S FUEL LEFT, AND I CANNOT SEE LAND."

That was the radio message sent out last night from her 'plane over the Pacific by Miss Amelia Earhart ("Lady Lindy") who started a "just-for-fun" round the world flight on June 1.

A coastguard cutter was this morning searching for the 'plane from Howland Island, between Hawaii and Fiji.

It was for this island that Miss Earhart was making when she set out on Thursday night from Lae, New Guinea—2,570 miles away.

WASHINGTON ORDERS SEARCH

Hours after the mid-ocean SOS, there was no sign of the 'plane.

From Washington, urged by frantic messages from "Lady Lindy's" husband, Mr. George Putnam, the wealthy publisher, orders were sent to Honolulu:—

"Send every available ship to search."

Howland island is two miles long, and only a few feet above sea level, and a difficult target for an aeroplane.

But, says Reuter, Miss Earhart had confidence that Captain Norman, her navigator, would find it.

Their all metal 'plane could not keep afloat for long, but carries a rubber lifeboat.

LOOPHOLES FOR CRIME

The present "inadequate" system of death certification for burials leaves many loopholes for crime," declared Lord Horder at the conference of the National Association of Funeral Directors at Portsmouth yesterday.

Lord Horder held that it should be made impossible for those engaged in certain trades to practise as funeral directors.

The Runaway Heiress

Seventeen-year-old Miss Martha Carr, whose millionaire father followed her to Scotland by 'plane, and foiled her dash to Gretna Green with Herr Richard Strausz-Hupe.

Foiled Lover

NOT TO FOLLOW SWEETHEART

BY A SPECIAL CORRESPONDENT

AFTER his romantic dash to Gretna Green with seventeen-year-old American, Martha Carr, Mr. Richard Strausz-Hupe, thirty-four-year-old Hungarian member of a New York firm of stockbrokers, is going to spend a quiet week-end in London.

While Martha was flown to the Continent early yesterday morning by her father, Mr. George Carr, Chicago chemical manufacturer, Mr. Strausz-Hupe sat disconsolately in his luxurious Chesham-place flat.

"I'm doing nothing at all for the next few days," he told me last night. "At the moment I am certainly not thinking of crossing the Channel after Martha.

"I prefer to remain in the background from now on."

Mr. Strausz-Hupe left his flat once only yesterday to visit his solicitors.

Martha and her father's luggage was packed before dawn, and after an early breakfast they left Claridge's for Croydon.

Mr. Carr had booked rooms at the fashionable Hotel Adlon, in Berlin, but they got to Croydon too late to catch the air liner to the German capital.

They left later in another air liner for Paris.

PLAY THRILL WAS A MISFIRE

BIG thrill in the Elmer Rice play, "Judgment Day" at the Strand Theatre misfired last night. . . . Because a revolver misfired!

"Down with tyranny!" roared Judge Slatarski, levelling a revolver at Vesnic, the Dictator, and pulling the trigger.

Nothing happened. The audience waited for the report; actors looked bewildered.

Then, with lightning presence of mind, Alan Wheatley collapsed and "died"

Hubert Harben, playing the judge, looked relieved and the play went on.

MYSTERY WARSHIP FIRES ON SPANISH PORT

FIFTEEN SHELLS WERE FIRED ON THE PORT OF SAGUNTO, EIGHTEEN MILES NORTH OF VALENCIA, LAST NIGHT, BY AN UNKNOWN WARSHIP.

DETAILS ARE SO FAR LACKING, SAYS BRITISH UNITED PRESS. **(Spain Crisis News—Page 3.)**

27 DIE IN PIT: MOTHER OF 11 WIDOWED

Twenty-seven men lost their lives yesterday in a series of terrible explosions in the Holditch mine of Brymbo Colliery, Chesterton, near Stoke-on-Trent.

FOUR bodies have been recovered, and five men have died in hospital, but eighteen more dead still lie beyond a barrier of flame in the pit.

Nine other men lie injured in hospital.

Wives and mothers were still standing in silence at the pit head last night—hoping against hope, refusing to believe that their men were dead.

Most tragic family of all is that of Josiah Cooke of London-road, Chesterton—one of the men who died in hospital.

"Need Never Have Gone"

His thirty-five-year-old widow is left with a family of eleven young children to provide for. Only a few hours after he had been brought out of the pit, relatives and neighbours have come to the help of the distraught young widow.

"The tragedy of it is," said one of the relatives, "that Josiah need never have gone down the pit.

'He left about 6.15 this morning, and from what we hear before he went down the pit there was a call for rescue volunteers.

"Josiah, we are told, was one of the first of the volunteers. That was the sort of man he was. He had worked in the pit since he was a boy, like his father before him.

"Save My Son"

There was a pathetic scene shortly before one of the rescue teams came up, when an old lady dressed in black, and sobbing, tottered to the pithead, fell on her knees and cried: "God, give me strength. My son is down there. Oh God, save my son!"

The dead are nearly all members of rescue teams who entered the pit after the first explosion which followed an outbreak of fire at 6.30 a.m.

The disasters began while a group of forty nightshift coal-cutters were working. There was a cry of "Fire." A cascade of sparks was seen near some machinery.

"Run for it," shouted the overman

The men ran for the pit bottom, three-quarters of a mile away. Then came the first explosion, which killed three miners.

Rescue teams descended, and while they worked, saving the injured from the blazing coalface and sealing off the affected areas, the second explosion occurred.

Late last night the fire was still blazing, and flooding was begun to damp it out.

TUESDAY, JULY 6, 1937

Daily Mirror

No. 10480 Registered at the G.P.O. as a Newspaper. ONE PENNY

BRITISH SHIP NEAR LADY LINDY

AS SHE RADIOS 'SINKING'

NEW hope for Miss Amelia Earhart, America's Lady Lindy, and her navigator Captain Fred Noonan was given last night by a faint radio message, giving their position as 281 miles north of Howland Island, in the Pacific.

A British freighter, the Moorby, was within ninet(miles of the position late last night, and was steaming full speed to the rescue.

Miss Earhart's message, says Reuter, reads:—

"281 North Howland . . . Call KHAQQ (Miss Earhart's call letters) . . . Beyond north . . . Don't hold with us much longer above water. . . ."

It was picked up by three U.S. Navy operators at Honolulu between 1.30 p.m. and 2.30 p.m. (B.S.T.).

The Mooby, bound for Sydney, reported that she heard a "strong continuous carrier wave frequency" at 10 a.m. B.S.T. and at 1.30 p.m. yesterday.

The U.S. coastguard cutter Itasca, which has searched north-east and north-west of Howland Island is also racing full speed to the position given. She is expected to reach the island early this morning.

Heavy Seas Running

But heavy seas are running, and there is fear that the 'plane may be swamped

There is a chance, however, that the 'plane may have grounded on a reef.

The Pan-American Radio Station yesterday instructed Miss Earhart to send out three long dashes if she were on the sea, four if she were on land.

According to her husband three long dashes were received on her wavelength almost immediately after the instruction was sent out.

Here is a timed list (all times B.S.T.) of the messages that made radio drama yesterday:—

8.5. a.m.—Honolulu reports definite radio signals on Miss Earhart's frequency, stated by Pan-American Airways to have been received in answer to instructions broadcast to missing flyers.

11.16 a.m.—Itasca hears the call letters "KHAQQ."

10. a.m-1.30 p.m.—British steamer Moorby hears a "strong, continuous carrier wave frequency."

1.30-2.30 p.m.—Honolulu picks up "sinking" message.

He Dropped in on a Friend!

The wrecked 'plane lying in the front garden of the damaged house. Inset is the pilot, Mr. J. K. Quill, photographed after the crash.

3,000 ft. DROP ENDS IN FRIEND'S GARDEN

LEAPING from a crashing 'plane 3,000ft. over New Malden, Surrey, last night, twenty-four-year-old test pilot, J. K. Quill, of Weybridge, landed safely by parachute on top of a fir tree and found himself in the garden of a friend he hadn't seen for years.

Captain L. Peety, of Brooklands Flying Club, was sitting at dinner with his wife in their home at Coombe-lane, Malden, when Mr. Quill landed in the garden.

"Hello," he said, as he helped him from the tree.

"Hello," grinned back his friend. "I think I would like a glass of beer." He was bleeding from the face and hands.

Sitting alone in a back room of her house in Woodlands-avenue, Coombe Hill, not far away,

(Continued on back page)

Tommy Farr, in the Big Money, Is "Fed Up"

WISHES HE WAS POOR MINER AGAIN

TOMMY Farr, lifted in a few months to the £10,000-£15,000 a year class as a heavy-weight boxer, wishes he was unknown again, and working in the pits of South Wales as a miner.

He left Paris last night for Le Touquet—and a rest. Before he went he told the *Daily Mirror*

"Everywhere I go I am surrounded by autograph-hunters and people wanting to talk to me. I am tired of it all.

"I Want to Get Away"

"I was far happier when I worked in the pits, when nobody knew me. I want to get away."

As Tommy talked in Paris, the big fight tangle in which he has become involved became more complicated than ever.

First it was announced by Ted Broadribb, Farr's manager, that Louis and Farr will meet in America, early in September.

Then Syd Hulls, Harringay promoter, declared that he has a contract for Farr to box Schmeling in London, also in September.

Peter Wilson's comment—page 30.

WARNING ALL THIEVES 'FUTILE' BURGLARY TEST

"FUTILE," was a comment at Sunbury Council last night when it was announced, following the council's demand for more police patrols in its streets, that the police were to hold a demonstration "burglary test" to try to prove that help can be speedily summoned in the event of burglaries.

Said Mr. G. Mason: "What is the use of a demonstration when everybody knows it is going to happen? It's futile. Are the police to drop like ghosts from heaven?"

Letters were read from Feltham Council, endorsing Sunbury's complaints, and from a local tenant, who wrote that he was giving up his property on account of the burglaries. As soon as he replaced stolen property it was stolen again—and he was leaving the district.

No decision was made pending a question in the House by Sir Reginald Blaker.

DE VALERA LEADS BY ONE

With eleven results still to be declared, Mr. de Valera last night had a clear majority of one seat over all other parties in the Irish Free State election.

The state of the parties late last night was: de Valera, 64; Cosgrave, 44; Labour, 11; Independent, 8; total, 127.

FRIDAY, JULY 9, 1937

Daily Mirror

No. 10483 Registered at the G.P.O. as a Newspaper ONE PENNY

JAPANESE BOMBARD CHINESE TOWN: TANKS, 'PLANES IN ACTION

She Says Buchmanites Are "Indecent"...

"It is to me as shocking—shocking in the Victorian sense—as indecent and indelicate as if someone took off all his clothes in the middle of Piccadilly-circus."

In these words, Margaret Rawlings, here seen as she appears in "Black Limelight," the play now running at the Duke of York's Theatre, yesterday attacked the Oxford Group practice of public confession.

Miss Rawlings, who was speaking at a literary luncheon in London, said that she wanted to make an appeal for modesty. **See story on page 3.**

As Mr. Chamberlain was warning a London audience last night that "We should not allow our attention to be wholly concentrated on Spain" war flared up between Japanese and Chinese near Peiping (Pekin), the great city in the north of China that was once the capital.

Negotiations to settle the dispute were at a deadlock at midnight.

MARTIAL law has been proclaimed in Peiping and train services have been stopped.

The city gates are closed and closely guarded to prevent the entry of Japanese troops.

While in Peiping itself Japanese troops placed machine guns in position and erected sandbag emplacements at the Japanese Embassy. Chinese youths in ragged grey uniforms manned the walls of Wanpin, the city at the northern end of the Marco Polo Bridge (north of Peiping), near where fighting first broke out.

They were in cheerful spirits. Armed with automatic rifles they said: "We will resist any attack."

Sandbags and Guns

Others were preparing positions at both ends of the Marco Polo Bridge, digging trenches and placing sandbags in position.

Officers said the Japanese had bombarded the town. More than 200 shells had been fired and many soldiers and civilians were killed.

Fighting broke out first when a section of Japanese troops were carrying out night manœuvres, part of which was a sham attack on the town of Wanpin.

According to the Japanese, Chinese troops in the town mistook the sham for a real attack and opened fire.

The Chinese say, however, that the Japanese trespassed o the Chinese garrison area

Tanks field-guns, tanks and aeroplanes are being brought up by the Japanese, and these tanks are patrolling the Chinese town of Tientsin

A spokesman for the Hopei-Chahar Political Council, said: "If the Japanese cross the railway north of the Wanpinghsin Wall (north of the Marco Polo bridge), then the Chinese will fire on them."

After battles between Japanese and Chinese troops near Peiping, negotiations in Peiping for a settlement were at a deadlock at midnight (5 o'c. B.S.T.)

Danger of a new flare-up was increasing with every hour's delay.

Soviet Protests

Meanwhile, a stern protest was made by M. Litvinov, Soviet Foreign Commissar, against alleged reappearance of Japanese and Manchukuoan forces on the disputed border islands of Bolshoi and Sennukha on the Amur River that divides Siberia (Soviet territory) from Manchukuo (under Japanese control).

The Japanese Navy Ministry has instructed the Third Fleet to stand by. The War Office has deferred Army discharges.

Japanese military chiefs were said last night to be drafting demands for the extension of their influence in North China.

Messages Reuter and British United Press

VILLAGE VICAR'S WIFE BANS "TRASHY" BOOKS—IS NO LONGER LIBRARIAN

FROM OUR OWN CORRESPONDENT

MARKS CROSS (Sussex), Thursday

THEY have been at cross purposes in Marks Cross about books. The vicar's wife who "censored" the village library, has resigned, and a working man's wife who called a parish meeting about it all is the new librarian.

This is the point of view of Mrs. Hamshere, ex-librarian: "Someone brought me a book from the village library and it was most suggestive.

"To avoid getting that sort of trashy literature in the library, some friends and I used to go through the batches as they arrived from Lewes and rejected all those we thought undesirable.

"If I can't have the right to sort out undesirable books, I will not be librarian."

Says Mrs. Lilliot, the new librarian: "Certain books sent out by the county library at Lewes were not available for the villagers. We don't want to be told what to read—and anyway the county library passes them. That ought to be enough.

"Not that I care tuppence for risque books or sexy novels, but I like to pick my own."

Marks Cross will now be free to choose what books it likes.

Mrs. Lilliot, a Dickens fan, has now formed a committee of five villagers to choose the literature.

"I know I am likely to be called a bright young thing for this," was her last word to me. "I don't care. I want to pick my own books. So does my husband—and that's that."

And she picked up the latest crime novel and sat down to a cup of tea

Have You PHOTO-BRAINS?

If you have a camera, prepare to use it now. It may win you substantial prizes in a fascinating new "Daily Mirror" competition, full details of which are given on page 3.

Each week throughout the summer prizes of £10, £5 and £2 will be awarded for the best photograph illustrating one of four ideas which will be printed in the "Daily Mirror" every Monday.

Now turn to page 3—and get your camera ready to shoot.

HUSBAND ON POISON CHARGE

BY A SPECIAL CORRESPONDENT

SIXTY-SIX-YEAR-OLD James Williams, shopkeeper, of City Garden-row, Islington, N., was arrested and charged last night with attempting to administer poison to his thirty-eight-year-old wife.

The charge followed inquiries by the police over a wide area in London.

Williams will appear at Old-street Police Court to-day.

Mrs. Williams, who is staying with relatives in London, is the daughter of a captain in the United States Navy.

Mr. and Mrs. Williams had been living above the shop for the past twelve months.

Mrs. Williams.

SIR ABE BAILEY: BULLETIN

Sir Abe Bailey, who has been suffering from a clot of blood in the artery of his leg, yesterday underwent a serious operation in London.

Sir Abe is seventy-three. He was stated last night to be "As well as can be expected."

MONDAY, JULY 12, 1937

Daily Mirror

No. 10485 Registered at the G.P.O. as a Newspaper. ONE PENNY

£200,000 'KING OF JAZZ' DIES —HE SHUNNED GIRLS, NIGHT CLUB REVELS

A "King of Jazz" . . . George Gershwin, creator of "Rhapsody in Blue," famous theme of which is seen below.

George ("Rhapsody in Blue") Gershwin, ex-£5-a-week show rehearsal pianist, who made £200,000 out of syncopated "hits," died yesterday at the age of thirty-eight in a Hollywood Hospital after an operation for a tumour on the brain.

AND last night in London, pale and shocked at the news, Louis Dreyfus, who gave Gershwin his first job, told the "Daily Mirror": "It never occurred to him to invest any of that £200,000 in a wife. He never seemed to think about girls.

"After 'Rhapsody in Blue' made him world famous he didn't alter. He was just the same—quiet and reserved. He was never one for gadding about and going to parties."

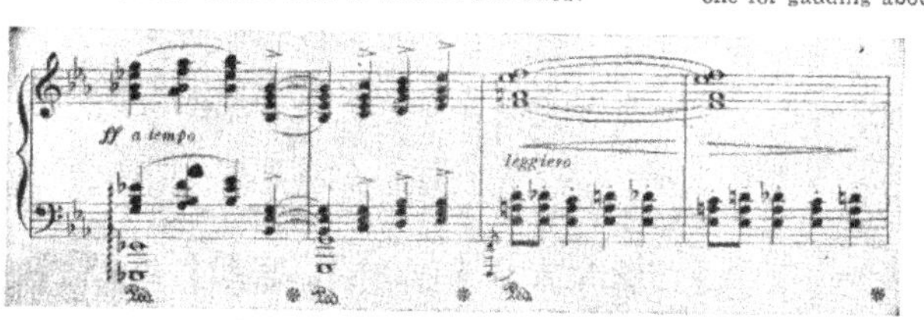

Louis Dreyfus, millionaire music publisher, attending a dinner party in Regent's Park, N.W., paused. His voice broke as he passed on to his fellow guests the "Daily Mirror's" news—"George Gershwin is dead."

He was so shaken that he left at once for the quietness of his own home in Wimbledon Park.

There he explained to the *Daily Mirror* that he and his brother are partners in Harms, one of the leading music publishing businesses in the United States.

"Years ago," he said "a young, serious, rather pale-looking fellow walked into our office. He said his name was George Gershwin, that he thought he could compose music.

His "Swanee" Success

"We told him to sit down at the piano and see what he could do. He only played a few bars, but Max looked over at me and said, 'That boy's got something.'

"We hired him at £5 a week. For a year he went around playing the piano at musical comedy rehearsals.

"That way he learned to compose stuff wi[th] a popular appeal.

"In his second year he told us he thought he had got something good. He played it. It was 'Swanee'—and you know how good that was.

"Then came the great 'Rhapsody in Blue.' George expressed himself in that. It was him, his thoughts, his way of expressing modern American music.

"It was a hit at once. It sold in thousands. It still does. It has had the longest run of anything we have published.

Collapsed in Studio

"But even after that he always wanted to do something more, something better."

Henry Hall's comment was: "Gershwin was a modern genius. His style was unique. 'Rhapsody in Blue' is going to live."

Only a fortnight ago Gershwin started work on a new Hollywood musical. Then he collapsed in the studio, and was taken to hospital.

Eight notes brought him fame—the eight notes that are the plaintive theme of his rhapsody which startled the world in 1925 as the first attempt to raise jazz to a symphonic level.

His syncopation genius brought him £30,000 a year—but he was ever professing that he had so much to learn of music, so little time to study.

HOST'S EGGSHELL SUIT AT ARCADIAN REVEL

Broken eggs with white and yolk glazed to the coat, breeches speckled with beetles . . . sounds like the latest in surrealist suitings but the picture is of Mr. Cecil Beaton, the photographer and artist, at the Féte Champetre which he gave at his Downland home, at Ashcombe, near Shaftesbury (Dorset) during the week-end.

His 300 guests, mainly Mayfair personalities, were asked to wear something rural and scores of Arcadian shepherds and shepherdesses drove to Ashcombe, guided by immense replicas of fauns and cupids.

Dancing went on till early yesterday morning, the host himself, changing his costume three times and finishing up as a scarecrow.

CROWDS SEE HATLESS MAN DIVE FROM PIER, DROWN

FROM OUR SPECIAL CORRESPONDENT

BRIGHTON, Sunday.

"IT'S not too rough to swim," John Phelps, a fifty-year-old man from Tilton-street, Fulham, London, said to a friend on Brighton Palace Pier to-day. He then flung down his hat, stood on the railings and dived fully clothed into the sea.

After swimming strongly for a few seconds he disappeared. Police brought his body ashore minutes later.

Phelps was a member of a charabanc party from London to Brighton organised by a Fulham club. Crowds on the pier and front saw Phelps dive into the sea.

Jack Phelps, the dead man's eldest son, of Tilton-street, Fulham, said to-night: "My father has always taken risks, and would do anything for a wager. As a boy he was known as "The Water Rat," because he was always swimming in the river.

"I can remember when I was a little boy how my father for a wager pulled me along in a rowing-boat from Putney to Mortlake by his teeth. He swam with the rope in his mouth for nearly five miles.

"He saw the sea to-day for the first time since 1919. He was very popular, and when the charabanc returned to London to-night every man in it was in tears."

Mr. Phelps leaves a widow and five children.

Have You PHOTO-BRAINS? See Page 3

5 UP FROM PIT TOMB

Five of the eighteen bodies entombed in the Brymbo pit, Chesterton, North Staffs, were recovered and brought to the surface late last night. They were those of Alfred James Bloor, fifty-one, Inspector of Mines, Newcastle-under-Lyme; H. L. Adkins, Basford, Stoke-on-Trent, under-manager of the colliery, and three workmen.

The rescue parties are now working in a pure atmosphere without breathing apparatus.

FRANCO SEEKS LOAN

General Franco is negotiating with British and American financiers for a loan of many millions, according to reports yesterday in Burgos, rebel capital, and Paris.

Representatives of the British group are said to have arrived in Burgos already (cables Reuter).

Eden Stops Yachting Trip: Page Three

WEDNESDAY, JULY 14, 1937

Daily Mirror

No. 10487 Registered at the G.P.O. as a Newspaper. ONE PENNY

INDIAN RULER'S GIRL WIFE

DIES AFTER OPERATION: WED AT 9

HIS RICHES COULD NOT SAVE HER

FROM OUR OWN CORRESPONDENT

BASLE (Switzerland), Tuesday.

MAHARANEE of Indore, beautiful, twenty-two-year-old wife of one of India's richest Princes, died in Kreis Hospital, Samadan, near here, in the early hours of the morning.

All the Maharajah's wealth—his income is £350,000 a year—had not enabled him to save the woman he loved and had married as a youth of fifteen fresh from school in England. The Maharanee was only nine when she became a bride.

The Maharanee died following an operation by Dr. Rappauer, world-famous surgeon; who was called in last night when she was raced by car to the hospital suffering from some form of infection.

The Maharajah, who was in Paris, was telephoned the news of his wife's sudden illness. He gave permission for the operation and then left immediately for Basle.

He reached the hospital a few hours after the Maharanee had died. Gently Dr. Rappauer broke the news to him, led him to his wife's bedside, where he remained for some time sitting with head bowed between his hands.

The Maharanee had one child—the Princess Usha Devi—born in the American Hospital, Paris, when she was eighteen.

The Maharanee of Indore with the Maharajah, one of India's wealthiest princes, on holiday.

Below is their only child, Princess Usha Devi, who was born in Paris

He Banned Child Marriages

The romance of the Maharajah and his girl bride was one of the most glamorous in India's history.

They came to the throne of Indore in 1926—two years after their wedding—when the Maharajah's father abdicated in his son's favour.

The abdication was caused by the ex-Maharajah's love for his favourite dancing girl, Mumtaz Begum.

One of the first acts of the young Maharajah was to sanction the introduction of a law prohibiting marriage of boys under eighteen and girls under fourteen.

The Maharajah, who is now twenty-eight, was educated partly at Cheam and later at Charterhouse.

His marriage to the Maharanee—the daughter of the junior chief of Kacal (Kolhapur) was celebrated by a month of ceremonial and feasting.

The Maharajah had to eat more than 300 dinners.

LLOYD GEORGE DISQUALIFIED

MR. Lloyd George, who for the last four years, has won the prizes for black currants at the Kent Fruit Show, was disqualified in all three classes, yesterday, because the baskets of black currants were not filled.

Had he complied with the regulations, he would have won all three prizes, the judges said.

Mr. Lloyd George's secretary told the *Daily Mirror* last night: "He was disappointed when told of the decision. But this set-back will make no difference to him.

"Set-backs, whether in politics or gardening, he is used to"

MOTHER KILLED IN ASYLUM WHILE VISITING ONLY SON

MRS. Louisa Rowley, sixty-three years old, of Bank-street, Bradley, near Bilston, Staffs, was sitting on the verandah at the County Mental Hospital, Stafford, talking to her son, whom she was visiting, when she was attacked with a plank.

She died soon afterwards. Her head was battered, it is alleged, as she lay on the ground.

An attendant rushed to her aid and Mrs. Rowley was attended by the hospital staff.

The assailant was thought to be recovering and was usually employed in the hospital grounds.

He had not shown violent tendencies before. Inquest is expected to be held to-morrow.

Mrs. Rowley's son, who is thirty-one, was admitted to the asylum in March, 1934.

REVENUE SHIP "SEIZES" YACHT

THOUSANDS of Margate visitors last night watched an Inland Revenue cutter cross the bows of a motor yacht, a mile and a half from the foreshore, and later bring her to Margate Jetty.

Inland Revenue officers later left the yacht accompanied by three men and went to Margate Police Station.

Three men will appear in court to-day on charges under the smuggling laws.

The yacht was proceeding to Herne Bay when she was stopped.

£10,000 Bank Theft Case

TWO MORE MEN ARRESTED

TWO men were arrested by Flying Squad officers late last night in connection with the £10,000 Manor Park bank robbery.

The men, a garage proprietor who is aged about seventy, and a motor mechanic, were charged and will appear at East Ham Police Court to-day.

The garage proprietor is said to live in Romford-road, Manor Park, and the mechanic in Thorold-road, Ilford.

Yesterday James Alfred Leslie Nicol, former cashier at Barclays Bank, Manor Park, was sentenced to two years' imprisonment accused of stealing £10,071 from the bank. See page 2.

LAST EARHART SEARCH

Sixty 'planes took off yesterday from the U.S. aircraft-carrier Lexington in a final attempt to locate Miss Amelia Earhart

MONDAY, JULY 19, 1937

Daily Mirror

No. 10491 Registered at the G.P.O. as a Newspaper. ONE PENNY

CHOCOLATE KING'S SON IN AIR CRASH: WIFE KILLED

Mr. Julian Rowntree with his twenty-four-year-old wife, Mrs. Beatrice Rowntree, who was killed instantly when their 'plane crashed at Brussels yesterday.

FIGHTING desperately to land his stalled monoplane at Brussels Airport yesterday, Mr. Julian Rowntree, son of the chairman of Rowntree and Co., Ltd., crashed to earth and his twenty-four-year-old wife—his sweetheart since boyhood—was crushed to death in the front cockpit.

The couple were married four years ago and Mrs. Rowntree was the mother of two sons, aged one and two.

Mr. Rowntree was taken to hospital unconscious but was allowed to leave later.

On Friday Mr. Rowntree and his wife arrived from Dusseldorf, Germany, and had just taken off for a flight to Paris on their way back to England when the disaster occurred.

Ten minutes after their machine took off from Brussels, it returned because Mr. Rowntree wanted further particulars of the route to Paris. When it was 100 feet above the landing strip i tlost speed and nose-dived.

Mrs. Rowntree, who was sitting in front, was killed instantly.

Loveliest Girl in District

The crash ended a romance which began when they were children..

Mr. Rowntree met his future wife, formerly Miss Ann Sorensen, when she lived with her Danish father at New Earswick, model village which houses the majority of the great Rowntree firm's employees.

She had red hair and a petite figure, and could act well and dance gracefully.

But it was the outdoor life that appealed to her. She was happiest when she could find time for her favourite hobby—gardening.

She left school when she was eighteen.

First Serious Accident

Mr. Rowntree told the *Daily Mirror* last night: "We arrived from Dusseldorf two days ago and spent two days in Brussels. To-day we were to have gone off to Paris. It is the first serious accident ever to happen to me."

When officials came to speak about his wife

(Continued on back page)

CHILD STOPS TAUBER SINGING

A CHILD on one of the balconies began to cry while Richard Tauber was singing in the Tower Ballroom at Blackpool last night.

Tauber stopped singing.

"I am sorry. I cannot carry on with this concert," he said. "I cannot concentrate."

A man then stood up in the audience and said: "We cannot bear with that child. This gentleman has come here to entertain us—so be reasonable."

"That goes for the people walking up and down here," cried another man in the top balcony.

The child was silenced. Tauber smiled—and went on singing.

Come as You Are..

. . . was invitation of the Rev. Donald Manners, Vicar of Felpham, near Bognor Regis, to these bathers yesterday as he showed them the hymns he had chosen for the first of his series of beach services.

During the service, attended by 200 people, many dressed in bathing costumes, shorts and beach suits photographers were asked to leave.

Special constables warned Mr. Manners that the foreshore was private property.

BISHOP BANS THE DUKE'S VICAR FROM HIS PULPITS

BALTIMORE Bishop Edward T. Helfenstein has closed every Episcopal (Anglican) pulpit in the city to Vicar Jardine, who married the Duke of Windsor and Mrs. Wallis Warfield.

Baltimore is the home town of the Duchess of Windsor.

There the Vicar has planned to tell the world on Thursday the "real reasons" for the Edward VIII abdication.

He told the *New York Times* that the Church of England had inspired his opponents in the United States to persuade charity organisations to drop their sponsorship of his lecture tour.

He indicated that he would make the accusation that a strong political alliance existed between Earl Baldwin and the Archbishop of Canterbury which forced the abdication.

Meanwhile Bishop Helfenstein declares: "I want to make it clear that I am not supporting Jardine—I certainly could not allow him to occupy a pulpit in my diocese.

"He would have to produce proper credentials from an English bishop before I should consider it."

And Vicar Jardine says to all this: "My agent Ernst has gone to Baltimore to unearth a boycott which is being planned against me."

Girls "Twin" Theft Victims

A girl assistant employed in a dairy shop in Fulham Palace-road, Fulham, went dog-racing at Wimbledon on Saturday. A thief stole £7 from her hand-bag.

The girl's friend remained at the shop on duty. While she was serving a customer, 8s. was stolen from her hand-bag.

STRANGLED

They are June Goldsmith, aged seven, and her four-year-old sister Una. See story on page 5.

TUESDAY, JULY 20, 1937

Daily Mirror

No. 10492 Registered at the G.P.O. as a Newspaper ONE PENNY

DIVORCE BILL MAY SAVE WIFE

"HAUNTED" BY GAOLED HUSBAND

LORDS last night passed the Third Reading of Mr. A. P. Herbert's Marriage Bill—and gave new hope to a woman whose tragic story horrified the assembled peers.

The woman is thirty-year-old Mrs. Christina Elizabeth Pearce, of Woolwich, S.E. Lord Eltisley, supporting the Bill, read this letter he had received from her:—

"I am married to a man who, after making my life a living hell, threw nitric acid over my face.

"For this he received seven years' penal servitude. He still threatens me from prison that when he comes out he will claim me if he can find me.

"I have spent nine months in hospital, and for two or three months my face was under plastic surgery. I shall be in and out of hospital for another twelve months.

"I wonder if it is worth while going on, as no doubt he may do me more damage next time.

"I only wish you and your fellow members could see how disfigured I am. It might help things very much.

"I am left with a baby to care for and my strength and health are gone. I cannot marry and secure the protection of another man until the Bill is passed. What am I to do?"

"I Wore a Mask"

Mrs. Pearce, once lovely, now scarred for life, revealed to the *Daily Mirror* last night how she has had three homes in five months to hide from the husband she fears.

So great is her fear that she is seeking to have her three-year-old girl legally adopted, and thus prevent the husband claiming her.

Said Mrs. Pearce:—

"It was last September, after I had applied for a separation order against my husband, that he attacked me.

"I had already left home but he invited me to the pictures, asked me to talk things over. On the way home he threw this terrible fluid all over me, almost burning away my face.

"When he was tried at the Old Bailey I went there wearing a mask.

"Afterwards, when he was in gaol, he wrote threatening letters to me and I realised that I was tied for life to this man who robbed me of happiness.

"For months I suffered, mentally and physically. Then, like a ray of hope, came the Marriage Bill.

"A few weeks ago I wrote to Lord Eltisley, put my case before him. I also wrote to Mr. Herbert.

"My Only Happiness"

"Apart from the misery of being stared at by curious people I am faced with the terrible fact that if my husband comes out of gaol he can legally claim both me and my child as the separation case had been adjourned when the trial took place.

"I shall never forget how, after fourteen weeks, I was allowed to see my little child Alma. I dreaded that she would not recog-

(Continued on back page)

HERE ON HOLIDAY

King Carol of Rumania coming ashore at Dover yesterday from the cross-Channel steamer Cote d'Argent. He's spending part of his five weeks' holiday in England.

Tommy May Get 1s. a Day Rise

The War Office is considering increasing regular soldiers' pay by a shilling a day, writes the "Daily Mirror" political correspondent.

This would add about two million pounds to the Army estimate.

Lack of recruits is worrying the Government, and concessions made so far are not securing sufficient soldiers.

Barley Sugar Soldiers—page 2.

SHE LOOKED AT DEATH AND PRAYED

Margaret Stewart, aged fifteen, was trapped with a girl friend on a sandbank in the Solway Firth. The water rose above their chins.

Margaret could swim but she stayed by her friend, holding her up. They held hands under the water . . . kissed goodbye.

Margaret prayed . . . they were rescued.

(Story on page 3.)

BISHOPS AND POLICE FIGHT IN STREET

FROM OUR OWN CORRESPONDENT

BELGRADE, Monday.

BISHOPS and priests fought a hand-to-hand battle with the police in the streets of Belgrade to-night.

A double row of armed police tried to bar a procession formed as a protest against the ratification of a new concordat with the Vatican, which is being forced through Parliament.

The Bishops and priests, waving holy banners and holding their crucifixes before them, pushed through, only to be met every twenty yards or so by new rows of police.

Crucifixes, torn from the hands of priests, were trampled underfoot in the struggle, and the holy banners, covered with crosses, torn to shreds.

The aged Bishop of Shabat fell to the ground, blood streaming down his face from a wound in the forehead, his great jewelled Bishop's crown dented and askew. Bishop Simeon was carried unconscious into the cathedral near by.

Five thousand followers of the priests dispersed after the police fixed bayonets.

GIRL GIVES SPEECH ON MOTHER'S CRUELTY, LEAPS FROM THIRD STORY

FROM OUR OWN CORRESPONDENT

NEW YORK, Monday.

EIGHTEEN-YEAR-OLD Alice Elizabeth Gallow, of Boston, was beaten with ropes by her mother and sister, then tied to a table for staying out after midnight.

She freed herself, made her way to a third-story fire escape.

There she made a speech to passers-by, telling them of the cruelties inflicted on her by her Puritanical mother and sister.

"I prefer death to being a prisoner," cried Alice. "Remember what you see so that you can tell it in court."

Jumped 45 ft.

Her horrified audience then saw her leap 45ft to the pavement.

The girl was taken to hospital in a critical condition.

Mother and sister are meanwhile facing charges of assault.

CUSTOMS CHARGES AGAINST WOMEN

MISS Stella Mary Locker-Lampson, of Markham-street, Chelsea, a daughter of Mr. Godfrey Locker-Lampson, former Under Secretary for the Home Office and Foreign Affairs, is among defendants against whom Customs summonses will be heard at Folkestone to-day.

Summonses concern the alleged importation of dresses, hats and other clothing.

The other defendants are: Elsie Nell Miller, Upper Cheyne-row, Chelsea, Vera K. Boys, Reeves Mews, W., and Marjorie Eve Thomas, North-row, Park-lane, W.

THURSDAY, JULY 29, 1937

Daily Mirror

No. 10500 Registered at the G.P.O as a Newspaper. ONE PENNY

LION ATTACKS EX-RECTOR OF STIFFKEY: GIRL OF 16 RESCUES HIM

Mr. Harold Davidson, sixty-seven-year-old ex-Rector of Stiffkey, was attacked by a lion in its cage at Skegness, Lincs, last night. He was rescued from certain death by sixteen-year-old Renee Somer, a girl attendant.

Davidson, doing a turn in " the lions' den " at the amusement park, tripped over a young lioness and her mate at once sprang on him.

IN a flash the angry beast had torn open both the ex-rector's shoulders with its claws, and though Davidson bravely tried to strike with his stick he crashed to the floor of the cage with the lion on top of him.

It gripped him by the back with its jaws and began to maul him, while spectators screamed in horror.

Picking up a whip and an iron bar Miss Somer leaped into the cage and rushed at the lion.

She rained blows on the beast with the whip, and when it raised its head and lurched forward to attack her she rammed the iron bar into its jaws.

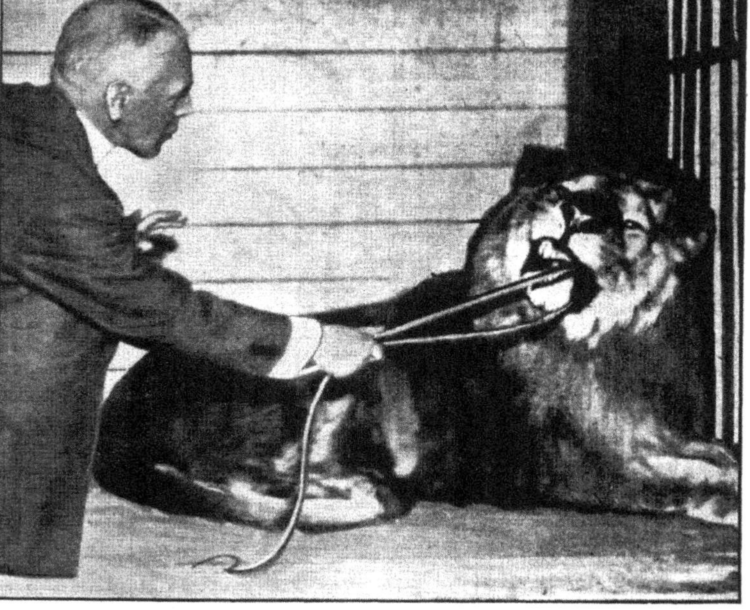

Mr. Davidson, in the cage at Skegness, with Freddie, the lion which mauled him.

Never Ceased Her Attack

Davidson was saved. Miss Somer drove the lion snarling into a corner, never ceasing her attack, though the lioness, now growling fiercely, seemed likely to spring on her at any second.

With one hand she dragged Davidson to the side of the cage farthest from the beasts.

Men attendants ran into the cage and carried him out.

When he was safe Miss Somer tottered out of the cage backwards and collapsed outside the bars in a dead faint.

While ambulance men were hurrying Davidson out on a stretcher many women fainted.

Miss Somers was given restoratives and sent to bed.

Davidson was detained in Skegness Cottage Hospital. His condition was stated early to-day to be " very grave," but Dr. O'Neill believes the ex-rector will recover.

Miss Somer, a diminutive girl with spectacles, told the *Daily Mirror*:—

" I could not do anything else but go to the aid of the rector. I have worked with

(Continued on Back Page)

Senorita Conchita Ocana, married by proxy in Spain to a Liverpool architect.

Bridegroom in Britain—Bride in Spain

MAN WAITS FOR TELEGRAM TO SAY HE IS WED

YOUNG Alfredo Martinez, Liverpool architect, sat in his office yesterday waiting for the most important telegram in his life.

He was waiting for a message which would read : " You were married to-day at the register office in Costellon de la Ptana, near Valencia."

It was the code he had agreed upon with his bride by proxy, Senorita Conchita Sanchez Ocana, daughter of a general fighting for the Madrid Government.

She was to telegraph as soon as the ceremony was completed at the litle village register office, with her uncle as representing the bridegroom.

Mr. Martinez and Conchita were to have been married last October,

As the senorita's parents feared that it would be unsafe for her to travel alone to England the wedding was put off indefinitely.

But they continued their courtship by letter, undiscouraged; finally decided on a wedding by proxy.

Mr. Martinez sent his bride a formal certificate of his bachelorship, accompanied by a birth certificate and a document authorising the bride's uncle to use his signature.

Conchita's part in this long-distance romance was to pledge her vows

The newly married couple are to meet soon at Marseilles and Mrs. Martinez will come back to Liverpool with her husband.

They will then go through a formal ceremony at St. Charles Roman Catholic Church

Halfpenny Off Petrol To-day

To-day the price of motor spirit is reduced ½d. a gallon to 1s. 7d., announces the National Petroleum Distributing Companies.

National Benzole will also be reduced by ½d. a gallon from 1s. 7½d.

When the price for best petrol was raised last April by ½d. a gallon, to 1s. 7½d., it was at its highest since 1932.

In 1896 petrol cost 9d. a gallon !

RIOT SOS TO BRITISH CRUISER

AS H.M.S. Apollo, 6,980 tons cruiser, landed marines at Bridgetown, chief town of Barbados, yesterday to quell thirty-six hours' rioting and street fighting, Reuter reported that six people had been killed and twenty-one injured in the fighting there.

Rioting continued last night and the situation was not yet under control.

A proclamation by the Governor appealed for a restoration of order and offered to help in investigating and attempting to remove the rioters' grievances.

The rioting followed a demonstration when workers demanding increased wages clashed with the police.

The rioters marched to see the Governor, Sir M. A. Young. They have smashed cars and many shops have been closed.

FRIDAY, JULY 30, 1937

Daily Mirror

No. 10501 Registered at the G.P.O. as a Newspaper. ONE PENNY

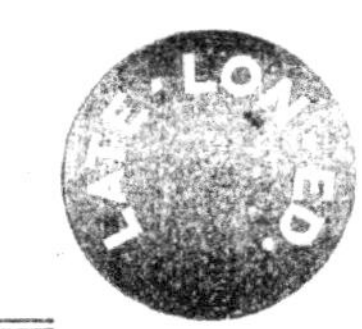

SIX MEN GUARD ROYAL BABIES

AFTER A PHONE CALL BY DUCHESS

BY OUR SPECIAL CORRESPONDENT

SANDWICH (Kent), Thursday.

Six detectives with field glasses guarded all approaches to Shingle End beach to-day when curly-haired Prince Edward, elder child of the Duke and Duchess of Kent, came down to the sands with his bucket and spade, soon after lunch.

TO-DAY, two more detectives were added to the staff of four who had been guarding Bloody Point House, holiday home of the royal children while the Duke and Duchess of Kent are on the Continent.

Beach Closed at Times

I understand that a stronger force of guards than usual is being maintained following a request by the Duchess of Kent.

Before she left for abroad she spoke over the telephone to the Home Office asking for a stronger force of police.

The public is still allowed on the beach at certain times—but only when the detectives have instructions that the royal children are not coming out.

When the Prince and Princess are there the detectives use the beach shelter as a look-out box, training their glasses on visitors

All approaches to Bloody Point House are similarly guarded.

Prince Edward, who wore a green suit and sun hat, stayed on the open beach for only a few moments.

Because of the strong north-easterly breeze

(Continued on back page)

ON HOLIDAY IN VENICE—the Duke and Duchess of Windsor. Both are following closely the recital of the gentleman on the left: and judging by his gesture he's telling a fishing story !

"I'LL EAT HIM —LIKE THIS!"

Tommy Farr, Britain's heavy-weight champion, is in America training to fight Joe Louis for the world title. We said training, but in this picture, taken at his quarters at Long Branch (New Jersey), he's being fed with ice-cream—by swimming champion Janice Lifson.

Bette Davis: Turn for Worse

HOLLYWOOD MAY BAN SUNBATHING FOR STARS

FROM OUR OWN CORRESPONDENT

HOLLYWOOD, Thursday.

HOLLYWOOD executives, alarmed by the illness of Bette Davis, who took a turn for the worse to-day after her collapse from sunstroke at Santa Barbara, California, are taking steps to check the tremendous financial loss such cases are causing.

Future contracts, I understand, will contain a clause forbidding stars to sunbathe unduly, and in future companies will refuse to pay salaries to stars ill from sunburn.

M.-G.-M. has already warned all stars against sun-bathing

Pat O'Brien, Deanna Durbin and Rosalind Russell håve all suffered from sunstroke in recent months and many expensive productions have been held up at various times.

Bette Davis, lying in a darkened room in her cottage on the seashore, will not recover for at least a month.

To-day her husband, Harmon Nelson, and family were called to her bedside, but Bette's doctor has assured them she will recover.

"Please give my love to all my friends in Britain and tell them I shall be quite well again in time," said Bette, through her mother Mrs. Ruth Davis, after being told the *Daily Mirror* was inquiring about her.

"It's done Bette a lot of good to know she had the sympathy of people in England," added Mrs. Davis.

"Her illness should be a warning to all sunbathers. She spent much time in the sun

CHILD STRANGLED BY SAFETY STRAP

TWENTY-SIX-YEAR-OLD Mrs. Fowler, of Tower Bungalow, Bricket Wood, Herts, yesterday left her thirteen-month-old baby, Robert, cooing happily in his pram. She returned in a few minutes to find him dead.

While she was giving her two other young children their dinner, Robert had become entangled in the safety strap of his pram and was strangled.

Mrs. Fowler screamed for help and quickly undid the straps, but all efforts to revive the boy were unsuccessful.

LORD TWEEDSMUIR'S ESCAPE

Lord Tweedsmuir, Governor-General of Canada, had a narrow escape during a mountain-climbing expedition in North-West Canada yesterday when a rock ledge he had jumped on collapsed. He managed to scramble to safety, says Reuter.

TUESDAY, AUGUST 3, 1937

Daily Mirror

No. 10504 Registered at the G.P.O. as a Newspaper. ONE PENNY

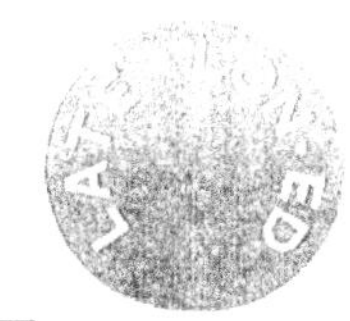

THOUSANDS STRANDED THIS MORNING IN HOLIDAY RUSH

" EVERYTHING ON WHEELS IS ON THE ROAD."

THAT was London Transport's way of describing the most amazing Bank Holiday homecoming ever early to-day.

Sun-bronzed, London's citizens rolled home from the country and the sea at the rate of 40,000 an hour this morning. But thousands only reached home in time for a wash and a meal before they returned to work. And thousands more never got home at all.

" We are inundated with S O S's from people who have been left stranded," a Southend police official told the " Daily Mirror " at 2 a.m.

" It has been the worst night in Southend's Bank Holiday history for out of door sleeping. Hundreds are left behind and there is nothing we can do but tell them to go down to the front.

" Every spare bit of grass in Southend has got a tent rigged up on it."

At Margate, too, hundreds of holidaymakers wrapped themselves in newspapers and slept in shelters and on the beach.

Special Trains at 2 a.m.

It was midnight before the rush on the roads began. Early to-day A.A. scouts reported a tremendous increase in traffic. On roads from the coast cars were running bonnet to tail in an endless, uninterrupted stream.

" Our garages are empty," said a Transport Board official.

" We have had to provide triplicate services to get the hikers home; double-deckers to deal with the coach services. S O S calls are coming in from trippers stranded in the country. We have had to run special buses and tell them to use their bus tickets on the railway."

" Despite our advance programme we have had to put on many extra trains," a Southern official told the *Daily Mirror*. Specials were still running into Victoria and suburban stations at 2 a.m. to-day

Found dying in her bath two days before she was to have given up her career to marry another doctor — Dr. Elizabeth Hutton, of Epsom (Surrey) Mental Hospital. See story on page 3.

IT'S A LIFE JOB, TOO!

The bridal coach surprise Miss Rose Samuels found outside Datchet (Bucks) Church after her wedding yesterday.

LORRY WENT TO CHURCH TO PROVE "OFFICE" BRIDE HAD SWOPPED JOBS!

FROM OUR SPECIAL CORRESPONDENT

DATCHET, Monday.

WHEN a bridal couple left Datchet parish church to-day they expected to find a wedding car waiting to take them on their honeymoon.

Instead they found a six-wheeled lorry.

On it, exposed to the laughing crowd of well-wishers, they found (as you see in the picture above)—

A perambulator, sewing machine, buckets, washbowls, and a clothes-line from which shirts and pants and other undergarments floated in the breeze.

At the other end of the lorry had been placed an office desk, complete with typewriter and telephone.

Along the side of the lorry, in big black letters, were the words, " The old job. The new job."

The surprise had been planned by friends of the bride, Miss Rose Samuels.

The bridegroom, Mr. George Streamer, is employed by a Staines motor firm.

Clambering on to the lorry amid a shower of confetti, Mr. and Mrs. Streamer drove to a hall nearly a mile away for their reception.

" We planned this surprise to remind Rose that she was leaving her office desk to become a housewife," a relative told me to-night, " and they both thoroughly enjoyed the joke.

" They had a shock when they found the lorry waiting outside. They left later for their honeymoon in the Isle of Wight by car."

£1,000,000 Went Down in Ice Cream

Holidaymakers spent £1,000,000 on ice-cream—2,000,000 gallons of it—yesterday.

At London museums there were 28,854 visitors. At Whipsnade Zoo 17,000 paid admission.

Navy Week attendances were: Portsmouth, 37,114; Chatham, 30,655; Plymouth, 20,063.

The State Apartments at Windsor Castle were visited by 13,000—a record. The Thames had its best day for years.

JOHN HAS A SILVER LINING

FIVE-YEAR-OLD John Joliffe, of Chickerell-road, Weymouth, has been saving for weeks to get a shilling to go to the circus. And now he can't see the lions and elephants after all.

The trouble is that John has swallowed the shilling

He was taken to Weymouth Hospital, and until an operation has been performed the shilling will probably remain inside him.

He Turned Blue

Said his grandmother, Mrs. Masters, yesterday:—

" John was lying on the sofa playing with the shilling when he swallowed it.

" At first we could not believe it, but he became blue and his grandfather turned him upside down to try to shake the shilling out."

WOOLWORTH HEIRESS GUEST OF DUKE AND DUCHESS

After entertaining Count Von Reventlow and his wife (formerly Miss Barbara Hutton, the Woolworth heiress) to tea, the Duke and Duchess of Windsor attended a performance of "Romeo and Juliet" at Ca Foscari, the old Palace in Venice last night.

The Duke and Duchess are leaving Venice to-night for Arnolstein, on the Austrian border, says Reuter.

60 SHELLS ON MADRID

Sixty shells fell in a quarter of an hour early to-day in the most intense bombardment Madrid has suffered since the war began, says a Spanish Press Agency report quoted by Reuter.

At 12.30 a.m. rebel batteries of six and ten inch guns opened fire on the city, shells falling at intervals of under twenty seconds. Casualty figures are not yet known.

SATURDAY, AUGUST 7, 1937

Daily Mirror

No. 10508 Registered at the G.P.O. as a Newspaper. ONE PENNY

BRITAIN PROMISED HOTTEST WEEK-END FOR MANY YEARS

BRITAIN faces the hottest week-end for years. Record temperatures are expected throughout the country for the next three days.

The march through the upper eighties began at four o'clock yesterday afternoon, when the temperature steamed up to 87deg. and hung there till 7 p.m.

Then it dropped—at the rate of one degree per hour—but nobody noticed it. At 11 p.m. it was 79 degrees. Baked bricks and pavements radiated a steamy atmosphere that drove millions from towns and cities into the open country.

Every pool and beach near town and village was thick with bathers.

Thousands prepared to bivouac out of doors for the night, and strings of cars, their occupants in swim-suits, vests and shorts, choked all outlets from London after sundown.

By 8 p.m. country lanes and fields were invaded by girls and men in bathing costumes.

Special police patrols on bicycles were sent out in Kent, Surrey, Essex and the other Home Counties to take charge of the emergency traffic.

GOING FOR A RUN IN THE CAR TO-DAY?

Then Turn to Page Five . . .

From noon south coast resorts had mass sun-bathing. In many places there were fourteen continuous hours of sunshine.

At Eltham the sun set fire to two acres of orchard there—and pickers plucked the fruit from blazing trees.

"It's impossible to tell when the heat wave will end," the Air Ministry declared.

An official drought has been proclaimed in some places.

AND JUST TO THINK THAT This Man Spent the Day

Trying to Avoid Frost-bite

. . . in the Port of London Authority cold storage building at Smithfield.

Driven Mad by Sunstroke

Sidney Lamb was found drowned in an underground tank at Broad Reed Farm, Forestside, Sussex. Medical evidence at a West Sussex inquest was that he had sunstroke on Bank Holiday Monday when he was spending the day with his sweetheart, Miss Violet Voller, at the seaside.

The coroner recorded a verdict of Su[illegible] while of unsound mind, due to sunstroke.

WAIT FOR IT! Wait for it! We all know the title for this picture of heavily-clad Guardsmen in yesterday's heat marching past children in bathing suits in the Mall. It's our old friend — Strip-TEASE.

Wrecked Own Elopement

GIRL'S NOTE BETRAYS ASYLUM RUNAWAY

A POSTCARD posted in Brighton from the woman he loves yesterday led to the recapture of twenty-six-year-old Ernest Hibbard, who eloped five days ago from Brookwood Mental Hospital, Surrey, with Winifred Mary Harding, aged twenty-three.

He was found at Staines about ten miles away. Winifred is still at large.

It was their second attempt to marry.

Eighteen months ago they tried to elope, but their plans were frustrated.

Their second escapade was ended yesterday, when Mrs. B, wife of one of the head attendants at the hospital, received in the morning a picture postcard bearing the message:

"We have had a lovely time. Ernie is going to Staines to-morrow to arrange for the wedding at Egham on Saturday at 2.30. Cheerio, Winnie."

Hospital attendants hurried at once to Staines, but a keen-eyed young constable of the Metropolitan Police had already recognised the would-be bridegroom and had detained him.

Brighton police also got busy. Officers visited a private hotel at Hayward's Heath, but they were too late.

The intended bride had paid her bill, packed her bag, and left, saying she was going to visit friends at Hounslow.

POLICE PAY 'UNLUCKY' PUNTERS FROM BOOKMAKER'S BAG

THREE horses were running in the last race at Lewes yesterday. Law Court, ridden by J. Marshall, was such a hot favourite that its starting price was 8—1 on

Gordon Richards was riding Knock-A-Penny in this race and the odds laid against his winning were 8-1. Thousands of Gordon Richards's fans gratefully accepted this price.

A number of bookmakers outside the ring were so confident that the favourite would win that they did not lay it at all.

Their optimism was misplaced. The favourite was beaten by half a length, and two of the bookies could not pay.

One bookmaker was taken to the police station on the course followed by about thirty of the unlucky punters.

There he said to the backers: "If you prosecute me you won't get anything at all, but if you're agreeable, you can share what I have between you."

Police then took particulars of each punter's claim and from the money in the bookmaker's bag were able to pay half of each amount due.

A number of bookmakers in the ring would not accept any bets on the last race.

MIDSHIPMAN FOUND HANGED IN WARSHIP

PAYMASTER Midshipman Sitwell, aged nineteen, was found hanging in the bomb store under the "middies'" quarters of the battleship Ramillies in Sheerness Harbour yesterday.

It is understood that a bomb was fastened to one end of a rope which was swung over a horizontal bar.

Sitwell's mother, a widow, is believed to live in Upper Norwood.

Ramillies arrived at Sheerness a week ago for summer leave.

TUESDAY, AUGUST 10, 1937

Daily Mirror

No. 10510 Registered at the G.P.O. as a Newspaper. ONE PENNY

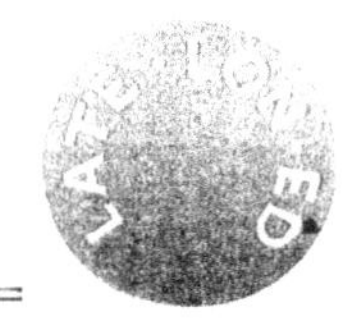

WIFE SHUNNED BY HUSBAND WHO WANTS CHILDREN: SHE SAID 'WAIT'

FROM OUR SPECIAL CORRESPONDENT

STOKE-ON-TRENT, Monday.

ALFRED Matthews, twenty-six-year-old husband, three years married, loves children. So does his wife, Cecily, who is twenty-four. But love of children has broken their marriage.

She believed that there was plenty of time ahead to have children; she hated to give up her job as a pottery artist. It meant that she and her husband could save money—ultimately to bring up a family at their little home in Ludwall-road, Longton, near Stoke.

Alfred, a lorry-driver, did not want to wait. When children did not arrive, he refused to have anything to do with her, she told magistrates at Longton to-day.

For Alfred and Cecily's quarrel brought them to the matrimonial court.

"I wanted my husband, and I wanted my home," she said. "But I had to leave him because he would have nothing to do with me."

Asked by the magistrates' clerk (Mr. George Hawley) the real reason for their parting, she hesitated and then replied in a low voice:—

"My husband is very fond of children, and I am, too. But I thought there was plenty of time.

"We were both working and I wanted to

(Continued on back page)

Mrs. Cicely Matthews.

Auburn-haired, beautiful Mrs. Dorothea Scott Wilkinson, of Hertford-street, London, W., who was carried moaning from court by policemen after she had been remanded in custody on a charge of publishing alleged defamatory libels concerning a man whose name was kept secret.

NAZI 'REPRISAL': TO EXPEL BRITISH JOURNALIST

The German authorities have decided to ask "The Times" to withdraw its chief correspondent in Berlin, Mr. Norman Ebbutt, within a fortnight, failing which his permit to remain will be withdrawn, says a Reuter message from Berlin.

The newspaper is requested to send out another correspondent who will carry out his task in a manner more acceptable to the regime.

This is regarded as a reprisal for the expulsion of three German journalists from this country.

Mr. Ebbutt, who is forty-three, has been "The Times" chief Berlin Correspondent since 1927.

B.B.C. Does It Again

WRONG ITEM BROADCAST FOR THREE MINUTES

BY A SPECIAL CORRESPONDENT

THE B.B.C. blundered once more last night.

They broadcast the wrong programme on the London Regional wavelength.

Puzzled listeners who tuned in at 8.40 to hear a talk entitled "Eccentrics" heard a woman's voice giving the "private views" of a waitress.

For three minutes this talk was broadcast, then an announcer interrupted and apologised to listeners

The Western Regional programme had been relayed by mistake, said the announcer.

While the anonymous woman waitress was speaking the talk on "Eccentrics" was being given on another wavelength. People in the studio were unaware that the microphone was not working.

"The hitch in the programme was due to a technical fault in the Bristol studio," an official of the B.B.C. told me

WOMAN DEAD IN STREAM

The body of Mrs. Ethel Gould, aged fifty-nine, wife of a Fulham builder, was discovered last night in a mill stream at Rochford, near Southend.

PNEUMATIC DRILL ROBBED HIM OF HIS MEMORY

FIFTY-NINE-YEAR-OLD Edward Vaux Wild, of Denzil-road, Willesden, N.W., missing for ten weeks, is believed to be suffering from loss of memory caused by the noise of pneumatic drills.

His bride of fourteen months, thirty-five-year-old Mary Wild, has walked hundreds of miles searching for him. She has even walked from London to Margate.

Advised to Rest

Wild was working on a new block of flats near his home. He complained of the noise of the pneumatic drills and a doctor advised him to rest.

He set out to work one morning ten weeks ago and has not been seen since.

CHILD WIFE, SPANKED FOR PULLING FACES, PLAYS TRUANT FROM SCHOOL

FROM OUR OWN CORRESPONDENT

NEW YORK, Monday.

NINE-YEAR-OLD Mrs. Eunice Winstead Johns, America's youngest wife, is playing truant from her school at Sneedville, Tennessee.

She refuses to go back there because she has been severely spanked for naughtiness by the schoolmaster.

Mrs. Johns had only been at the school for two days. But during that time she had caused an uproar by making faces at her teacher, egging on her classmates to naughtiness and interrupting classes with gossip about her husband and home life

The teacher warned her that she would be punished; but Eunice replied: "You can't do that to me. I'm a married woman."

Education authorities appealed to her twenty-two-year-old husband, Charlie, to use his influence.

FRIDAY, AUGUST 13, 1937

Daily Mirror

No. 10513 Registered at the G.P.O. as a Newspaper. ONE PENNY

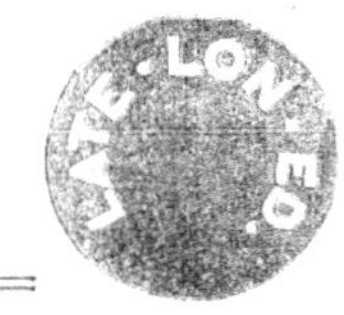

SINGING GIRL FALLS 80 FEET FROM TOP OF LONDON STORE

How Ivy Smith fell from the roof of Selfridges to the pavement 80ft. below. The sun-blind, breaking her fall, saved her life.

HOME-GOING shoppers in Oxford-street, London, paused last night as a girl's voice raised in a wild song echoed from the frescoed front of Selfridge's store. As they looked up, the girl, dressed in black, still singing, hurtled down from the roof gardens, 80ft. above.

Somersaulting in the air she crashed on her back on the sun blind screening the ground floor windows, and rolled off on to the pavement at the feet of a woman passer-by.

The sun blind saved her from certain death. She was still alive when she reached Middlesex Hospital, where she was identified as twenty-two-year-old Mrs. Ivy Ida Smith, of Manor Way, North Harrow, but she was critically ill with fractures to her skull. All night her husband watched by her bed.

Clung on by Her Hands

Miss E. Nash, of Swiss Cottage, N., at whose feet the girl fell, told the *Daily Mirror* :—

"It happened an hour after the store had closed, I heard the singing and looked up and saw the girl appear from behind the Coronation decorations

"Still singing, she seemed to slip, clutched the decorations with her fingers, hung on a minute and then crashed down.

Mrs. Smith had only lived at the Harrow address for two days.

Mr. F. Goodall, of Manor-way, North Harrow, told the *Daily Mirror*: "Mr. and Mrs. Smith engaged a room here two days ago. They told me that they had recently sold the bungalow where they had been living nearby and were looking for another house

"Mrs. Smith said they were married several years ago in Scotland and she had recently returned from a holiday with some relatives there and had left her baby with them.

"She told me that she hoped to return to Scotland and bring her baby to live with them as soon as she found a new home.

"This morning her husband went to business in London and she went out, but did not say where she was going. She seemed perfectly happy."

With his arm in a sling, Alfred—and his umbrella parachute.

Gamp Let Him Down—with a Bump

"PARACHUTIST" RETIRES, AGED 9

FROM OUR SPECIAL CORRESPONDENT

WINDSOR, Thursday.

ALFRED, aged nine, has retired from the parachuting game. And if his former hero, James Cagney, could kill himself parachuting in a film, Alf isn't even going to the funeral.

"It's a mug's game," Alfred told me. His arm was in a sling and his right side covered with bruises. Earlier in the day, as Master A. Vickers, of East-crescent, Dedworth, he had been discharged from Windsor Hospital, where he had been treated for multiple injuries.

"I'd seen Cagney do it in the pictures," Alf explained bitterly, "so we borrowed an umbrella from a lady We hadn't go no aeroplane see?

Slipped Taking-Off

"So I climbed a tree, but slipped when I took off. It was a nice day for parachutin', too—clear sky, no wind, everything perfect

"*Exceptin'* the lady's umbrella. That was a bit of no good. I'd like to see Mr. Cagney parachutin' with a lady's umbrella

"I was unconscious for half an hour. I must have landed a bit heavy.

"Was I hurt? Not on your life. Didn't hurt a bit. Not for long, anyway."

Windsor's Public Parachutist No. 1 scratched his head with his free hand when I asked him about the future. As the only boy in the family, with five sisters, he realises that life is not going to be a bed of roses.

"I'll get a job all right. I'm not afraid of anything. At least, not on the ground"

Yard Warns Bad Police Drivers

A circular has been issued from Scotland Yard to all drivers of Metropolitan police cars, warning them that they have failed to set a good example to motorists by not bringing their cars to a standstill where there is a "halt" sign.

Traffic patrols are warned that a special watch is to be kept and that action will be taken against any driver disregarding such signs.

There is also a hint to the drivers to make a special point of "setting an example" to other road users.

McMAHON RELEASED

GEORGE Andrew McMahon, sentenced to twelve months' hard labour at the Old Bailey in September last year for "producing a revolver with intent to alarm the King," was freed from Wandsworth Prison in secret last night.

His wife, warned of his release, met him at the gates and they drove off together in a car.

McMahon, an Irishman of thirty-four, was arrested in July, 1936, when his revolver fell at the feet of the horse ridden by King Edward, now Duke of Windsor, as he passed down Constitution Hill after the Trooping of the Colour ceremony.

[illegible] wife, reading of the incident in the evening papers, rushed [illegible] gaol. "If you will only stick to me," he sobbed, "I [illegible]." She promised.

George Andrew McMahon.

SATURDAY, AUGUST 14, 1937

Daily Mirror

No. 10514 Registered at the G.P.O. as a Newspaper. ONE PENNY

RIVERS SWEEP LONDON STREETS AFTER GREAT STORM

So deep was the water in the main street at Kingston (Surrey) during the terrific storm yesterday evening, that these people spent half an hour **SWIMMING** ! Other storm pictures on pages 12, 13 and 24.

FLOODS STOP TRAINS, DELUGE HOMES

BY A SPECIAL CORRESPONDENT

BATHING GIRLS SWAM IN THE STREETS LAST NIGHT WHEN GREATER LONDON WAS SWEPT BY THE HEAVIEST STORM FOR TWENTY YEARS.

MORE than 102,094,000 tons of rain, equal to 2.13 inches, fell during the day, flooding thousands of houses and shops, submerging miles of roads and railways, and causing tremendous damage.

Within half an hour streets had been turned into rivers.

Trams, buses and trolley-buses were brought to a standstill, hundreds of cars abandoned, and many of the railway arteries carrying home-going thousands were paralysed.

In Richmond-avenue, Highams Park, early this morning people were still marooned in houses flooded to a depth of three feet.. From upstairs windows they cheered firemen engaged in pumping away the water—a task which was expected to last another twenty-four hours.

Others were still waiting at 2 a.m. to return to their homes, and efforts were being made to procure a horse and cart to take them through water four feet deep.

The storm started in the afternoon on the south-west outskirts of London and moved in a broad semi-circle around to the north-east.

And the cause of it all, said the Air Ministry last night, was—

"A small depression moving up from the south-west end of the Channel to north-east England.

"Most of England will have rain for the next twelve hours."

Kingston, Surbiton and the West London area covering Acton and Ealing suffered most in the deluge.

Under the railway bridge at Kingston floods were so deep n the road that girls put on bathing costumes and swam in the water. Several schoolboys joined them.

Brentford High-street and Uxbridge-road at North Ealing rose a foot before the eyes of shoppers taking shelter from the rain.

Mr. F. L. Perry, owner of a wireless shop,

(Continued on back page)

Sir W. Monckton Resigns a Post

Sir Walter Monckton, Attorney-General to the Duchy of Cornwall, has resigned the office of Recorder of Hythe, which he has held since 1930.

This was stated in a Home Office announcement last night.

Sir Walter played a prominent part in the negotiations which preceded the abdication of King Edward VIII.

He attended the Duke of Windsor's wedding.

MOTHERS PUSH BABES TO SAFETY—KILLED

FIRST thought of two mothers, as they saw a skidding bus mount the footpath in Victoria-road, Woolston, a suburb of Southampton, yesterday, was for the safety of their children.

Both mothers Mrs. Jessie Smith, twenty-eight, of Highlands-road, Itchen, and Mrs. Harriet Downie, thirty, of Mortimer-road, Itchen, were crushed to death.

They were standing outside a shop, both holding perambulators containing babies. Just before the bus struck them they pushed the prams to safety. The children in them were unhurt.

Mrs. Downie's five-year-old son, Jimmy, who was holding his mother's hand, was injured and lies in hospital in a critical condition. A passenger in the bus was also injured.

Mr. Henry Bowyer, of Netley, driver of the bus, said: "Another two feet and I should have missed the women."

He added wryly: "This would happen on Friday the Thirteenth. The driver of this bus was taken ill to-day, and I was told to take his place."

'IN THE MONEY'—BUT OWES 5s.

FROM OUR OWN CORRESPONDENT

NEW YORK, Friday.

FRANCIS O. French cannot pay the 5s. he owes his Chinese laundryman, although he is father-in-law of John Jacob Astor, whose fortune is estimated at millions of pounds.

French is used to these ups and downs. Once after a stock market crash he took a job as taxi-driver.

Few doubt that the Astor millions would have been at his disposal to settle the debt. But French seems to enjoy giving harrowing moments to his wealthy family.

MONDAY, AUGUST 16, 1937

Daily Mirror

No. 10515 Registered at the G.P.O. as a Newspaper. ONE PENNY

BRITISH WOMEN ORDERED TO LEAVE SHANGHAI AS CHINESE MASS FOR WAR

ALL women and children among the 11,000 British people in Shanghai are to be evacuated.

Decision was reached at a Foreign Office conference last night as the cables told of a great "general offensive" by the Chinese, and of firing near the British Consulate.

At the conference were Sir Robert Vansittart, Permanent Under-Secretary of the Foreign Office, naval and military experts and technical advisers.

Plans for the evacuation are complete. Seven hundred women and children will go aboard the liner Rajputana for Hong Kong to-morrow. Another party will leave on Thursday.

Reinforcements of British troops are to be rushed to Shanghai, where £200,000,000 of British capital is invested.

Sailors and marines were landed yesterday, and to-day the Royal Ulster Rifles will sail from Hong Kong on the liner Empress of Asia. Half of the 1st Battalion 2nd Punjab Regiment, stationed at Taiping (Malay States), has been ordered to stand by to go to Hong Kong.

After an air raid on the Chinese positions west of the city the Japanese began a combined land, sea and air offensive this morning.

70,000 Men Ready

Heavy Japanese reinforcements are near the mouth of the Yangtse River.

Six Japanese bombers went into action, dropping bombs on—and near—Hungjao Aerodrome.

The Chinese have massed 70,000 troops for reinforcements.

Sir H. M. Knatchbull-Hugessen, the British Ambassador at Nanking, has protested to the Chinese Government regarding the bombing of H.M.S. Cumberland at Woosung, and at the bombing of the International Settlement, where 506 people were killed and 903 wounded.

Chinese airmen were trying to hit the Japanese flagship, anchored off the Settlement, but missed.

Dr. Robert Cecil Robertson, of the Lester Institute, Shanghai, reported killed in the bombing, is alive and well, according to a cable to Mr. Donald Robertson, his brother, at Sheerness.

(*Messages: Reuter British United Press and Exchange.*)

DO YOU KNOW THEM?

Five of the six children who were left by a woman at a house in Percival-road, Enfield, London, on Friday night.

From the top are: Ernest, eight; Joan, seven; Richard, six; Peter, five; and Ronald, four. The sixth child is Marjorie, aged two. All are being cared for in a home.

HITCH HOLDS UP JUNE'S WEDDING

WEDDING of June, formerly Lady Inverclyde, to Mr. Edward Hillman, jun., of Chicago, which was to have taken place at Nice within a few days, is postponed owing to a hitch in the verification of documents concerning her divorce.

The documents have to be verified by the British Consular authorities before the wedding can take place, says British United Press.

"This delay is most disappointing," June said last night.

"My lawyer in Nice is trying to hasten matters, and he is hopeful of having everything in order in a few days

Star-Maker's Wife Ill

Seriously ill in Hollywood, where she is expecting a baby. . . . Mrs. Ernst Lubitsch, wife of the famous film director, who is seen with her on holiday. Lubitsch is keeping constant vigil at his wife's bedside. Formerly Vivien Gaye, a London girl and her husband's secretary, she was married to Lubitsch two years ago.

"DUMPED" CHILDREN CLUES LAST NIGHT

IMPORTANT clues which may trace the parents of the six mystery children left by their mother at the home of strangers in Enfield were revealed last night by *Daily Mirror* inquiries.

The children were left at the home of Mr. and Mrs. Rossiter, of Percival-road, Enfield, on Friday, by a woman who gave her name as Mrs. Lucy Smith.

She said her car had broken down and asked Mrs. Rossiter to look after them for ten minutes until it was repaired. She never returned.

The children are now being cared for in a Willesden Home.

Last night the *Daily Mirror* learned that the family lived in Rosebank-avenue, Sudbury, near Wembley, until a week ago.

Early last week a man and woman, who gave the name of Smith, went to Wembley Police Station with six children, who were left outside in a car. They asked if the children could be sent to a home.

When they were told that if the children had to be taken care of, the parents would have to go to the workhouse, they left, saying they would return later.

Mr. Smith had been out of work for some time. His wife had worked as a barmaid at a Sudbury hotel, but when police waited at the hotel for her on Saturday she failed to arrive.

Eight-year-old Ernest Smith, eldest of the children, told the *Daily Mirror* last night:—

"We used to live at Sudbury until about a week ago, when some men came and took the furniture away."

"Daddy, who is a painter and decorator, had been out of work for some time. A few days ago we went to an empty house at Elstree, where we had to sleep on the floor.

"Daddy and mummy cried a lot all the time, and on Friday mummy told us to get dressed and get into the car to go and see grandfather.

"We got to a house at Enfield and mummy took us inside and, after kissing us, told us to wait for ten minutes. But she never came back."

SATURDAY, AUGUST 21, 1937

Daily Mirror

No. 10520 Registered at the G.P.O. as a Newspaper. ONE PENNY

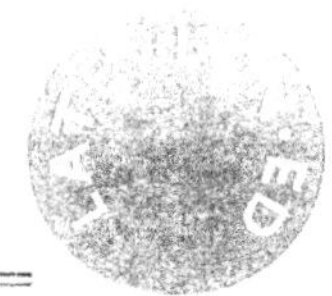

VANISHED BABY FOUND SAFE

—ABANDONED 200 MILES FROM HOME

BY A SPECIAL CORRESPONDENT

SIX-WEEKS-OLD Ivor Pearce, for whom the police of all Britain have searched since he vanished in his perambulator from a London street on Tuesday night, was found yesterday at Oldham, Lancs, 200 miles away.

To a mother sobbing in Lambeth Hospital, where she has lain exhausted for two days since collapsing after a seventeen-hour search for her baby, Scotland Yard officers carried the news that to-day he will be back in her arms.

White woollens and a little blue coat identical with those Ivor Pearce was wearing had established his identity beyond doubt.

The mystery of his journey across half England to arrive safe and sound in an Oldham lodging house, the police have still to solve.

Late last night they announced that they are anxious to interview a seventeen-year-old girl with dark bobbed hair named "Ena," who they believe can solve the riddle.

Ena was the girl Mrs. Minnie Pearce, of Waterloo-road, S.E., told the police she left her baby with when she went shopping in the New Cut, Lambeth, on Tuesday night.

Travelled by Lorry

And it was a girl answering Ena's description who arrived at a common lodging-house in Grimshaw-street, Oldham, on Wednesday with baby Pearce in her arms.

The girl with the child had apparently made her way from London to Newcastle-under-Lyme in Staffordshire by motor-lorry. There, it is believed, she obtained a lift in a private motor-car to Manchester

Last night the husband of Mrs. Mary Hall, another lodger in the house, told me how a message from his wife to the police brought the search for Ivor to an end.

"The girl asked for lodgings and she and the child slept in the room next to my wife and I. On Thursday morning she told us that the baby belonged to her sister. Later she denied this and said it was her own child.

"She said she had been living with an Irishman and that the boy had been born in Lambeth Hospital, London, in July.

"She said she was fed up with looking after him and asked us to adopt him. We told her we were finding it difficult enough to keep ourselves alive

"Then she said she had a chance of a job in Liverpool and asked us to mind the baby while she went there after the post. When she did not return we informed the police."

EXPLOSION ON BOARD BRITISH STEAMER

"Motor vessel Benguela, of London, is arriving Falmouth to-night. Serious explosion on board. Requires doctor on arrival."

This radio was received last night at Land's End wireless station.

Early to-day, when the ship reached Falmouth, she reported one man lost overboard and another badly burned in an explosion that carried off the hatches.

16 Luckiest People

TRAIN TURNS OVER BUT NO ONE HURT

FROM OUR OWN CORRESPONDENT

NORWICH, Friday.

THE sixteen luckiest travellers in Britain stepped from a special train at Norwich this afternoon.

They had been transferred to the special from a Leicester-Norwich train, which was derailed at Hindolvestone, nineteen miles from Norwich.

All three coaches of that train were wrecked and overturned. One ran into and demolished a platelayers' hut. An uprooted rail tore through another coach like a sword. Four hundred yards of permanent way were twisted like steel snakes.

BUT NOT A SINGLE PASSENGER RECEIVED AS MUCH AS A CUT OR BRUISE.

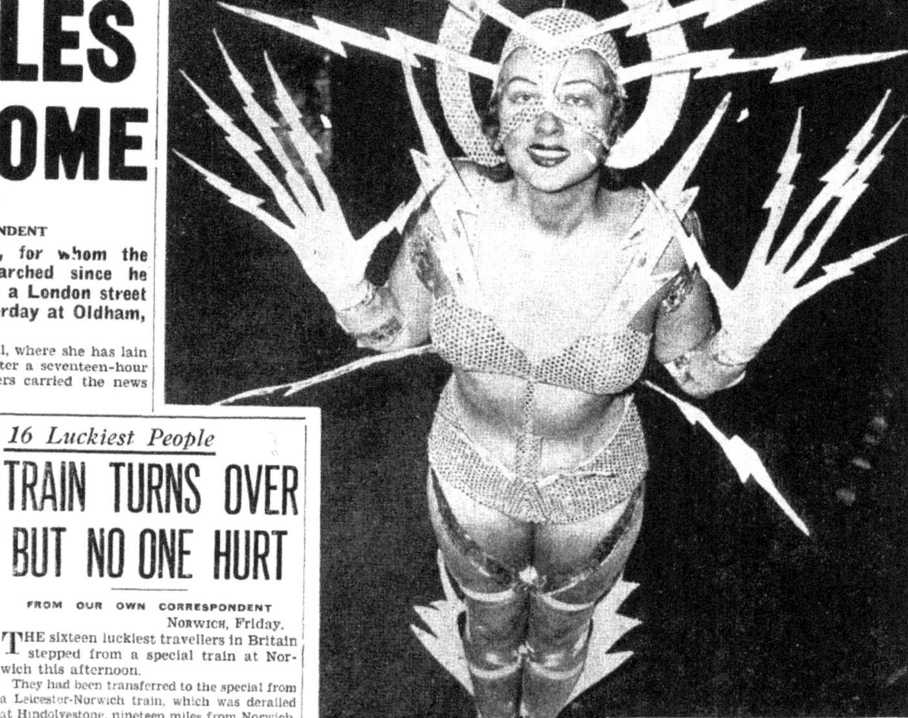

She's the genie inside your wireless set; she's the "Spirit of Radio." You'll see her, nineteen years old Elmina Humphreys at Radiolympia, next month.

SIR JOHN AND LADY REITH INJURED IN CROSS ROADS CAR COLLISION

SIR John Reith, Director-General of the B.B.C., and Lady Reith were injured last night in a collision between their motor-car and a lorry near Stredda, Cornwall.

Sir John suffered a cut over the left eye, crushed ribs and abrasions to the leg when he was flung from his seat by the impact.

Lady Reith had severe shock and a badly bruised right arm. She was driving the car.

A nurse and a baby riding in the car were injured also. The baby was badly gashed in the face. The nurse suffered shock.

The car, a 25 h.p. coupe, was badly smashed. The party were on a holiday tour and on a by-road from St. Austell to Bodmin. The collision occurred at a cross-road.

Mr. E. J. H. Robins, of Colenso-place, St. Austell, was the driver of the lorry.

The car party was taken to Sir John's holiday headquarters at Veryan, where a doctor awaited them.

Sir John Reith is forty-eight. He was married in 1921.

Sir John was trained as an engineer. He was wounded in the war and spent two years working with the Ministry of Munitions.

In 1922 he became the first general manager of the British Broadcasting Company, Limited, and the following year he became managing director. He was knighted in 1927.

Sir John has one son and a daughter.

FRIDAY, AUGUST 27, 1937

Daily Mirror

No. 10525 Registered at the G.P.O. as a Newspaper. ONE PENNY

BLINDFOLDED BOY DROWNED: CAME ROUND ON WAY TO MORTUARY

FROM OUR OWN CORRESPONDENT

BATH, Thursday.

SYDNEY Toms, fifteen-year-old errand boy, fell blindfolded into the Avon here to-night as he showed off his cycling prowess to a friend on the river bank. An hour and three-quarters later he came to life again—on his way to the mortuary.

He survived for a few minutes before relays of doctors, nurses, police and ambulance men fighting for his life in Bath Royal United Hospital gave him up—for the second time to-night—as dead.

Toms was three-quarters of an hour in the river before his "body" was recovered. For an hour rescue men worked to restore a spark of life to the boy. They failed and gave up in despair.

Stretcher men lifted the body and carried it to a waiting van. But a doctor's shout halted them. SYDNEY HAD MOVED.

Instead of the mortuary Sydney was rushed to a hospital ward.

Oxygen masks, every appliance known to science, every doctor available, were requisitioned to keep that spark alive.

At once an SOS was sent to the Central Police headquarters for relays of officers, among them Superintendent Ashworth, the Deputy Chief Constable, to act as reliefs in the work of artificial respiration.

For an hour the fight went on. Once more it ended in defeat.

"I Screamed"

Toms lived in Great Stanhope-street, Bath. The fall into the river that cost his life was described to me by his friend, David Mortimore.

"Sydney and I went to the river bank together," he said. "He was on his cycle.

"When we got there he decided to blindfold himself and then started to circle near the river.

"I shouted to him to turn right, but he must have lost his head, and went left over the bank, bicycle and all, into the river.

"I screamed for help, and then I fainted."

Mortimore's screams were heard by a man on the bank, who 'phoned for an ambulance while another rushed for a pole.

An ambulance equipped with floodlights arrived and the river was searched for three-quarters of an hour before Toms was found.

Pretty and popular barmaid at the Northwood Hotel, Northwood (Middlesex), Mrs. Lily Chamberlain was found murdered in her flat yesterday. This, the last picture taken of her, shows her in the hotel bar.

'Lord Godiva' Captured After 70 m.p.h. Chase

FROM OUR OWN CORRESPONDENT

New York, Thursday.

Naked at the wheel of his car, a man drove through New York streets to-day at seventy miles an hour. Behind him raced a car from which leaned two policemen firing their revolvers.

Hundreds of New Yorkers watched the chase, which ended in the arrest of Robert Morris Young, Wall Street clerk, identified as the mystery "Lord Godiva" who for two months terrorised women.

"Lord Godiva," always nude in his car, cruised the streets by night frightening women. Then, with a gay laugh, he would drive off at a terrific speed.

3 NURSES ARE FOOD POISON VICTIMS

THREE nurses from the Finsbury Day Nursery, Baker-street, N.W.1, were admitted to the Royal Free Hospital last night suffering from food poisoning.

Only a few hours before they had eaten some corned beef bought in the King's Cross-road district, where food poisoning broke out last week-end. Another victim of the epidemic died in hospital yesterday. **(See page 6.)**

The nurses, whose conditions were stated to be serious when they were admitted to the hospital, are:—

Joan Robertson, eighteen, of Hardie-street, Dagenham, Essex; May Blumm, twenty, of Reservoir-road, Southgate; and Florence Herbert, sixteen, of Portobello-road, Dalston.

They were stated later last night to be improving.

'PAULETTE': BOXER SOUGHT

Detectives searched the Belsize Park, N.W., district yesterday for a tall, fair man, "possibly a boxer," whom they wish to question regarding the murder of Elsie MacMahon (Paulette), who was found strangled in her burning flat in Bath-road, Euston-road.

THE JEEP O.K.-D HIS WEDDING

FROM OUR SPECIAL CORRRESPOND ENT

LUTON (Beds), Thursday.

MR. Billy Costello, thirty-one-year-old variety star, whose voice is famous throughout the world as the voice of Popeye, was to-day married by special licence to Miss Florence Baines, of Stockton-on-Tees, Yorkshire, at the St. Albans Register Office.

He was a very happy sailor when I saw him to-night at the Alma Cinema, Luton.

"Yesterday Florence and I consulted the Jeep," he told me. "Says I to the Jeep, 'Is August 26 a lucky day for me?' Up goes the Jeep's tail like a periscope.

"'Will I get some money?' says I. Up goes the Jeep's tail.

"Then says Florence, 'Is August 26 a happy day for me to get married?' Up goes the Jeep's tail and it stays up.

"So to-day Florence and I were married.

"Half an hour after we were married I gets a cable from New York. Me old uncle has died and left me £4,000."

UNDERGRADUATE LOST ON ALPINE PEAK

BRITISH visitors helped yesterday to search for Leslie Corcos, a twenty-year-old Cambridge undergraduate who has been missing since Wednesday on the Frohnalpstock, a 6,306ft. peak, near Brunnen, Switzerland.

Late last night, says Reuter, there was little hope that Corcos would be found alive, but the search will be resumed to-day.

Corcos went alone from Brunnen, where he had been staying with his mother, brothers and sisters, to climb the peak, from which there is a famous view of the lake of Lucerne.

When he had not returned at nightfall, Alpine Club members set out and searched till dawn. Then they were relieved by tourists and villagers with a police dog.

"Kultur" Spreads to the Embassies

"Cultural attaches are to be appointed to all German embassies, legations and major consulates," Herr Hans Johst, President of the Reich Chamber of Literature, announced last night in Berlin.

First "cultural attache" will be appointed to the German Embassy in London, he said.

Duty will be "to spread German cultural ideas."

Young Germans, said Herr Johst, must be "broadminded, like the English." They are "far too romantic."—British United Press.

MONDAY, AUGUST 30, 1937

Daily Mirror

No. 10527 Registered at the G.P.O. as a Newspaper. ONE PENNY

ROPES CUT TO KILL GIRL ON 135 FT. MAST

Unconcerned after her narrow escape from death, Miss Camilla Mayer—a "Daily Mirror" picture last evening.

FROM OUR SPECIAL CORRESPONDENT

CLACTON-ON-SEA, Sunday.

DETECTIVES are investigating an attempt to imperil eighteen-year-old Camilla Mayer, German "Stratosphere Girl" who performs balancing feats on the top of a 135ft. steel mast at the amusement park here.

Guy ropes supporting the mast have been found deliberately cut on two days.

Before the cutting was spotted on the first occasion the attempt to wreck the mast nearly succeeded.

Horrified attendants saw it sway perilously to one side as Camilla was poised on the top.

Cut Almost Through

They examined the hawsers and found that one of the main ones had been cut almost through and that the strain of Camilla's acrobatics had caused the last few strands to snap.

Through a loud-speaker she was told in German to remain perfectly still, and she sat at the top of the high mast until the hawser had been made safe. Then she continued her act.

This morning, a careful examination of all the ropes and hawsers was made before Camilla began her performance.

It was found that another rope had been neatly cut, leaving only a few strands to take the strain.

This was at once made good, and the police were called in. A day and night guard will now be kept on the ropes.

Mr. Stanley Wells, manager of the amusement park told me: "It seems absurd that anyone could have a personal grudge against Miss Mayer, who has been here only a fortnight and does not speak much English.

"We are completely at a loss to find any reason for the dastardly attempt."

Miss Camilla Mayer, the "Stratosphere Girl," poised on the frail 135ft. steel mast from which she would have plunged to certain death had the alleged cutting of the guy ropes not been discovered.

CHEERED FRANCO IN WRONG PLACE

SIX-FEET-THREE-INCHES Rupert Belville, wealthy old Etonian fighting for General Franco, is in the hands of Spanish Government troops at Albeqicia, near Santander.

With a Spanish friend he landed in a light 'plane at Albeqicia. They believed wireless reports that Franco had taken Santander, and gave several loud cheers for the General.

They were immediately arrested—by Government troops—and informed that they had landed at the wrong aerodrome.

Mr. Belville's friend says the Central News, was Senor Gonzalez, member of the famous sherry firm.

WEDDING CAR IN CRASH

Five people on their way to a wedding at St. Peter's Church, Forest Gate, had to continue their journey on foot after a sports car had come in collision with their car.

The sports car overturned. Harold Bridges, St. George's-avenue, Forest Gate, and John Seedoss, Grove Lane-road, Leytonstone, were trapped underneath. They were taken to hospital.

HIKER M.P. STARTS HEATH BLAZE

HIKER M.P. Mr. Dingle Foot started a fire which devastated thirty acres of heather-clad country around the Devon beauty spot at Woostan Castle, Moretonhampstead, yesterday.

Mr. Foot, son of Mr. Isaac Foot, and member for Dundee, is spending a walking holiday with his wife in South Devon. Last night he confessed:—

"I was trying to be tidy burning a piece of paper in which my lunch had been wrapped, when the gorse and grass caught fire. I tried to stamp it out, but failed, and hurried for help."

The fire gained a rapid hold, and police, firemen and dozens of others worked into the night to beat out the flames.

Two Hawks Led Glider to Victory

Two hawks circling high above the valleys of Great Hucklow, Derbyshire, brought Captain R. S. Rattray, of the London Gliding Club, the daily prize in the national gliding contests held there yesterday.

After being launched into the air he immediately headed in their direction. They led him to a current which caused him to soar quickly.

Circling in the path of the birds he gained a height of 3,400ft.—the best of the day.

LOUIS ODDS ON DOWN TO 2-1

POLICE ARE READY FOR FARR WIN

Farr v. Louis fight to-night at New York Yankee Stadium—if it doesn't rain. Forecast is: Probably occasional rain.

FROM OUR OWN CORRESPONDENT

LONG BRANCH (New Jersey), Sunday.

TOMMY Farr's stock is soaring as the battle hour approaches. Odds on Louis had got down to 2—1 to-night.

But—some prophets back rain at about the same odds, and it is hinted that a twenty-four-hour postponement may be needed.

Losing confidence that Louis will win, Police Chief Valentine is to draft hundreds of extra police into Harlem, the city's negro section. It is feared that a victory by Farr might start rioting, with attacks on whites.

Farr is more confident than Louis now.

"I'm sure I can out think Joe in a crisis beat him mentally to the punch," he said.

"I am going to win to-morrow night. I honestly believe I will have less trouble with Louis than I did with Baer."

The two will weigh-in at noon in New York to-morrow.

Ticket sales picked up over the week-end and Tommy envisages at least £10,000 jingling in his pockets.

He says that win, lose or draw he will box Jimmy Braddock in London's National Sporting Club on November 22.

TUESDAY, AUGUST 31, 1937

Daily Mirror

No. 10528 — Registered at the G.P.O. as a Newspaper. — ONE PENNY

LOUIS BEATS TOMMY FARR:

POINTS DECISION

JOE Louis beat Tommy Farr, British heavy-weight champion, at Yankee Stadium, New York, this morning, and retained his world title.

Victory went to Louis on points after a magnificent fight, both men giving a superb exhibition. Farr finished with a tremendous attack, smashing blow upon blow onto Louis.

The decision was loudly booed by the crowd.

As challenger the Briton was first to enter the ring, and he was greeted uproariously. Louis's ovation was not so good.

Farr opened the attack in the first round forcing Louis against the ropes and pounding away with his right. Again in round two he continued the attack landing blows on the body and face. Louis was cautious.

By the third he was jabbing constantly and peppering Louis's face with light lefts and appeared to be getting the negro worried. Louis replied desperately with some swift jabs that brought blood to Farr's right eye.

Cheers for Britisher

In the fifth round Louis hit Farr with all the force of his famous right. Louis was fighting viciously, but Farr was not even disturbed.

Farr led easily in the sixth round, hit Louis almost at will with real fury in his fists.

Round seven found Farr's face bleeding badly after a hurricane of blows, but after the bell for the eighth he came back gallantly, fighting hard and mixing them freely. He won both this and the ninth.

Still hitting strongly in round ten Farr carried the fight to Louis, who was playing all the time on Farr's bad eye.

The ringside crowd was now definitely in favour of the Briton, owing to his wonderful fight, and cheered his efforts again and again. His face was bathed in blood, but he fought unflinchingly—the fight of his life—and took round eleven.

Twelfth round went to Louis, who was now forcing the pace. He took the next two rounds, but in the fifteenth Farr made a tremendous attack and forced the negro against the ropes in a last desperate effort.

Encouraged by the great improvement in the weather, which had turned clear and warm, a crowd estimated at over 40,000 had crammed the Stadium to about three-quarters of its capacity an hour before the fight began.

1,000 Police on Guard

There was a large percentage of negroes among the crowd, and in the anticipation of racial riots, a squad of at least 1,000 policemen were on duty in and around the Stadium, says Reuter.

Celebrities from all walks of life occupied reserved seats at the ringside. The Marquis of Queensberry and Sir Noel Curtis Bennett were distinguished visitors from England.

The stage and screen were represented by Douglas Fairbanks, George Raft and Al Jolson.

Famous boxing figures present were James J. Braddock, Jack Dempsey, Jack Sharkey, Jack Johnson and Max Schmeling, all ex-heavy-weight champions of the world.

Max Schmeling is hoping to be matched with the winner.

When the preliminaries were begun, the "gate" was estimated at 240,000 dollars (about £48,000) plus £21,000 from film and broadcasting rights, which made the total within reach of £60,000.

Farr's confidence in his own ability had brought the odds down to 3 to 1 against him yesterday, but when he entered the ring odds of 8 to 1 were offered by gamblers at the ringside.

With her American bridegroom. . . . June, the actress, and Mr. Edward Hillman, junior, Chicago store magnate, after their marriage at Cannes Town Hall.

June's marriage to Lord Inverclyde was dissolved in 1933.

JUNE ASKED GROOM FOR ANOTHER KISS

FAMOUS ex-actress June, married at Cannes yesterday to Chicago store magnate Edward Hillman, jun., received a kiss from him as they were married in the Town Hall.

"Do it again," she begged—and he kissed her repeatedly.

Men and women of all nationalities, on holiday on the Riviera, were among the crowd which mobbed the couple after the ceremony.

"This is worse than a Hollywood first night," said the bridegroom as the couple left the Town Hall, where they were married by the Mayor, M. Pierre Nouveau, amid a shower of rice.

After Mr. Hillman had put the ring on his bride's finger he kissed her. It was then she asked for more.

Gift from Maharajah

June arrived at the Town Hall just before 5 p.m., wearing a pale blue frock, with a large spray of white and mauve orchids.

Round her wrist was an emerald and diamond bracelet—the bridegroom's present.

Outside the Town Hall June gasped with delight when she saw a magnificent car waiting for her. It was a wedding present from her cousin, Mr. Maurice Strauss.

Another wedding present was a gold cigarette case studded and initialled with diamonds from the Maharajah of Rajputana.

As June is suffering from a bad cold the first night of the honeymoon was spent in the hotel at Cannes.

To-day the pair will leave for a secret destination, where they will spend three or four days before going to Paris.

They will sail for America in the Normandie on September 8 and will set up house at Mr. Hillman's home in Beverly Hills, Hollywood.

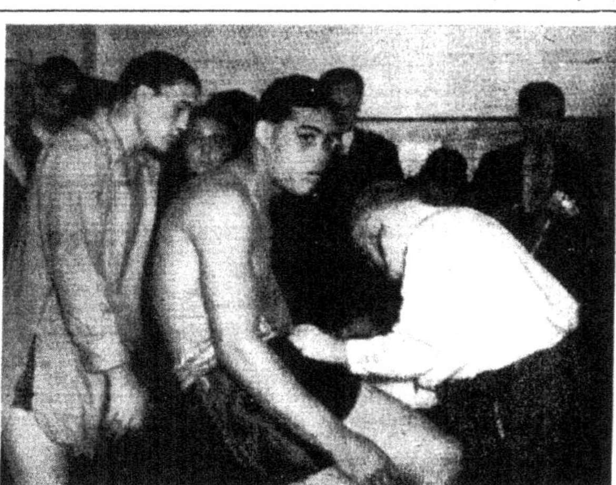

Radio picture of Tommy Farr and Joe Louis weighing-in before last night's fight.

SATURDAY, SEPTEMBER 4, 1937

Daily Mirror

No. 10532 Registered at the G.P.O. as a Newspaper. ONE PENNY

MILLIONAIRE OFFERS £20,000 TO GET RID OF FOURTH WIFE

Even before he shaves in the morning, Tommy Manville buckles on this cartridge belt with two revolvers, in case any of the threats against his life should materialise.

FROM OUR OWN CORRESPONDENT

NEW YORK, Friday.

MILLIONAIRE playboy Tommy Manville, "alimony king" of U.S.A., has spent thousands of pounds to-day on full page advertisements in New York newspapers "for a lawyer with enough guts to get him a divorce" from his glamorous blonde wife, formerly Marcelle Edwards, beauty queen of Broadway.

As soon as the evening newspapers were on the streets crowds of panting lawyers started to battle and clamour outside the locked gates of the multi-millionaire's city home.

While Tommy romped with his secretary and other pretty girl friends on his estate, Bon Repose, hundreds of City lawyers, scenting a fortune, went wild with excitement.

They dashed off telegrams, inundated the Manville mansion with telephone calls and raced out in cars to waylay him.

At Bon Repose they found the way barred by armed guards

Ex-wives as Judges

Little Jewish lawyers waving brief cases pleaded for admittance, and when that failed, cried: "Let us in in the name of the law. Manville's sent for us."

The heavy-jowled guards' reply was: "Law or no law, you've got to scram until Manville tells us he sent for you."

Poring over hundreds of legal telegrams and sipping champagne with his pretty friends, Manville remarked:

"The trouble is that my wife, Marcelle, won't be content with £200 weekly, although my past three wives have been content with £200 weekly alimony.

"But I must be careful in the process of elimination. I'm going to find a super lawyer

He sat back in thought, while his girl friends purred their approval. Then he got another "cute" idea.

Smacking his fist on his palm, he proclaimed: "I'll have my lawyer get my first three wives to sit on the jury when Marcelle's claims are heard."

(Continued on back page)

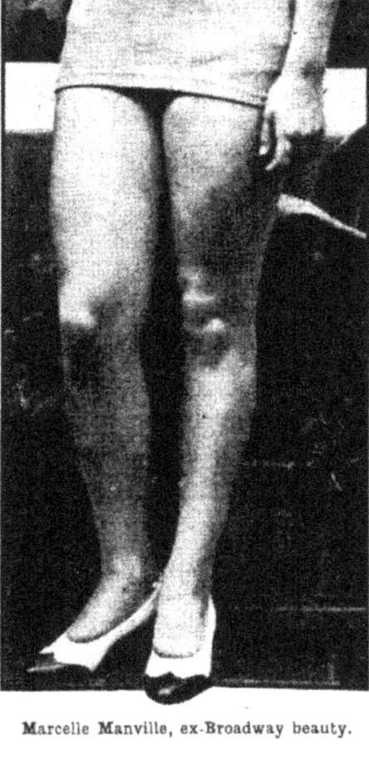

Marcelle Manville, ex-Broadway beauty.

SEAMAN SAVES DOG IN QUARRY

Hundreds of people at Chatham, Kent, last night watched Able-Seaman Elcoat climb down a 100ft.-deep quarry and rescue a dog. He went down on a rope made of a clothes-line and pieces of cord.

Police-Constables Bodimeade and Talbot knotted the ropes together and lowered Elcoat over the edge with the rope tied round his waist.

The dog, maddened with fear, tried to bite its rescuer, who was cheered when he brought it to safety.

ENGLISH BUTLER LEFT £100,000 IN U.S.

Mr. William Lowe.

WILLIAM Lowe, English butler, whose mother, Mrs. Lowe, lives in Gresley-road, Hornsey-lane, London, is jointly to share with a maid the £200,000 fortune of Mrs. Julia Marshall Foster, ninety-year-old New York widow, who died in July.

Lowe had been Mrs. Foster's butler for seventeen years; Olive Olsen, her maid for twenty-nine years. The bequest was for "faithful service."

Last night Lowe's mother told the "Daily Mirror": "I am perfectly happy here in my little home. My son's wife and baby boy are on holiday in this country and will be returning in the Queen Mary in a few weeks. I am not going to let the fortune make any difference to me."

Lowe and Mrs. Olsen yesterday took possession of Mrs. Foster's large house in Tukedo Park, fashionable New York district.

Schmeling to Fight Joe Louis

Max Schmeling has signed a contract to fight Joe Louis for the world heavy-weight title over fifteen rounds in June, 1938, in the United States, reports British United Press.

Schmeling beat Louis last year and signed to fight Braddock for the title. Braddock, however, avoided the fight and lost his title to Louis.

Mike Jacobs, the promoter, said last night that Schmeling had agreed to take twenty per cent. of the purse, while Louis would take thirty-seven-and-a-half per cent.

At the same time Schmeling has placed himself under contract to Jacobs for eighteen months after the title fight.

The winner of the Schmeling-Louis bout will be matched in September, 1938, in a fifteen-round title fight with the winner of the heavy-weight elimination contest to be held by Jacobs this winter, in which Farr, Braddock, Baer and Pastor are concerned.

Did Not Hear S O S

THE PATIENT BROUGHT THE BOTTLE BACK

"THIS medicine is the wrong colour. I've brought the bottle back," said a man who walked into the out-patients' department of the Metropolitan Hospital, Kingsland-road, Hagerston, E., last night.

He did not know that an S O S had been broadcast by the B.B.C. warning patients that a mistake had been made with a man's medicine, and that it would be dangerous to drink it.

There was almost panic in parts of East London when it became known that the mistake had been made, and after the S O S had been broadcast, scores of people called at the hospital to see if their medicine was all right.

The man to whom the medicine was issued did not hear the broadcast, but noticed when he got home that it was a different colour from that usually given to him.

R.A.F. PILOT KILLED AS 'PLANE HITS WARSHIP

TRYING to land his 'plane on the aircraft carrier Furious, off the Isle of Wight, Sub-Lieutenant Charles Anthony Knocker, R.N., Flying-Officer R.A.F., hit the side of the vessel, fell into the sea, and sank at once.

His death was announced last night by the Admiralty, who stated that the accident occurred on Thursday.

There have now been fifty-nine R.A.F. aeroplane accidents this year, resulting in ninety-five deaths compared with a total of fifty-four accidents and ninety-six deaths during 1936.

TUESDAY, SEPTEMBER 7, 1937

Daily Mirror

No. 10534 — Registered at the G.P.O. as a Newspaper. — ONE PENNY

RUSSIA ACCUSES ITALY OF PIRACY: EMBASSY MOBBED

POLICE guards surrounded the Italian Embassy in Moscow last night to protect diplomats from the fury of a Russian mob, as Stalin threw a thunderbolt in Europe, openly accusing Italy of torpedoing two Soviet ships in the Mediterranean.

To the Soviet demand for reparations and punishment of the "guilty" submarines—two are said to be named—Mussolini replied with a complete denial of the allegations and a refusal to discuss the matter that is described in Moscow as "the limit of arrogance."

All Russia went anti-Italian last night and thousands of mass meetings and demonstrations were held.

Breach of diplomatic relations between Moscow and Rome is expected at any time.

Italy, it is stated, may refuse to take part in the twelve-Power piracy conference, planned at Nyon, near Geneva, on Friday, when Britain and France are expected to force through a "shoot-to-sink" policy that would end the submarine menace in the Mediterranean.

These dramatic developments came shortly after an announcement that Mussolini, who had already planned to go to Germany toward the end of September, would fly to Berlin this week to confer with Hitler before the conference began.

Stalin Calls Cabinet

It is impossible to foresee the effect Russia's accusations may have on the Nyon talks.

Stalin, who is reported to be "deeply insulted" by Mussolini's reply to the Russian note, last night summoned his Cabinet

Moscow is said to be considering strong measures to protect her ships, and it is believed that Russian submarines and warships will be ordered into the Mediterranean.

Britain and France have agreed to tolerate no quibbling with their demand for a "shoot-to-sink" policy when the conference meets on Friday, writes the *Daily Mirror* Political Correspondent.

None of the time-wasting subterfuges—references to committees or experts—will be tolerated.

All the Mediterranean Powers, and Russia and Germany, will be bluntly asked whether they are prepared to put an immediate stop to piracy on the high seas.

British Ship Seized

Last-minute example of piracy in the Mediterranean was flashed to London by cable last night.

It told how the British steamer Burlington, captured by one of Franco's cruisers off Palermo, Sicily—hundreds of miles from Spanish territorial waters—had been taken to Palma, Majorca. Her cargo, 7,000 tons of oil, was confiscated.

Burlington is a 5,000-ton tanker owned by the Finchley Steamship Company, of London.

Messages from "Daily Mirror" Warsaw correspondent, Reuter and Central News

She's Glamour Girl No. 1

Sixteen-year-old Thelma Bain, of Worthing, who, although she has never been on the stage or seen a cabaret, yesterday won the title of Glamour Girl No. 1 and an £8-a-week contract to appear in London, Paris and New York.

See story on page 3.

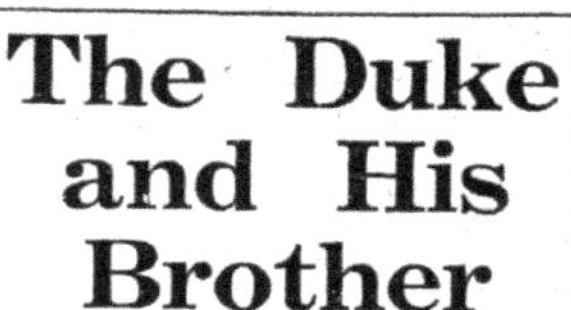

The Duke and His Brother

The Duke and Duchess of Windsor will leave Castle Wasserleonburg, Austria, where their short tenancy ended yesterday, without having seen the Duke and Duchess of Kent, says British United Press.

The following statement was made last night:—

"His Royal Highness is very sorry that he has been unable to see the Duke and Duchess of Kent, who were expected as guests at the Castle yesterday or to-day, but he has just received a communication from Yugoslavia stating that they have changed their plans."

FAIRGROUND CROWD SCATTER FROM MAN RUNNING AMOK WITH A RIFLE

MEN and women dashed screaming across Barnet (Herts) Fairground late last night from a man running amok with a rifle.

The man was firing at a rifle range when he suddenly gave a wild shout, whipped round and fired two shots at people on a roundabout.

Fairground attendants closed with the man and there was a struggle, in which the rifle was again fired.

Eventually they succeeded in forcing the man into a caravan at the edge of the fairground.

Poli[illegible]re called, but when they arrived they [illegible]at the man had escaped.

T[illegible]D SCARE IN LINER

The Hamburg-America liner New York was delayed nearly an hour at quarantine yesterday by a suspected case of typhoid fever, reports Reuter from New York.

The crew and passengers were released after the patient—a steward—had been sent to hospital pending a definite diagnosis.

Liner, Minus Propeller, Crosses Ocean

When the French liner Normandie arrived at Havre yesterday divers found that her port central propeller had vanished.

She struck a submerged log as she was leaving New York harbour, but in spite of the mishap she averaged 29.61 knots to make the ocean crossing on scheduled time.

It was announced last night that she would sail again to-morrow according to programme.

SATURDAY, SEPTEMBER 11, 1937

Daily Mirror

No. 10538 Registered at the G.P.O. as a Newspaper. ONE PENNY

BRITAIN, FRANCE TO POLICE THE SEAS: EDEN'S BLUNT SPEECH

FROM OUR DIPLOMATIC CORRESPONDENT

NYON (Switzerland), Friday.

MR. Anthony Eden, Britain's Foreign Minister, pale, weary but determined, made the shortest, bluntest speech of his career at the Mediterranean anti-piracy conference, here, to-day.

He brought the public session of the conference to an end within a few minutes by urging the importance of a quick decision. A committee was appointed immediately to draw up a plan to end the submarine terror of the Mediterranean.

This committee will create a force to patrol the Mediterranean, which will not only deal with the violation of the submarine protocol by sinking at sight, but will also act as a deterrent to illegal submarine activity.

Veiled Threat

This is the speech: Division of the Mediterranean into zones to be allotted to, chiefly, Britain and France, for policing.

Other nations, including Italy, will be invited to co-operate.

Mr. Eden followed Soviet Russia's M. Litvinov as a speaker.

Litvinov was even more blunt than Eden. He did not talk of piracy in the Mediterranean, but of the attacks of one Power on peaceful shipping.

Everyone knew that he referred to Italy.

Litvinov's speech also included a veiled threat of reprisals against Italy, and Rome was indignant last night.

A spokesman said: "We shall regard Russian measures against us as aggression, for we have done nothing to merit reprisals."

Mr. Eden buried his face in his hands as Litvinov spoke. Then he stood up and said:

"I regret that certain States whose co-operation was desired are not present. I propose to keep them informed of the progress made with a view to their eventual co-operation.

"Immediate Task"

"We have an immediate task to perform. Let us press it on to a speedy conclusion. I propose that we should at once resolve ourselves into a Standing Committee."

This was agreed to. The public session ended and the conference of ten Powers went into private committee.

The Conference finally agreed, it is learned, to entrust to Britain and France the task of patrolling the Mediterranean, west of Malta, to end submarine piracy (says British United Press). If Italy refuses a zone, Britain and France will take over.

The Conference reached agreement in principle on all major points, but the details will be worked out this afternoon

Most Amazing Air Crash Picture Ever Taken

In this picture, more amazing than any other of its kind, you see one of the most remarkable of air tragedies ACTUALLY HAPPENING.

It is the crash in which two competitors in the King's Cup air race were killed at Scarborough yesterday. As the aeroplane is tossed upward by a squall of wind, one of its two occupants is flung through the roof . . . YOU SEE HIM IN MID-AIR.

He fell to death on the cliff below. The machine crashed, killing his co-pilot as well. Full story back page—further pictures on page 1[illegible].

Below are the two airmen, Wing-Comdr. Percy Sherren (dark suit) and Wing-Comdr. E. G. Hilton.

"Stowaway" with Script of New Play

Robert Oliver, the New York office boy who disappeared with the script of a new play addressed to actor Laurence Olivier, in London, has been found on the high seas—travelling to England in the Queen Mary to deliver the script in person!

Robert was told to deliver the play to someone on board just before the liner sailed. Now the authorities are wondering whether he stowed away—or merely misunderstood his boss's orders.

But the agent said yesterday: "He is such a faithful, loyal boy that I am sure he would not deliberately have done this."

OXFORD COLLEGE HEAD AND WIFE DIE IN 'PLANE CRASH

CANON Burnett Hillman Streeter, Provost of Queen's College, Oxford, and Mrs. Streeter, his wife, were killed when the Berne-Basle regular passenger 'plane in which they were returning from a Swiss holiday crashed into a mountain side in the Juras yesterday.

The pilot, M. Eberschweiler, was also killed.

The 'plane, which was one of the Alpar service, left Berne at 2.50 p.m. yesterday. Nothing more was heard of her till the wreckage was found 3,770ft. up on a peak in the canton of Basle-Campagne late last night.

"We received a letter from him this morning," the college porter told the "Daily Mirror" last night. "He wrote that he and his wife were returning this evening and asked me to wait up for them."

Canon Streeter, who was sixty-three, was elected Provost of Queen's in 1933.

He was a distinguished scholar and published many outstanding books on theological subjects. He had the reputation of being one of the finest preachers in the Church of England.

MONDAY, SEPTEMBER 13, 1937

Daily Mirror

No. 10539 Registered at the G.P.O. as a Newspaper. ONE PENNY

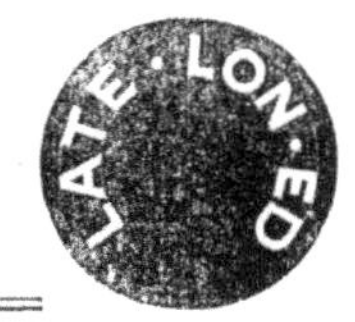

UNKNOWN SUBMARINE 'UNABLE TO RISE' OFF COAST OF SPAIN

A damaged submarine of unknown nationality lies, unable to reach the surface, in deep water near the Spanish Mediterranean coast. The crew is still alive, but their air supply is running low.

THE submarine was located by officials of the Cartagena naval base, according to a Febus (Spanish Government) news agency report, quoted by a British United Press message from Madrid yesterday.

Officials refuse to give any indication of the identity of the submarine, but it was reported on Saturday that a submarine had been sunk by Government shore batteries.

The salvage of the boat may cause a major sensation should it be one of the submarines, with distinguishing marks painted out, that are responsible for piracy in the Mediterranean.

The Cartagena naval authorities are now carrying out a diving examination and combing the vicinity with a view to "producing proper convincing facts for the world," says Reuter.

BRITAIN TO PAY FOR TRIUMPH

FROM OUR POLITICAL CORRESPONDENT.

GENEVA, Sunday

Britain will have the lion's share of the naval work in connection with the Mediterranean anti-piracy control.

If Italy refuses to sign the Nyon Treaty, the British ships will have even more to do. France, too, will rely more on our ships as the time goes on.

A Supplementary Naval Estimate is therefore anticipated when Parliament meets this autumn.

But Britain has scored a big diplomatic triumph Mr. Anthony Eden is elated; he looks as if a great weight were lifted from his shoulders Admiralty experts are delighted.

Staunch Allies

At Nyon and Geneva during the week-end Britain and France have become staunch allies. The French and British flags are seen flying together everywhere. The Swiss loudly praise the two countries.

Italy, Germany and the Soviet Union remain unsatisfied.

The Mediterranean Treaty will be signed at Nyon even if Italy remains aloof. Piracy against neutral shipping will be brought to an end.

Soviet Russia was, I am told, quietly snubbed at the Conference when she asked if

(Continued on back page)

11 Proposals—Beauty Queen Says "No"

Beautiful eighteen-year-old Queenie Buckland was chosen Queen of Ruislip, Middlesex, less than a month ago. Since then she has received eleven offers of marriage. But she says she is not interested in men.

Last night she told the Daily Mirror": "I have read only one letter myself. All the others are in the hands of my employers, at the place where I work as a waitress. I am not answering them.

"I am old fashioned and have never even been to a dance. I have never had a boy friend in my life."

Piracy Patrol to Cost Us £14,000 a Day

Britain's taxpayers have yet another burden to face. Our share in the anti-pirate patrol of the Mediterranean, it is estimated, will cost her approximately £14,000 a day.

Britain will contribute thirty-five destroyers and France twenty-five to the force that will keep control in the Mediterranean.

Riding on the box seat beside the picturesquely - costumed driver . . the Duke of Windsor out for a drive at Borsodivanka, near Budapest.

The Duke took the reins part of the time.

POLICE RUN DOWN STOLEN CAR

POLICE on patrol in a wireless car in Edgware-road, London, N., last night recognised the number and description of a saloon car which had been reported stolen from Fleetwood, Lancs, last week, and signalled it to stop.

Ignoring the signal, the driver accelerated and dashed through the traffic with the police in pursuit.

Along Harrow-road the cars sped, turned into Bishop's-road, then doubled back up Bayswater-road, with the police car gradually gaining.

Drawing alongside the police car headed the saloon into Clanricarde-gardens—a cul-de-sac.

Here the two cars became interlocked and travelled for forty yards before they could pull up.

Later two men were detained and the Lancashire police were informed.

He Carries His Clothes Under His Arm

FARMERS, HIKERS, HUNT NUDIST

FROM OUR OWN CORRESPONDENT

NELSON (Lancs), Sunday.

HIKERS, local farmers and residents here turned amateur detectives to-day and banded themselves together in an all-day hunt for a naked man seen on Pendle Hill.

Several people reported seeing the man walking naked in the fields, carrying his clothes under his arm.

As soon as they approached him he dashed for shelter into woods or undergrowth.

At nightfall the army of searchers disbanded —unsuccessful.

Once they sighted a man in the first stages of undressing—he was taking his jacket off.

Down swooped the searchers, to receive this indignant explanation:

"I was only rolling my sleeves down. It's getting cold"

But the people here are still convinced that nudism is rampant on Pendle Hill, determined to stamp it out.

Farmer Hartley said: "I've seen ten or a dozen naked men at a time on top of the hill in the summer. They are supposed to be sun-bathing

"During hay making we had a girl in one of our meadows that had just been cut.

"She was on the ground with nothing on.

"The cart taking hay from the next meadow passed her several times. As it went past she simply threw a coat over her body

TUESDAY, SEPTEMBER 14, 1937

Daily Mirror

No. 10540 Registered at the G.P.O. as a Newspaper. ONE PENNY

GIRL DRINKS POISON, CRYING TO JACK DOYLE, "I LOVE YOU!"

FROM OUR OWN CORRESPONDENT

NEW YORK, Monday.

LOOKING across at Jack Doyle, the Irish boxer, over the crowded tables of a Hollywood terrace cafe last night, a beautiful red-haired girl drank poison, staggered towards Doyle and collapsed at his feet, crying, "You are the man I love."

Doyle knelt by her side, tried to revive her. Then he picked her up in his arms and carried her to his car through the crowd of diners, which included many film stars and directors.

He rushed her to hospital where doctors fought for her life, and won, although she had mixed herself a cup of deadly poison.

To-night the girl was identified as Betty Liza Strathmore, aged twenty-three, a dancer

"I Hardly Know Her"

Doyle, who had gone to the cafe—at the famous Hotel Knickerbocker—with a party including Miss Betty Bronson, the society girl, told me to-day:

"I am puzzled. I hardly know Miss Strathmore. Some time ago she was casually introduced to me by a film director, and we talked a little. But that was all.

"It all happened as I had just gone into the cafe.

"I noticed the girl sitting alone at a table clutching a blood-red cup in her hand.

"She raised it and drank. Then she ran towards us, stared in my face, and said, 'You are the man I love.' Then she fell, apparently dead."

Miss Strathmore is alleged to have told the police that she took poison to "get even" with Doyle. "He laughed at me when I said I loved him," she declared.

A month ago, says Reuter, Miss Strathmore claimed that she was engaged to Doyle. This he immediately denied.

He is now engaged to marry Mrs. Delphine Dodge Godde, daughter of Mr. Henry Dodge, the millionaire car manufacturer.

By Mule Track and 'Plane on Stretcher

Crippled by infantile paralysis, thirteen-year-old Pamela Sargent, daughter of Dr. Malcolm Sargent, the composer and conductor, had to be carried on a stretcher down a steep mule track by Red Cross men yesterday.

She had been taken so severely ill while staying at her parents' mountain villa, near Portofino, Italy, that her body had to be encased in plaster for the journey. She is being brought to England by 'plane, states Reuter.

BENCH OVERRULES MOTHER

"KIDNAPPED" GIRL TO STOP WEDDING

SEVENTEEN - YEAR - OLD Kathleen Deverill, of Stratford Tony, Wilts, wants to marry Harry Lloyd Thick, twenty-four-year-old gardener.

They bought furniture for their home and she left her job.

Then her father and mother who, says Kathleen, had consented to Harry's suit, objected

"They removed me by force to a diocesan home at Devizes," Kathleen told Salisbury magistrates yesterday, when she obtained their consent to marry her sweetheart.

"I struggled, but mother held me down so that I could not get away."

Days later, Kathleen was released and then went to live voluntarily at Salisbury Diocesan Refuge.

"The trouble arose when I would not give up my bicycle and leave it at home," said the bride-to-be.

Harry said, "Kathleen's parents never objected until the last moment."

Mrs. John Deverill said Harry was "too jealous" to marry her daughter. And she denied that she knew early about the courtship.

But the Bench granted Kathleen's application to be allowed to marry.

Miss Deverill left Salisbury Diocese Refuge last night, telling the sisters she would marry to-day by special licence.

BEERY WOUNDED IN FILM

Wallace Beery, the film star, shot himself accidentally in the thigh during the filming of a Wild West picture yesterday, says Reuter, and was taken to hospital

THEY BOTH LOVED THE SAME MAN

And because he duped them both, Mrs. Williams, wife of Alfred Henry Williams, and Kathleen Griffiths (taller), London mannequin, met at the Old Bailey yesterday and left united in firm friendship.

They had seen Williams, who wore an Old Etonian tie, sentenced to eighteen months' hard labour. He married Mrs. Williams twelve years ago; left her after two years. He bigamously married Miss Griffiths.

STABBED TAXIMAN STAGGERS FROM CAB AFTER CRASH

A POLICEMAN on duty in Cambridge Park-road, Wanstead, last night, saw a taxi swerve and collide with a lorry which was coming in the opposite direction.

The taxi driver staggered from his seat, and began stabbing himself in the chest and neck with a large knife.

The policeman ran to him, and, with the aid of the lorry driver managed to take the knife away, but not before he had inflicted several serious injuries on himself.

The taxi driver, George Bellingham, aged fifty-six, of Horne-road, Barkingside was taken to Whipps Cross Hospital, where he was detained.

Detectives sat at his bedside through the night.

"My husband, who drives all day in the City area, has held a licence for over thirty years," Mrs. Bellingham told the *Daily Mirror*.

"Recently, however, he has been in ill-health. This is his first accident. I think it must have caused him to have a brainstorm."

Picture of wrecked taxi—page 2.

Discovery I Man Drowned

STRICT SECRECY ORDER

BY A SPECIAL CORRESPONDENT

STRICT secrecy is being kept about the strange death of Mr. Duncan A. M Watts, member of the skeleton crew of Captain Scott's famous ship Discovery I, whose body was found in the Thames near Battersea Bridge last night.

Watts was reported missing from the ship—which is moored near Waterloo Bridge—on Sunday night.

Members of the crew told me last night that they had been warned by the Boy Scouts Discovery Committee not to discuss the tragedy.

"Watts was a married man aged about forty," one of the crew said to me. "I understand he lived at Southsea. He had not been with the ship very long.

"I cannot say whether Watts fell into the river while working or how he met his death."

WEDNESDAY, SEPTEMBER 15, 1937

Daily Mirror

No. 10541 Registered at the G.P.O. as a Newspaper. ONE PENNY

MINER HURTLES TO DEATH AS HE SEEKS LOST BOY DOWN SHAFT

Mr. Ted Peckham.

WHEN about to make a search last night for the body of nine-year-old Aubrey Gilbert, who last week fell down a shaft at disused tin mines at Camborne, Cornwall, Jack Curtis, a miner, hurtled 120ft. to death.

Curtis secured grappling irons, and, with four men at the windlass, got in the bucket and gave the order to lower him down the shaft.

He had descended only three feet when the winch slipped out of gear and, at terrific speed, Curtis shot to the bottom of the shaft.

Police Post Patrol

Frantic efforts were made to stop his fall, and an iron bar was used in an attempt to jam the gear wheels, but in vain.

The wire rope ran out to its full length. Men and women at the pithead hauled the bucket to the surface, but it was empty.

The bottom of the shaft contains a great depth of water. It has not been possible to ascertain how deep the shaft really is.

Hundreds of people gathered round the pithead, but police had strict orders that no further attempts were to be made at present to descend the shaft, and posted a guard.

Curtis, who was aged forty-two, lived at Redruth. He was a married man with several children

CHORUS-BOY PEERS BAR "STRIP TEASE"

BY A SPECIAL CORRESPONDENT

THREE English peers are willing to appear as chorus-boys on the New York stage—but they won't stand for 'strip-tease"!

They 'phoned Ted Peckham, young American chief of a New York guide-escort bureau, in London yesterday in reply to an advertisement which he had inserted in an evening newspaper:

"How Much Dough"

"Six peers of the realm wanted immediately for New York production," ran the advertisement. "Salary, expenses and passage paid. Telephone for appointment in the first instance to Mr. Ted Peckham, Central 2771."

"I had three lords on the 'phone within a few hours of the appearance of the advertisement," Mr. Peckham told the *Daily Mirror* last night.

"The first thing they wanted to know was how much dough they will get.

Would Not Give Names

"They were scared that they would have to do a strip-tease act, but I told them they would just have to play a small part in the show, and be polite to the ladies like a real lord.

"The funny part of it was that they would not give their names. I guess they're rather shy.

"I'm staying here until Wednesday, and I'm expecting to hire a few lords by then.

"The name of the show is 'Gentlemen for Hire.'"

BILL POWELL "VERY TIRED," WANTS REST

AFTER keeping to his cabin all the way across the Atlantic, screen idol William Powell was surprised when confronted with news cameras and reporters when the liner Statendam arrived at Plymouth yesterday.

He refused to discuss his vigil at the death bed of Jean Harlow, saying:—

"I am very tired. I am going to Holland for a couple of days' rest and then I shall go on to Paris. I shall rely on inspiration alone as to where I go after that.

"I am due back in Hollywood in November to make a picture for 20th Century Fox."

Wendy Barrie Storms: "I'm Not Wed!"

Centre of the controversy—film star Wendy Barrie (below).

FROM OUR OWN CORRESPONDENT

New York, Tuesday.

Wendy Barrie, the twenty-four-year-old British film actress who made her name in "The Private Lives of Henry VIII," opened a newspaper in Hollywood to-day to read that she was honeymooning hundreds of miles away at Joliet, Illinois, after a New York wedding to Bill Lawrence, an actor of nineteen.

"This wedding story is an absolute outrage," Wendy stormed over the 'phone when I rang he up to-night.

"Who is this Bill Lawrence? I've never heard of him in my life I haven't married anyone."

Then I telephoned the Joliet home to ask Bill's mother, Mrs. H. A. Skeas, if it were true that Bill had married film actress Wendy Barrie:

"Indeed, it is," replied Mrs. Skeas, her voice ringing with pride. "Bill vanished from home a fortnight ago. The other day he returned saying he and Wendy had married secretly in New York. Two days later Wendy, who had been held in New York by business, joined hi mhere. The happy things have gone out for the day."

AIDED MOTORIST, LOST LEG

Alan Frederick Ward, Woodside-avenue, Coventry, was helping to push a stranded car near Coventry to a garage yesterday when a van, driven by Sidney Edward Rayner, of Mount Pleasant, Alperton, Wembley, crashed into him.

Trapped between the vehicles, Ward was so severely injured that his right leg had to be amputated.

CLOTHES GAVE HIM AWAY

Walking home to dinner at midday yesterday, sixteen-year-old van boy Frederick Slack, of King-street, Exeter, saw a man struggling in the River Exe and being swept towards a weir.

He dived in, brought the man—Charles Willis, unemployed, of Newport (Mon.)—ashore, waited till artificial respiration had brought him round, and then walked away without giving his name.

Only when he returned to work in his best clothes did the story of the rescue come out

BY LAND, SEA AND AIR: FAMILY RALLY TO SICK QUEEN'S BEDSIDE

BY air, land and sea her family rallied yesterday to the bedside of Queen Alexandrine of Denmark, who was taken suddenly ill on Monday with gastric trouble, and was rushed to hospital for an operation.

The operation, says Reuter, is believed to have been successful, but four doctors are still in attendance.

King Christian, who had watched by his wife's bedside all night was able to snatch a few hours' rest yesterday.

The Crown Prince, after being informed of his mother's condition by wireless on board the warship in which he was at Danish naval manœuvres, left by aeroplane to be at his mother's bedside

His wife, Crown Princess Ingrid, is on her way to the hospital at Skagen by car, while the Queen's younger son, Prince Knud, and his wife arrived at Skagen by steamer from Copenhagen.

The King's sister, Princess Ingeborg of Sweden, and Princess Margareta, wife of Prince Axel of Denmark, also arrived by air

SATURDAY, SEPTEMBER 18, 1937

Daily Mirror

No. 10544 Registered at the G.P.O. as a Newspaper. ONE PENNY

FIRST KISS FOR 40 YEARS

BELISHA GOES "NAP"

Mr. Hore-Belisha, War Minister, struck this pose while watching, yesterday, French Army manœuvres. All he wants is the hat, and he's Napoleon !

TOUR OF DUKE'S VICAR COST £1,500

FROM OUR OWN CORRESPONDENT

NEW YORK, Friday.

THE Rev. Anderson Jardine, "the Duke's Vicar," has finished his lecture tour of America and gone home. Somebody lost £1,500 on the venture. Some of it came out of the pocket of the "poor man's parson," he admitted, as he stood to-day, a dejected figure in a cold drizzle on the deck of the homeward-bound American President.

Mr. Jardine would not name the loss, but Hugh C. Ernst, backer of the vicar's tour, was not so hesitant. "The project landed us £1,500 in the red," he stated.

AS LOST WIFE IS FOUND

FROM OUR OWN CORRESPONDENT

LETCHWORTH (Hertfordshire), Friday.

LITTLE, grey-haired Henry Tillyer, seventy-three-year-old hermit of Harlington, Middlesex, stepped from a bus, clasped hands and kissed a weeping, trembling old woman in the road at Letchworth to-night. It was Ellen, his wife. He had not seen her for forty years.

Their kiss was the pledge that two broken lives will be linked again in the village where their romance ended after five years of married life.

For years Henry Tillyer searched the country for the woman he had loved and lost, before settling in a hut at Hartlington near the spot where he had courted her.

"I Have Never Forgotten

"If I could find her and she would forget the past I would start a new home," he told the *Daily Mirror* on Tuesday night. Their meeting to-day was a sequel to that vow.

"I forgive you. I will come down to your hut and talk about the future," was the answer he received when he met his sixty-four-year-old wife.

Twenty-four hours before they met Mr Tillyer saw his daughter Ada in a London hospital for the first time since she was a baby in arms. From her he learned that Mrs Tillyer was in service in Letchworth and set off by road to see her.

In the road the old couple clasped hands and kissed but both of them were too distressed to talk.

"I feel to ill to talk to my husband now" Mrs Tillyer told the *Daily Mirror*.

"I still wear my wedding ring, and have never forgotten that I am his wife.

"It is forty years since we separated in our little cottage in Harlington. I had two babies Ada and Albert. They were both in arms

(Continued on back page)

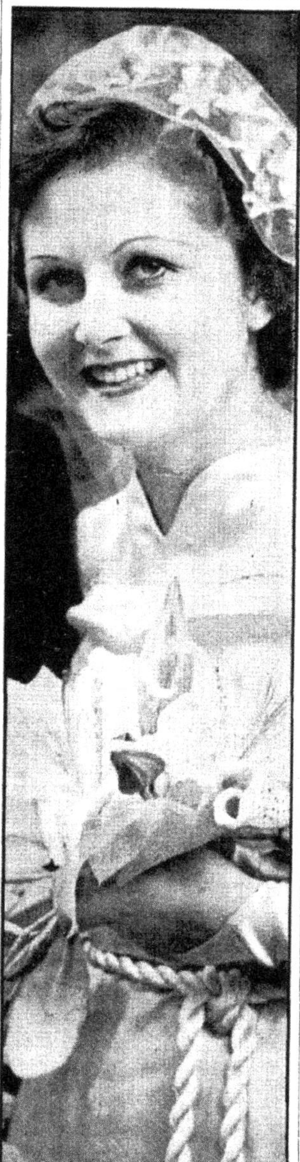

Lovely, in a girdled wedding gown, Miss Dorothy North, daughter of the Hon. Mrs. Dudley North, and a relative of Lord North, after her wedding at St. James's, Spanish-place, London, yesterday, to Mr. R. A. C. Graham.

Two Mice in "Lost World"

The fifteen scientists who have scaled 2,000ft. into the sky to the "Lost World" above the Grand Canyon of Arizona, have so far discovered—two mice.

Not a sign of the mammoths or any of the prehistoric monsters which peopled the "lost world" of Conan Doyle's story.

But they also found chippings of stone arrowheads—proving that the scientists are not the first men to have reached the summit of the plateau.—British United Press.

ROOSEVELT ATTACKS THE DICTATORS

PRESIDENT Roosevelt, speaking at the foot of the Washington Monument in Washington yesterday—Constitution Day—condemned dictatorships as a "threat to world civilisation."

"The known and measurable danger of becoming involved in war, we face confidently," he said, reports Reuter early to-day.

"But it takes even more foresight, intelligence and patience to meet the subtle attack which the spreading of dictatorship makes upon the morale of a democracy."

What happened in Europe affected them in America. Lately there had been a clear challenge in various parts of the world to the democratic idea of representative government.

"Their leaders laugh at all Constitutions, predict the copying of their own methods and prophesy an early end of democracy throughout the world.

"Both that attitude and that prediction are denied by those of us who still believe in democracy—that is, by the overwhelming majority of the nations of the world and by the overwhelming majority of the people of the world."

He pledged himself to seek, within the limits of the Constitution, the reforms he felt were essential to preserve American democracy.

Mrs. Petre's 90 m.p.h. Crash

WOMAN CAR "ACE" HURT

PETITE, dark-haired Kay Petre—Britain's ace woman race-driver—was unconscious in Weybridge Hospital last night with a fractured skull following a 90-m.p.h. crash while practising at Brooklands for the 500 kilometre race there to-day.

Shortly before midnight her condition was said to be "critical."

Her car and another, driven by Mr. R. Parnell, are believed to have touched in passing, causing Mrs Petre's to overturn while the other crashed over the Byfleet bank. Mr. Parnell was unhurt.

"Her crash helmet undoubtedly saved her life," said an official of the British Racing Drivers' Club, last night. "Wreckage from her car was strewn over the track for more than a hundred yards

"The two cars passed the timekeeper's box within six seconds of each other. Mrs. Petre was in front but Mr. Parnell was travelling about ten miles an hour faster. The track was wet and as Mrs. Petre was overtaken the two cars must have touched."

Pictures on page 15.

TREBITSCH LINCOLN AGAIN

TREBITSCH Lincoln, ex-M.P. for Darlington, who was accused of being a German spy, was reported by Exchange last night to have arrived at Peiping

He is now a Buddhist monk going under the name of Chao Kung.

Fears for Japanese liner—Page 2

MYSTERY SEAPLANE OVER BRITISH PORT

FROM OUR OWN CORRESPONDENT

FALMOUTH, Friday.

SAILORS on the decks of the Spanish Government destroyer Jose Luis Diez, in the harbour here ran for cover to-day when an unidentified seaplane, flying in from the open sea, dipped and circled over the warship before making off in the direction in which it had come.

It had no markings by which it could be identified.

The 'plane's mysterious disappearance added to the wild rumours circulating here since it was stated the Jose Luis Diez, after undergoing repairs, was expected to leave at any moment.

Evidence that a Franco submarine is lurking outside Falmouth Harbour for the Jose Luis Diez was given me to-night by Captain G. Parks, master of the tug Lynch, when he anchored in the harbour. He saw the submarine two days ago about three miles south-east of St. Anthony Lighthouse, he said.

MONDAY, SEPTEMBER 20, 1937

Daily Mirror

No. 10545 Registered at the G.P.O. as a Newspaper. ONE PENNY

WINNIE MELVILLE DIES ON EVE OF HER STAGE "COME-BACK"

WINNIE Melville, propped up in bed in a London hospital yesterday, read over the copies of songs which helped to make her famous—and talked of the stage "come back" that she planned. Her dreams will never come true. Within a few hours of reading those old songs she was dead. She was forty-two.

At her bedside in St. Mary's Hospital, Paddington, where she had been ill for some months, were copies of melodies which she helped to make famous in "The Vagabond King"—in which she and her husband, Derek Oldham, the actor and singer, took the leading parts—and other musical plays.

In "The Vagabond King" Winnie Melville and Derek Oldham established themselves as the best-loved stage lovers of the day. The balcony scene in which they sang the duet, "Only a Rose," thrilled thousands.

At the Starting Place

At sixteen Winnie Melville won a singing competition. She was in the Folies-Bergeres at the end of the war.

Four years ago she parted from her stage, and life, partner, Derek Oldham, actor and singer, whom she married in 1923. There was a decree of judicial separation.

After four years' absence from the stage she was examined in bankruptcy last October at Windsor.

Then she determined to "come-back." She sang at the Pavilion, Worthing, where she had begun her career, as a girl of sixteen, by winning a singing competition and a £2 10s. a week job.

After this "come-back" appearance she said that she had been "snowed under" with offers to appear in the provinces, the West End and the U.S.

But illness defeated her. Last April she was compelled to seek help from the Actors' Benevolent Fund.

She was taken seriously ill

Help Repaid

Mr. W. G. Gray, secretary of the Actors' Benevolent Fund, and friend of Miss Melville, told the *Daily Mirror* yesterday:

"Only a short while ago Derek Oldham arranged through his solicitors that she should receive a regular allowance which would have made her independent.

"While living with her mother at Cambridge Court, Hyde Park, four or five months ago, she applied to the Fund for help.

"Derek Oldham got to know of this and repaid all the money we had given her—on condition that we kept it secret.

"Then, in July this year she slipped. She was taken to Middlesex Hospital.

"Again Derek Oldham came forward. And when she was discharged he arranged that she should have two or three months' holiday at his expense.

Bid to Save Another's Baby

Mrs. Thomas Dack mother of the twins.

Seen here with her own little daughter, Mrs. Amy Abbott, of Chelmsford (Essex) answered a broadcast S O S for a foster mother to save survivor of twins born at Wells, Norfolk, to Mrs. Thomas Dack

But in vain—the second twin died shortly after she arrived. **See story on page 5.**

"Swing" Music Is Immoral

FROM OUR OWN CORRESPONDENT

New York, Sunday.

A campaign for banning swing music as "highly dangerous to morality" has been started by the American Creative League of Music Students following a "Peeping Tom" test on a young couple.

Announcing that the League planned to introduce an anti-swing music Bill into all American State Legislatures, Mr. Arthur Cremin, its president, described one of several experiments on which the move is based.

"We placed a youth and a girl in a room where we could see them without being observed," he said. "First we arranged a radio programme of good music, classical pieces and popular songs, such as waltzes.

"They were friendly, but that was all. Later we arranged another meeting. This time we played swing music. They were both much bolder, and the result was shocking."

LADY TREDEGAR DIES AT 37

FORMER leader of young London society, Viscountess Tredegar died suddenly on Saturday in Budapest at the home of a friend with whom she was staying. She was thirty-seven.

Her brother, Lord Alington, flew to Budapest yesterday after hearing the news.

Lady Tredegar married the Hon. Evan Morgan in 1928 at a brilliant ceremony in Brompton Oratory. Six years later he succeeded to the title.

As the Hon. Lois Sturt she was a great friend of Lady Diana Duff Cooper, with whom she appeared as Nell Gwyn in the film "The Great Adventure."

She often had lunch hatless at fashionable West End restaurants, could speak several languages and had passed her flying tests.

Her husband inherited the bulk of the £2,300,000 estate of his father.

Winnie Melville with Derek Oldham in "The Vagabond King."

TRAIN DERAILED: STATION 'SIEGE'

CANNON-STREET Station, usually the quietest of the London main line stations on a Sunday, was yesterday beseiged by hundreds of anxious friends and relations waiting to meet passengers in the Continental boat trains.

The reason—traffic had been diverted there after the engine of the 12.35 p.m. Dover to Victoria boat-train—"The Swiss Special"—had jumped the rails after passing Brixton Station, blocking the main line to Victoria.

About 500 passengers were on the train, but none of the coaches left the rails, and no one was hurt.

Nearly a hundred porters and customs officials were rushed to Cannon-street in three coaches to deal with the crush there.

People waiting at Victoria to greet the later Continental trains hurried by taxi, bus and train to Cannon-street, and for some time chaos prevailed.

The station forecourt was packed with taxis, coaches and private cars, and extra police were called to deal with the situation.

Shortly after 5 o'clock the derailed engine was replaced on the lines and proceeded to Victoria

Seven Years Nearer Freedom, but— HATRY IS NOW SERIOUSLY ILL

CLARENCE Hatry, who was sentenced to fourteen years penal servitude in 1930 on charges in connection with various companies, is seriously ill in Maidstone prison suffering from phlebitis.

A close friend who has received a letter from him said yesterday that Hatry, who is forty-eight, had already spent four months in bed. After being up for a short time, he had now been ordered to bed again.

"He never suffered from phlebitis before he went to prison," the friend said.

"Hatry,' he added, "has made gardening his chief hobby while at Maidstone. Friends have sent him gifts of rock plants for his rockery, which has become almost famous. It has been seen by many visitors to the prison, including the Archbishop of Canterbury."

SATURDAY, SEPTEMBER 25, 1937

Daily Mirror

No. 10550 — Registered at the G.P.O. as a Newspaper. — ONE PENNY

MOTHERS FIGHT OFF WOMAN

RAIDER'S ATTACKS ON THEIR BABIES

FROM OUR SPECIAL CORRESPONDENT

TWO babies, two mothers, a nursemaid and a man were attacked by a woman in Eastholme, Golder's Green, N.W., last night.

She crouched over one baby's pram with a tricycle raise[illegible] in her arms, as though she were going to smash it down, and in another house tried to grab a baby out of the arms of a nurse.

The first house she entered was that of Mr. and Mrs. Charles Howard.

Mrs. Howard said: "She crept in through the back door, which was unlatched, and entered a room in which my fourteen-month-old girl was sitting with her nurse.

Nurse Fights Her Off

"When she saw the woman, the nurse picked the baby up in her arms and the woman leapt towards her.

"She tried to grab the baby, but my nurse beat her off. For five minutes they struggled and during that time the woman had dragged both the nurse and the baby towards the back door.

"Then I heard the commotion and rushed into the room. I saw it was a woman with whom we were friendly, but it seemed as though she had gone quite mad. I fought to help baby and the nurse, and finally we beat the woman off.

"Ten minutes later I saw the back door opening slowly again and once more the woman entered.

"She made another lunge at the baby, and for a few minutes the room was like Bedlam. My hair was torn down and my dress ripped.

"Then the woman ran out of the house and I telephoned the police."

"Crouching Over Pram"

Mrs. F. Hallgarten, who lives in the same street, saw the woman bending over the pram in which her three-month-old baby daughter was lying.

"I said 'Good evening' to her as I knew she lived somewhere in the street," said Mrs. Hallgarten.

"She didn't answer but made as though to strike me. I ran into the house and took baby with me.

"I heard the woman run round to the back of the house and when I went through I saw her crouching over the pram with a tricycle raised as though she were going to smash it down on the baby."

"When she saw me she made off."

Mr. H. Hammersmith, who lives next door to Mrs Hallgarten, was also attacked.

He was walking along Eastholme when the woman dashed across the road towards him shouting something about "toys and torture."

She then hit him hard three times

Later the woman was found hiding in her house in Eastholme and was taken away by four policemen

LUCKIEST DOG IS THE MAN

You see the crashed aeroplane in this picture? You see the airman sitting beside it, playing with a couple of dogs? WELL, HE WAS IN THE 'EROPLANE WHEN IT CRASHED — at Gunthorpe, Notts, yesterday. Some folk are just born lucky!

Love Takes a Holiday and—

POLICE TAKE THE LOVER

FROM OUR OWN CORRESPONDENT

MINEHEAD, Friday.

ALLAN Down, twenty-seven-year-old groom, of Cutcombe, near here, had three days' holiday. He spent it with his sweetheart in Brendon, North Devon . . . and wondered how he could prolong his stay.

This, according to evidence at Dunster to-day, was his idea:

On the day he was due to return, he telephoned his employer, the Hon. Mrs. Drury Lowe, at Cutcombe, saying he had been knocked down by a car containing three men, was injured and was unable to return.

Mrs. Drury Lowe told the police. They sought Down's assistance in tracing the driver of the car.

Finally he admitted that there had not been an accident.

And now Allan, accused of commiting a public mischief, is committed for trial

STAGE STAR WEPT, THEN—

Boos from the gallery at the Palace Theatre on Thursday night sent Barbara Blair, star of the new show, "Take It Easy," weeping to her dressing-room.

Last night there were cheers instead as Miss Blair appeared before the footlights. S[illegible] she to the *Daily Mirror* later:

"I feel better now and feel sure we shall have a show worthy of a long run at the Palace."

Peter Panna Neagle

Miss Anna Neagle, the actress, and star of the British film "Victoria the Great," has been engaged by Daniel Mayer Company, Ltd., to play Peter Pan at the Palladium on Christmas Eve.

BOY SHOOTS HEADMISTRESS

'TOUGH GUY' AGED 12

FROM OUR OWN CORRESPONDENT

NEW YORK, Friday.

TWELVE-YEAR-OLD Robert Snyder, of Toledo, thrilled by radio gangster dramas, determined to become a "tough guy" himself.

He stole an automatic pistol from his father, cracked into the office of fifty-nine-year-old June Mapps, principal of the local high school

Said he: "I want to see Gloria Moore."

Miss Mapps said: "No"—and received five shots from the young gangster's pistol.

Snyder then fled, and on the way between school and his home shot himself in the head. He now lies between life and death.

Pretty Gloria Moore said to me to-night:—

"I don't know why he wanted to see me. I only knew him as a casual classmate acquaintance"

THURSDAY, SEPTEMBER 30, 1937

Daily Mirror

No. 10554 Registered at the G.P.O. as a Newspaper. ONE PENNY

ENDEAVOUR IN PORT TO-NIGHT —WOODROOFFE IS TO BROADCAST

FROM OUR SPECIAL CORRESPONDENT

GOSPORT, Wednesday.

LIEUTENANT-COMMANDER Thomas Woodrooffe, the man who said " The Fleet's lit up," will give a radio commentary on the homecoming of Endeavour I.

In making this announcement to-night, the B.B.C. said that the time and place was still uncertain, but all Gosport is confident that Endeavour will sail into port here to-morrow night, and is preparing a welcome worthy of its triumph.

Presumably the broadcast will take place from here. Listeners in America are to hear it.

Lieutenant-Commander Woodrooffe gave the broadcast description of the illuminations of the Fleet at Spithead in May—" The Fleet's Lit Up " commentary. Later the B.B.C. announced that he was to be transferred, after sick leave, to duties which, for a time, would not involve his speaking at the microphone.

Yesterday the Belgian motor-tanker Esso Belgium wirelessed Lloyd's that she had just sighted Endeavour about 160 miles off the Lizard. Air Ministry reports indicated last night that the yacht will be aided by a calm sea in the final phase of her homeward journey.

Captain V-rnon H. Alcock, master of the Cheyenne, broadcasting to-night an account of his meeting with the Endeavour, said that he proceeded after learning that Endeavour was all right because he knew that Captain Heard would wish to continue himself, having gone so far.

Scores of men were busy putting up flags bunting and welcome messages—" You made it after all "—at Gosport to-day, while the Mayor Major C. F. O. Graham, arranged for a civic reception at the local cinema.

A Wife's View

The feeling among local people, however is that all the work will have been in vain.

Captain Ned Heard, skipper of Endeavour I, is known as a dour sailorman who dislikes any kind of fuss, and it is thought that he will sail quietly into the harbour and refuse to attend any such " modern nonsense " as a civic ceremony.

This evening Mrs. Heard and her daughter Mrs. Rice, wife of another member of the crew, arrived in the town to stay with friends and greet their husbands on their arrival.

Both of them were surprised at the enthusiasm of the port.

" I am sure I don't know what all this fuss is about," Mrs. Heard said to me.

" My husband reckoned to get across within two weeks and he has done so. He has done nothing wonderful and I've not worried about him at all for one moment."

Other relatives of members of the crew are expected to-morrow morning.

The First Picture of the Gallant Endeavour I

The first picture of Endeavour I to be taken since she parted from her mother ship in mid-Atlantic. While all Britain felt anxiety for her safety, the yacht was bowling merrily along as you see in this picture—all sails set and riding the waves like a conqueror. It was like this that she was snapped by a steward from the steamer Cheyenne, 250 miles from the Irish coast.

The man who first saw Endeavour I—A. Allison (dark suit), mate of the Cheyenne, with P. H. King, jun., second engineer.

Radio Kills Canary

Jimmy, the canary pet of a Sheffield woman, was a grand singer. From morn till night he warbled in his cage resting on a radio set.

This week he was singing as usual to music coming from the radio. His song became stronger and stronger, then suddenly it ceased, and Jimmy was found dead.

In trying to beat the wireless he had burst his heart.

TWO BRITONS CRASH IN ITALY

TWO London people were gravely injured near Udine, North Italy, yesterday, when the chauffeur of their motor-car lost control while passing another car.

They are: Mrs. James Margaret Woodhouse and Mr. William Woodhouse Lane.

Mrs. Woodhouse received multiple fractures of the skull and last night was unconscious in hospital while doctors fought for her life.

Lane sustained fractures of the right hip and head injuries.

SURPRISE £5,000 GRANT TO SHOT BRITISH AMBASSADOR

THE Government has made the unprecedented decision to grant £5,000 compensation to Sir Hughe Knatchbull-Hugessen, the Ambassador shot from a Japanese warplane as he was travelling with his staff by car from Nanking to Shanghai.

Last night the Foreign Office made the following announcement:—

" In view of the grievous injuries sustained by H.M. Ambassador in China, and the possible prejudice to his future health, his Majesty's Government propose to ask Parliament to vote him the sum of £5,000."

Sir Hughe, who was severely injured in the back, left hospital on September 26, and on Monday will sail with his family on a tour to the Dutch East Indies. He is expected to return at the end of November.

At the end of a war it is quite common for

(Continued on back page)

BRITAIN URGES CONFERENCE

Lord Cranborne, Under-Secretary of State for Foreign Affairs, stated in the Committee of twenty-three at Geneva last night, says Reuter, that the British Government would be ready to concur in a conference of Powers to arrange some settlement of the Far East conflict if all the other Powers interested would agree.

4 DETAINED AFTER STREET FIGHT

FOR twenty-five minutes a struggling screaming group of men and women defied the efforts of the police to separate them in Clerkenwell-road, E.C., late last night.

" It was a lovely scrap," an eye-witness told the *Daily Mirror*. " It began just after the pubs closed and started by being a family affair. The main combatants were two men and two women.

" When the police tried to interfere the crowd joined in, and the women were flung, screaming, to the ground.

" Eventually more police arrived and four people were taken to Gray's Inn-road police station."

SATURDAY, OCTOBER 2, 1937

Daily Mirror

No. 10556 Registered at the G.P.O. as a Newspaper ONE PENNY

ENDEAVOUR MEN JOKED WHEN WITHIN ACE OF DEATH

"It was useless to try to pilot the ship—she was completely out of control and we were at the mercy of the waves. And all the time one or two of the fellows would try to keep up our spirits by cracking jokes."

THESE words of one of the Endeavour I heroes yesterday summed up their heroic battle with an Atlantic hurricane after they had broken adrift from their towing ship.

As if to make amends for Endeavour's fight with the elements nature had stage-managed with wonderful effect the homecoming of Endeavour I to Gosport yesterday.

Crowds had gathered since dawn to greet the yacht and her gallant crew. Her progress up the Solent had been reported from point to point. As the haze lifted at the mouth of the harbour, the slim shadow of the mast of Endeavour I could be seen towering above the anchored shipping.

Captain Heard, skipper of the Endeavour, with his wife and the Mayor of Gosport. Another welcome picture on pages 16 and 17.

Bunting stretched across the approaches to the harbour and flags fluttered a welcome both from England and America.

Roar after roar of cheers crashed out as the yacht glided gracefully to her moorings, towed by the motor vessel Viva II.

The quayside was black with thousands of eager watchers. Speed-boats flashed over the sunlit waters, trumpets sounded, and as one after another vessel riding at anchor sighted Endeavour, great bays from their sirens rent the air.

When Endeavour was first sighted some of the wives of the crew, who were being brought from the village of Tollesbury, Essex, to greet their husbands, had not reached Gosport.

Relatives of the skipper and crew were ferried across the narrow strip of water between one of the landing stages and the Endeavour.

There were touching scenes as relatives greeted their men folk. Some of the wives had brought their children.

Little by little a story that will rank as one of the great epics of the sea was told.

One of the most dramatic accounts was that given by Joe Uglow, second cook, as he showed his relatives from Looe, in Cornwall over the yacht.

Joe piloted them through the various quarters of Endeavour where for nearly nineteen days they had been more or less imprisoned in what he described "as a submarine."

He told how the water rushed down the hatchways like a Niagara, and then took them into the compartment aft of the ship, which had been used more or less as a wireless room.

The water was rising rapidly and it was every man to the pumps.

"We worked frantically during that nine hours' hurricane, which none of us will ever forget.

"During the whole of this time it was impossible to raise a sail or to go on deck.

(Continued on back page)

GOLF A 'DANGEROUS GAME' SAYS OSTEOPATH

AS an exercise, golf is fallacious.

This view was expressed by Mr. T. Mitchell-Fox, speaking at the Osteopathic Association of Great Britain conference in London yesterday.

"Golf is a positive source of income for the osteopath," he said. "It is the most dangerous game in the world. You get everything from a bad toe to a bad temper.

"Any exercise the golfer gets is lost by the nineteenth hole. You get as much exercise going for a walk in the country, kicking a ball, or knocking the head off a daisy.

"The majority of people who play the game do so at week-ends, when they are not prepared for sudden athletic activity.

"Tempers are frayed, and they hit like fury, and something happens. Everyone of any age, who wants to play golf, should be conditioned for the game."

Pam Barton, girl golf champion, chuckled when I suggested that golf was dangerous.

"Rubbish," she said. "I've never had a bad toe or a bad temper in all the time I've been playing. Golf is one of the easiest of all games for a woman. Of course, you have to be fit, but it doesn't require strenuous training."

BRITAIN ROUNDS UP ARAB LEADERS IN DRASTIC PALESTINE PURGE

Mr. L. Y. Andrews, District Commissioner of Galilee District, whose murder brought situation to a head

Hussein Khalidi, Mayor of Jerusalem, for whose arrest a warrant was issued in Palestine

PALESTINE—land of death and unrest for years—was the stage for swiftly-moving drama yesterday. British authorities, tired of the work of the terrorists, launched drastic measures. Arab leaders, threatened with arrest and exile, rushed into hiding. Strong guards of troops were posted at key spots.

Warrants were issued for the arrest of the Mayor of Jerusalem—and other leaders. They will be deported.

The Grand Mufti of Jerusalem—head of the Palestine Arabs—has been turned out of office as President of the Supreme Moslem Council.

The Arab Higher Committee is declared illegal.

Jerusalem "Gag"

When the country woke yesterday it was to find that all telephone communication had been cut off—and officials, troops and police were very active.

An Arab challenged by sentries refused to halt. He was shot dead.

Censorship was clamped down on Jerusalem by the District Commissioner.

At Haifa troops armed with machine guns surrounded the offices of the District Commissioner while police searched the offices.

Action is said to have followed an Arab "ultimatum" demanding release of the 200 prisoners arrested after the Nazareth murder of Mr. Andrews, District Commissioner of Galilee.

"Wanted" Men

A Government communique announced that the Government had been "gravely concerned by the existence of an organised campaign of terrorism and assassination directed against individuals."

It recalled the attempt to assassinate Mr. R. G. B. Spicer, Inspector-General of Police, on June 14, the murders of Jews and Arabs, and, finally, the murder of Mr. Lewis Andrews and his bodyguard, Police-Constable Peter McEwan.

Arrest warrants were issued for: Jamal Husseini, Ahmed Hilmi Pasha, Fuad Saba (secretary of the Higher Arab Committee), Yacoub Husseini and Dr. Hussein Khalidi (Mayor of Jerusalem).

Jamal Husseini was arrested at Beersheba.

—Reuter, British United Press and Central News.

THAT'S A FIRM—THAT WAS

"My firm went out of business suddenly," said a defendant at Clerkenwell County Court, yesterday.

Mr. Registrar Friend: It must have been very suddenly. I see it happened between the letter you wrote to the Court and the postcript!

FIVE DROWN AS SHIP CAPSIZES

FIVE men belonging to the small Sunderland steamer Taylor (204 tons) were drowned when their ship capsized off Buchan Ness, Aberdeenshire, early yesterday.

The only survivor, Captain John Olsen, aged fifty-six, the Norwegian skipper, was in the water for five hours, clinging to two railway sleepers, until he was rescued by the Aberdeen trawler, Ocean Princess (203 tons).

The trawler ran into wreckage from the Taylor and then heard shouts from the water. James Innes, a deck hand, dived overboard in the darkness with a line and rescued Olsen, whose first words were, "There are another five men in the water."

A thorough search failed to reveal any trace of the men.

Skipper Alexander Bruce, of the Ocean Princess, stated that they heard a cry as they struck the wreckage.

It was a dark night, raining, and the sea was choppy, but one of the crew saw the light of the ship shining on what proved to be the peak of Captain Olsen's cap.

Olsen told them that his ship took a heavy list and the engine-room filled with water. She turned over and sank before they could get to the small boat.

The rest of the Taylor's crew are: William Dedling, mate, Fulwell-road, Sunderland; Alexander Forbes, able seaman, Barrasgate-road, Fraserburgh, Aberdeenshire; George Oag, first engineer, Louisebergh-street, Wick; John Blair, second engineer, Ballet-place, Fraserburgh, and James Joiner, ordinary seaman.

CATS RAID HOUSES

For neglecting two cats, George Neave, of Natal-road, Thornton Heath, Surrey, was fined 5s., with one guinea costs, at Croydon yesterday.

Prosecuting for the R.S.P.C.A., Mr. Gordon Jones said, "This is a typical case of people moving away and leaving behind cats without troubling to see that they will be in any way cared for."

It was stated that for three weeks the cats roamed about homeless and starving. They raided houses for food. One of the cats got into a kitchen and, jumping on to the stove, tried to nose open the lids of the saucepans. When given food the cats fought one another for it.

TUESDAY, OCTOBER 5, 1937

Daily Mirror

No. 10558 — Registered at the G.P.O. as a Newspaper. — ONE PENNY

BRITISH WARSHIP ATTACKED BY PIRATE SUBMARINE OFF SPAIN

H.M.S. Basilisk, 1,360-ton destroyer, taking part in the British Mediterranean patrol was attacked by a pirate submarine yesterday off Cape San Antonio seventy miles south-east of Valencia.

Basilisk and another destroyer were steaming down the Spanish coast twenty-five miles off shore when the pirate's periscope was sighted to landward.

A few seconds later the periscope was submerged and three torpedoes were launched at the destroyers.

Seeing their danger the destroyers steamed full out in circles.

Ocean Hunt

Three terrific explosions followed, were heard in the San Antonio semaphore station.

Exchanging radio signals, the destroyers continued to zig-zag over the spot where the periscope of the pirate disappeared.

In a few minutes five more British warships raced up and joined the hunt.

Thud after thud was heard ashore as the warships dropped depth charges over the trail of the fugitive.

In the listening-posts deep down in the destroyers' hulls men at the hydrophones followed the throb of the pirate's engines as she raced shorewards, and kept the officers on the bridge and in the gun control towers close on her heels as she raced for cover.

The pursuers divided into two groups of four and three.

The first group scoured the sea for twenty miles east of the Cape and the second sailed along the coast in a south-easterly direction

Smoke on the Sea

Three Navy seaplanes joined the search and eventually converged at a point in-shore near the second group of destroyers.

Soon afterwards watchers at the semaphore station saw dense clouds of smoke rise from the sea near the destroyers.

It hung over the water for twelve minutes and the search party steamed away to the south.

Basilisk is captained by Commander E. Dangerfield, and is one of ten British warships which went to the Mediterranean recently to join the anti-piracy patrol.

It was stated officially in Gibraltar later that Basilisk had been attacked and had taken retaliatory action, the result of which was unknown. The search for the pirate was continuing early to-day.

H. M. S. Basilisk. Laid down at Clydebank as part of 1928 programme and launched in 1930, she carries eleven guns and eight torpedo tubes.

ON A BENCH IN THE PARK

As part of the "brighter parks" campaign of Sir Philip Sassoon, First Commissioner of Works, new benches were installed in St. James's Park, London, yesterday . . . and the Prime Minister, Mr. Neville Chamberlain, was one of the first to try them, as you see in this picture.

The seats are being paid for by public subscription. The King and Queen and Queen Mary have each provided one.

UNIVERSITY GIRLS PHOTOGRAPHED NUDE "FOR SCIENTIFIC PURPOSES"

FROM OUR OWN CORRESPONDENT

MICHIGAN, Monday.

HUNDREDS of horrified parents were telephoning Wayne University, Michigan, to-day, protesting vehemently at the University permitting their daughters to be photographed in the nude "for scientific purposes."

They had heard an amazing story of how hundreds of Wayne undergraduettes were stripped of their clothes, masked, then photographed with "candid cameras" by officials of the university's health faculty

Barely surviving the storm of protest, Dr. Irwin Sander, chief of health faculty, told me: "I am astonished at the publicity given this photography. Hundreds of students have been photographed since the project was mooted. Only three objected.

"All the photographs were taken with the aim of correcting posture defects."

But the Board of Education is to appoint a committee to inquire

Hitler To Be An Angel: Official

"I am convinced that when the Leader passes into eternity the Supreme Judge will not have to judge long but will open Heaven to him."

Herr Julius Streicher, Governor of Franconia, made this declaration in a Harvest Day speech at Nuremberg.

TIGER KILLS TWO BRITONS IN CAR

MR. H. G Mills, British resident of the United Provinces, and his wife have died in hospital after being attacked by a man-eating tiger while motoring from Dehra Dun to Sirmur, says a Reuter message from Lahore.

The tiger appeared in the road, and when they hooted at the beast it sprang on the car and mauled both occupants.

A party has gone out to track the tiger.

TUESDAY, OCTOBER 12, 1937

Daily Mirror

No. 10564 Registered at the G.P.O. as a Newspaper. ONE PENNY

WIDOW'S LOVE NOTES PESTER COUPLE FOR TWO YEARS

FROM OUR SPECIAL CORRESPONDENT

READING, Monday.

For two and a half years, Mr. and Mrs. William Clancy, grey-haired couple, have sat in fear of the postman's knock—boarded their letter-box and the foot of the door of their villa in Wantage-road, here—so that the letters sent by a woman should not be delivered to them.

AT Berkshire Quarter Sessions to-day the couple came face to face with their woman tormentor. Forty-eight-year-old Mrs. Rose Elizabeth Kempster, of Forest Gate, London, E., was sentenced to six months' hard labour on eight charges of sending indecent letters through the post.

Grey-haired, his face lined, William Clancy, trainer of Reading Football Club, told me to-night how he and his wife have faced a campaign of abuse and obscenity from the pen of Rose Elizabeth Kempster.

"Thank God it is all over," he said. "It has been a terrible time for my wife. She has gone straight to bed, as she collapsed in the court.

"It all began some years ago when Mrs. Kempster boarded members of the football club.

"In one of the letters she alleged she had seen me with all kinds of women.

"This July, when I was visiting my mother in Wales, she wrote to my wife here saying she was having a holiday with me in Torquay.

Still Attached to Him

"I never knew what else was in that letter. My wife destroyed it."

In Court Mrs. Kempster said she cut four photographs of Mr. Clancy from a newspaper and preserved them

When the chairman asked her why, she replied: "I was very fond of the gentleman at one time."

Mr. R. G. Micklethwait (prosecuting): You are still very much attached to Mr. Clancy, aren't you?—Yes.

Dr. Anna R. Glover, medical officer at Holloway Prison, said that Kempster was not certifiable.

A "SMILING PRINCE" AGAIN

Remember the smiling Prince? These pictures show you how he came back again yesterday when the Duke of Windsor began his study of labour conditions at Berlin factories.

Above: The Duke laughing as he talks to workers with Dr Ley, Labour Front leader, also seen with the Duke in circle

A. STANDS FOR 8 IN FAMILY BUT WHICH?

BY A SPECIAL CORRESPONDENT

AS eight of her nine children have Christian names beginning with the letter "A" life has been a complicated business for sixty-four-year-old Mrs. Fanny Stevens, of Parnell-road, Old Ford, E. Last night she told me that when the postman came with letters addressed to "Mr. A. Stevens," she had to open them to see if they were for Alfred, Arthur, Albert, Archie or Andy.

If any young men called and asked to see "Miss Stevens," she used to ask if they meant Annie, Alice or Ada.

The only one she never had any doubt about was Willie—who broke the sequence in honour of two favourite uncles.

Yesterday the names complication was carried into Clerkenwell County Court. Arthur was sued for £6—cost of alleged damages to a motor-car. But brother Archie appeared and said he was driving the car which was said to have caused the damage.

First Come–

"I must abandon my brief—I am defending the wrong man," observed Mr. Quintin Hogg, son of the Lord Chancellor.

Judge Earengey gave leave to amend the name in the summons.

"What happens," he asked Archie, "when you get a letter? Do you have to hold a conference?"

(Continued on back page)

Outstretched arms as members of the crowd seek to shake the Duke's hand when he left his hotel to visit the factory. Similar scenes marked his arrival at the hotel with the Duchess. A great throng filled the wide street as he entered the building, and there were shouts to him to appear at a window. See story on page 3.

THE MAN WHO PUT HIS FOOT IN IT

FROM OUR OWN CORRESPONDENT

SOUTHAMPTON, Monday.

IT had been raining. A man, collar turned up, head down, hurried along.

He walked through a puddle, and on the next dry paving-stone his rubber-soled shoe left a wet footprint—a peculiar print.

Behind the man came Detective-Inspector William Moore, of the Southampton police. He saw the print. He had seen one very much like it before.

In fact, he had in his pocket a photograph of a similar print left behind in a shop which had been broken into three days before.

The detective stopped the man, questioned him, and as a result Ernest George Carter, aged twenty-nine, a valet, pleaded guilty at Southampton Police Court, yesterday, to a charge of shopbreaking and larceny. He was committed for trial.

WEDNESDAY, OCTOBER 13, 1937

Daily Mirror

No. 10565 Registered at the G.P.O. as a Newspaper. ONE PENNY

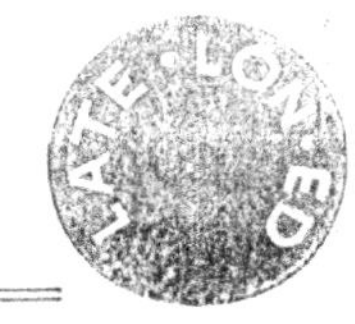

I SEE GANGSTERS SHOT DOWN BY G-MEN IN STREET FIGHT

Two gunmen were shot dead and another was wounded by G-men in one of the most amazing street battles of American history at Bangor (Maine) yesterday. They had been betrayed by the wife of one of them.

The "Daily Mirror" Correspondent, warned by the police that arrests were expected, stood by and saw the whole battle, while bullets spattered his car.

By JOHN B. WALTERS

"DAILY MIRROR" SPECIAL CORRESPONDENT

BANGOR (Maine), Tuesday.

CROUCHING in the shelter of my car in the main street of this little town to-day I saw Al Brady, America's Public Enemy No. 1 and triple murderer, fight to death with two of his henchmen as G-men raked the street with a machine-gun.

As the hail of bullets began, screaming women shoppers flung themselves to the pavement or crouched terrified behind the counters of stores, dragging their children to safety.

Men raced for cover; motorists jerked their cars to a stop and doubled down for shelter on the floor.

Bullets flicked past my head as I leaped to safety behind my car.

He Filmed It

In the middle of it all Shap Hurd, young shop assistant whose tip-off led the G-men to prepare their ambush, calmly knelt on the pavement filming the battle with a miniature movie camera as the bullets flew around.

The first shots rang out as Brady and two notorious gunmen, Clarence Shaffer and James Dalhover, slipped into the street from the sports shop where Hurd is employed.

From an empty building opposite a machine-gun, concealed by G-men earlier in the morning, stuttered out its deadly hail.

Above its din came the shouts of men warning the women and children lying on the pavements to lie flat and keep their heads down.

Brady and his killers fought like madmen. I saw G-man Walsh plunge to the ground, a smear of blood across his temple.

Then Brady tottered, his gun dropped from his hand, and he fell dead, shot through the head. Shaffer was next. I heard him snarl like a dog as a bullet struck and killed him.

Dalhover, his face blood-smeared, threw up his hands and surrendered.

G-men sprang at him, snapped the handcuffs on his wrists.

Squads of uniformed police poured into the street. "It's all over, it's all over," they

(Continued on back page)

ACTRESS TO WED SON OF AN ARCHDEACON

Fair, vivacious Miss Myrtle Stewart, known to thousands by her acting in "Wild Violets," "Lilac Time" and "Bitter Sweet," is to marry Lieutenant-Commander A. O. Watson, R.N., on Saturday. He is the son of the Archdeacon of Ripon.

* * *

Miss Stewart, who has signed contracts to play in pantomime at Christmas, may leave the stage next year. "I met my fiance at Portsmouth, at a cocktail party given by a friend," she told the "Daily Mirror" yesterday.

* * *

"His ship is refitting at Devonport now, and he can only come up to town on odd days to help me with the arrangements."

* * *

Well-know people from the Navy, the Church, the B.B.C. and the stage will attend the wedding "Tommy Rose, the airman, Laddie Cliff, if he is well enough, Admiral Tyrwhitt and Charles Brewer, of the B.B.C., hope to be there," Miss Stewart said.

RANG UP GIRL FRIEND

LOCKED IN P.O. THREE HOURS

BY A SPECIAL CORRESPONDENT

TWENTY-ONE-YEAR-OLD John Evans went down to the sweet-shop post office on the corner of Woolwich-road, Greenwich, last night to make a ten-minute 'phone call to a girl friend. The time was twenty minutes past seven.

AT 7.30 he noticed the lights in the shop go out.

AT 7.40 he came out of the telephone box into the shop and found all doors leading from it locked and bolted. He had been forgotten.

Three hours later, after messages had been flashed on the screens of two local cinemas asking Mr. A. Cook, the postmaster, to return immediately, and after six policemen had been trying to find some way of letting John Evans out, Mr. Cook suddenly turned up.

"What's all this about?" he asked.

John Evans later told me of his three-hour predicament among the sweets.

"When the lights in the shop outside went out I naturally thought Mr. Cook, who knows me, was at hand to let me out

"But he had forgotten all about me. When I found that I was locked in I 'phoned up the police

MRS. SNEYD IS NOW MRS. KURTTISBENET

THE following announcement was issued yesterday:—

"I, Irene Marguerite Campbell Kurttisbenet, of No. 26, Pond-place, Chelsea, S.W., former wife of Ralph Sneyd, heretofore called and known by the name of Irene Marguerite Campbell Sneyd, hereby give notice that on the first day of October, 1937, I renounced and abandoned the use of my said surname Sneyd and assumed in lieu thereof the surname of Kurttisbenet."

Mrs. Sneyd was formerly married to Colonel Ralph Sneyd, but the marriage was dissolved in 1926.

At the Old Bailey last month Mrs. Sneyd gave evidence during a case against a thirty-nine-year-old London accountant who was found not guilty of breaking into her Chelsea flat and stealing £5. The accused man was defended by Mr. Derek Curtis-Bennett.

In his searching cross-examination of Mrs. Sneyd, Mr. Curtis-Bennett referred several times to her past life.

Mrs. Kurttisbenet, asked by the *Daily Mirror* last night why she had chosen such an unusual name, replied:—

"Everybody is at liberty to draw their own conclusions. At the moment, I have no reason to give."

Asked if it was coincidence that her new name was so similar to that of Mr. Curtis-Bennett, the counsel, she said:—

"Is there a counsel of that name? I cannot remember him. You see, I have so many cases and so many counsel I cannot remember them all."

Mr. Derek Curtis-Bennett was surprised when he was told of the announcement.

"There is nothing I can do about it," he said, through a clerk. "I have nothing to say."

NUFFIELD'S NEW £1,300,000

LORD Nuffield has offered another £1,300,000 to Oxford University.

One million pounds of it he has staked on a great social experiment—the foundation of a new college that will "bridge the gulf" now dividing the scholars planning the progress of civilisation from the men of affairs and workers who carry on the world.

With the formal announcement last night came the statement that there are to be no more Nuffield benefactions—at present. His gifts have now reached a total of £10,000,000.

Lord Nuffield's offer, conveyed in a letter to the Chancellor of the University, includes:—£900,000 for the erection of a college "worthy of the highest traditions of Oxford architecture; a site valued at £100,000; £200,000 as additional endowment to his previous gift for medical research; £100,000 for a laboratory of physical chemistry.

Deploring the comparative scarcity of university graduates in the highest posts in industry, he says it must be partly due to the failure of employers to appreciate the qualities which a university education fosters in a young man or woman.

"But my own experience convinces me that it is also partly due to the gulf which exists between academic studies and practical affairs."

Duke at 12 p.m. Film Show

The Duke of Kent wanted to see the new Marx brothers film, "A Day at the Races"—and he did last night, at a private request performance in a Dudley cinema that began at 11 p.m., after the public had gone. There was an audience of five.

The Duke flew to Himley Hall, residence of Lord Dudley, yesterday, to fulfil a public engagement in Birmingham to-day.

Late in the afternoon the cinema manager was notified of his wish to see the film, and special arrangements were made to bring it from Birmingham for the midnight show.

MONDAY, OCTOBER 18, 1937

Daily Mirror

No. 10569 Registered at the G.P.O. as a Newspaper. ONE PENNY

MAROONED WIFE'S NOTE FROM SWAMP SNATCHED BY SWOOPING R.A.F. 'PLANE

Brigadier-General A. C. Lewin.

Using two struts and a cord from the wreckage of their 'plane, Mrs. A. C. Lewin, wife of Brigadier-General Lewin, got a message to the world yesterday from the swamps of the Nile, 300 miles south of Khartum, where they have been stranded for a week.

SHE used a trick of the Australian desert flyers of the last war—the "clothes-line post."

Across the two struts, stuck firmly in the ground, she stretched a cord weighted on the ends, and with her SOS firmly tied in the middle.

Attracted to the post by her signals, an R.A.F. pilot on search patrol flew low over the cord, trailing a grab, and drew her message to the 'plane. It read:

"We appreciate all the efforts that are being made for us, and we are deeply grieved and upset at what has occurred.

"My husband hopes that nothing untoward has happened to anyone who has been searching for us."

After stating that they have sufficient food and water for three days, the message adds that Mrs. Lewin does not think she and her husband can tackle the journey through the swamps, and requests a supply of hammocks.

The pilot, racing off with the message, saw only one figure—that of Mrs. Lewin. It is assumed that her husband is ill, and was lying in shelter of the 'plane.

Smoke-Puff SOS

Ever since their forced landing in the swamp on October 9, Mrs. Lewin and her husband, the sixty-three-year-old "flying General," have burned a fire to guide the rescue patrols.

On Saturday, says Reuter, one of the big R.A.F. bombers carrying food to their aid saw Morse SOS puffs of smoke from the fire and swooped low. Then the pilot saw the clothes-line post.

He curved away while his observer got the grappling line ready and then with his engine roaring skimmed over the rugged face of the desert, his wheels close to the ground over the "post."

Again and again he passed over missing the "string" by inches until coming down so low that it seemed he must strike the swamp, he at last snagged and secured the message line.

It was a most delicate manœuvre. The broken surface of the desert is impossible for aeroplanes—a landing is out of the question—it was this which brought disaster to the General.

The pilot waving farewell to Mrs. Lewin raced off to relay the message to Khartum.

Beauty Hath Charms!

She believes in luck! June Knight, U.S. screen star, seen here leaving Croydon for a Continental holiday after filming at Pinewood, carries the chainful of mascot charms you see below . . . and adds to it in every country she visits.

GAS KILLS SLEEPING FAMILY OF 4

FROM OUR OWN CORRESPONDENT

KIDDERMINSTER (Worcester), Sunday.

A FAMILY of four—one of them a five-year-old child—were gassed to death early to-day as they slept in their home in Sutton-road here.

They were: Mrs. Alice Elizabeth Ayres, sixty-one; her son-in-law, Leonard Walters, twenty-six; his wife Marian, twenty-four, and their daughter, Jane Yvonne, aged five.

It is assumed that a gas meter standing on a shelf became displaced, causing gas to pour into the house.

Walters a moulder in a local foundry, was sleeping on the couch in the kitchen and his wife was lying near the door leading from the kitchen to the stairs.

The fact that the lights were on downstairs suggests she smelt gas, came down to investigate, and was overcome.

Child Had Fever

Mrs. Ayres was lying at the foot of her bed in a back room upstairs, and the child in the front bedroom, which she had shared with her mother.

Walters slept in the kitchen because the child had scarlet fever and, by permission of the health authorities, was being nursed at home.

The tragedy was discovered because the smell of gas penetrated to the house next door, and two youths living there, twins aged sixteen, showed signs of being overcome.

They recovered later.

A neighbour, Mr. W. J. Harris, forced a window and saw Walters lying dead on the couch.

He called the police.

GIRL WHO DOESN'T WANT TO BE FOUND TALKS TO "DAILY MIRROR"

FROM OUR OWN CORRESPONDENT

EASTBOURNE, Sunday.

I TALKED to-day to the girl who does not want to be found. She has been kept in hospital here for two weeks, defying all attempts by police and specialists to make her tell them who she is and refusing to be photographed.

Since she was taken to hospital by the police, who found her hungry and penniless on the front here, nearly twenty parents have visited her, hoping to find a lost daughter.

When I suggested that her name was Annie Moran, she replied, "Yes, if you like." Asked if she had any friends, she said, "No, there is no one who knows me."

She wouldn't say where she had come from, and said, "No," when I asked her if she knew Eastbourne or other parts of Sussex.

Then I remarked, "You appear to be like Topsy." She said, "Who was Topsy?" She smiled when I replied, "Haven't you ever heard of 'Uncle Tom's Cabin,' and how Topsy said she was not born, but 'just growed'?"

I pointed out that her brown hair appeared to have been permed, and said, "You must have had that done somewhere. You couldn't

(Continued on back page)

LONDON'S FIRST FOG OF WINTER

FIRST fog of the winter descended on the outskirts of London and many parts of the Home Counties last night.

In some districts visibility was reduced to five yards.

Flares were lit on the Great North road at Stanborough, near Hatfield, and on the Barnet by-pass.

London remained comparatively clear, but there may be a heavy fog early this morning. Transport was not delayed.

A spell of fine weather with clear skies and no wind is likely to lead to early morning fogs as long as the fine weather lasts.

Thick patches of fog delayed traffic returning from the east coast along Southend arterial road, and in Ilford and Wanstead cars had to go at walking pace.

The fog in the south was not general. Brighton reported "all clear," but at Guildford the fog was "getting thicker every moment."

There was slight fog in the Thames estuary, and shipping was held up in some places.

TUESDAY, OCTOBER 19, 1937

Daily Mirror

No. 10570 | Registered at the G.P.O. as a Newspaper. | ONE PENNY

FOG BELT 200 MILES WIDE

HOLDS UP HALF ENGLAND

WHILE Air Ministry officials were cheerily forecasting a farewell to fog to-day—" a breeze will probably blow it away, except from some districts in the south-east "—traffic in half of England was held up last night by a 200-mile-wide belt of dense, billowing cloud.

The King and Queen and the Duke and Duchess of Kent were travelling through the fog this morning—the King and Queen on their way to Hull, where they start their Yorkshire tour, and the Duke and Duchess to Swansea for a two-day visit to South Wales.

The special train which took the King and Queen from King's Cross passed through Peterborough only nine minutes behind schedule. The Duke and Duchess left Paddington at 12.55 a.m., when conditions on the line were reported to be " not too bad."

Seven People Killed

At least seven deaths were caused by the fog, which disorganised bus services, " grounded " air liners, stopped greyhound racing on all National Greyhound Racing Club tracks in London, and slowed down rail services.

While shunting on the G.W.R. line at Coronation-road, Park Royal, Acton, last night, a truck became lost in the fog and crashed through the level-crossing gates into the middle of the road.

It narrowly missed two cars, but no one was injured.

Many bus services in the suburbs of London were an hour late.

Late last night inspectors with hurricane lamps and wax torches had to be stationed along the routes.

Motorists found mile-long jams on Western-avenue, Westway, the Barnet and Watford by-pass roads where scores of A.A. traffic scouts dealt with long convoys of traffic while erecting traffic flares at roundabouts and crossings.

Children gave up collecting for fireworks to guide motorists at 2d. a time.

The fog postponed the wedding of Mr. L. E. Husderg, a twenty-two-year-old Swedish student in London.

While he was waiting at the Swedish Legation for her to arrive for the ceremony, his bride, Miss Maj Palmer, of Longsund, Sweden, was still on board the steamer Suecia, fog-bound in the Thames since early morning, after travelling from Sweden.

The marriage will be performed to-day.

THE GIRL WITH THE SECRET FEAR

Found, hungry and penniless, on the sea front, this girl has for the past two weeks been in St. Mary's Hospital, Eastbourne, defying all attempts by police and specialists to make her tell them who she is and refusing to be photographed.

Haunted by a terror the cause of which she will not disclose, she sits all day long with her hands over her face, as you see in the picture below.

But yesterday, at the request of the police, a photographer secured the picture on the left. To get it he had to lie flat on his stomach, pointing a long-distance camera through a doorway 50ft. away. For three hours he waited in vain.

Then luck took a hand. Someone upset a wheelbarrow laden with flowerpots outside the window. Startled, the girl looked up . . . and the picture was taken.

NOW DOES ANYONE RECOGNISE HER ?

DIED WITH "DREAM CHILDREN" BY HER

BY A SPECIAL CORRESPONDENT

AS children of Grenaby-road, Croydon, Surrey, played in the street, a small, old woman, always wearing the same long, grey coat, the same bonnet, and always carrying the same wicker basket, watched them in silence, smiling wistfully.

She lived alone in a small house nearby. No tradesman, no visitor ever stopped at the door. She never spoke to anyone.

Found After Months

The woman, widowed fifty-seven-year-old Mrs. Anne Jeffrey, was found dead in her bed during the week-end. She had been dead for two months.

In the poorly-furnished room where she lay was a large pile of children's story books and on a table near her bed was a volume of Charles Lamb, open at his famous essay, " Dream Children."

Sir Bernard Spilsbury carried out a post-mortem examination yesterday.

BLUNT TO MISS THE KING

The Bishop of Bradford, Dr. Blunt, who had accepted an invitation to be presented to the King when he visits Bradford to-morrow, will be unable to do so owing to indisposition.

BECAME ENGAGED THROUGH PRISON BARS

SPECIAL " DAILY MIRROR " NEWS

SEVENTEEN-YEAR-OLD Irene Scott, of Chorley Wood, has become engaged, through the wire netting barrier of the visitors' room at Brixton Prison, London, to John Rodgers, the London barman facing his trial on a murder charge.

"I did it t. prove my devotion," she told the " Daily .firror " yesterday as she sat at her home in Solesbridge-road twisting a pretty engagement ring on her finger.

" A month ago Jack calmly asked me to knit him a sweater, as it was very cold in prison. He wore it in the dock at the Old Bailey to-day."

Last night, after the opening day of Rodgers's trial at the Old Bailey for the murder of Lily Chamberlain, his married barmaid friend, Miss Scott sent him a telegram.

Since he was arrested six weeks ago, she has visited him nearly every day in prison. They have also corresponded daily.

Miss Scott has known her fiance for three years. They were young sweethearts together while she was still at school.

Yesterday she sat through the first day of his trial with Miss May Scott, her sister.

Opening of trial—page 6.

THURSDAY, OCTOBER 21, 1937

Daily Mirror

No. 10572 Registered at the G.P.O. as a Newspaper. ONE PENNY

HITLER SPURS DUCE

TO NEW SPAIN PEACE MOVE

BY OUR POLITICAL CORRESPONDENT

SIGNOR MUSSOLINI, ACTING ON ADVICE FROM HITLER, YESTERDAY REVERSED HIS SPANISH POLICY, BROUGHT A NEW ASSURANCE OF PEACE TO EUROPE—AND ASTONISHED THE WORLD.

His spokesman, Count Grandi, electrified the apparently dying non-intervention talk in London by announcing that Italy was prepared to agree to:—

1. A "token" withdrawal of volunteers from Spain;
2. The dispatch of commissions to count the number of foreign troops on both sides of the Spanish war, and
3. Granting of belligerent rights to both the Franco and Madrid Governments.

The secret of Italy's move is linked with Herr von Ribbentrop's sudden departure to Germany on the eve of the committee's first meeting.

He told Herr Hitler that Britain and France were prepared to take a much firmer line of action towards Italy in the event of non-intervention breaking down. Hitler advised Mussolini to go warily. Hence Italy's diplomatic change of front and the revival of non-intervention.

Both Hitler and Mussolini have steered their countries into strong diplomatic positions. They can now announce to the world that they have saved the Non-Intervention Committee and that they desire peace above all things.

Count Grandi recanting, at the non-intervention session, almost everything he had said at the previous day's hearing, agreed not to press the claim that had threatened to wreck the talks—the claim for granting belligerent rights to Franco before foreigners are withdrawn.

Eden's Elation

Dr. Woermann, the German minister, gave complete support to Italy, but M. Maisky, for Russia, announced that he would have reservations to make later.

Mr. Eden, the chairman, showed his bewilderment and his elation. He adjourned the meeting until to-morrow, and added: "If we make as much progress as we have made to-day we shall be well on the way to a settlement."

News of Mussolini's dramatic decision startled Rome itself, but its newspapers hastened to approve.

In Valencia Signor Luis Companys, President of Catalonia, declared: "We have unlimited reserves. If no more foreign troops were sent to Franco the end of the war would be a matter of weeks, at most of a few months."

The news was cheered in the City. There was an immediate burst of activity in late street trading. Leading industrial, rubber and oil shares were in strong demand.

A wave of buying developed last night on Wall Street. The market closed with some stocks nine points higher.

4 HOURS WAIT ON KERB FOR DEAD MOTHER

FROM OUR SPECIAL CORRESPONDENT

BIRMINGHAM, Wednesday.

BECAUSE his father had always told him to be "a little soldier," eight-year-old Raymond Allaway stood guard over his two-year-old brother in a Birmingham street for four and a half hours.

They did not know that their mother, Mrs. May Eveline Allaway, had been knocked down and fatally injured by a lorry—just after she had left them, with the bidding, "Wait here until I get back."

Mrs. Allaway, thirty-seven, of Gospel-lane, Acocks Green, had gone to draw her husband's last unemployment pay—after three years "on the dole," he had found a job.

When she was knocked down passers-by who ran to aid her heard her cry, "Oh, my baby," and in the ambulance she kept muttering, "My children! Look after my children."

Police officers began searching. But they did not find the boys until four and a half hours later. Roy was standing at attention beside the baby's pram at the spot where their mother had told them to wait.

Mrs. Allaway had called at the Labour Exchange on the previous day, but was given a wrong form. She was on her way to change it.

There are two other boys—Victor, aged ten, and Donald, twin of Raymond.

When I saw the father, Leslie Allaway, at his home to-night, he said to me:

"I joined the Army when I was fourteen and went all through the war, and was always telling Ray to be a good soldier.

"When the policemen found him he had not budged an inch, cried or asked anyone for help."

At the inquest to-day the verdict was Accidental death.

Here's Gracie in Fresh Fields

Meet Gracie Fields and her tough-guy husband, Victor McLaglen, in "He Was Her Man," £200,000 film of the gold rush of the 'eighties.

Gracie's costume is something new in the fields she's conquered. She's a saloon girl. The picture is being directed by Monty Banks at the Denham (Bucks) studios.

STEVE'S RADIO GOODBYE TO BROWN JACK

STEVE Donoghue, just before he was guest of honour in London last night at a jockeys' dinner to mark his retirement, bade an affectionate good-night by radio to one of his favourite mounts, Brown Jack, the wonder horse, which won the Queen Alexandra Stakes six years in succession.

Brown Jack recognises Steve's voice instantly, and when his present owner, Sir Harold Wernher, heard of the proposal for Donoghue to broadcast last night, he arranged for a radio receiving set to be installed in the stable where Brown Jack lives in retirement.

"Hallo, old boy," said Steve, as he finished his broadcast. "I can see you now, you beauty. I hope your ears are burning, because I am thinking of you all the time. We are jolly old pals."

After the broadcast Donoghue went on to the Picadilly Hotel, where he was the guest of famous jockeys.

Donoghue is to become a trainer next year.

'BANKRUPT' BY TOUR OF DUKE'S VICAR

SAYING that he was bankrupt by the American lecture tour he backed for the Rev. Anderson Jardine ("the Duke's Vicar"), publicity agent Hugh Ernst, of New York, appealed yesterday to Mr. Jardine for Help.

"Expenses were £1,720 and the thirty lectures brought in only £120," Ernst told our New York correspondent. "If Jardine can afford it I hope he will help me recoup."

Mr. Jardine told the *Daily Mirror* last night: "The statement is not true. Ernst was financed from London. I did not see any of the money. Nor did I see the books. But I know that he was paid 500 dollars for one of my broadcasts. I gave seven radio talks in seven days, so he must have made a good deal of money out of broadcasting."

MONDAY, OCTOBER 25, 1937

Daily Mirror

No. 10575 Registered at the G.P.O. as a Newspaper. ONE PENNY

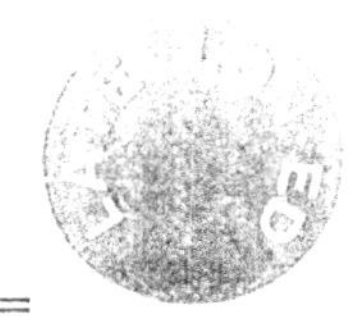

POLICE QUESTION HUNDREDS

ON HEIRESS'S DEATH RIDDLE

FROM OUR SPECIAL CORRESPONDENT

BATH, Sunday.

HUNDREDS of people have been interviewed by the Bath police in an attempt to solve the death riddle of Ellen Ruddle, heiress, drug addict and woman of mystery, who, two months ago, died in a Poor Law institution.

The Home Office are expected to issue an exhumation order this week.

Queue to See Grave

Sir Bernard Spilsbury, the pathologist, Sir William Willcox and Dr. Roche Lynch, the Home Office analyst, have been consulted.

The report of exhumation proceedings brought crowds of people to-day to St. James's Cemetery, just outside the city, where Ellen Ruddle is buried. By eleven o'clock, when the gates opened, a queue had formed.

But the grave is unmarked and the keepers had had strict orders not to indicate it to the sightseers.

Ellen Ruddle died on August 31 this year. Next day she was buried

There were only five mourners. They were her father, Mr. Edwin Ruddle, who had not seen or heard of his daughter for nine years her aunt, two girls cousins, and a solicitor.

Mr. Ruddle, a retired farmer, who now lives at Barton-on-Sea, Hants, told me:—

"When the funeral service was over the solicitor led me to a spot under a tree in the cemetery and read to me Ellen's will.

"She had left all her property and estate to Dr. Ronald Gordon, the doctor who had attended her 'in gratitude for his many kindnesses.'

"I was not even mentioned in the will."

Shortly after the funeral a young woman gave certain information to the Bath police.

Hardly had they begun to inquire into that information before a letter was received from the Home Office raising the question of Miss Ruddle's death certificate.

On that certificate the cause of death was given as heart failure and chronic morphine poisoning.

Ellen Ruddle had lived in Bath for the seven years before her death.

Few people there knew her as Miss Ruddle. To them she was known as Mrs. Gray, wife, she said, of a doctor living abroad.

Four years ago, in a Bath nursing home, she

(Continued on back page)

Miss Ellen Ruddle—a picture taken some years ago.

Dr. R. G. Gordon.

SHE MADE THIS SHED HER HOME

In this wooden shed at the end of her garden at Marlborough Buildings, Bath, Miss Ellen Ruddle lived like a recluse, surrounded by cats and dogs, and living on milk and ice-cream.

Here she was found in a coma and taken to Frome-road House Infirmary, where she died on August 28, a week later.

WOMEN HUNT HUMAN 'FOX' FOR SPORT

FROM OUR OWN CORRESPONDENT

NEW YORK, Sunday.

NEARLY 130 whooping hunting fans galloped miles over the countryside near Martinez, California, to-day, after a human fox—a convict.

There were no dogs, but thirty-five smartly-groomed women rode in the hunt and merrily ran the panting "fox" to earth after three and a half hours of "wonderful sport."

Bluff Sheriff John Miller, of Contra Costa County, had the idea to entertain his sporting friends and to "demonstrate the ability of horsemen in tracking down prisoners should a real gaol-break occur."

This morning the sheriff released a twenty-four-year-old prisoner from Contra Costa Gaol, telling him he had two hours in which to run before the hunt started after him.

Hid in Brush

The quarry, whose name the sheriff refused to reveal, dashed into the hills and hid in the underbrush.

This afternoon Mr. and Mrs. Pat Shaw, who, like other members of the hunt, carried a photograph of the convict, ran him to earth.

He was then allowed to join in a giant dinner given by the sheriff and generously awarded £2.

"It will help him on his way," said Sheriff Miller, "as his term is just ending."

Everyone agreed that a fine time was had by all—except the fox.

Master Radios "Daily Mirror"

"BRITISH 'PLANE BOMBS SUBMARINE" STORY

VIVID story of how he saw a seaplane bomb a submarine of unknown nationality in the Mediterranean was wirelessed to the *Daily Mirror* this morning by the master of the British liner, Kaisar-I-Hind, due at Gibraltar to-day.

His message said:

"Seaplane seen cruising five miles distant. Subsequently submarine sighted on surface.

"Seaplane seen dropping two heavy bombs, from which columns of water shot up great height. Submarine apparently submerged and seaplane proceeded on its original course.

The bombing, which took place between Alicante, Spain, and Cape Tenes, on the North Africa coast, was first reported in a general call sent out by the liner last night.

"Observe seaplane dropping bombs on submarines."

The Admiralty stated last night that the flying boat belonged to a British squadron, but denied the presence of a submarine.

"The aircraft dropped two bombs at flame floats in practice," said the statement. "No doubt the flame floats were mistaken for a submarine by the Kaisar-I-Hind, which was five miles distant."

French cargo boat Oued Mellah, with grain from Morocco to Port Vendres, France, was bombed by an aeroplane "of unknown nationality" fifty miles from Barcelona yesterday.

The crew took to the boats.

Messages: Reuter, Exchange, Telegraph.

MRS. SELF BARRED FROM KENYA

KENYA immigration officials yesterday refused Mrs. Hedwig Self permission to land at Mombasa.

She was a passenger in the liner Llangibby Castle, from which Mr. Gervase Lambton, the twenty-five-year-old cousin of the Earl of Durham, was lost overboard yesterday week.

It was stated that Mrs. Self could not comply with the money regulations.

She would say nothing about the disappearance at sea of Mr. Lambton.

Before he met his death, Mr. Lambton left Mrs. Self a note, which read:

"I have kept my promise sooner than you imagined. By the time you receive this I shall be in the sea."

One of the crew of the Llangibby Castle described how he saw Mr. Lambton in the sea making no effort to save himself, says Exchange.

30 MISSING ON BLAZING SHIP

Thirty of the crew of the British steamer Kaitangata (1,983 tons, owned by the Ling Nam Steamship Company, of Hong Kong) are missing in a blaze on the vessel, which was carrying a cargo of petrol.

Picking up an S O S at midnight, the British steamer Nanning raced to the spot and took off the officers, radio operators and thirteen of the crew. A search is being made for the remaining thirty, says Exchange.

FRIDAY, OCTOBER 29, 1937

Daily Mirror

No. 10579 Registered at the G.P.O. as a Newspaper. ONE PENNY

MOTHER KILLS SON'S WIFE, SAYS 'SHE WAS NOT GOOD ENOUGH'

JOSEPHINE MORY, A FORTY-SEVEN-YEAR-OLD MOTHER, THOUGHT HER DAUGHTER-IN-LAW WAS NOT GOOD ENOUGH FOR HER SON. SO SHE STRANGLED HER.

Then, to give the appearance of suicide, she hung the body on the back of a door.

As the murderess was sentenced to death in Douai, France, last night the spectators in the public gallery, who had been shouting, "Give her death," broke into rounds of applause.

The trial revealed a mother's growing hatred of the woman who had married her son, and the son's battle for happiness with the wife who had been his mistress.

Wed in Defiance of Parents

The wife, formerly Mlle. Yvette, had lived with Madame Mory's son, a lieutenant in the French Army Reserve.

They married, despite his parents' opposition, just before a baby was born.

A second baby was due when the wife was murdered.

In court yesterday Mme. Mory told of her ambitions for her son, of her dismay when he married beneath him.

"We made every sacrifice for him," she cried, "so that he could complete his studies. He should have recompensed us for our sufferings." She planned for him a rich marriage into a comfortable, respected family.

M. Mory, her husband, had told the Court how he had gone to the girl's uncle and aunt and tried to persuade them not to permit the marriage.

"The girl told me then that she would soon be a mother," he said. "I told her she could raise the brat herself."

The report of a private detective hired by Mme. Mory to investigate the girl's past was laid before the Court. From statements picked up from people in Rouen, the detective said:

"I concluded that this girl was a prostitute, and a private one at that. She was not serious."

"My Mother Cursed Me"

M. Louis Mory, the son, said that his parents gave him the detective's report, but he immediately checked all the allegations himself and found them completely untrue.

"My parents continued to complain to me," he said. "They said, 'This girl is not made for you.'

"I attempted numerous visits to conciliate them, but in vain. They had wanted me to make a rich marriage. My mother was continually cursing and threatening me, and every time she visited us it was perfect hell."

The son, says British United Press, refused to look at his parents during the trial, though Mme. Mory called to him, "Come, my son, come and kiss me."

Madame Mory in court yesterday. "Your tears deceive no one," said the prosecutor, as he tore her defence to shreds.

It's a SON for Dr. Cronin

"If you want a baby, have it now!" Britain's most provocative writer of the century, Dr. A. J. Cronin, author of "The Stars Look Down" and "The Citadel," told "Daily Mirror" readers in a full page article yesterday.

Lest he was accused of preaching what he did not practise, he divulged an intimate secret. "We are expecting another child in our family very soon," he wrote. "And, heavens! don't I hope it's a girl." Dr. Cronin already has two sons.

Yesterday this notice appeared in the Press:—

CRONIN.—On October 27, 1937, at 19, Bentinck-street, W.1, to Agnes Mary, wife of A. J. Cronin, a son.

"COLLECTED" CAR AT POINT OF REVOLVER

BY A SPECIAL CORRESPONDENT

"I'll show you the way we do things in South America!"

A WELL-DRESSED young man who spoke with a foreign accent snapped out these words as he whipped a silver-plated automatic from his pocket, and rammed it into the stomach of Mr. Dave Lee, manager of Rickett's Garage, Drummond-street, Euston-road, N.W., late last night.

A few minutes later he drove off in a £1,800 Lagonda Napier—bearing a Diplomatic Corps number plate.

The car was brought into the garage on Wednesday for repairs, and the "gunman" had called for it.

Mr. Lee tendered his bill and there was a dispute over the amount. Mr. Lee refused to accept less and also refused to sign a receipt which stated that the amount was paid under protest.

"When the car was brought in," Mr. Lee told me last night, "I didn't take the name of the owner. He was accompanied by a friend and this friend called for the car.

"He said he wanted the car at once, and I refused to hand it over till the bill was paid. He then asked me to sign a receipt which said that the amount was paid under protest.

"I refused. Suddenly he pulled a revolver from his pocket and rammed it into my stomach.

"Another customer was in the garage at the time, and he made a dive for the telephone.

"'Stay where you are,' ordered the man with the gun, 'or I'll do you in after I've fixed this chap.'

"Then he turned to me. 'Now sign that receipt,' he said and, feeling the gun pressing into my stomach, I wasted no time and signed.

"He didn't try to take any money from the till and paid me the amount of the bill."

Mr. Lee was put under police protection.

TOMMY FARR SUMMONED BY A YOUNG MOTHER

A SUMMONS against Tommy Farr has been granted by the Bridgend (Glamorgan) magistrates on the application of a young Porthcawl woman for an affiliation order. The summons is returnable at Bridgend Police Court to-morrow.

Mr. W. M. Thomas, a Bridgend solicitor, is appearing for the woman, twenty-two-year-old Miss Clarice Switen, of Fuchsia Cottage, New-road, Porthcawl, and Farr will be represented by Messrs. Morgan, Bruce and Nicholas, of Pontypridd.

Childhood Friends

The two families lived next door at Tonypandy until the Switens moved fifteen years ago, and Farr and the girl played together as children.

It is expected that both parties will ask for an adjournment until a week to-day to facilitate the attendance of witnesses.

Farr will attend to contest the case.

TRAPPED 5 DAYS IN HOLD

When the Canadian Pacific liner Empress of Britain reached Southampton last night from Canada it was revealed that Arthur John Brown, twenty-three, homeless, had been trapped in a hold for five and a half days without food or drink on the outward voyage.

Brown, in a statement, said he boarded the liner at Southampton on October 16 as a workman and "lost his way."

WOMAN STRUCK BLIND

"My eyes, they won't open," cried Mrs. Sarah Allen, sixty-seven, of King-street, Stanley, Co. Durham, while she was drying her face with a towel.

That was a week ago. Yesterday mystified doctors told her relatives that she will never see again.

Mrs. Esther Allen, granddaughter-in-law of the blind woman, said last night, "She was joking just before she was struck blind."

PEER FIGHTS BLAZE

Lord Egerton, of Tatton, Knutsford, Cheshire, led firemen and estate workers in an effort to save a joiners' shop on his estate last night.

They were able to prevent the flames from spreading, but the shop was destroyed.

FELL 80 FEET—AND SMILED

"PASSED at the post," said sixty-year-old Mr. Jimmy Thomas, a well-known figure on southern racecourses, after he had fallen 80ft. down a shaft from a platform at Liverpool-street Station last night without hurting himself.

Returning from Newmarket, Mr. Thomas had just greeted his wife on the platform, when he stepped back into the open shaft of a Post Office lift.

A goods lift was quickly commandeered by officials, who hurried to his assistance.

When they opened the door at the bottom of the shaft Mr. Thomas was waiting for them, smiling and brushing the dust from his clothes.

SATURDAY, OCTOBER 30, 1937

Daily Mirror

No. 10580 Registered at the G.P.O. as a Newspaper. ONE PENNY

DIVER-MAYOR IN BATTLE WITH 20-FT. SHARK ON SEA BED

SHE'S SUING FARR

Granted a summons against Tommy Farr cn her application to Bridgend (Glamorgan) magistrates for an affiliation order to be heard to-day. . . . Miss Clarice Switen walking on the promenade at Porthcawl, where she lives at Fuchsia Cottage, New road.

FROM OUR OWN CORRESPONDENT

PENZANCE, Friday.

DIVER C. A. Chard, Mayor of Falmouth, was working 40ft. under water at the bottom of St. Ives Bay this afternoon, when he turned round and found himself face to face with a 20ft. shark.

Mr. Chard made a grab for his safety line, but the shark moved quicker. It seized the lire in its mouth and dragged him across the sea bed.

For minutes that "seemed an eternity" Mr. Chard trailed zig-zag on the end of the line at the mercy of the plunging shark. Then the line snapped—and friends in a boat on the surface drew him to safety by his air line.

He told me the story at his home in Florence-place to-night

"Saw Monster Overhead"

"I was working at a depth of about 4. ... laying pipes in the bay," said Mr. Chard, "when I saw the monster above my head.

"It must have either seized the line in its jaws or become entangled in it, for in a moment I was being dragged this way and that along the sea bed.

"The shark darted across the top of my head like a torpedo about 8ft. above me. Several times I hit the bottom.

"I thought my last moment had come. It seemed an eternity before the line parted—I think the shark must have bitten it through.

"None the Worse"

"Those in the boat above promptly hauled me to the surface by means of the air line.

"I feel pretty sore," he added, "but otherwise I am none the worse for my experience. Needless to say I do not hope for a repetition of it."

Presence of a shark in the bay has been reported for several days.

A shark bit through his lifeline . . . Councillor C. A. Chard, Mayor of Falmouth, in his diving kit.

CHURCH DRAWS RENTS FROM 'IMMORAL HOUSES,' SAYS EX-M.P.

THE Church is drawing ground rents from houses of "dubious reputation morally"—according to a charge to be made at the autumn session of the Church Assembly.

When the Assembly meets on November 15, in Westminster, ex-M.P. Mr. G. W. Currie will move a motion containing the statement that "the Church has been participating in ground rents of houses of 'dubious reputation morally' in part of the London Bishopric estate described as 'Maida Vale Proper' in Paddington."

Another charge to be made in the motion is: "That on the Ecclesiastical Commissioners' Walworth No. 1 estate near Lambeth Palace 'every house' in one 'bad patch of property from which ground rents are drawn seems to be infested with vermin.'"

Mr. Currie who lives in Cadogan-place S.W., is a life governor of the Corporation of Sons of the Clergy, chairman of the Poor Clergy Relief Corporation and treasurer of the Mothers' Union.

The Rev. P. T. R. Kirk, vicar of Christ Church Broadway, Westminster, in a motion referring to the recent report of the League of Nations' Mixed Committee on Nutrition will urge:—

Increased allowances for children under Unemployment Assistance and Insurance, free milk daily at elementary schools, free school dinners for children where necessary, and cheap milk for children under school age and for expectant and nursing mothers

Hence the Pyramads

FROM OUR OWN CORRESPONDENT

NEW YORK, Friday.

Samuel Goldwyn's Press agent has wired from Hollywood asking Mohammed Amine Youssef, Egyptian Minister to Washington, for rates and conditions for advertising on the Pyramids the forthcoming film "Adventures of Marco Polo."

£2,000 JEWELS MISSING

Stock-taking at the German pavilion of the Paris Exhibition, the general commissaire discovered yesterday that £2,000 worth of jewels were missing.

It is not known yet whether they were stolen at once or in a series of raids since the last check a fortnight ago.

HITLER TO ACT ON COLONIES

HITLER is to take direct action on his demand for colonies, forecast General Von Epp, Chief of the Reich Colonial Association, in a speech at Munich yesterday.

Speaking to the Colonial Committee of the Reich Academy of Law, he said: "We must work out a legal foundation for the coming action of the Fuehrer which will bring about a happy solution of the colonial problem," reports Reuter

LORD HOWE CHALLENGES DR. BURGIN

LORD Howe, British racing driver, last night called on Dr. Burgin, Transport Minister, to name his seconds—for a road driving duel.

Speaking at the British Racing Drivers' Club dinner at the Park Lane Hotel, London, Lord Howe said Dr. Burgin had claimed that road dangers were "much exaggerated."

"If the Minister of Transport would like to try driving from Brighton towards London any fine Sunday about 10.30 a.m. and lives—I think he'll only live to eat his words," he said.

MYSTERY BLAZE AT SEA

Shoreham Harbour lifeboat was warned to stand by late last night after a report from the Brighton Police that an aeroplane had been seen to come down in flames into the sea off Brighton.

Mr. Frederick Beard, landlord of the Cabinet Makers' Arms, Brighton, said that while out in a boat he saw a bright flash of flame light up the sea. He cruised around but could find no trace of wreckage.

No 'plane is missing from any south coast aerodrome.

FORFEIT KILLER CARS

A new Bill presented to the House of Lords by Lord Newton plans the forfeiture of the motor-car of any person convicted of manslaughter.

MONDAY, NOVEMBER 1, 1937

Daily Mirror

No. 10581 Registered at the G.P.O. as a Newspaper. ONE PENNY

U.S. TO BUILD ROYAL TRAIN FOR THE WINDSORS' GREAT TOUR

FROM OUR OWN CORRESPONDENT

NEW YORK, Sunday.

AMERICA has designed a palace on wheels to carry the Duke and Duchess of Windsor on the most spectacular tour ever planned in the States.

The most famous decorators in the country have been assisting Washington experts to plan into the train every detail of comfort found in the most up-to-date modern hotels.

The foundation is to be the chassis of the State private train used by President Roosevelt on his Government tours.

It will be "christened" the Royal train, and will be painted throughout with the Duke's colours and crest.

In addition to the "royal suite," the movable palace is designed to provide suites for official hosts, quarters for the guard of honour.

A miniature broadcasting station will be installed, telegraph and cable stations and unlimited accommodation for journalists, newsreel operators and camera-men.

The plans are to be submitted immediately to the Duke and Duchess.

Men who have managed many national tours for President Roosevelt are behind the scheme.

They compare their plans for the "Royal train" to the "White House on Wheels."

Here are the plans in detail.

Like the President, the Duke and Duchess will occupy one private coach. This coach will be equipped with loudspeakers on the rear platform so that the Duke can address crowds at the stations along his route.

Special Guards

Both the Columbia and the National Broadcasting Companies will have radio engineers and crack announcers aboard the train to arrange national broadcasts.

Dining and lounge cars will be wired for sound so that correspondents may hear the Duke's voice as they sit at their typewriters when he is speaking from the rear platform of the train.

Representatives of Western Union and the postal, telegraph and cable companies will be aboard to transmit news stories.

The Duke and Duchess will be provided with special guards to protect them against cranks and gate crashers.

It is planned to engage former Secret Service men or G-Men for this duty.

In addition, the train will carry picked railway police and its itinerary will be flashed in advance to police in all towns and villages along the route.

At Washington, only accredited correspondents already working in the city will be allowed to interview the visitors

"Welfare Leader"

There were reports in New York last night that the Duke is planning a world-wide organisation, of which he would be the leader, for the study of industrial welfare and the establishment of living and working conditions.

The Duke and Duchess, it was stated, would devote much of their time and fortune to the organisation, which would be supported by wealthy industrialists.

An official statement in Paris to Reuter on behalf of the Duke said he could make no comment on the report

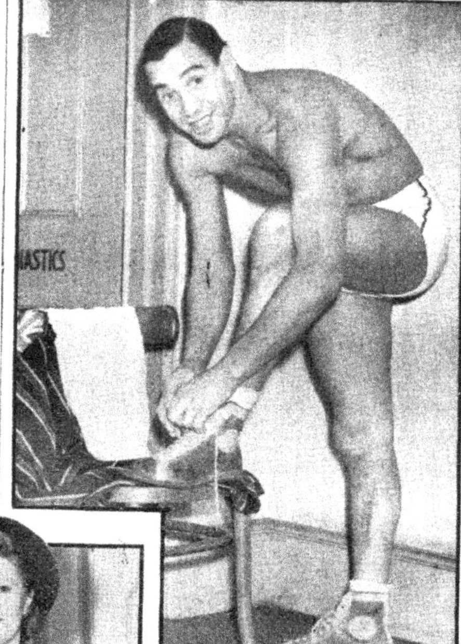

All-in wrestler Bob Gregory's fiancee, Miss Valerie Brooke (Princess Baba).

Princess to Wed Wrestler

BY A SPECIAL CORRESPONDENT

Twenty-one-year-old Miss Valerie Brooke (Princess Baba), youngest daughter of the white Rajah and Ranee of Sarawak, is engaged to an all-in wrestler.

He's Robert Gregory, and you see him lacing his boots for a match in London yesterday. Bob, who is twenty-five, met his Princess three months ago and fell in love at first sight.

Last night the Ranee refused to make any comment.

This morning she will hold a round-table conference with her daughter and Bob Grégory, and reveal whether the Rajah, Sir Charles Vyner Brooke, 10,000 miles away in his Eastern State, approves of an all-in wrestler for his new son-in-law.

Already there has been an interchange of cables between the Ranee and Rajah.

Bob Gregory told me last night: "This engagement of mine was private. It was never meant to leak out as it has done. What the Rajah will think when he sees it in the front pages, I do not know.

"I have had no real opportunity of interviewing Valerie's mother, the Ranee, and all the publicity has taken me by by surprise.

Princess Baba's elder sisters are Lady Inchcape (Princess Gold) and Mrs. Harry Roy (Princess Pearl), wife of the dance band leader.

WOMAN ATTACKED AND ROBBED IN WEST END FLAT

C.I.D. officers were last night called to a flat in Upper Berkeley-street, London, W., where the occupant, Miss Nancy Feldman, aged twenty-seven, told them that she had been attacked by a man and robbed of a handbag containing £10.

She said she had been gagged with articles of underclothing and tied up with stockings.

Miss Feldman was not injured. She was able to give detectives a description of her assailant.

SHIP SUNK BY 'PLANE

BRITISH CREW GUNNED AS THEY TOOK TO BOATS

A "FLYING pirate," with skull and crossbones painted under her wings, sank the British steamer Jean Weems (2,455 tons) off the Catalan coast on Saturday, after raking the decks of the ship with her machine-guns as the crew tumbled over the side into the lifeboats.

The story of how she gave them five minutes to clear the ship, then sent her to the bottom with twenty bombs, was told by Captain Thomas Eversett, of Cardiff, and the members of his crew, at the little fishing village of Palafrugel last night.

The twenty-six members of the crew, thirteen in each boat, had rowed for seven hours until they reached the village, a few miles from the French frontier

Nine of them were British officers and men, and thirteen seamen not of British nationality. Two observers of the Non-Intervention Control were also on board.

Mr. Clifford Davies, the first mate, said the

(Continued on back page)

PREMIER MISSES DEBATE TO-DAY

MR Neville Chamberlain, the Prime Minister, will not be in the House of Commons to-day to wind up the debate on the Address.

He has been suffering from gout, and is not able to walk yet

Sir John Simon will end the debate for the Government, and he will not therefore be able to attend the Cutlers Feast at Sheffield. His place as chief guest will be taken by the Minister of Transport, Dr. Burgin.

The Premier returned to Downing-street with Mrs. Chamberlain yesterday after a week-end at Chequers.

His general health is good, and he is not likely to be away from the House more than a day or two.

SATURDAY, NOVEMBER 6, 1937

Daily Mirror

No. 10386 Registered at the G.P.O. as a Newspaper. ONE PENNY

THE DUKE POSTPONES U.S. TOUR: 'MOTIVE NOT UNDERSTOOD'

THE DUKE OF WINDSOR DECIDED LAST NIGHT TO POSTPONE HIS VISIT TO THE U.S.

HE and the Duchess were to have sailed in the Bremen to-day, but, after receiving a dramatic cable from Mr. C. Bedaux, who was to have managed the tour, he changed his mind.

A statement was issued explaining :—

"His Royal Highness arrived at this decision with great reluctance and after much deliberation, but he feels that, owing to the grave misconceptions which have arisen and the misstatements which have appeared regarding the motives and purpose of his industrial tour, there is no alternative but to defer it for the present.

"The Duke emphatically repeats that there is no shadow of justification for any suggestion that he is allied to any industrial system or that he is for or against any political or racial doctrine, and he expresses the earnest hope that after this announcement his real and sincere motive for his proposed visit to America will be properly understood."

"His Royal Highness will personally convey his thanks to those industrial companies who so generously extended invitations to him and to all who have assisted in the arrangements."

The Duke and Duchess were finishing their packing when they were handed the cable from Mr. Bedaux, who has earned the enmity of U.S. trade unionists because of his factory speed-up methods.

The cable said:—

"SIRE, I am compelled in honesty and friendship to advise you that, because of a mistaken attack upon me here, I am convinced that your proposed study will be difficult under my guidance.

"My Deepest Wish"

"I respectfully suggest and in your behalf implore that you relieve me completely from all my duties in connection with your American tour.

"I will be happy to extend to the person designated by you as my successor, every possible assistance and co-operation.

"Grateful as I am for your request that I should continue, I nevertheless beg you to be guided by the knowledge that my deepest wish is the full attainment of the object of your visit to the United States.

"I remain, Sire, your devoted friend, Charlie F. Bedaux."

Mr. Joseph P. McCurdy, of the Baltimore Federation of Labour, which started the outcry against the Duke's trip, said to a special correspondent of the *Daily Mirror* last night:

"Our complaint was more against Bedaux than against the Duke of Windsor.

"Bedaux's stretch-out system created more havoc in American industry than anything in a decade.

"But our attitude towards the Duke of Windsor is naturally coloured by the fact that his tour of Germany was conducted by the notorious Dr. Ley, who was largely responsible for the destruction of German free trade unions.

"We thought and think Bedaux was bring-

(Continued on Back Page)

A Woman's Life Is Being Saved Here

This wonderful fire rescue picture shows Mrs. Montgomery, mother of four children, descending from the window of her blazing flat above a radio store in High-road, Kilburn, by two ladders placed together by twenty-five-year-old Donald Houghton, greengrocer's assistant, of Aldridge-road Villas, W.11.

Previously he had taken down in turn eleven-year-old Alan, who has only one arm; Beryl, aged nine; Heathbrook, aged six, and Irene, aged five. Then he went back for their mother.

BRIDE DID NOT SEE JOCKEY OFF

BY OUR SPECIAL CORRESPONDENT

WEST HORSLEY (Surrey), Friday.

PEGGY Thrale, twenty-one-year-old daughter of Mr. Peter Thrale, was not at Croydon to-day to say good-bye to her jockey husband, Kenneth Gethin, whom she married secretly before he left England to ride in India.

Her mother had taken her into the country.

Her parents, angered because she motored to London for a register office wedding without disclosing her intentions, kept their word not to allow her to see her husband leave.

Right up to the moment when he boarded an aeroplane at Croydon for Marseilles, Gethin stood scanning faces on the aerodrome as if expecting that his bride's parents would relent.

Members of the household would not disclose where his wife and her mother had gone.

Shirley Temple's Libel Suit

Messrs. Joynson-Hicks and Co., of Norfolk-street, W.C., have issued a writ on behalf of Shirley Temple, Twentieth Century Fox Film Corporation and Twentieth Century Fox Film Company, Ltd., in respect of an alleged libel contained in a recent issue of the magazine "Night and Day."

MONDAY, NOVEMBER 8, 1937

Daily Mirror

No. 10587 — Registered at the G.P.O. as a Newspaper. — ONE PENNY

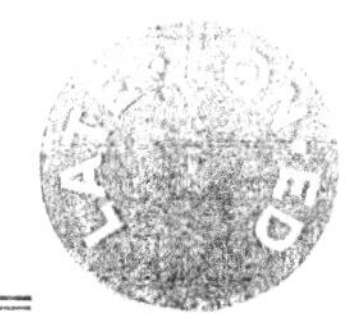

FAMOUS PREACHERS ATTACK FREE SEX LIFE OF 1937 GIRLS

Two great preachers—Jesuit Father Woodlock and Dr. Herbert Williams, Anglican Bishop of Carlisle—used plain words yesterday about sex and love. Both gave warning that the lack of self-control was increasing.

FATHER Woodlock, pastor of famous Farm-street Church, Mayfair, London, declared that many girls and young women "no longer draw the line in conduct where, in pre-war days, convention and prudence, if not conscience, drew it for women who wished to be socially respectable."

He was preaching at Oxford, beginning a course on "Modern Morals and Christian Marriage."

After his phrase about the line of conduct, he said: "To-day the amateur enters more and more into competition with her professional sister, because she is so often amoral in regard to such relations and untroubled in conscience on such matters."

Many people lived, in other social relations, by the Christian code.

"They are honest, charitable, unselfish, sensitive to the injustices and sufferings resulting from present-day social inequalities; they hate cruelty of war, and are eager and active to right wrongs and help the 'down-and-out,' but their sex life is free and uncontrolled by the Christian ideal and moral law."

Many feared that any form of self-denial of instinct, appetite or passion, any withholding of complete self-expression, was dangerous to psychologic health and crippled personality.

The Bishop of Carlisle, in a sermon at Hayton, North Cumberland, spoke of the National Health campaign, and asked:—

"Would there be any need for this immense expenditure for hospital services if people were living righteously? How much disease is the result of wilful sin?"

Though modern science kept increasing the means by which consequences of sin could be escaped, he said, the moral evil persisted. Lack of self-control became greater.

HER HUSBAND IS HER CHAMPION: Mrs. W. F. Long, the Mayoress of Bath, an alleged "slight" to whom is said to have caused the Mayor, Councilor W. F. Long, to threaten to resign.

A dinner to be given to them by the City Council was cancelled two days before it was due to be held.

Cancellation followed a protest by the Mayor, who declared that the Mayoress had not received a formal invitation to the dinner.

But Alderman A. W. Wills, chairman of the committee in charge of the dinner, said: "Our invitation took exactly the same form as invitations to all Mayoresses for the last twenty years."

The Curls Are Different—

But there's no mistaking Shirley Temple. She's got a new coiffure for her forthcoming picture and it's the first time in her screen career that the famous curls have been arranged in any but their natural way.

Ex-Friend Says—

MRS. GODDE OFFERED DOYLE £200 A WEEK

FROM OUR OWN CORRESPONDENT

NEW YORK, Sunday.

CHICAGO heiress, Mrs. Delphine Dodge Godde offered Jack Doyle £200 a week to marry her, declared Judith Allen's lawyers to-day, striking the latest blow in the Doyle-Allen battle.

Statement is based on a deposition made by Doyle's former friend, James McIlvenn.

In her bid to buy Doyle's affections, says the deposition, Mrs. Godde also paid £2,000 of his debts and promised to sell her £200,000 house in Washington and buy him another in California next to Robert Taylor's estate.

Indignantly Doyle denied the charges to me to-night

Cruel Lies

"These are cruel lies to soil the reputation of the woman I love," he said. "Mrs Godde has provided me with no financial resources."

"I have had only gifts of sentiment from her—simple things like my harmonica. She never gave me anything worth more than a shilling."

Doyle broadcast from New York to-day

CONSUL IN HOLD-UP

British Acting Consul-General, Mr. J. G. Baillie, and his wife were victims of an armed hold-up in Caseros, a suburb of Buenos Aires, early to-day, says Reuter.

Mr. Baillie, who was driving their car, accelerated to escape a hail of bullets and, despite a punctured tyre, no one was hurt.

3 SOMERSAULTS—4 ESCAPE

After a collision on the Cambridge arterial road at Enfield last night, a car somersaulted three times across the road, but three of the four people in it escaped without a scratch, and the fourth was only bruised.

The occupants of the car were Mr. and Mrs. Calmels, of Flamstead End, Cheshunt, Herts, a boy aged twelve and a baby.

JULIANA APPOINTS HER NURSE

FROM OUR OWN CORRESPONDENT

AMSTERDAM, Sunday.

PRINCESS Juliana this afternoon engaged a nurse for the child which she is expecting in January.

She to-day entertained the nurse to tea at the Palace of Svestdyk. Both the Prince and Princess had a long talk with her. After a while, the Prince left them alone, saying: "The ladies will now have some more to discuss."

Broadcasting on June 15 she told the Dutch people: "For joyful reasons of health, which I know you will approve, I am prevented from joining in all festivities (connected with her return to Amsterdam after her honeymoon).

The Prince and Princess were married last January. Their child, the heir presumptive, will be called the Prince or Princess of Orange-Nassau.

TOO OLD TO PARADE

Ex-Servicemen did not parade to Hersham, Surrey, Parish Church Remembrance Sunday services yesterday.

The Rev. E. R. Brittain explained that it had been decided to drop the parade this year because members of the Legion were getting older, and could not walk long distances in bad weather.

The fire brigade and local Territorials paraded, however.

WEDNESDAY, NOVEMBER 10, 1937

Daily Mirror

No. 10589 Registered at the G.P.O. as a Newspaper. ONE PENNY

RAMSAY MACDONALD DIES IN LINER ON WAY TO S. AMERICA

MR. Ramsay MacDonald, three times Premier of Britain, died last night in the liner Reina del Pacifico which was taking him and his daughter Sheila to South America. He was seventy-one.

His body has been embalmed and will be taken to Bermuda where the liner is due on November 15.

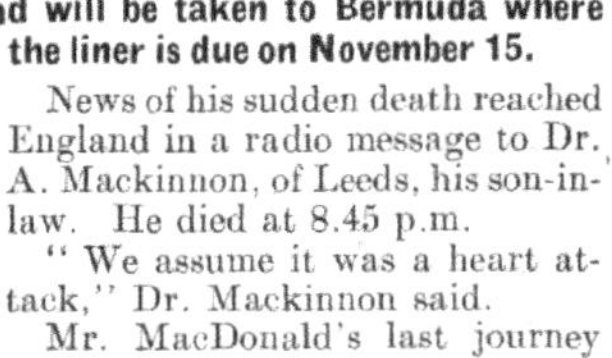

News of his sudden death reached England in a radio message to Dr. A. Mackinnon, of Leeds, his son-in-law. He died at 8.45 p.m.

"We assume it was a heart attack," Dr. Mackinnon said.

Mr. MacDonald's last journey began last Thursday.

"I am going in search of that most elusive of all forms of happiness—rest," were his words just before he embarked.

"It is the first holiday I have ever had free from care," he added.

Two other members of his family received news of his death last night—Miss Ishbel MacDonald and Mr. Malcolm MacDonald, his Cabinet Minister son, now attending the Brussels Conference.

To Be Buried at Wife's Side

Mr. MacDonald's death will cause a by-election in the Scottish Universities, for which he was M.P.

It was his last constituency. He could have vacated it when he resigned Ministerial rank after the Coronation and was offered a peerage by the King.

"My Lossiemouth friends call me Jamey," he said. "I can't ask them now to call me Milord."

Mr. MacDonald often expressed the wish that when he died he should be laid to rest beside his wife in the little cemetery outside Lossiemouth.

He often used to go to Lossiemouth to kneel for a while at the graveside of his wife.

"He often expressed a wish to be buried in the little town in which he was born." Dr. Mackinnon, his son-in-law, said last night.

"I saw him a fortnight ago, and he told me he was feeling very tired.

"He had no presentiment that he would never return alive."

Poor Boy to Premier.—See his life story in page 4.

Mrs. Ella Hesketh-Wright.

GAGGED MAID TELLS OF £20,000 RAID

THREE masked raiders entered the £1,200-a-year penthouse of Mrs. Ella Hesketh-Wright in Park-lane, London, yesterday, bound and gagged her maid, and after forcing the mistress from bed at the point of a revolver, rifled her safe of £20,000 in cash and gems.

All day thirty-five-year-old Mrs. May Goodwin, the maid, talked with detectives at Scotland Yard to aid in their search for the men behind Britain's most daring jewel robbery for years.

Last night, returning to Aldford House, Park-lane, she told the *Daily Mirror*:

"I have been giving information to detectives at the Yard since ten this morning. That twelve hours has been an ordeal.

"All I have been able to say is that the three men—one in chauffeur's uniform—rang at the door. I asked them, 'What is all this about.' They threatened that they would fire if I opened my mouth.

"With that they forced me into my mistress's bedroom and bound me while the safe was burgled."

Men in Silk Masks

The men walked up the carpeted main staircase to the entrance hall of the flat in Aldford House, eight floors above Park-lane, then at its busiest with people going to work.

Mrs. Wright told the *Daily Mirror*: "I woke to find the three men, each with a black silk handkerchief over the lower half of his face, standing at the foot of the bed, pointing revolvers at me.

"They gave me no chance to put on a wrap," said Mrs. Wright. "I got the key to my safe and two of the men covered me to the room where I have my private safe.

"Two of them bound me with the stripped sheet while the other scooped the safe of my diamonds, all my jewels, and about £100 in cash, mostly £1 notes.

HAUNTED BY A MAN'S SMILE: HE LOOKED AT HER—THEN CRASHED

HAUNTED by a young man's smile, pretty, fifteen-year-old Bridget Sheehy has been unable to sleep since she saw him crash to his death on a motor-cycle five days ago.

At the Ealing inquest to-day on Stanley Bridges, aged twenty, of Tavistock-road, Greenford, Middlesex, Miss Sheehy told the coroner that as Bridges passed her on his motor-cycle he turned and smiled.

Next moment he crashed into a car.

"I think the cause of the accident was the fatal moment when he looked round," said the coroner Mr. Reginald Kemp recording a verdict of Accidental death.

"Unable to Sleep"

Miss Sheehy looked pale with sleeplessness when I saw her afterwards at her home in St. Kilda's-road, Harrow, writes a Special Correspondent.

"His face has haunted me since the accident," she said. "I have been unable to sleep

"I nearly fainted at the inquest," she went on. "I was out walking with my dog on the Greenford-road when a young man passed me on a motor-cycle.

"He turned round and smiled. I had never seen him in my life before. He turned round a second time and then there was a terrible crash. I was too terrified to look at him or to give any help

Mrs. Goodwin, photographed last night after she had been questioned at Scotland Yard for twelve hours.

TWO NURSES AT INQUIRY

INTER-DEPARTMENTAL committee to inquire into the recruitment, training, registration and terms and conditions of service of nurses, includes one hospital matron and one staff nurse among its twenty-one members.

Personnel of the committee was announced last night by the Ministry of Health. The Earl of Athlone is chairman.

The matron is Miss D. M. Smith, of the Middlesex Hospital, and the nurse Miss Frances Wakeford, on the staff of the Kingston and District Hospital of the Surrey County Council.

Other members include several M.P.s, professors of medicine, doctors, officials of nursing organisations and educationists.

The Minister of Health, Sir Kingsley Wood, has arranged for the services of women inspectors to be placed at the disposal of the committee for the purpose of advice and inquiries on technical nursing matters. **Nurses' Letters, page 14.**

THURSDAY, NOVEMBER 11, 1937

Daily Mirror

No. 10590 — Registered at the G.P.O. as a Newspaper. — ONE PENNY

THE DUKE AND CANON IN ARMISTICE SURPRISE

THE Duke of Windsor's announcement (reported on page 2) that he would attend the Armistice Day Service at St. George's Church, Rue Auguste Vacquerie, Paris, to-day, was followed late last night by an amazing statement from Canon T. L. C. Dart, the vicar.

Canon Dart, who declared that he was acting on his own responsibility and without any prompting from his Bishop, said:—

"I would rather the Duke of Windsor did not attend the service.

"I am glad for all that he did in the war. I have a certain respect for his memory and am thankful for the good things he has done in the past.

"But the attitude of the Church in the matter of divorce and remarriage is very definite. A marriage only ends before God when it is ended by death.

"Given the Best Seats"

"The Duke comes to my church because he is the Duke of Windsor and because he was once on the throne. I have given him the best seats I can.

"Colonel Crowther, an official of the British Legion, will take him to his seat. He will go out with the British Legion."

Lord Brownlow visited the Duke in his apartment at 1.30 a.m. this morning, but later when he left with Mr. Dudley Forwood, the Duke's equerry, they would make no statement as to whether the Duke would attend the service or not.

The service, which is held annually, is attended by the British Legion, Boy Scouts and Girl Guides.

The Two Minutes Silence is observed and the Reveille and Last Post are sounded by buglers.

St. George's is one of the two chief Church of England churches in Paris. The other, known as the British Embassy Church, is usually attended by members of the Embassy

A lost golf ball led to their wedding yesterday. . . . Mr. Leslie Rowlands, Monmouthshire golf champion, and his bride, Miss Joan Parlour, off for a golfing honeymoon.

Two weeks ago Mr. Rowlands was about to drive off from the thirteenth tee at St. Mellon's Golf Club, Newport, when a woman player wandering about in the rough distracted his attention. Mr. Rowlands went to remonstrate, stayed to help Miss Parlour to find a lost ball. It was the first time they had met. Four days later he proposed and was accepted.

600 YEARS AFTER...

They say its the latest in feminine fashions . . . . a pointed hat and flowing veil; a Persian lamb coat and muff. But the style, seen at Waterloo Station (London), yesterday, was familiar to Londoners over six hundred years ago, when Plantagenet women thought a veil hanging from the pointed crown of a hat was the last word, my dear . . .

SIX-STORY HOTEL FIRE EARLY TO-DAY

BY A SPECIAL CORRESPONDENT

WHILE flames crackled on the top floor and smoke filled the building, scores of firemen in gas-masks groped through the deserted rooms and corridors of the six-story Belgravia Hotel, Grosvenor-gardens, near Victoria Station, S.W., early to-day, searching for a caretaker who was later found to be safe.

As the firemen dashed through the 120 empty rooms of the hotel, which has been unoccupied for about three years, comrades poured water on to the flames from several water-towers.

One hundred firemen with twenty engines fought the blaze.

Flames lit up the sky, and crowds, many from hotels nearby with coats flung over their pyjamas and others in evening dress, raced to the scene believing that Victoria Station was ablaze.

The caretaker, Mr. J. Patrick, who is the only occupant of the building, knew nothing of the fire until he saw the glow reflected in the windows and heard the bells of the fire engines.

"I knew nothing of the blaze until I saw the reflection of the flames," he told the *Daily Mirror*.

"No one else was on the premises. Workmen have been reconstructing the building and there was a large quantity of wood about."

Several shops and a bank beneath the building were damaged by water which poured from the upper floors.

At 3 a.m. the outbreak was under control, but firemen were still playing their hoses on the burning rooms.

NIGHT SCOT IN EUSTON CRASH: MANY HURT

BY A SPECIAL CORRESPONDENT

PASSENGERS were flung from their bunks in all directions and a porter was thrown on to the line and badly hurt when an empty train, shunting into Euston Station crashed into the Night Scot shortly before midnight last night.

"Twelve passengers and three railway employees were taken to hospital, most of them suffering from severe cuts and bruises.

The Night Scot, due to leave Euston at 11.45 p.m., was standing full of passengers waiting for the engine to be coupled when the empty train, which was to have left for Glasgow at 12.40, ran into the front coach.

Woodwork splintered, glass flew wide from broken windows as the impact wrecked the front coach of the Night Scot—a parcel van and a dining car—and drove the rear engine through the buffers.

Trucks as Stretchers

Joseph Good, a porter, of Windsor-terrace, City-road, was loading parcels into the front van when a truck of ice-boxes overturned on him and flung him on to the line.

Porters and officials ran to the carriages and assisted injured passengers on to the platform, where luggage trucks were hastily improvised as stretchers until the ambulances arrived.

Many passengers who jumped unhurt from the sleeping berths were only half clad. Clutching bags and satchels, they streamed through the station yard to the hotel.

Among the passengers were a number of Scottish soldiers who had attended the unveiling of the Haig memorial in London yesterday and were returning to Scotland.

None of these was seriously injured, although a number were severely bruised.

Company Sergeant-Major J. Docherty, of the 1st/6th Argyll and Sutherland Highlanders, told me: "I had arrived early and was half dozing in my compartment. I felt a terrific impact and was flung across the compartment, banging my head on a window."

Hurled from Berth

Behind the splintered car were a number of sleeping cars containing passengers.

Miss F. Gordon, a young American, said: "I got the shock of my life when I was hurled from my sleeping berth to the floor. Fortunately, I am only slightly bruised, but some passengers in the same coach were badly cut."

Injured detained in hospital were:—

George Edgar Ingram, of New Cavendish-street, W.C.1.

Robert Marshall, High-street, Rochester.

Monsieur A. Assiede, of Rue de Suffrise, Paris.

Mr. Sokoloff, Tanza-road, Hampstead.

Passengers who were unhurt were transferred to later trains at St. Pancras and King's Cross. At 2 a.m. breakdown gangs were still busy clearing the line.

"I'M A TOUGH GUY, DADDY"—HE DIED

THE night before he died two-year-old John Rowles, of Harold-street, Old Trafford, Stretford, "played at fighting" with his father. "I'm a tough guy, daddy," he said.

Next day he was being pushed in his perambulator across Chester-road by his mother when a heavy motor lorry came along.

Mrs. Rowles tried in vain to push the pram out of the way, but little John was thrown under the lorry wheels, and he died soon afterwards in hospital. Mrs. Rowles escaped.

Mr. John Rowles, the father, said last night: "John was a fine little kiddie. Our other two children, aged six and four years, keep asking for him."

SATURDAY, NOVEMBER 20, 1937

Daily Mirror

No. 10598 Registered at the G.P.O. as a Newspaper. ONE PENNY

TYPHOID BELT RADIO SOS:

NEW CASES DUE TO INFECTED WATERCRESS

URGENT warning came over the radio last night that "three members of one family outside Croydon showed positive typhoid tests last night," bringing the total of new cases on the eve of the end of the incubation period to twenty-one.

Already six victims have died, others are seriously ill and the number under treatment is 116.

All the three cases reported in the S O S last night are "believed to have contracted infection from watercress grown near Croydon."

Mr. E. Taberner, Croydon Town Clerk, authorised the broadcast.

Mother Sees Second Son Die

To-day ends the sixteen-day incubation period—the time necessary for latent cases to develop into fever. On November 4 the outbreak was first reported, and the infected Croydon well sealed.

Throughout the district last night residents were apprehensive and alarmed fearing that to-day might bring the scourge to their children—into their homes

Mothers, eager to protect their families from infection, have crowded the hospitals. Hundreds have been inoculated, not realising that inoculation can only prevent the contraction of the fever; not allay infection once contracted.

Every home in the district will spend an anxious Saturday to-day.

Most tragic figure in the fever belt is Mrs. A. J. Hill, of South Park Hill-road, Croydon. Yesterday she saw her second son, Clifford, twenty-four, die of the fever.

A week ago her eldest boy, Dr. Roland J. Hill, died—one of the first victims

"My wife is in a state of collapse. We are terrified lest our sole surviving child, Muriel, who is twenty-seven, may contract the fever," Mr. Hill told the *Daily Mirror* last night.

The Danger Signs

One of the new victims is Lord Rochester, of Park Hill-road, Croydon.

Lord Rochester, formerly Mr. Ernest Lamb, was Paymaster-General in the first years of the National Government.

A doctor, speaking of the epidemic, told the *Daily Mirror* last night: "Typhoid must run its course

"At the first symptoms—headaches and general sickness—the patient must be treated for high fever.

"Boil all suspected water before drinking it.

"Keep all sinks, drains and domestic water courses clean and well disinfected."

Last night the municipal authorities reported that Department of Health officials are in close co-operation with the local authority.

The bacteriological reports show officially that Croydon water is "pure and wholesome

THEY BOTH WEAR WINNING SMILES

. . . and they've reason to smile because they're winning through—Flying-Officer A. E. Clouston with his co-pilot, Mrs. Kirby-Green.

CLOUSTON, ON LAST LAP, MAY CRACK RECORD BY 42 HOURS

TIRED out but still game, Flying-Officer A. E. Clouston and his co-pilot, Mrs. Betty Kirby-Green, took off from Cairo Airfield at 12.28 a.m. to-day to fly non-stop to Croydon by noon—and keep the promise Clouston made as he climbed into his 'plane last Sunday.

He said then they would be back in time for lunch. If they succeed they will have beaten H. L. Brook's record for the Cape-London flight by forty-two hours, as well as capturing the London-Cape and round flight records.

The flight nearly ended in disaster last night. Flying non-stop from Khartum, 1,000 miles down the Nile, Clouston and Mrs. Betty Kirby-Green were over the Cairo landing field at 7.30—after five hours flying.

A great crowd was waiting for them.

Rose Safely

Deaf, sleepy, and tired, Clouston glided to land, then suddenly opened up his throttle and rose again into the air for another try.

At the second attempt he was again unsuccessful. The 'plane ballooned four times across the aerodrome while spectators held their breath.

Then again Clouston opened up the "gun" and the big Comet safely rose.

The third time was successful.

He grounded thirty-seven and three quarter hours after leaving Capetown, says Reuter—over a day ahead of Brook's record, despite a delay of eight and a half hours at Broken Hill, Rhodesia, with engine trouble.

Prince Cantacouzenie, of Rumania, left Croydon at 12.36 a.m. to-day on an attempt to break the London-Cape air record.

Dying Boy, Trapped by Bus, Jokes

Cycling to school yesterday George Wochner, a fifteen-year-old scholarship boy, of Pottersdown-street, Tooting, S.W., fell under a bus in Upper Tooting-road.

He joked with firemen as they jacked up the front of the bus to release him, but collapsed and died on the way to hospital

DEAD GIRL HELD FIANCE'S PICTURES

BY A SPECIAL CORRESPONDENT

PICTURES of her fiance, whom she was to have married in three months, were clutched in the hands of nineteen-year-old Doris Ivy Eccleston, whose body was found on the underground railway line near Stepney Green yesterday.

Ivy, who lived at Thorpe-road, Forest Gate, was engaged to good-looking Ralph Aldous, of Eastbourne-road, West Ham. Yesterday she left her home for her work in a Stratford shirt factory. Instead of going by bus as usual she went by the underground.

Shortly after leaving Stepney Green Station passengers saw her fall from the carriage before an oncoming train.

Her fiance told me last night: "I had known Doris for two years, and we were to have been married early next year.

"I saw her last night, and, although she was not very well, she seemed quite cheerful. We arranged to meet again to-night. We had never quarrelled."

BRITISH SHIP DOCKS WITH ARMED GUARD

WITH an armed guard on board, the British steamer African Mariner arrived at Malta from the Eastern Mediterranean last night. She was escorted by the cruiser Greyhound, Reuter says.

The ship was taken over by the Court authorities.

The Admiralty stated that the ship had been taken in for search under the Merchant Shipping (Carriage of Munitions to Spain) Act, which makes it an offence for British ships to carry munitions to Spain.

The African Mariner (6,581 tons) was once the Bois-Soleil, French-owned. Her new owners are the Africa and Continental Steamship Co., Ltd., London

British warships have powers to stop carriage of arms to either side in Spain's war.

Early in September the African Mariner figured as a "mystery ship." For five days she was anchored off Folkestone, receiving no visitors, sending no one ashore

MONDAY, NOVEMBER 22, 1937

Daily Mirror

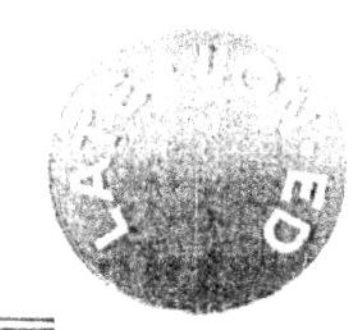

No. 10599 Registered at the G.P.O. as a Newspaper. ONE PENNY

DEATH REVEALS A WOMAN'S MASQUERADE AS MAN FOR 12 YEARS

BY A SPECIAL CORRESPONDENT

FOR twelve years Alfred Grouard served Mr. Joseph Hamblen Sears, wealthy New York author and publisher, as the "perfect chef"—to be revealed by death as a woman.

Last night, on the Transatlantic telephone, Mr. Sears told me the story of one of the longest masquerades on record.

All that twelve years Grouard worked night and day: never asked for time off—never once left the house or the cottage in the grounds in which the servants lived.

"I was amazed," said Mr. Sears, "when the undertakers made the discovery.

"I realise now that my chef's whole life was a mystery that ought to have made us suspicious. But Grouard never looked or acted as anything but a man.

Refused to See Doctor

"He came to me with grand references as a chef. I took him on and, by gosh, he certainly could cook. . . .

"True, he was also a trifle queer, but, after all, a man doesn't inquire into the private life of his domestics, and I just put him down as a sort of eccentric.

"You see he never went out of the place. He had his own room in the cottage in the grounds where all my servants live, and he seemed content to work and pop over there to sleep.

"Everything went fine until last February. Then he was taken ill. I did everything I could, but he absolutely refused to see a doctor or go into hospital. . . . Now I know why.

"Actually he hardly did a day's work since, but he never had anyone but a Catholic priest to come to see him until the day he died.

"Then I had the shock of my life. Along came the undertakers to tell me that my 'perfect chef' was a woman.

"Naturally I wouldn't believe it at first. "She was probably trying to protect herself from the advances of men. Though why she should want to do that when she was about sixty years old I can't understand.

"Besides she looked like a man and talked like one. Perhaps she had been doing it so long that she became like a man in the end."

Yesterday, as police checked the records for forty years back trying to unveil her past, the woman was buried in a plain wooden coffin. It bore the one word "Grouard."

FLYING-BOAT'S DEBUT

The arrival of the Cordelia—the first Empire class flying-boat ever to have come to the Far East—was witnessed by a large crowd yesterday morning, says Reuter from Singapore.

It is believed that a regular flying-boat service will be extended to Singapore from Karachi in January.

This Hat's Hot News

This steeple-like hat is the latest from Paris. You may laugh at it but it shows that the French, too, are able to laugh—at peril.

Modelled on the hood of the dreaded Ku Klux Klan it's designed by a milliner inspired by the round-up of the Cagoulards (Hooded Men) and the seizure of their secret arsenals.

Another 12 Hours of Fog

Fog and frost which caused hundreds of crashes yesterday will be worse to-day.

The Air Ministry forecasts another twelve hours of weather which will be bad enough to stop all transport around London. Then it will clear up.

Saturday night was the coldest for four years, twenty degrees of frost being recorded at Amersham, Bucks.

Six hundred calls for help from drivers who had crashed were received by the A.A. in four hours yesterday.

(Full Fog Story on back page.)

CROYDON PRAYS AS TYPHOID SPREADS

BY A SPECIAL REPRESENTATIVE

HUNDREDS of people joined in prayers offered last night in Croydon's churches for sufferers from the typhoid epidemic—which has already cost six lives and shows no signs of abating.

The seventeen-day incubation period expired at midnight on Saturday but at noon yesterday eleven new cases had been reported and there have been more since then bringing the total to nearly 150.

The epidemic has also spread to Kensington, London's royal borough, where five cases have occurred and two have died.

No more figures for Croydon will be published until mid-day to-day, but according to a public health official incubation may take anything from seven to twenty-one days.

Eighteen cases were recorded on Friday, thirteen on Saturday.

Croydon is fighting typhoid on two fronts—Addington in the East and Haling Park in the West.

Between them lies the Brighton road "isthmus," which is lower lying and does not take its water from the suspected Addington Well, closed on November 4.

Every housewife in the town, which has nearly 250,000 inhabitants, is playing her part in the battle. On the hob in every home a kettle is kept constantly boiling.

All day yesterday the Town Hall was kept open while officers in four departments—water, town clerk, public health and sanitary inspectors—were busy recording and investigating new cases and causes

Four Cases in One House

Watercress is believed to have caused the Kensington typhoid outbreak.

All five cases occurred in Becher-street, in the poorer, crowded quarter of Notting Dale.

Four cases were in one house, and it is there that a husband and wife—Mr. Sidney Newman, fifty-five, and Mrs. Newman, forty-seven, have died.

Mrs. Newman died at her home on Thursday and Mr. Newman died in hospital on Saturday. Their fifteen-year-old daughter, Mary, is in the Seagrave Road Fever Hospital, Fulham.

Mrs. Ada Stanley, who lives in rooms below those of the dead couple, is also in hospital.

The fifth case, reported yesterday, is Mrs. Kathleen Beale, daughter of Mr. and Mrs. Newman.

Mrs. Beale lives on the opposite side of the street. In that house there are three families.

Dr. J. Fenton, medical officer of health for Kensington, said last night: "There is no reason to suspect a spread of infection

BLOODHOUNDS TRAIL VANISHED WOMAN

FROM OUR OWN CORRESPONDENT

FARNHAM (Surrey), Sunday.

BLOODHOUNDS were used by Farnham police to-night in a search for thirty-three-year-old Mrs. Catherine Ellacott, of Maycot, Hale, near here, who disappeared from home early yesterday wearing an overcoat over her nightdress.

Late to-night there was no clue to her movements.

In thick fog villagers helped the police to scour miles of heath and commonland without result. Then a pair of bloodhounds, kept by a police officer at Ash, were brought to the house.

They picked up a faint trail for a few yards, but the fog made it impossible for the searchers to continue.

A horsepond a mile away from Mrs. Ellacott's home has been dragged without result.

They Want To Be Happy

"As a tribute to a woman who has guided and helped him, I ask the man who has a happy, comfortable home to help the clubs to enable the girls of to-day to make a happy home for other men."

. . This appeal to husbands was made by Lord Aberdare, chairman of the National Fitness Council, in a broadcast on behalf of the National Council of Girls' Clubs last night.

WATERSPOUT HIT BOAT

When a waterspout 20 ft. high swamped their fishing-boat off Rottingdean, near Brighton, at the week-end, two Londoners saved it from sinking by baling out with their hats. They lost an oar and rowed to shore with a floor-board.

They were Robert Gordon, twenty-three, of Wood Green, N., and Arthur Deacon, twenty-seven, of Shepherd's Bush, W.

WEDNESDAY, NOVEMBER 24, 1937

Daily Mirror

No. 10601   Registered at the G.P.O. as a Newspaper   ONE PENNY

Mona Tinsley.

REBEL "ARMY'S" PLOT TO SEIZE PARIS BY SEWER MARCH

THE Hooded Men of France plotted to overthrow the Republic, march through the sewers of Paris, arrest the Ministers, and to restore the Monarchy.

At a given signal, members of the French Parliament were to be seized, Paris buses commandeered, arms and ammunition distributed, and a coup d'etat carried out.

That revelation of the extent of the Cagoulard plot—officially announced by M. Marx Dormoy, Minister of the Interior—startled France last night.

"It was a veritable plot against Republican institutions," M. Dormoy declared.

"We were confronted by a secret military organisation entirely copying the lines of the army.

"The organisation comprises a general staff, a first, second, third and fourth bureau and a medical service.

"The separation of its effectives into 'divisions,' 'brigades,' 'regiments' and 'battalions' shows how this organisation has been designed for civil war.

"Documents seized show that those responsible had chosen as their aim the replacement of the Republican form by a dictatorship which would precede the restoration of the monarchy."

[The Duc de Guise, Pretender to the throne of France, on Monday announced his intention of reconquering "the throne of my fathers," and called upon Frenchmen to restore the monarchy as a solution to their difficulties.]

Secret Instructions

Then M. Dormoy gave details of the plot uncovered by the police—of hidden maps and secret instructions, of specially-drawn plans of the sewers of Paris and underground routes to the Chamber of Deputies.

The sewers of Paris, through which the rebels planned to march, resemble vast underground canals, stretching for miles, and are provided with paths at either side.

Among other papers discovered are:—

Information regarding the State's forces in Paris and environs with the names of officers commanding the units;

Plans of the interiors of offices occupied by Left Wing newspapers and plans of the flats of Socialist Deputies;

A list of Ministers and Members of Parliament to be arrested when the signal was given.

But M. Dormoy declared that the attempted revolt had been crushed before the rising was due.

Last night detention warrants were issued against Eugene Deloncle, consulting engineer to the company which built the Normandie, who is now in Italy, and four other people, including a former naval captain and an Air Force sergeant.

The four will be questioned to-day on their alleged complicity in the plot.

(Messages from "Daily Mirror" correspondent, Reuter and British United Press.)

NODDER SMILES AT DEATH: "CONSCIENCE CLEAR," HE CRIES

Frederick Nodder . . . to die.

"I SHALL leave this court with a clear conscience," cried Frederick Nodder, found guilty at Nottingham Assizes yesterday, of the murder of ten-year-old Mona Tinsley.

Impassive, standing stiffly to attention, he gazed fixedly ahead as Mr. Justice Macnaghten pronounced sentence of death in the tense stillness of the court-room.

At the last words, "May God have mercy on your soul," the forty-five-year-old Hayton (Notts) motor-engineer, turned in the dock, glanced round the court and, as he went to the cells, smiled.

"Justice has slowly but surely overtaken you," the Judge had said before pronouncing sentence on Nodder, who was brought from the cells where he was serving a sentence of seven years for abducting Mona Tinsley, passed at Birmingham Assizes on March 10.

"It may be that time will reveal the dreadful secret you carry in your heart," Mr. Justice Swift then told Nodder.

Mona vanished on January 5. Her body was found in the River Idle on June 6.

After once retiring the jury came back to hear additional evidence. Forty minutes later they returned again, and within half an hour Nodder was on his way to Lincoln Prison, where he will be hanged.

Mona Tinsley's father and mother sat behind the dock, where a wooden partition prevented them seeing more than Nodder's head.

Witness Recalled

People in the crowded court thought the jury had reached their verdict when they returned for the first time. Instead, Mr. Maurice Healy, K.C., defending Nodder, had a witness recalled and said, "Something has come to our knowledge since you were in the box."

The first witness to be recalled was Mr. Walter Victor Marshall, manager of Bawtry Gas Company, who had told of the discovery of the body when boating with his family on the River Idle.

Then Dr. Webster, a medical witness for the Crown, again gave evidence.

Nodder, in evidence, declared that he "thought too much about Mona to harm her," while his counsel complained that the prosecution were "hypnotised by the idea" that Nodder murdered the child.

Husband Thought Love Letters "Silly"

Mrs. Elsie Lee, of Kensington, of whose husband, Engineer-Lieutenant-Commander Francis Lee, Mr. Justice Bucknill said yesterday:—

"He showed a complete lack of the very necessary give-and-take if the marriage was to be a success. He regarded love letters as silly.

"From an engineer's point of view they may be. But from a human point of view they are not."

Engineer-Lieutenant-Commander Lee's petition for the dissolution of the marriage was dismissed. **See story on page 5.**

STAGE LEOPARD MAULS TRAINER

BY A SPECIAL CORRESPONDENT

AFTER slim and lovely Ruth Hasse, twenty-four-year-old German acrobat, clad in a leopard skin, had finished her act in front of two full-grown leopards chained to the stage at Lewisham Hippodrome last night, one of the beasts attacked the trainer, Edrick Eckahart, and his assistant.

"One of the leopards was going to attack Miss Hasse, and Eckahart and his assistant held it back and tried to get it into its cage," the manager of the Hippodrome told the "Daily Mirror."

Eckahart and Vincent McKenna, who helped him, were both mauled, and had to be taken to Lewisham Hospital.

The beast which attacked the trainer only arrived from Germany earlier in the day. At the first house it was calm and obedient.

HE SAW IT ALL—BUT CANNOT TALK

THE only one who could provide a clue which might solve the mystery of eleven-year-old Edith Louisa Perring's disappearance is her baby brother, aged two.

He was the last person to see her before she vanished three days ago. But he cannot talk.

Edith, who lives in Mill-lane, South Kirby, Yorkshire, was seen nursing him in their back-yard.

A little later the boy ran into the house crying bitterly. His parents found Edith had gone.

Edith is about four feet tall, has blue eyes and dark hair, and was wearing a red jumper, tweed skirt, white socks and black patent shoes.

"BIG ADVENTURE" END

Two missing Brighton schoolgirls—thirteen-year-old Joyce Cowley, of Russell-street, and fourteen-year-old Helen Portrait, of Norfolk-road—were found wandering penniless in Bournemouth last night.

FRENCH PREMIER AND LONDON TALKS

The French Premier, M. Chautemps, and his Foreign Minister, M. Delbos, have been invited to London to discuss the results of the recent meeting between Lord Halifax and Herr Hitler.

Mr. Eden yesterday had a talk with the French Ambassador in London, when the date for the discussions was considered.

FRIDAY, NOVEMBER 26, 1937

Daily Mirror

No. 10603 Registered at the G.P.O. as a Newspaper. ONE PENNY

FOUR DIE IN FOG COLLISION: RADIO ARTIST LOST

TWO men and two women in a small saloon car were killed in last night's fog, when they were in a head-on collision with a bus on the Kingston by-pass road.

One of the men is believed to have been Alfred John Deverson, of Replingham-road, Southfields, S.W.

The fog completely encircled London, except for a gap in the south. In some suburbs buses had to be convoyed. Motorists took hours to complete journeys that normally take thirty minutes.

One of them was Reginald Dixon, the famous radio organist, who was lost while driving from Greenford, Middlesex, to Clapham, S.W., where he was to have appeared in the "Voices of Variety" *relay from the Granada Cinema.*

For the first time in his career he was too late to broadcast. But he rushed on the stage in his overcoat, and played to the cinema audience.

Police sent messages all over London trying to find Mr. Dixon, and his wife, who is expecting a baby in a few days, heard over the radio, in their Blackpool home, that he was lost.

Her anxiety turned to tear. Then the telephone rang, and she heard his voice.

"Is that you, darling," he said, "I'm all right—I've been lost."

"And sure enough I was, though I was having plenty of adventures," Mr. Dixon told the *Daily Mirror* after he had given his performance at Clapham, three hours late.

"Don't ask me," he said, "where I went—I don't know, and I am sure the man who was driving me doesn't, either.

Fell Down Embankment

"We seemed to go for miles, running on to the pavements and narrowly missing walls. Then, somewhere near Shepherd's Bush, another car ran into us."

Mrs. E. F. Patrick, of Russell-road, Northolt Park, thought that the train in which she was going to Wembley Hill had arrived at the station when it was stopped by signals at St. John's-road bridge.

She opened the door, fell out of the train, and rolled down an embankment. Afterwards the train went on without her.

When the train reached Wembley Hill the station staff were told what had happened.

The signals were set at danger while porters went along the line and searched for Mrs. Patrick.

They thought she would be badly injured, but she had found her way through the fog to the signal-box, and was only bruised.

Smashed almost out of all semblance of a car . . . The wreckage from which the bodies of two men and two women were lifted after the collision, in thick fog, on the Kingston by-pass

Shot Father—Not Murder

RICH WOMAN BEFRIENDS BOY

FOURTEEN-YEAR-OLD John Stone, reared in misery and suffering, was yesterday acquitted of murdering his cruel father, whose butt and whipping post he had been.

And, when he stepped from the dock, he was befriended by a wealthy widow, Mrs. Morris Eyton, who plans to introduce him to happiness and give him a new start in life.

John Stone shot his father outside their home in Mitton, Penkridge, Staffs, but declared he had not meant to do so. "I was going to try and hit out with the gun if he came for me," he explained.

The jury were told of the boy's miserable life since his mother died, and his counsel declared, "If he gets justice it will be the first time in his life."

Soon after, freed, the boy was surrounded in the waiting-room by women, who showered kisses and congratulations on him.

Danced for Joy

He was smuggled from the court by a back door, where Mrs. Morris-Eyton was awaiting him with her car.

She drove him to her home, Calvington Manor near Newport, Shropshire, *where last* night he was so excited by his release that he was dancing in glee around the servants' hall.

Mrs. Morris-Eyton told the *Daily Mirror*: "I have taken John under my care because I want to see that he has a real start in life.

"He will go to work for me on my farm at Calvington. I want him to grow up and live an ordinary, natural life.

"To Forget"

"The best thing for everybody—especially the boy himself—is that he shall be allowed to forget this terrible happening.

"I have known the family for several years. His step-sister is my parlourmaid, and it will be nice for them to see each other.

"His mother was employed as the nursery maid for my late husband's family for a number of years.

"So I felt I had a close personal interest in the boy's future."

BOOT-HAND TO WED HEIRESS

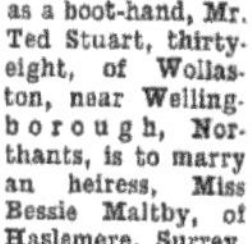

Earning £3 a week as a boot-hand, Mr. Ted Stuart, thirty-eight, of Wollaston, near Wellingborough, Northants, is to marry an heiress, Miss Bessie Maltby, of Haslemere, Surrey, daughter of Mr. Thomas Maltby, a yacht owner. Picture shows them at Wollaston Church bazaar at which Miss Maltby had a stall.

Their friendship began some years ago when he visited his aunt, who is nurse-companion to Mrs. Maltby. Plans for the marriage are not yet definite, but a house, described by the villagers as bigger than the vicarage, is being built at Wollaston.

Women, Beware Typhoid Thief

One London sneak-thief has already "cashed in" on the typhoid scare.

He called at a house in Williamson-street, Islington, N., yesterday, told the startled wife who answered the door that he was a Ministry of Health inspector testing water for *typhoid* germs.

When he left he had more than a few samples of water . . . he had the housewife's purse and the money in it.

Other Typhoid news—page 3.

£15,000 FARR-DOYLE FIGHT RUMOUR

SYNDICATE of London business men were stated last night to be planning a £15,000 fight between Tommy Farr and Jack Doyle in the new Earl's Court exhibition building early in the New Year.

Interested parties said last night:—

Jack Doyle: It will all be settled in twenty-four hours.

Tommy Farr: If Doyle wants a contest with me he must first accredit himself with the British boxing public.

See Peter Wilson, page 30.

THE QUEEN'S NEW STANDARD

The Queen's new Standard flew over Buckingham Palace for the first time yesterday.

It shows the Queen's personal arms, the arms of England coupled with those of the Bowes-Lyon family, and indicates that her Majesty is in residence alone at the Palace while the King is at Sandringham.

MONDAY, NOVEMBER 29, 1937

Daily Mirror

No. 10605 Registered at the G.P.O. as a Newspaper. ONE PENNY

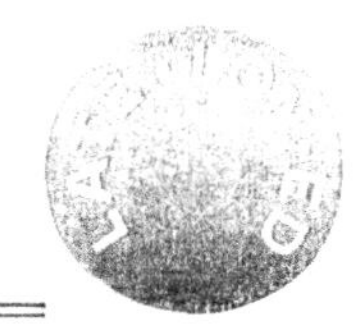

BOY WITH A BROOM FIGHTS DEATH DUEL, SAVES 2 WOMEN

BY A SPECIAL CORRESPONDENT

RONALD Prior, seventeen-year-old London draughtsman, saved the lives of two women last night when, armed only with a broom, he fought a duel with a madman who had attacked them with a knife and an iron bar.

Prior, sitting in his home in Belgrade-road, Stoke Newington, N.16. heard screams from the flat above.

He dashed upstairs, found two women crouching on the floor while Edwin Stanley, sixty-one, a shoemaker, attacked them.

The women, Stanley's wife and stepdaughter, Miss Elsie Smith, aged nineteen, had been wounded with the razor-sharp cobbler's knife which Stanley brandished.

Mrs. Stanley was trying to shield her daughter from the rain of blows.

Ronald Prior.

"I seized the first thing that came to my hand," Prior said later. "It was a broom.

"I fenced with him desperately as the women backed out of the room.

"For a second it seemed certain that Stanley would get me with that wicked knife and, since my broom was no real match for him, I was about to close with him when the fight suddenly ended.

"Stanley wheeled round, muttered an incoherent sentence, then stabbed himself in the throat.

"When the police arrived Stanley was dead."

Elsie Smith was badly injured. She had been struck again and again on the chest. She was hysterical and had concussion.

Her brother also injured, was taken with her to the Metropolitan Hospital and detained.

Prior's father told me that Stanley had recently been ill and added :—

"I think he was jealous of his stepdaughter."

POLICEMAN SHOT IN STRUGGLE

Lying in Willesden General Hospital, with his wife watching over him, is Police-Constable Alexander Carmichael, who was shot during a struggle with men in the pitch darkness of deserted Dollis Hill, London, railway station at 2 a.m. yesterday.

With his mate, Police-Constable Murphy, he went towards the men, who were close to the window of a tobacconist's kiosk. Murphy challenged one man who dashed across the electric lines. Carmichael turned to the other, and Murphy heard sounds of a struggle. Then the pencil flash from a revolver cut through the foggy darkness. When Murphy looked round he saw his colleague fall to the ground.

At the hospital Carmichael gave a statement to his C.I.D. colleagues. After an operation, he told the "Daily Mirror" that the bullet went into the fleshy part of his leg and came out above the knee. Two men were questioned at Willesden Police Station shortly after the shooting and detained.

Below, Scotland Yard experts examining a counter cash plate from the kiosk for finger-prints

ARAB GANGSTERS SLAY CONSTABLE

A British constable named Pierce was shot dead last night while a police patrol was trying to arrest an Arab gang in the plain of Jezreel.

The Arabs had fired on a lorry in which Jews were returning from the colony at Nahalal.—Exchange.

TOWN PLANS TO FINE PEOPLE WHOSE CLOCKS TELL THE WRONG TIME

FROM A SPECIAL CORRESPONDENT

GUILDFORD people are determined to stop the nuisance of missing trains and appointments through street clocks which tell the wrong time.

Owners of public clocks which do not register the correct time, and who will not remove them are to be fined if the Corporation has its way.

In a General Powers Bill to be presented to Parliament next session a clause provides that the occupier of any building from which a clock is suspended must remove the clock within twenty-eight days of receiving notice from the Corporation that it is registering incorrectly.

Failure to do this means that he will be liable to a fine of £5, and to a daily fine thereafter of £2.

"There is a growing tendency nowadays to erect clocks in the streets over shops as an advertisement," said Mr. G. H. R. Wilson, town clerk of Guildford, to me yesterday.

"As the number of clocks increases we get more and more confused about the right time. This leads to people missing trains and is generally unsatisfactory.

"Lately there has been many more applications to us from tradespeople wishing to erect clocks in the streets and we cannot dissuade them."

IT'S HEART-BURNING!

Fate has played an ironical trick upon the students of the Kent Farm Institute, Sittingbourne, which was badly damaged by fire during the week-end

From their canteen, which was destroyed, the only article salvaged was the "tick" book, in which all the canteen debts are entered. The book was found in perfect condition.

In future it will be known as "Phœnix."

FRANCO'S NEW THREAT

General Franco has declared a blockade of Republican Spain, abolishing all neutral zones for shipping, says the British United Press.

On November 22, last year, Franco declared a limited blockade of Republican ports, neutral ships being assured of safety only in certain limited anchorages off Valencia, Tarragona, Alicante, Cartagena and Barcelona.

BANDITS ESCAPE IN FOG

Fog covered the escape last night of motor bandits who raided a sub-post office in Norwood-road, West Norwood, and took a safe, containing money and postal orders.

LAST CHANCE MAY SAVE HIS LIFE

WHILE awaiting a cable calling him to Canada to give a blood transfusion, Mr. Edgar Harding Stanford, of Ilford, was summoned to Croydon General Hospital where a man was lying dangerously ill.

The man, Harold Ralph Day, a traffic manager, of Croydon, had been ill for two months suffering from endo-carditis, a rare disease of the blood stream affecting the heart.

Dr. James Sinclair, of Thornton Heath, read that Mr. Stanford had been cured of a similar disease and knew he would be one of the few men able to survive an injection of mercurochrome into his blood-stream.

It was the once chance to save his patient, and he immediately got in touch with Mr. Stanford. The transfusion was performed late last night.

"It is the only cure known to medical science," Dr. Sinclair told the *Daily Mirror*.

WEDNESDAY, DECEMBER 1, 1937

Daily Mirror

No. 10607 — Registered at the G.P.O. as a Newspaper. — ONE PENNY

GHOST-LIKE FIGURE STABS BOY AT CHURCH, VANISHES

FROM OUR OWN CORRESPONDENT

SITTINGBOURNE, Kent, Tuesday.

JUMPING from behind the war memorial at the door of Borden Parish Church, near here, a ghostlike figure, dressed in white, knocked down and stabbed a ten-year-old boy who was on his way to choir practice.

The boy, Peter Ingram, of Bobbing Hill, Sittingbourne, was following the vicar and choirmaster into the church from the unlit churchyard.

Some distance behind him were seven other choirboys, who rushed up to him as the figure in white leaped away in the darkness among the tombstones.

Peter was bleeding from two stab wounds, one below the left ear and one on the left jaw, which had penetrated through the flesh to the inside of his mouth.

Wounded Twice

He was carried to the district nurse for first aid and was afterwards wheeled to a doctor's in a borrowed perambulator.

The choirmaster and several of the older boys searched the churchyard, but found no trace of the figure in white.

Peter could give them no clue. "I just caught a glimpse of someone all in white," he said. "Then I felt a blow on my head that knocked me down."

Other boys say the ghostlike figure was that of a man. "But right from head to foot it was all in white," said one, "and we couldn't be sure."

BABY ILL: S O S FOR MISSING PARENTS

BY A SPECIAL CORRESPONDENT

BABY Albert Pendleton, eighteen months old, has lost his parents, but is too ill even to cry for them.

He is lying in the County Hospital, Farnborough, Kent, critically ill with pneumonia, and last night London was being searched for his mother and father, Mr and Mrs William Pendleton.

They were last heard of months ago at Anerley, S.E.—before their baby was taken ill and sent to hospital—and to help in the search an S O S for them was broadcast last night.

"I CRASHED THERE"

Mrs. Kay Petre, still bearing the scar of the crash that nearly cost her life, pointing out at Brooklands yesterday the spot where she skidded. Though the crash was as long ago as September 17, the skid marks are still visible.

She was travelling at 90 m.p.h. in practice for the "500" when the crash came. For days she lay in hospital between life and death, and when life won she was still under the shadow of blindness.

It was her courage that brought success to the doctors' efforts to save her and courage again that took her yesterday to the scene of her disaster.

It is courage that is sending her back to hospital this week-end to have the last trace of her injury removed.

And courage, too, that has made this decision: "My wife is waiting to enter her next race early next year," Major Henry Petre told the "Daily Mirror" last night. "She has made a wonderful recovery and we are confident that the scar will be entirely removed."

Left: A picture of Mrs. Petre taken before the crash.

JAPANESE PERIL TO SINGAPORE BASE

JAPAN is on the road to Britain's Far East base—Singapore. And nothing less than Europe can bar the Emperor's advance. General Sir Ian Hamilton gave the startling warning last night.

It was at a dinner of the Royal Scottish Corporation in London last night that the General talked of Japan's war aims.

Singapore could be captured by a land army, he declared.

"Road Clearly Marked"

"How monstrous it will seem to posterity," he said, "that throughout 1937 the European nations should have been quarrelling like dogs over a bone about Spain . . . at a moment when we ought to be having military conversations between the general staffs of Europe.

"The Emperor's road is clearly marked—Hangkow, Hong-Kong, Singapore, Bhamo, Assam, Bengal. Nothing less than Europe can definitely hold up that army.

"A land army can lay siege to and capture Singapore exactly as Port Arthur was captured."

British 'plane fired on.—Page 4

WAR HORSE REFUSED ALL FOOD. FOLLOWED MASTER TO DEATH

TOMMY died yesterday—a broken-hearted war horse that had refused all food since his master, Mr. J. A. Krupp, of Clifton-villas, Paddington, W., died a fortnight ago.

"Tommy was over thirty and had been with my father for nearly twenty years," said a son of Mr. Krupp. "When we bought him there were still shrapnel marks on his body."

He was in such a weakened condition that he had to be humanely destroyed. He had served throughout the war in France and Belgium.

THURSDAY, DECEMBER 2, 1937

Daily Mirror

No. 10608 Registered at the G.P.O. as a Newspaper. ONE PENNY

MOTHERS ASKED: 'IS HUSBAND FATHER OF YOUR CHILD?'

BY OUR POLITICAL CORRESPONDENT

"Is your husband the father of your child?"

MOTHERS of newly-born babies in London maternity homes have been asked this question by visiting registrars, and to-day in Parliament an explanation will be demanded from the Minister of Health.

It is a further revelation of official prying into private lives, and M.P.s, already determined not to allow the Popular Statistics ("Nosey Parker") Bill to become law, will undoubtedly be strengthened in their resolve by these disclosures.

Mr. E. Thurtle (Soc., Shoreditch) will ask the Minister:—

Is he aware that registrars attending nursing homes in London for the purpose of registering births state that they are obliged by law to ask mothers of newly-born children whether their husbands are the fathers of such children, and do in fact, put such questions to mothers, and will he say by what authority such duty is imposed upon registrars?

"I have positive proof that registrars do go to maternity nursing homes and ask patients whether their husbands are the fathers of their newly-born children," Mr. Thurtle told me yesterday.

"If the Minister says he has no knowledge of this, more than one member of the House will support me. We are determined to stop this form of inquisition."

M.P.'s Wife Questioned

One M.P., whose name I am not permitted to reveal, told me that when his wife was in a London nursing home, she was asked whether he was the father of their child.

The registrar said he was bound to ask patients this question, and that it often caused scenes and deep distress.

The M.P.'s wife in this case treated the registrar's impertinent question as a joke.

But on the following afternoon Mr. Nosey Parker came to the same nursing home and put his question to a mother who was just recovering from a serious confinement.

The patient promptly went into hysterics and her screams could be heard throughout the nursing home.

The M.P. told me he was willing to support Mr. Thurtle's condemnation of such practice

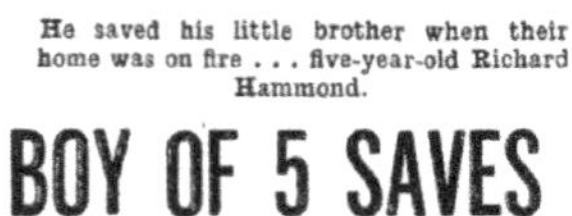

He saved his little brother when their home was on fire . . . five-year-old Richard Hammond.

BOY OF 5 SAVES BROTHER IN FIRE

"FLAMES, Mummy. All the chairs were burning," was all five-year-old Richard Hammond could tell his mother last night of the fire from which he dragged his three-year-old brother to safety.

Mrs. Lilian Hammond, wife of a lorry-driver, left Richard and his brother Harry playing in the attic of their home in Doris-road, Ashford, Middlesex, while she went with her five-month-old baby to the welfare clinic.

"While I was at the clinic," Mrs. Hammond told the *Daily Mirror*, "a friend rushed in shouting, 'Your home is on fire!'

"My two boys were in a friend's house when I arrived, and Richard was still holding his little brother's hand.

"He is too excited to tell me what happened; but I am sure he must have seen the room ablaze and led his brother out. He has always been a brave boy."

Richard and Harry and their seven-year-old sister, who was at school at the time, slept in a neighbour's house last night, but Mr. and Mrs. Hammond made up a bed in their ruined home.

The house was not insured

FRANCO'S TOKIO LEGATION

Japan yesterday recognised General Franco's Government.

Mr. Hirota, Japanese Foreign Minister, says British United Press, exchanged documents with Senor Castillo, General Franco's representative in Tokio, where Franco's Legation will open to-day.

To walk up the aisle alone on her wedding day . . . Miss Rosemary Cohen.

SOCIETY BRIDE WILL WALK TO ALTAR ALONE

BY A SPECIAL CORRESPONDENT

WHEN Rosemary Cohen, of Great Cumberland-place, W., walks up the aisle of St. Margaret's Church, Westminster, on December 16, to meet her bridegroom she will be the first London society bride to do so alone.

Defying tradition, Rosemary will walk to the altar unattended except for her nine-year-old train-bearer, Barbara North, daughter of Lord North, who will carry her ten yards square train of white tulle.

Mother at Her Side

The reason is that Rosemary's father is dead and she has no close male relatives, so she has decided to do without an arm to lean on when she walks down the aisle.

Her mother, Mrs. Arthur Cohen, will step to her side as she takes up her position for the marriage service to give her away.

Last night at her home the tall, slim bride-to-be told me: "I thought it would be much more sensible to go alone as I have no brothers to attend me. I will probably be frightfully nervous, but I'm not worrying.

Fiance Says "Good Idea"

"All I hope is that my little train-bearer will be able to manage the train, which has five yards of width at each side and ten yards flowing behind."

Rosemary's barrister fiance, Mr. Dick Brewster Thornton, of Norfolk-street, W., agreed that it was a good idea. "It's a long way to walk when all eyes are upon you," he said.

Miss Cohen is the only daughter of the late Mr. Arthur Cohen, who was senior partner in the firm Cohen, Laming and Hoare, stock-brokers, of Austin Friars.

The couple will spend their honeymoon in America and the West Indies

Took Camping-Out Kit with Him

YOUTH AND GIRL MISSING: POLICE APPEAL

TAKING a complete camping-out kit with him, seventeen-year-old Cecil Reed has vanished from his home in High Wycombe (Bucks). It is believed that Miss Minnie Essex, also seventeen, of Grenfell-avenue, has gone with him.

They have been friends for several weeks, and last night High Wycombe police circulated a description of them and appealed for information.

Both were missed from their homes early on Tuesday morning.

Reed, who lives at New-road, Sands, High Wycombe, is said to be about 5ft. 10in. in height, clean shaven, with brown eyes, dark hair, dressed in brown overalls and tweed jacket of dark brown colour, dark blue trousers.

The statement adds: "He is in possession of a brown army kitbag containing a ground sheet, two eiderdowns, a blanket and a blue camping-out tent.

"He is believed to be accompanied by Miss Minnie Essex—5ft. 6in. in height, slim build, dark hair and dark complexion, wearing either a dark tweed overcoat or a blue coat."

"Bridging" Their Divorce

FROM OUR OWN CORRESPONDENT

NEW YORK, Wednesday.

After their proposed divorce, the Culbertsons, America's famous bridge pair, will live next door to each other, Mr. Ely Culbertson told me to-day when he sailed for England in the Queen Mary.

In his suitcase he carried a big picture of his wife. He repeated that their bridge partnership would not be affected.

One reason for their parting is that Ely, against his wife's advice, is soon to publish a sensational book about his life—"The Strange Life of Ely Culbertson." "Mrs. Culbertson thinks it will be hard on our children," he said. "I disagree. Truth never hurt anyone."

FRIDAY, DECEMBER 3, 1937

Daily Mirror

No. 10609 Registered at the G.P.O. as a Newspaper. ONE PENNY

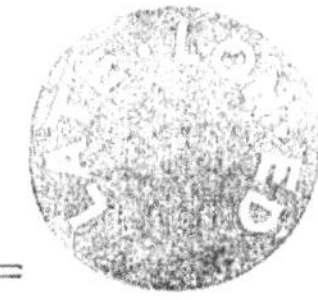

ARMY CHIEFS RESIGN

YOUNGER MEN CALLED IN BY HORE-BELISHA: V.C. IN COMMAND

To be the new Chief of Imperial General Staff . . . Major-General Viscount Gort, V.C.

Major-General C. G. Liddell, who will become Adjutant-General, and Engineer-Vice-Admiral Sir Harold A. Brown (bare-headed), to be Master-General of the Ordnance.

REVOLUTIONARY CHANGES IN THE CONSTITUTION OF THE ARMY COUNCIL, INVOLVING THE RESIGNATION OF THREE OF THE FOUR MILITARY MEMBERS AND THEIR REPLACEMENT BY YOUNGER MEN, WERE ANNOUNCED LAST NIGHT BY THE WAR OFFICE.

WITH ONE BOLD SWEEP, MR. HORE-BELISHA, FORTY-THREE-YEAR-OLD MINISTER OF WAR, BEGINS HIS TASK OF CREATING AN ARMY ADAPTED TO THE WAR OF THE FUTURE AND BRITAIN'S VAST PLANS OF RE-ARMAMENT AND DEFENCE.

After six months of office devoted to an intensive study of the problem he has made his plan. For the Army it means:—

Red tape to go;

Promotion by merit, instead of seniority;

A fresh flow of ideas from an Army Council whose average age is fifty-two instead of sixty-three;

A superior War Council reinforced by the fighting Generals of the field.

Ready for War

No such drastic reorganisation of the executive has taken place in the whole history of the British Army.

Mr. Hore-Belisha's action has been dictated by the determination that the army, one of the smallest in the world, must be made absolutely efficient and ready to take the field whenever necessary.

Deciding that ability and initiative count far more than seniority, he has defied the seniority rule and appointed a number of men over the heads of their elders.

These are the chief changes in personnel:—

Field-Marshal Sir Cyril Deverell, Chief of the Imperial General Staff, is succeeded by Viscount Gort—a V.C.—and the post of Deputy-Chief of the Imperial General Staff has been revived and given to Colonel (temporary Major-General) Sir Ronald Adam, Bart.

(Continued on back page)

"TIGER" GORT WON V.C. WITH GUARDS

THE man his students called The Tiger, Viscount Gort the new Chief of the Imperial General Staff, becomes Britain's leading soldier at fifty-one—probably the youngest man ever to have held the office.

He has been in the Army for thirty-two years; has won the V.C., the D.S.O. three times and the M.C

His V.C. was won during the charge of the Guards at the Canal du Nord in September 1918.

Although severely wounded, he directed the attack until it had succeeded.

He has two children, a son and a daughter. His marriage to his cousin Miss Corinne Vereker, was dissolved in 1925

Adjutant at 25

Major-General C. G. Liddell, the new Adjutant-General, who is fifty-four, entered the Army from Sandhurst when he was nineteen, and rose rapidly to captain and adjutant when he was only twenty-five.

Major-General Wavell, who now comes home to take over the Southern Command, has said that every infantryman should combine the qualities of a poacher, cat burglar and gunman, is now fifty-four; was the youngest General in the Army; is a Scotsman, a Black Watch man.

Lieutenant-General Sir John Dill retains the most important home command—the Aldershot Command; is fifty-six, an Irishman.

Won his reputation as a staff officer with Allenby.

Mr. Hore-Belisha, Minister for War, with some of the younger members of Britain's fighting forces.

FLANNELFOOT'S WIFE LIVED AS WIDOW 5 YEARS

FROM OUR SPECIAL CORRESPONDENT

READING, Thursday.

FOR five years neighbours here knew grey-haired, middle-aged Mrs. Harry Vickers as a widow struggling to provide a decent livelihood for her fifteen-year-old daughter.

This afternoon Mrs. Vickers knew that soon her friends would learn that she was the wife of Flannelfoot, burglar of the century, who was sent to five years' penal servitude at Middlesex Sessions.

With her daughter, Elsie, she went to her parents' home in York-road, Reading.

She still protects the man who deserted her in 1932, took her daughter away to London and left her penniless.

"I know a great deal about Flannelfoot," she said, "but I will never tell it. I cannot."

"Flannelfoot" Sentenced—page 4: picture, back page.

MR. CHURCHILL ISSUES WRIT

BY A SPECIAL CORRESPONDENT

A writ for alleged libel has been issued on behalf of Mr Winston Churchill by Messrs. Nicholl, Manisty and Company, his solicitors, against Messrs. Heinemann, the publishers, and Mr. Geoffrey Dennis, the author.

It is understood that the alleged libel is contained in a passage in Mr. Dennis's book, "Coronation Commentary."

This book was the basis of an action in the King's Bench Division ten days ago, when the Duke of Windsor sued Messrs. Heinemann and Mr. Dennis.

NEW JAP THREAT TO HONG KONG

UNLESS Great Britain "reconsiders her attitude towards Japan" — regarding alleged supplies of arms to China through Hong Kong—Japan will be "forced to check military supplies by cutting communications between Hong Kong and Canton, or to close the China coasts to China by declaring war."

This threat was made in Japanese newspapers yesterday, says Reuter.

General Chiang Kai-Shek is reported in Hong Kong to have rejected terms of peace proposed by Dr. Oskar P. Trautmann, the German Ambassador to China, on the ground that they constitute complete surrender.

SATURDAY, DECEMBER 4, 1937

Daily Mirror

No. 10610 Registered at the G.P.O. as a Newspaper. ONE PENNY

LOST LOVERS LIVE 5 DAYS ON LEMONADE, BISCUITS

Seventeen-year-old Minnie Essex, of Grenfell-avenue, High Wycombe (Bucks) and her sweetheart of the same age, Cecil Reed, who disappeared from their homes five days ago after they had been forbidden to see each other, were found last night.

FROM OUR OWN CORRESPONDENT

HIGH WYCOMBE, Friday.

SHAKEN with sobs and drenched by lashing rain, Minnie Essex, who disappeared with her sweetheart, Cecil Reed, son of a policeman, knocked at the door of her home in Grenfell-avenue to-night.

"Mummy," she gasped, "come quickly. Cecil is lying ill in the woods."

Then, like a hare, she darted off before her mother could even get her coat on.

Mrs. Essex ran to young Reed's home in New-road and told the boy's father and mother.

Searched in Vain

Quickly a search party was organised and in the gathering dusk Mr. Reed, Mrs. Essex and relatives plodded through the wet grass to the woods about three miles away.

Knowing that the couple had taken with them complete camping equipment and blankets when they first disappeared, the search party looked for signs of their camp.

In an old shed near a quarry they found a glove, but there was no sign of Minnie or her sweetheart.

Then they came upon the barn of a deserted farm and there found the tent, blankets and some empty lemonade bottles. There was still no sign of Minnie or the boy.

Downcast, the search party returned home.

But at eight o'clock Cecil Reed, unshaven, shivering with cold, walked into his home.

"I am glad to be home, mum," was all he would say.

Walked in Circles

He told his parents that Minnie had taken refuge in a one-roomed, lonely cottage because she did not wish to go home.

I crossed some fields and found Minnie at the cottage home of Granny Pearce, who lives alone.

Minnie told me the story of how she and Cecil had lived in the old barn for five days with nothing to eat except a few biscuits and lemonade.

"On Monday night, after my parents had gone to bed," she said, "I sat there waiting for Cecil. He came along early in the morning

(Continued on back page)

THE BOAT TRAIN'S IN!

Ploughing its way through floods caused by continuous rain for the past twenty-four hours. . . . The Newcastle-Cardiff express goes through Beighton (Derbyshire) station.

For floods story see page 2.

Missing for five days, she returned home yesterday . . . Miss Minnie Essex.

HANDLESS MAN TO MARRY GIRL WHO NURSED HIM BACK TO LIFE

FROM OUR SPECIAL CORRESPONDENT

NOTTINGHAM, Friday.

LOSING both hands in an accident at his work, Mr. George Roland Cullis was nursed back to health by Miss Dora Fantom, of Paxton, Derbyshire. To-morrow he will marry his nurse, and the clergyman will place the wedding ring on the bride's finger.

Mr. Cullis, who lives at Birkin-avenue, Nottingham, lost his hands through falling into a vat of boiling dye. Miss Fantom nursed him at Nottingham General Hospital. He says he owes his life to her nursing.

They will be married by Rev. J. A. Page at St. Paul's, Nottingham. Sixty guests will attend the reception.

Anonymous Card

After the amputation of his left hand, Mr. Cullis received an anonymous card saying, "Please get well quickly." A year passed before he learned that the sender was the girl he will marry.

The couple will manage a grocery and general store.

SKATER DIVES INTO ORCHESTRA

FIVE thousand spectators at the ice hockey revue "Marina" at Earl's Court last night saw Red McCarthy, acrobatic skater, jumping at 35 miles an hour over a 4ft. barrier of barrels, pitch headlong into the orchestra.

The conductor was struck, music stands and scenery were shattered, and the show was stopped while attendants dashed on the ice to McCarthy's aid

He was assisted, semi-conscious, to his dressing room. He had broken his left wrist and hurt a knee.

Wrist in Plaster

McCarthy appeared in the final act, his wrist in plaster.

"This is nothing," he said. "I have now broken forty-one bones since going into the ice business. This is the sixth time my left wrist has gone."

A Queen Wants More "Pay"

High cost of living has become a problem for the Queen of Mohilla, tiny island in the Indian Ocean.

Queen Salima Machimba's income, granted by the French Government, is £66 a year, and she wants more than that to help her husband, who is a policeman, support her family.

So the Queen has applied for an "increase"—and has suggested that France should issue special postage stamps bearing her portrait to defray the extra cost, says British United Press.

WANDERING IN THE RAIN

A man of sixty, wearing a clergyman's collar, was found during the night wandering on the main road at Margaretting, near Chelmsford, Essex, suffering from loss of memory.

His clothing was drenched by rain. The man is in St. John's Hospital, Chelmsford.

WEDNESDAY, DECEMBER 8, 1937

Daily Mirror

No. 10613 Registered at the G.P.O. as a Newspaper ONE PENNY

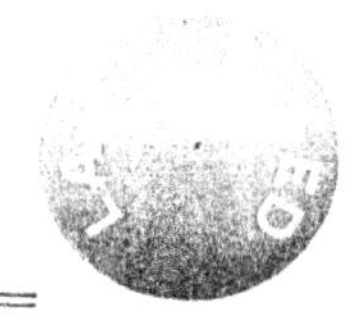

£20,000 HEIR READ NEWS OF FORTUNE IN SANDWICH WRAPPINGS

William Seddon, 65s.-a-week steeplejack painter, of Ansty-road, Coventry, has found himself the heir to what he believes to be a £20,000 fortune through a notice in a newspaper used to wrap up a workmate's lunch.

THE fortune was left to him by an uncle whom he had never seen—the late Mr. Isaac Richard Seddon, New Zealand Labour Leader and brother of a former Premier of New Zealand.

And now let Bill Seddon tell his own story of his amazing good fortune, as he told it to the *Daily Mirror* last night during a game of dominoes in his local "pub."

"We were working on a new factory," he said, "and I was sitting round with the rest of the fellows having my lunch.

"One of the chaps finished his sandwiches and started reading the paper they had been wrapped in

"Suddenly he leaned over, handed me the paper, and said, 'Bill, is this anything to do with you?'

"I read what he pointed out and saw that it was a London solicitor advertising for me—if still alive—to communicate with him at once

"I left work right away and was in London the same night. I found that my uncle Isaac, whom I had never seen because he had been living in New Zealand, had left me his entire fortune

Uncle's Dying Calls

"They tell me uncle thought a lot of me and kept calling my name as he lay dying.

"'You'll find my nephew somewhere around Wigan way,' was what he said.

"You see, I used to be a good Rugby and Soccer player when I was younger. My family were well known in Lancashire as sportsmen.

"My brother Walter at one time played centre half for Arsenal."

But although it is a big jump from 65s.-a-week to a bank balance of £20,000, Bill does not mean his sudden wealth to interfere with his happiness—and his job

"I'm sticking to those who have stuck to me, and I'm going to continue with my job," he added. "I'm a steeplejack-painter by trade and I fill in my spare time doing odd jobs in the decorating line."

Bill is forty-six years old, served in the war and was blinded in one eye

★ Lovely eighteen-year-old Lady Patricia Douglas (right), who is to marry Count John Bendern, better known in the golfing world as John de Forest. (Story on back page.) ★

2 AIR RAID DICTATORS FOR BRITAIN

BRITAIN is to have two Air Raid Dictators—an Inspector-General of Air Raid Precautions and a Deputy-Under-Secretary of State to supervise the administration of the work

Appointments were announced by Home Secretary Sir Samuel Hoare in the House of Commons last night

The Inspector-General is to be Wing-Commander Hodsoll, who has been in charge of the Air Raid Precautions Department for the last two years. He is only forty-three.

The new Under-Secretary is to be Mr. C. W. G. Eady, now secretary to the Unemployment Assistance Board, described by Sir Samuel as 'one of the most competent organisers in Whitehall." He is forty-seven.

Wing-Commander Hodsoll is to concentrate on the planning and technical side of the work and on the development of schemes

He will undertake research and advise local authorities in protection plans.

"Like Monsters"

Mr. Eady will control the department dealing with the actual carrying out of the schemes.

Sir Samuel Hoare, announcing the appointments, said "The Air Raids Precautions Department must be organised on a Service basis.

"What we are forced to do seems to run counter to most of the ideals and most of the chief movements and tendencies of civilised life.

"Civilised life has been developed by generations of progress and here, in 1937, we are making conditions and setting the clock back thousands of years, making men, women and children disperse over the country to the most remote districts and abandon all these amenities and necessities of civilised life.

"For generations we have been developing more rational clothes. Under the provisions of this Bill we are making arrangements for dressing people up in gas masks and gas-proof suits, making them look as if they were monsters out of the dark ages."

Earlier Sir Samuel had said: "We shall gather experience when we make a further and more extensive investigation into these two very difficult problems of shelters and

(Continued on back page)

MR. GOTOBED IS MR. CHAPMAN

A MACHINIST at Witney, Oxfordshire, has changed his name from Gotobed to Chapman, it was announced in last night's *London Gazette*.

The name originated in Cambridge and Norfolk round about the year 1200.

London Gotobeds—there are three in the London 'phone book, but about 200 in the British Isles—discussed the family name with the *Daily Mirror* last night.

Bertram Gotobed, a professional accompanist, said:

"I've had my leg pulled all my life. When my old headmaster called out 'Gotobed,' I used to reply, 'Thank you, sir!' instead of 'Yes, sir.'

"My grandfather went from Bedford to Dorset many years ago. These Witney ex-Gotobeds may be distant relatives."

Mr. James Gotobed of Pinner, said: "I never had my leg pulled much. I think the name is too obvious for the pun-maker."

LADDIE CLIFF DIES: WIFE AT BEDSIDE

LADDIE Cliff, the famous comedian, died this morning at Montcalm, Switzerland. His wife, Phyllis Monkman, was at his bedside.

He had been lying ill in a sanatorium for nine weeks

2,000 Performances

Laddie Cliff, who was forty-six, was to have co-starred with Stanley Lupino in "Crazy Days" when it opened at the Shaftesbury on September 15., but was taken ill with pleurisy during the trial run at Streatham

For seventeen years he had been making Britain laugh.

With Stanley Lupino he had played for 2,000 performances, a record on any stage.

He was married in 1926 to Phyllis Monkman. It was a romance of the Co-optimists, of which they were original members.

OPERA FOR A WEDDING

Symphony conductor Dr. Leonard Walker landed at Plymouth from New York last night. He is to conduct a specially written opera at the wedding celebrations of seventeen-year-old King Farouk of Egypt on January 20

Duke of Windsor House-Hunting

FROM OUR OWN CORRESPONDENT

Paris, Tuesday.

The Duke and Duchess of Windsor are searching for a home near Paris. They want to rent for two years, from March 1, a villa or chateau not far from the golf course of St. Cloud, where the Duke plays nearly every day.

Aubrey Boomer, the professional there, is an old friend of the Duke.

After spending Christmas at Cannes, the Duke and Duchess will return to Paris. They are expected to sail on January 15 for America, where they will stay for about two months.

Their tour will be entirely private.

SATURDAY, DECEMBER 11, 1937

Daily Mirror

No. 10616 Registered at the G.P.O. as a Newspaper. ONE PENNY

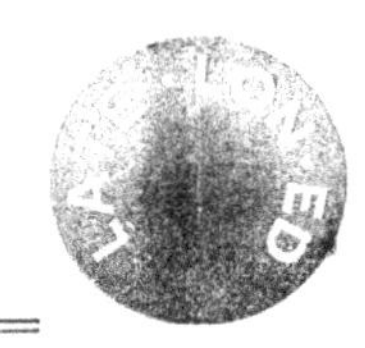

34 KILLED AS TRAINS CRASH IN BLIZZARD: WRECK ABLAZE

Thirty-four people were killed and ninety-two injured in the snow of a Scottish blizzard yesterday when an Edinburgh-Glasgow express crashed into a stationary passenger train 200 yards from Castlecary Station, lonely hamlet in Stirlingshire.

Twenty-six bodies had been recovered early to-day. Fire broke out in the wreckage at midnight and Falkirk fire brigade were called to prevent flames spreading to eight bodies still trapped in the wreckage.

A breakdown gang of more than 100 men were at work in the light of torches and bonfires alongside the track when there was a shriek in the darkness of "Save my husband! Save my husband!"

A rescue worker groped his way to the voice, searched among the wreckage of the compartment, found nothing.

Many people were so gravely injured that it is feared the death roll will mount still higher in the worst British railway disaster since, in 1915, 227 people were killed in the Gretna troop tain smash.

50 m.p.h. Collision

The guard of the stationary train, which was going from Dundee to Glasgow, missed death by seconds. He had just stepped down on to the snow-covered track to find why his train had stopped, when the express engine crashed into his train, flinging the last two coaches across the line.

Its whistle shrieking warning the Glasgow-bound express—most popular business man's train of the day—roared at fifty miles per hour through Castlecary Station.

The engine-driver, peering through the snow, suddenly saw the last coach of the train in front. Frantically, helplessly, he braked.

The first two coaches of the express snapped from the coupling of the engine as it ploughed into an embankment, piled themselves up on each other. The third coach—a dining car—reared itself up like a gigantic crane, the front 30ft. above the back.

It was in those coaches that passengers were killed and gravely injured.

From the wreckage clambered the less severely injured. Men, blood streaming down their faces slithered through the snow and in the darkness pulled frantically at smashed doors, climbed through shattered windows to pull those trapped, those dying, on to the side of the line.

Lit Wreckage as Flares

There were no lamps. Wreckage was dipped in oil and lit as flares. Coats, mackintoshes, seats from the train were placed on the snow, the injured laid on them.

Above the screams of the maimed was heard the hissing of steam from the wrecked engine's boiler. A railwayman clambered on to the footplate, shut off the pressure and averted an explosion.

One man, whose legs were cut clean from

(Continued on back page)

THE TERRIFIC CRASH OF THE TRAINS CAN BE SEEN FROM THIS "DAILY MIRROR" PICTURE, TAKEN EARLY TO-DAY. THE WRECKAGE UNDER THE UPLIFTED COACH WAS ANOTHER COACH. BODIES IN IT WERE FOUND 15FT. ABOVE THE TRACK. THE WHITE LIGHT IN THE RIGHT FOREGROUND IS WRECKAGE BEING BURNED IN ORDER TO PROVIDE LIGHT FOR RESCUE WORK.

Dead Men Saved Him

One man was found alive in the wreckage resting between the bodies of two men. Standing between the two men at the time of the crash, he was cushioned between them.

Mr. Gordon Dickson, of Edinburgh, flung through a window, refused first-aid and crawled in the snow to help rescue work. The first woman he pulled out was his mother, who was travelling in the train unknown to him.

William McLeod, a Glasgow commercial traveller, left his seat a few minutes before the crash to speak to a friend in another compartment. The compartment he left was smashed to matchwood.

MONDAY, DECEMBER 13, 1937

Daily Mirror

No. 10617 Registered at the G.P.O. as a Newspaper. ONE PENNY

JAPANESE SHELL AND BOMB TWO BRITISH WARSHIPS: SAILOR KILLED

CABINET MINISTERS HAVE BEEN HASTILY SUMMONED TO LONDON THIS MORNING BY THE FOREIGN SECRETARY, MR. EDEN, TO DISCUSS THE SHELLING AND BOMBING YESTERDAY OF BRITISH GUNBOATS, STEAMERS AND TUGS IN THE YANGTSE RIVER BY JAPANESE ARTILLERY AND WARPLANES.

The Japanese fire killed sick berth attendant T. N. Lonergan of H.M.S. Ladybird, who lives at Fulham, S.W., and wounded Flag Captain C. E. M. O'Donnell, Petty Officer D. H. Smallwood and several ratings.

Four separate attacks were made by bombers and howitzers and continued until the British guns began to pump shells into the batteries and round the attacking 'planes.

The steamers, the Tsingtah (British Lumber Co.), the Suiwo (Jardine Matheson), and a concentration of tugs and junks were attacked as they were being escorted by the British river gunboats Scarab and Cricket.

Shower of Bombs

Without warning a flight of Japanese bombers high in the sky turned nose to earth and loosed a shower of bombs.

Then Scarab and Cricket opened their anti-aircraft artillery pom-poms and Lewis guns on the warplanes.

Bursts puffed all round the Japanese. Their 'planes rocked with the concussion of the explosions, then raced away.

The warships attacked were the gunboats Ladybird and Bee.

Ladybird, which was anchored at the Asiatic Petroleum Company's installation, got under way as soon as the Japanese artillery began to drop shells round the Tsingtah and the Suiwo.

Shells on Deck

She was fired at until she got out of range four shells landing on her decks.

The gunboat Bee, flagship of the Yangtse Fleet, was fired on as she came down the river at a point two miles from Nanking.

Later in the day the British steamer Whangpu and a hulk, both belonging to Messrs. Butterfield and Swire, were bombed by Japanese 'planes, and several other British ships and a U.S. gunboat which was crowded with refugees and Embassy staffs, were under a heavy barrage of shells.

Sir Charles Little, Commander-in-Chief, China Station, was informed of the attacks, says Reuter, and on his instructions, Captain Dundas, senior naval officer at Shanghai, lodged official protests with Admiral Hasegawa.

FILM OF DUKE HAS 'PREMIERE' AT AN INN

ONE hundred and fifty men and women sat in the lounge bar of the Coach and Horses, London-road, Hounslow (Middlesex) last night and saw a film based on the life of the Duke of Windsor.

They were the first audience in Britain to see the film, which was entitled "The Life of Edward ex-King of England, who gave up the world's greatest throne for the love of an American woman."

Sent from U.S.

The film arrived from America in the Queen Mary only three days before. This was the first full length picture programme to be shown in a public-house in Britain.

Dealing with the life of the Duke of Windsor, it showed extracts from his youth, including his triumphant American tour, and concluding with his abdication speech.

During the performance, barmen walked among the audience with trays of drinks, but dart-boards and pin-tables in other bars were deserted.

Picture on back page.

ATTACKED MAN MYSTERY

Detectives were waiting to-day by the bedside in Hackney Hospital of an unknown man who was found seriously injured in the street at Clapton Common late last night.

The man, who was suffering from a broken leg and facial injuries, is believed to have been attacked by a gang.

A STAR STORKS OUT

"I WANT A BABY"

FROM OUR OWN CORRESPONDENT

NEW YORK, Sunday.

Film star Dorothy Lamour bought two storks a little while ago.

TO-DAY SHE ASTOUNDED HOLLYWOOD WITH THE ANNOUNCEMENT THAT IN A YEAR'S TIME SHE WILL RETIRE FROM ACTING TO PREPARE FOR A BABY.

Film company has replied: "You can't retire. You are under seven-year contract. Art comes first. Why not wait or adopt baby like other stars."

And Miss Lamour, who is twenty-three, retorted: "No contract can interfere with a woman's right to become a mother.

"I WANT A BABY OF MY OWN BEFORE I AM TWENTY-FIVE, AND I AM GOING TO HAVE IT."

"I'll quit pictures December 10, 1938," repeats star firmly, "when preparation for baby will begin."

MISS LAMOUR'S SEVEN-YEAR CONTRACT BRINGS HER IN £200 A WEEK.

P.S.—The two storks Miss Lamour bought are housed in an aviary in her Hollywood home.

GERMANY APPROVES ITALY'S DECISION

GERMANY will never again join the League of Nations, according to an official statement issued in Berlin last night.

Germany's approval of Italy's decision to leave the League is also announced in the statement, says British United Press.

"The Fascist Government's decision to withdraw from the League of Nations, as well as the significant arguments with which the Duce explained the decision, finds complete understanding and the warmest sympathy in Germany," says the statement.

"Concerning the material character of Italy's attitude towards the League, no doubt could have existed for a long time past. Signor Mussolini's words about the false gods of Geneva, spoken last September on the May Field in Berlin, still linger in our ears."

"At no time in its existence had the League been able to make a useful contribution to any of the pending problems of international policy.

Italy leaves the League—page 18

THEY WANT STALIN CROWNED TSAR

SOVIET Army leaders, headed by Marshal Voroshiloff, Minister of Defence, are urging Stalin to crown himself Tsar of All the Russias.

Stalin was "victorious" in yesterday's elections, in which more than 90,000,000 Russians went to the polls, and is entitled to proclaim himself President of Russia. He received a 100 per cent. vote in Moscow and returns late last night showed heavy polling everywhere.

By crowning himself Tsar, Stalin would be following the example of Napoleon, who set the crown on his own head when he became Emperor of France.

TUESDAY, DECEMBER 14, 1937

Daily Mirror

No. 10618 Registered at the G.P.O. as a Newspaper. **ONE PENNY**

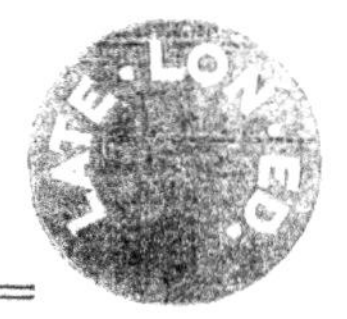

GIRL, DYING IN SNOW, BEGS FRIENDS TO GO ON

Nora Leary.

DYING from cold and exhaustion, seventeen-year-old Nora Leary, trapped with three other hikers—two men and a girl—in a blizzard on the desolate moorland of the Yorkshire-Derbyshire border, pleaded with them to leave her and save their lives.

They refused, stripped off their own coats to give her warmth, and stayed with her in the little dug-out they had scraped away with tin lids and their frost-bitten hands.

When dawn came, with the snow still whirling round them, they found she was dead. They did not know when she died, although throughout the night they had kept themselves awake by nudging each other and singing hymns.

Then they set out to fight against the blizzard once more. This time they were successful, stumbled on Garlick Farm, owned by Mrs. Caldwell.

There the second girl was left and the men pushed on to Broomhead Hall, home of Captain Rimington Wilson, where a "chance shot in the dark by telephone" brought them in touch with rescue parties who were about to seek them.

Mother Pleaded "Don't Go"

Nora, whose home is in Birch-road, Sheffield, had only been rambling for about six weeks. Her mother, fearing the danger of bad weather, h~d pleaded with her not to go.

The girl's companions—all Sheffield ramblers—were Albert Garfitt, twenty-six, of Fitzwilliam-street, Fred Glaser, twenty-three, of Normanton-street, and Margaret Dearnley, of Stamford-street.

The four set off on Sunday for a ramble between Ewden Beck and Derwent.

Late last night, Garfitt and Glaser set out with police, gamekeepers and a horse-drawn sledge to bring in Miss Leary's body.

Before they left Glaser told the *Daily Mirror*:—

"We had only gone a few miles when we were struck by the blizzard, and Miss Leary complained of feeling tired and ill.

"She told us she felt she was becoming a burden to us and pleaded with us time after time to leave and go for assistance.

"We told her we could not do that, and as the weather was getting worse all the time we decided to rest. We found a bank and started digging with tin lids to make a sort of dug-out to shield ourselves from the weather.

Night in Dug-Out

"Then Nora became delirious, and although we tried our best to pacify her, she kept on saying childish things until she absolutely collapsed and became unconscious.

"She was very cold and we thought she was dying, but we don't know when she died.

"We had only one sandwich between us and only one flask of tea. All through the night we stayed in our improvised dug-out, and almost as soon as daylight dawned we set off, leaving Nora behind.

"It took us four hours' hard walking to reach Garlick Farm."

When Nora and her companions failed to return members of the Associate Rambling Club, to which they belonged, and police began to scour the moors.

Then, early yesterday, Mr. T. W. Hopkins, chairman of the rambling club, put in a chance call to Captain Wilson at Broomhead Hall.

The Little More, How Much It Is

"A woman who is just ahead of fashion is popular, but if she were too far ahead she would be arrested for indecent exposure," said Mr. James Laver, of the Victoria and Albert Museum, South Kensington, at the English Speaking Union dinner in London last night.

Fashion plates, he added, could not raise the standards of taste; the best they could do was to expedite the change of fashion.

ROOSEVELT WARNS EMPEROR: TALK OF ANGLO-U.S. NAVAL PARADE

President Roosevelt has taken charge of the crisis following the sinking of the U.S. Gunboat Panay by Japanese bombers, and grave action may be taken if his demands are not met.

The demands—for a full apology, compensation and guarantee against further attacks—were dictated by the President himself, and conveyed by Secretary of State Cordell Hull to the Japanese Ambassador in Washington, Mr. Hirosi Saito. President Roosevelt has also asked for a message to be conveyed to the Emperor of Japan.

Through his secretary, Mr. Stephen Early, the President has asked America to give him "full support in whatever action is taken and face the situation on a basis of national patriotism, freed from all partisan consideration."

The U.S. Note to Japan was preceded by frenzied official activity not unlike that before her participation in the Great War, but it is unlikely that the Panay will be allowed to become a second Lusitania and embroil America in another war.

✦ ✦ ✦

Britain's action in regard to Japan will now even more closely depend on America, writes the *Daily Mirror* political correspondent. Late last night Mr. Anthony Eden and the Prime Minister were in conference over reports from China and Tokio.

One said that the British community in Shanghai was urging a Joint Naval demonstration by Britain and America.

Japanese sink U.S. warship—page 3.

To give up her career . . . famous American actress, Mary Newcombe, who was confirmed by the Bishop of Salisbury last night in the village church adjoining her home at Stinsford (Dorset).

STAGE STAR KNEELS WITH VILLAGERS

FROM OUR OWN CORRESPONDENT

DORCHESTER (Dorset), Monday.

MARY NEWCOMBE, the American stage and film star, was admitted to full membership of the Church of England tonight when the Bishop of Salisbury confirmed her in the little village church at Stinsford, near here.

The service was held in the village church adjoining the house—once the home of monks—where she lives with her husband, Mr. A. H. Higginson, a wealthy American, who is the squire and is Joint Master of the Cattistock.

A congregation of eleven villagers and a choir of six men and women witnessed the ceremony, at which the others who knelt before the Bishop were a farmer's wife, a schoolboy, two village girls and the church organ-blower.

The girls were in white, but Miss Newcombe, like the farmer's wife, wore a simple black dress with a white confirmation veil flowing to her waist.

Miss Newcombe, I understand, intends to leave the stage and to devote her time to the district, which is the Mellstock of Hardy's novels.

She hunts frequently with the Cattistock pack and, with Mrs. Ruxton, the other Joint Master, who is also an American, this season set a new hunting fashion for women.

Both appeared at meets wearing smart black-peaked hunting caps, instead of the bowlers usually worn by women.

HANDCUFFED MEN SAVE THEIR WARDERS

FROM OUR SPECIAL CORRESPONDENT

BRIGHTON, Monday.

THREE handcuffed prisoners on their way to serve sentences at Lewes Gaol, helped their warders to freedom from the wrecked prison van when it overturned on the main road from Brighton to Lewes tonight.

The prison van, driven by a Brighton police constable, with the three prisoners and two warders in the back, had just passed a bus on the way to the gaol when it turned over in the high wind and threw the prisoners and warders in a heap inside the locked van.

The two warders—gaolers from Brighton Police Station—were injured, and the three prisoners, who were not hurt, dragged them to safety.

After helping the gaolers the prisoners, who were sentenced at Brighton Police Court this morning, then jumped on a passing bus, stepped off at the gaol and were taken inside. The warders were taken to hospital.

CHAINED SKELETON FOUND IN FOREST

The skeleton of a man, chained and padlocked to three trees, was found by a hunter yesterday in a forest near Dijon.

In a small bag nearby were a few English banknotes, some Swedish and French money, a card bearing the name of a Swedish countess and a receipt in the name of Berger.

Small phials, empty, were also near the body, says the British United Press.

SATURDAY, DECEMBER 18, 1937

Daily Mirror

No. 10622 Registered at the G.P.O. as a Newspaper. ONE PENNY

THE QUEEN BEATS THE KING IN FIRST DARTS GAME

"I've Never Thrown a Dart Before"

"I WILL WIN"—AND SO SHE DID

The Queen throwing her second dart. It scored thirteen, bringing her total to twenty. Her third dart scored only one . . . but this didn't matter, for the King, playing immediately after her, got only nineteen with his three shots.

FROM OUR OWN CORRESPONDENT

WINDSOR (Bucks), Friday.

FACTORY workers and clerks to-night saw the Queen beat the King at darts in the bar lounge at Slough Social Centre.

Three or four matches were in progress when the King and Queen—paying an informal visit—entered the room.

Mr. Fred Draper had just scored double one.

"I would like to try that," said the Queen.

Mr. Draper handed her three feathered darts.

"I have never thrown a dart before. What do I do and where do I stand?" inquired the Queen.

Mr. Draper told her what to do and she then turned to the King.

"I will beat you," she said with a laugh.

With the first dart she scored a seven, with the second thirteen, and then—aiming for the twenty—she scored a one—twenty-one in all.

Then the Queen handed over the darts to the King. He threw a seven, a three and a nine—a total of nineteen. The King turned to the Queen. "You have won all right," he said.

"I have never thorwn a dart before," the Queen explained. 'What a very sporty game it is."

Before leaving the centre the King and Queen listened to a male voice choir which included several Welsh miners, and went into the main hall, where 1,600 members sang the National Anthem.

They then drove direct to Royal Lodge, Windsor Great Park, where they will spend the week-end.

CAR DIVES INTO RIVER—TWO DEAD

Two young men lost their lives late last night when a motor-car in which they were travelling crashed through a chain stretched across the road at Sculcoates Bridge, Hull, and plunged into the River Hull, 50ft. below.

The bridge had been opened to allow ships to pass through.

"I Shall Never Live . . ."

The victims were William Padley, aged nineteen, coal porter, of Drypool, Hull, and James Lawson, aged eighteen, son of a coal merchant of Spyvee-street, Hull.

"I shall never live to see Christmas" Padley told a friend a few days ago, joking about an asthma complaint.

MAN FOUND SHOT THROUGH EYES

SHOT in both eyes, an Army captain was found by a gamekeeper in a lonely wood between Trowbridge and Westbury (Wilts) yesterday. A twelve-bore shotgun lay near him.

A visiting card, found on the body, bore the name of Captain C. F. Mermagen, Royal Artillery, of Buxton-road, Brighton.

A woman left Brighton last night to identify the body.

Captain Mermagen, his beautiful blonde wife, and their daughter, five-year-old Mavis, moved to a house in Buxton-road, Brighton, about three months ago from a flat in Chilton-road, Brighton.

Mystery is added to the tragedy by reports that a stranger has been haunting the neighbourhood of Trowbridge for several days.

At Trowbridge Royal Artillery Depot it was said the dead man was not known there.

Mr. Jim Davis, a local resident, said that on Tuesday a man answering to the captain's description called at his house and asked for some food.

"He looked very cold, and we gave him a meal and he went away," said Mr. Davis.

Police took from Westbury Station last night a brown paper parcel left there by the man some days ago.

Royal Christmas Tree for Abbey

Gift from the King, a Christmas tree will stand in the nave of Westminster Abbey near the grave of the Unknown Warrior.

It will be decorated with children's toys, and near it will stand a box for offerings in aid of the infant department of Westminster Hospital.

The tree was offered by the King to celebrate his first Christmas after the Coronation, and was at once accepted by the Abbey authorities.

It is expected to arrive on Monday.

WEDNESDAY, DECEMBER 29, 1937

Daily Mirror

No. 10629 Registered at the G.P.O. as a Newspaper. ONE PENNY

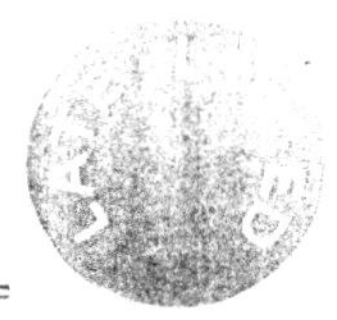

JAGUAR PROWLS SHIP: HOLDS CREW AT BAY FOR 4 DAYS

SLINKING behind bulkheads, lifeboats and deck housings for four days and nights, a Peruvian jaguar stalked the crew of the British steamer Lobos bound for Liverpool.

By night the flash of the great cat's green eyes as it prowled the decks and companionways kept the crew in a constant state of alarm.

During the day the jaguar took shelter in the after part of the ship, snarling savagely when anybody approached its lair.

Engineers crammed on all steam to reach Liverpool before the jaguar should be driven desperate by hunger and make a sortie by daylight against the crew.

On Monday night as the ship drew near the English coast a stoker, exhausted, fell asleep on his bunk.

A few moments later the snarling of the jaguar awakened him.

Staring Eyes Beside Bunk

Looking over the side of the bunk he found himself staring into two wicked eyes. Roaring a warning he leaped out and dashed on deck.

The jaguar, apparently scared, made off and took refuge on the poop. Its cage was brought as close as possible, and the animal, after being cornered, was forced into it.

The beast, trapped in the Andes Mountains, Peru, for the London Zoo, was caged and brought aboard the Lobos, a Pacific Steam Navigation Company's motor-vessel, at Callao.

Four days before reaching the Mersey the animal chewed through the woodwork of its cage during the night and disappeared.

Members of the crew with lanterns searched the ship from end to end.

The jaguar eluded them that night, but next night, becoming bolder, began to prowl round the ship.

At Liverpool yesterday he was transferred to a new cage and entrained for Regent's Park, London.

(Continued on back page)

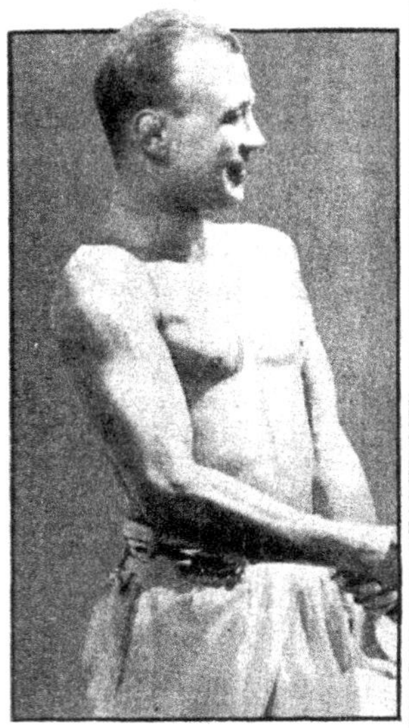

Dead after an all-in wrestling bout. . . . Twenty-seven-year-old ex-public schoolboy Michael (Micky) Flack, who took up wrestling six years ago. He died on Christmas Eve. The inquest was adjourned yesterday for further evidence to decide whether he received a fatal injury in a wrestling match. See story on back page.

Earl's Daughter Follows in Father's (Stage) Footsteps

By A SPECIAL CORRESPONDENT

Her blue eyes twinkling with excitement, Lady Patricia Wellesley (below), nineteen-year-old daughter of Earl Cowley, stopped in the middle of a note at her singing lesson last night to confess to me: "It must be in my blood, I suppose, but I am determined to take up a stage career like my mother and father."

Her father, now living on a ranch in Nevada with his second wife, earned his living on the stage for years; her mother was Mae Picard, an American actress.

"What's more," Lady Patricia added, "mother is delighted that I am serious about going on the stage. And now I am getting down to the job."

Her father, as a young man, gave up his career in the Army because it was not adventurous enough. He took a job as a labourer to a scenic artist at 25s. a week, and then joined the male chorus of a musical comedy. Later, as Arthur Wellesley, he toured the provinces in leading roles in many famous hits. He does not know his daughter is following in his footlight footsteps.

"I don't mind starting in the chorus," she told me. But she will first try the easier way—a small part in a straight play which she hopes to get within a few months.

Her teacher, Mr. Laurence Leonard, says she is "one of the best pupils I have had."

SHIP BLOWS UP IN HARBOUR

FROM OUR OWN CORRESPONDENT

POOLE (Dorset), Tuesday.

HOUSES two miles away were rocked when an explosion wrecked the 409-ton Norwegian steamer Inna in harbour here to-night.

In houses near the harbour people were shaken out of their beds and scores of windows were smashed.

Police, firemen and ambulance men who rushed to the ship found that decks, winches and masts had been blown away and fire had broken out.

One man, Karl Heugan, had been thrown overboard and killed.

Three other members of the crew—the chief engineer, Dieter Petersen; the mate, Berga Jansen, and the mess-boy, Hans Henrikson—were injured.

The skipper, Captain Soerkeli, told me that the vessel seemed to heave bodily out of the water. Everything in his cabin was smashed.

The ship listed over to an angle of 45deg., and was only saved from turning turtle by its nearness to the quay wall.

The explosion is believed to have been caused by gases from the cargo of artificial fertiliser and calcium cyanide.

MORE WARSHIPS FOR U.S.A.—"MUST FACE THE FACTS"

PRESIDENT Roosevelt stated yesterday that he might recommend to Congress the construction of more warships.

Since it was decided to build two battleships, two light cruisers, eight destroyers and six submarines, world events, he said, had caused him "growing concern."

"In speaking of my growing concern," he added, "I do not refer to any specific nation or any specific threat against the United States. The fact is that, in the world as a whole, nations are not only continuing but enlarging their armament programmes."

He added, reports Reuter:

"I have used every conceivable effort to stop this trend and work towards a decrease of armaments. Facts nevertheless are facts, and the United States must recognise them."

BOROTRA HURT ON SKIS

Jean Borotra, French tennis star, injured his right leg while ski-ing at St. Moritz and must stay in bed for a week.

The doctor hopes that his tennis ability will not be affected. The leg will be X-rayed to-day, says Reuter.

Borotra, first victim of the St. Moritz season, said: "I was going faster than my ski-ing knowledge justified."

Burglars Sent Back Stolen Wedding Ring

Cat burglars who broke into the home of Mr. and Mrs. Ronald Pearce, of Plomer Hill, High Wycombe, Bucks, while the family were listening to a late-night wireless programme, yesterday returned by post, and with their compliments, a wedding-ring which they took among other jewellery.

"It is very nice of them to return the ring," said Mr. Pearce "It is of very little value, but to me it has a very deep sentimental value."

£20,000 RAID: WOMAN ARRESTED

ONE woman was arrested and another detained at Liverpool last night in connection with the raid on the Park-lane flat of Mrs. M. E. Hesketh-Wright last November, when £20,000 in jewels and money was taken.

Policemen met the women as they stepped off a train from London and questioned them.

One will appear in court at Liverpool to-day. The other is awaiting an escort from London.

On December 11 a salesman, James Hynes, who was alleged to have been one of three armed men who broke into the flat of Mrs. Hesketh-Wright, was committed for trial accused of robbery.

Most of the jewellery alleged to have been stolen has been recovered.

www.ingramcontent.com/pod-product-compliance
Ingram Content Group UK Ltd.
Pitfield, Milton Keynes, MK11 3LW, UK
UKHW052327191224
452677UK00017B/197